The Terrorism Ahead

The Terrorism Ahead

Confronting Transnational Violence in the Twenty-first Century

Paul J. Smith

M.E.Sharpe
Armonk, New York
London, England

Library of Congress Cataloging-in-Publication Data

Smith, Paul J., 1965–
  The terrorism ahead : confronting transnational violence in the twenty-first century /
by Paul J. Smith.
    p. cm.
  Includes index.
  ISBN 978-0-7656-1987-7 (cloth : alk. paper)—ISBN 978-0-7656-1988-4 (pbk. : alk. paper)
  1. Terrorism. 2. Terrorism—Prevention—International cooperation. 3. Terrorism—Religious
aspects. 4. Weapons of mass destruction. I. Title.

2008

HV6431.S6415 2007
363.325′16—dc22   2007003968

Printed in the United States of America

The paper used in this publication meets the minimum requirements of
American National Standard for Information Sciences
Permanence of Paper for Printed Library Materials,
ANSI Z 39.48-1984.

∞

BM (c)   10   9   8   7   6   5   4   3   2   1
BM (c)   10   9   8   7   6   5   4   3   2   1

To Tamayo, Erica, and Alisa,
my fellow travelers on the great adventure.

Contents

Preface

Terrorism has emerged as one of the top security challenges of our age. Countries around the world are engaged in unprecedented efforts to counter this threat and to confront the underlying conditions that give rise to it. The United States, at the forefront of this campaign, has characterized the struggle as nothing less than "war." The 2006 National Strategy for Combating Terrorism states that "America is at war with a transnational terrorist movement fueled by a radical ideology of hatred, oppression, and murder."[1] Moreover, it is a war that requires sacrifices and unprecedented measures at home, some of which are controversial, particularly as cyber-terrorism expert James Lewis testified to Congress recently, "Americans do not like the idea of domestic intelligence."[2]

One of those measures was revealed on January 14, 2007, when the *New York Times* reported that both the U.S. Department of Defense and the Central Intelligence Agency (CIA) had been using National Security Letters "to obtain banking and credit records of hundreds of Americans and others suspected of terrorism or espionage inside the United States."[3] National Security Letters allow the government to obtain, without a warrant, useful personal and private information about an individual being investigated for a particular security-related reason. The *Times* article noted that the practice of issuing such letters had been proceeding despite the fact the CIA and Department of Defense had long been prohibited from engaging in domestic surveillance or law enforcement activities.[4]

Defending the practice, Vice President Dick Cheney stated that the intrusions did not violate people's civil rights and in fact the Defense Department "has legitimate authority in this area" which goes back at least three or four decades and "was reaffirmed in the Patriot Act [USA PATRIOT Act]."[5] The USA PATRIOT Act[6] was passed by the U.S. Senate on October 11, 2001, and the House of Representatives on October 12, 2001, "in response to the terrorists' attacks of September 11, 2001."[7]

The Act contains a number of provisions that dramatically increase the power of law enforcement in the context of terrorism investigations, including allowing roving wiretaps and warrantless searches of residences, authorizing eavesdropping in certain situations, promoting cooperation between law enforcement and foreign intelligence investigators, reinforcing federal money laundering laws, and expanding the number of terrorism-related inadmissible categories for potential immigrants, among many others.[8]

As for National Security Letters, the Department of Justice Office of the Inspector General issued a report in March 2007 describing how the USA PATRIOT Act had lowered the evidentiary threshold required for such letters, thus making their use more common.[9] The report also noted that the FBI commonly shares analytical products (containing National Security Letter–derived information) with the intelligence community and the U.S. Department of Defense.[10]

Many Americans reluctantly accept the USA PATRIOT Act because they believe it protects them, a view that was emphasized by President George W. Bush in January 2006, when he remarked: "The American people expect to be protected, and the PATRIOT Act is a really important tool for them to stay protected."[11] But if protection from harm is the goal, Americans are remarkably exposed to deadly risk regardless of any protection provided by the PATRIOT Act. Barring any unforeseen catastrophic terrorist event, most Americans can be reasonably certain that they will not become victims of terrorism. However, past experience does show that approximately 42,000[12] Americans will lose their lives annually on the nation's highways as a result of automobile accidents and another 225,000 Americans will die annually from "preventable hospital and pharmaceutical drug errors."[13]

Yet few Americans are clamoring for a PATRIOT Act for bad drivers or wayward doctors, nurses, or pharmacists. These deaths are accepted, however reluctantly, as the price of freedom and the American way of life. Such tolerance does not extend to terrorists, however, and this fact raises an interesting question—what is it about terrorism that spurs the American public to so readily and sheepishly accept a curtailing of their freedoms and civil liberties? Why do many Americans uncritically accept a host of other dramatic military, legal, and political actions by the U.S. government conducted in the name of countering or preventing terrorism?

Many terrorists themselves could probably answer these questions without any hesitation or difficulty. They would most likely assert that terrorism thrives on its ability to strike ruthlessly without warning and to hit its target indiscriminately. These actions, in turn, generate and perpetuate fear, which is ultimately the weapon of choice for terrorists. Historically, terrorists have always tapped into humanity's darkest fears and exploited human beings' deepest insecurities. Society can tolerate road accidents, plane crashes, medical mistakes, and lethal bathtub falls, even when such events are sudden and unexpected. These events are viewed as simply part of life. Society dismisses these episodes as unfortunate, but nevertheless foreseeable.

Terrorism, however, is something different altogether. Perhaps it is because it manifests in a dramatic, shocking, and sensational manner. Perhaps, also, it is the macabre fascination related to the fact that, unlike an airplane disaster or an earthquake, terrorist violence is intentional and man-made. In cases of terrorism, fellow human beings, motivated by some grievance or political ambition, deliberately generate the destruction and human carnage. Chaotic images of terrorism are often plastered across various international media outlets. Bloody photographs, video footage, and scenes of destruction are transmitted to television audiences globally and are seen over and over again. Although most people in the world will most likely not die from terrorism, in the end that fact really does not matter. Terrorists win because they terrorize; they ignite fear and overreaction.

In addition, the cultivation of fear also partially explains why terrorists conduct suicide bombings and plan for attacks involving chemical, biological, radiological, and nuclear (CBRN) weapons, known colloquially as "weapons of mass destruction" (WMD). Regarding suicide bombings, Osama bin Laden has praised such methods because they have become "a great source of terror for the enemy."[14] Suicide terrorism symbolizes the nondeterrable commitment of terrorist groups. Terrorism scholar David Rapoport has argued that suicide terrorism is one of the key hallmarks of contemporary "fourth wave" religious terrorism: "'Suicide bombing,' reminiscent of anarchist bomb-throwing efforts, [is] the most deadly tactical innovation" of contemporary religious terrorists.[15]

Regarding CBRN, many experts—and perhaps even the terrorists themselves—recognize that many CBRN weapons are not necessarily more destructive than most conventional bombs or rifles. In addition, CBRN weapons are expensive, hard to get (usually), and technically difficult to construct or deploy. Nevertheless, such weapons would generate a profound psychological effect and this is why they have been used in the past, and will almost certainly be deployed in the future. If a CBRN event occurs in the United States, according to Bruce Hoffman, it is not likely to be "the destruction of an entire city" depicted in fictional novels or movies but rather a "far more deliberate and delicately planned use of a chemical, biological, or radiological agent for more discrete purposes," which would generate profound and far-reaching psychological consequences.[16]

Because fear is at the heart of terrorism, this book seeks to assuage and mitigate such fear by providing in-depth exploration into terrorism past, present, and future. The rationale for this book and its title *The Terrorism Ahead* is to present the case that terrorism is a constant feature of human civilization—it is neither new nor is it likely to ever end. This is not intended to be a "defeatist" admission, but rather a realistic observation.

Terrorism is, and has always been, a form of "propaganda by the deed" used throughout history by aggrieved or frustrated groups seeking to bring about some sort of political change. However, the confluence of demographic, technological, and social factors—which will be explored in greater detail throughout the book—has created the conditions that make the world particularly vulnerable to terrorism today. Thus, it is critical that the phenomenon be understood as completely as possible so that terrorism can be intelligently and effectively countered.

The real challenge, however, is containing terrorism while preserving those attributes—freedom, civil liberties, judicial fairness—that make the United States a country worthy of global admiration. As one U.S. Senator has stated, "Freedom is at the heart of who we are as a Nation, and as a people. We cannot be a beacon of freedom for the world unless we protect our own freedoms here at home."[17] Clearly, the threat of terrorism is real, but so is the imperative to preserve those values that this country holds dear. It is hoped that this book will contribute to an understanding that can preserve the balance between these two compelling realities.

Paul J. Smith
Jamestown, Rhode Island

Acknowledgments

This book is the product of more than ten years of inquiry, investigation, teaching, and overall research into terrorism and related transnational crime subjects. I am extremely grateful to my former employer, Asia-Pacific Center for Security Studies (APCSS) in Honolulu, Hawaii, and my current employer, the U.S. Naval War College in Newport, Rhode Island, for providing me the institutional support (including access to terrorism professionals from around the world) that enabled me to complete this project. On a personal level, I want to acknowledge the four other members of our counterterrorism team at APCSS, namely, Carleton Cramer, Chris Jasparro, Eric Shibuya, and Philip (Terry) Klapakis, who kept me stimulated and always "on my toes" with regard to the field of terrorism. In addition, I am grateful to "fellow travelers" in the field, including terrorism scholars Anthony Marsella, Greg Barton, Peter Chalk, Rohan Gunaratna, Zachary Abuza, Kumar Ramakrishna, and Shyam Tekwani, all of whom introduced me to the field of terrorism studies in their own way and were active in numerous terrorism conferences conducted in Hawaii.

I would also like to acknowledge the support and assistance provided by current colleagues at the U.S. Naval War College, including Joan Johnson-Freese, Tom Fedyszyn, Dana Struckman, Ambassador Gene Christy, Derek Reveron, Chris Fettweis, Terence Roehrig, Stephen Emerson, Andrew Stigler, and Jeffrey Norwitz. I am also grateful to other former colleagues at the Asia-Pacific Center for Security Studies in Hawaii with whom I spent hours discussing and debating all aspects of terrorism and transnational issues, as well as numerous other topics. In particular, I want to acknowledge Ambassador Charles Salmon, Rouben Azizian, Don Berlin, Eugene Bose, Elizabeth Van Wie Davis, Lee Endress, Butch Finley, Robert Forte, Tina Grice, Mark Harstad, Maurice Hutchinson, Dorothy Kaneshiro, Mohan Malik, Alexander Mansourov, John Miller, Christine Paige, Tom Peterman, Denny Roy, Yoichiro Sato, Anthony Smith, Ian Storey, Virginia Watson and Robert Wirsing. I would like to especially acknowledge the former president of APCSS (and my former boss), Lt. General Henry C. Stackpole, III (USMC-Ret.), who understood and appreciated the emerging security environment of the twenty-first century, which would feature new and more destructive forms of transnational violence. I also want to thank my University of Hawaii political science professors, Richard Chadwick, Kate Zhou, and John Wilson, who provided critiques (including plenty of helpful debate) and guidance during earlier versions of this manuscript. I also thank the numerous military, law enforcement, and intelligence officials from around the world—some who were my former students—whom I cannot name for security reasons, but whose influence and ideas permeate this book. I must also acknowledge Admiral Lloyd (Joe) Vasey (USN-Ret.), founder of Pacific Forum Center for Strategic and International Studies (CSIS) in Hawaii, who set me on the course that ultimately led to where I am today. Finally, since terrorism is sometimes an emotional and controversial topic, I must remind readers that any and all opinions or assertions made in this book are my own (unless otherwise referenced), and do not represent the opinions, positions or policies of the U.S. Naval War College, the U.S. Department of Defense, or the U.S. Government.

The
Terrorism
Ahead

1

The Nature and Definition of Terrorism

On April 20, 2004, Jordanian counterterrorism officials disrupted a plot involving the use of chemical weapons that was organized and financed by Abu-Mus'ab al-Zarqawi, who at the time was alive and living in Iraq. The goal of the plot was to bomb the Jordanian Prime Minister's Office, the U.S. Embassy, and the General Intelligence Department (GID) in Amman.

The attack plan, which would employ suicide terrorists, envisaged a convoy of vehicles that would enter the compound, where all three targets were located. The first vehicle, a conventional sedan, would attack the guard post and destroy it. The trucks in the back of the convoy would proceed into the compound and position themselves near their targets, and then detonate. The planners hoped that in addition to the conventional explosives, the use of toxic chemicals would enhance the effects of the blast and create "a cloud of toxins that would disperse around the GID compound and out in the city, inducing mass casualties."[1] In addition, the emission of chemical gases was expected to "cause physical deformities and direct damage to the lungs and the eyes."[2]

Preparations for the attack were extensive and were led by Azmi al-Jayyusi, who took direct orders from al-Zarqawi. Al-Jayyusi actually began planning for the attack while in Iraq, following his transfer from Afghanistan, under the direct orders of al-Zarqawi. Subsequently, he moved to Jordan to oversee logistical planning for the attack. In Jordan, the attack planners—including al-Jayyusi—purchased more than twenty tons of chemicals from local companies, which were intended to be part one of a two-part explosion design, one chemical and the other conventional.[3] Funding for the plot exceeded US$170,000, most of which was supplied by Al-Zarqawi in smaller payments ranging from US$10,000 to US$15,000.[4]

The plot designers calculated that the two explosions would have had an impact within a two-kilometer radius. Overall, it was anticipated that 80,000 people would die and 160,000 would be wounded.[5] According to Husayn Sharif, one of the co-conspirators in the plot, the Jordan attack was intended to be the "first suicide chemical attack by al-Qaeda."[6] Fortunately, it was disrupted prior to its execution.

The attempted attack in Jordan was followed three months later by the issuance of a final report by the National Commission on Terrorist Attacks on the United States (*The 9/11 Commission Report*) on July 22, 2004. The report was the product of a multiyear effort by current and former U.S. officials to understand the background and motivations underlying the September 11, 2001, terrorist attacks in the United States. The report described how nineteen young men, mostly citizens of Saudi Arabia, boarded four planes within the United States and flew three of them into the World Trade Center in New York City and the Pentagon, in Washington, DC, with the fourth crashing in Pennsylvania. The individuals who perpetrated this incident acted as part of, or on behalf of, a conservative and militant Salafist terrorist organization known as al-Qaeda, which at the time was based in Afghanistan.

Although 9/11 and the disrupted chemical attack in Jordan were separate and unrelated plots, they shared a common characteristic in that each exhibited varying degrees of what might be called progressive tactical evolution. In other words, specific terrorist plots are often a single node in a long line of progressive learning, including attempts, failures, and then redeployment of the same or similar tactics. The 9/11 attack, for instance, was the culmination of conceptual thinking and planning by Khalid Sheikh Mohammed ("KSM") beginning in 1993. KSM had already been tied to the first attempt to bomb the World Trade Center in 1993.[7] According to *The 9/11 Commission Report*, by the year 1995, KSM and others "speculated about striking the World Trade Center and CIA headquarters."[8]

Moreover, a Joint Intelligence Inquiry conducted by the U.S. Congress revealed numerous planned, attempted, or aborted suicide plots involving airplanes that were being planned against the United States or other Western countries in the mid- to late 1990s. Among the plots catalogued by investigators was the hijacking in December 1994 of an Air France flight in Algiers by members of the Algerian Armed Islamic Group.[9] The terrorists had threatened to crash the plane, in a suicide operation, into the Eiffel Tower. A year later, in 1995, Philippine authorities uncovered the Bojinka plot—partly engineered by KSM—which featured a plan to bomb eleven U.S. airliners as they crossed the Pacific Ocean. Another stage of Bojinka, as described earlier, involved the crashing of an airplane into CIA headquarters and other targets.[10]

In January 1996, another plot surfaced involving a planned airplane suicide plot targeting the White House.[11] Later, in October 1996, intelligence agencies learned of an Iranian plot "to hijack a Japanese plane over Israel and crash it into Tel Aviv."[12] Roughly two years later, in August 1998, the intelligence community learned that an al-Qaeda-linked group "planned to fly an explosive-laden plane from a foreign country into the World Trade Center."[13] In September 1998, intelligence officials learned of a bin Laden-directed operation that "might involve flying an explosives-laden aircraft into a U.S. airport and detonating it."[14]

In November 1998, intelligence officials in Turkey uncovered a possible plot by an Islamic extremist group to conduct "a suicide attack [involving an airplane packed with explosives] to coincide with celebrations marking the death of Ataturk, the founder of modern Turkey."[15] In April 2000, the U.S. intelligence community was told by a "walk-in" source to the Federal Bureau of Investigation's Newark, New Jersey, office that he had learned hijacking techniques and "was to meet five or six persons in the United States" for the purpose of taking over a plane and flying it to Afghanistan.[16] Finally, in August 2001, U.S. intelligence officials learned of a plot to "bomb the U.S. embassy in Nairobi from an airplane or crash the airplane into it."[17]

Similarly, the Jordan chemical plot could also be viewed as a single node in a long line of tactical evolution. Since the 1980s, al-Qaeda has been fascinated by the prospect of deploying chemical weapons in a mass casualty attack (often in conjunction with a conventional attack). In the 1990s, al-Qaeda had constructed chemical laboratories in Afghanistan and was actively conducting experiments to determine the efficacy of certain chemical weapons. Moreover, recent evidence suggests that al-Qaeda and affiliated groups have been very interested in conducting a chemical weapons attack. In Iraq, for instance, insurgents operating in Al Anbar province and elsewhere—many of whom are believed to be linked to al-Qaeda—have conducted a number of suicide attacks involving trucks loaded with chemicals such as chlorine. In addition, in April 2007, a truck loaded with nitric acid overturned before it could hit a joint security station manned by American and Iraqi troops.[18] These attacks suggest a new form of progressive tactical evolution, consistent with al-Qaeda's past practices. Some U.S. officials have downplayed the significance of these attacks, asserting that they cause mere "psychological effects" instead of "killing effects."[19] Nevertheless, these attacks imply that al-Qaeda and affiliated groups or individuals are learning and evolving. These groups have noted, for instance, the powerful psychological effects generated by the 1995 Sarin gas attack in the Tokyo subway system. As a *Jane's Terrorism and Security Monitor* report noted, "such [a chemical] attack would finally cement al-Qaeda's reputation as a force that is capable of fielding weapons of mass destruction."[20]

Moreover, it would probably not matter for terrorists that such an attack might actually result in fewer casualties than an attack using conventional explosives (an observation that is often made regarding the 1995 Tokyo subway attacks). The successful execution of a chemical attack—which would be deemed a weapons of mass destruction (WMD) event by the target state and international media—"would be a propaganda victory for the global jihad movement."[21]

"Massive Intelligence Failure"

Terrorism incidents often provoke deep introspection by governments, which are under pressure from their publics to explain why they were unable to prevent the attacks. Not surprisingly, in the days, weeks, and months following the September 11, 2001, attacks in the United States, many pundits, analysts, and scholars began to question how such an attack could have occurred; U.S. Senator Richard Shelby described the events surrounding September 11, 2001, as a "massive intelligence failure."[22] *The 9/11 Commission Report* would later observe that "the road to 9/11 again illustrates how the large, unwieldy U.S. government tended to underestimate a threat that grew ever greater."[23]

It is perhaps understandable that such underestimation was allowed to flourish; after all, the U.S. intelligence and security establishment had been geared for decades to focus on state-based threats, and particularly those threats emanating from the Soviet Union. What 9/11 demonstrated was a willingness on the part of nonstate actors to execute a mass casualty attack on an unprecedented scale. Similarly, the planned chemical attacks in Jordan demonstrated a "specific intent"—despite its disruption by the Jordanian government—to bring about even greater casualties, on a level that would far exceed the death toll of 9/11. Moreover, both attacks, one inchoate while the other completed, demonstrated the power of religion—however distorted and manipulated—to motivate and justify such massive harm. When asked about why he joined the Jordan operation, for instance, Husayn Sharif stated: "I agreed to carry out this operation because I believe it serves Islam."[24]

Perhaps most important, both events demonstrated a fundamental transformation of terrorism and its role in international politics. No longer could terrorism simply be viewed as a "nuisance" on the world stage, nor could it be handled exclusively as a law enforcement matter.

On the point of nuisance, former U.S. presidential candidate John Kerry was quoted in an article in the *New York Times Magazine* (just weeks before the November 2, 2004, election) as saying "we have to get back to the place we were, where terrorists are not the focus of our lives, but they're a nuisance."[25] President Bush subsequently criticized Senator Kerry's remark by stating that it reflected a fundamental misunderstanding of the terrorist threat the United States was now facing. Directly referencing Senator Kerry's "nuisance" standard, President Bush was quoted as saying "Our goal is not to reduce terror to some acceptable level of nuisance. Our goal is to defeat terror by staying on the offensive, destroying terrorists, and spreading freedom and liberty around the world."[26]

Despite the political rhetoric associated with discussion of the "nuisance" standard, one can find validity on both sides of the argument. In Senator Kerry's defense, the "nuisance" standard was presented as an alternative to perpetual war that is implied by an open-ended campaign designated the "global war on terrorism" (or GWOT, as it is known within government circles). Senator Kerry stated that terrorism, like prostitution, could never be eliminated, but it could, with the appropriate measures, be managed so that it does not disrupt society or exact too heavy a price in terms of its destructive capacity. However, President Bush was also correct in asserting, in essence, that terrorism could no longer be viewed through the lens that it had been understood in previous eras, such as during the cold war, or earlier periods, when terrorism was indeed seen as a nuisance. The convergence of chemical, biological, radiological, and nuclear (CBRN) technology and unrestrained desires on the part of modern terrorists to bring about catastrophic destruction—whether through conventional or nonconventional weapons—meant that terrorism could never again be viewed through the nuisance paradigm.

Indeed, terrorism now reflects—and is arguably a product of—powerful forces of globalization both functionally and ideationally (i.e., the competition and power of ideas). Weapons and technology once thought to be safely under "lock and key" in state armories or laboratories are now increasingly available on the gray and black markets. For example, Aum Shinrikyo, the Japanese religious cult that conducted the 1995 attack on Tokyo's subway system, was able to obtain "technology and blueprints for producing Sarin, a deadly nerve gas" from official contacts that it maintained in Russia in the early 1990s.[27]

In addition, globalization has brought about a revolution in communications and transportation that has enabled terrorist plots to be planned and executed at transcontinental distances. The 9/11 plot was organized in Afghanistan, Pakistan, Malaysia, Germany, and other countries. Moreover, cheap and efficient air transportation has allowed terrorists, often with forged passports in hand, to travel the world for purposes of raising funds, spreading their ideology, or recruiting new members.[28] The Internet, perhaps the ultimate expression of the power of the information revolution, has emerged as the communication platform for contemporary terrorists; "the great virtues of the Internet . . . have been turned to the advantage of groups committed to terrorizing societies to achieve their goals."[29]

Moreover, some analysts and scholars have noted that the brand of terrorism represented by 9/11 and similar plots reveals the onset of a new type of terrorism. In 1996, Walter Laqueur published an article titled "Postmodern Terrorism" in the journal *Foreign Affairs* in which he detailed the emergence of this "new" terrorism, which would feature the absence of state sponsorship, the presence of religious or millenarian ideologies, and the inclination to use

CBRN weapons. Laqueur also wrote: "Society has also become vulnerable to a new kind of terrorism, in which the destructive power of both the individual terrorist and terrorism as a tactic are infinitely greater."[30]

Laqueur's analysis would be echoed a decade later when a U.S. congressional research report noted that "looming over the entire issue of international terrorism is the specter of proliferation of weapons of mass destruction."[31] The attempted chemical attack in Jordan is evidence of the validity of such concern. In addition, the "new" terrorism would also feature suicide attacks, not historically unique but nevertheless unprecedented in terms of scale and destructive capacity. Recently, for example, the Sri Lankan Liberation Tigers of Tamil Eelam conducted a suicide attack on a convoy of buses that killed more than ninety Sri Lankan navy personnel.[32]

Terrorism and State Terror

To understand terrorism in the contemporary context, it is important to recognize that terrorism is generally considered a tool or tactic, not an ideology or philosophy. This "tool" can be used as part of a larger political or military campaign, such as an insurgency. When al-Qaeda conducted the 9/11 attacks, it was using the "tool" of terrorism to achieve the larger purposes of diminishing American political influence in the Middle East, among other objectives.

One way to define terrorism is to describe it as simply the "systematic use of coercive intimidation, usually to service political ends."[33] The word "terrorism" itself was adopted from the French word *terreur,* which was derived from the Latin word *terrere* (to frighten). The word *terreur* began to be commonly used in France during the French Revolution during a period known as the Reign of Terror (1793–94).[34] During this period, Maximilien Robespierre used the Revolutionary Committee of Public Safety to institute terror throughout France. The committee pursued, investigated, and arrested individuals who disagreed with, or even appeared less than enthusiastic about, its policies.[35] The result was that over 300,000 to 400,000[36] suspects were arrested on generally unsubstantiated political charges under the "Law of Suspects," and up to 40,000 were executed, many of them not having the benefit of a trial.[37] The guillotine was commonly used as the execution method, in part because of the broad public spectacle that was generated.[38]

Ironically, as Audrey Kurth Cronin describes, the terrorism associated with the French revolution was essentially state terror—"the means whereby the nascent revolutionary state consolidated power and imposed order"—whereas today the term is typically reserved for nonstate actors.[39]

R. Thackrah describes the differences between state terror and terrorism in terms of law enforcement by the state versus defiance of the state: "Terror practiced by a government in office appears as law enforcement and is directed against the opposition, while terrorism on the other hand implies open defiance of the law and is the means whereby an opposition aims to demoralize government authority."[40] Jerrold Post defines state terror as "the state turning its resources—police, judiciary, military, secret police, etc.—against its own citizenry to suppress dissent, as exemplified by the 'dirty wars' in Argentina. When Saddam Hussein used nerve gas against his own Kurdish citizens, this was an example of state CBW [chemical and biological weapons] terrorism."[41]

Others have characterized the difference between state terror and nonstate terrorism as enforcement terror versus agitational terror. Enforcement terror is used "by those in power who wish to suppress challenges to their authority"[42] and is most identifiable with terror conducted by states. Agitational terror is generally associated with individuals who are interested in disrupting the existing order so that they might ascend to political power themselves.[43] In general, agitational terror would almost always apply to nonstate actors.

In early twentieth-century Russia, for example, Vladimir Lenin eschewed agitational terrorism; he was extremely suspicious of using terror tactics to achieve political goals. However, after 1905, Lenin "increasingly became an enthusiastic supporter of all types of terror" and moreover, his position hardened to such an extent that he came "to justify the most ruthless terrorist means," an attitude that would persist once he had attained power and could then use the instruments of the state to mete out terror.[44] Richard Drake writes that by 1917, Lenin had totally abandoned any reluctance to employ terrorist tactics: "The Bolshevik leader claimed that all resistance to the communist revolution would have to be met with maximum force. . . . The terrorist potential in Lenin's program was unmistakable, as his fellow Bolshevik, Trotsky, proudly acknowledged [in his book] *Terrorism and Communism: a Reply* (1918)."[45]

In later years, Joseph Stalin would take state terror to new heights, generating human carnage to such a level that some have described the former Soviet Union as a "country built on bones."[46] The hundreds of thousands of bodies, the result of Soviet terror, have been "discovered in practically every Soviet city, including the center of Moscow."[47] Thus, when comparing Lenin to Stalin, one can see the primary difference being that Lenin experienced the full spectrum, engaging in (or advocating) terrorism at certain stages of his life when he was not in power, and then having gained power, using the instruments of the state against its own population (state terror). Stalin, however, was primarily known for being simply a purveyor of state terror. Thus, as can be seen in these examples, although there are similarities between terrorism and state terror, "they are ultimately, two entirely different creatures."[48]

Other examples of state terror in the form of political pogroms and ethnic cleansing campaigns orchestrated by a state include the Turkish-sanctioned policy implemented between 1915 and 1916 to slaughter more than 650,000 ethnic Armenians.[49] Subsequently, in Germany, during the period leading up to World War II—in addition to the war years—state terror reached a new level of violence. Between 1933 and 1945, Nazi Germany pursued a policy of persecuting and systematically exterminating nearly 6.5 million Jews and others, including "asocials" (Gypsies, homosexuals, the handicapped, the mentally ill, and Soviet prisoners).[50]

Clearly, the loss of life in the context of state terror in the modern era far overshadows the violence and death count attributable to nonstate actor terrorism, at least thus far in history. As Walter Laqueur notes: "No one denies that the number of victims and the amount of suffering caused by oppressive, tyrannical governments has been infinitely greater than that caused by small groups of rebels: a Hitler or a Stalin killed more people in one year than all terrorists throughout recorded history."[51] This partly reflects the simple fact that states generally had more efficient means—and more powerful weapons—to conduct terrorist actions against their own populations, or those of neighboring states or outlying colonies.

In the future, this "body count asymmetry"—as macabre as the notion may sound—between state terror and nonstate actor terrorism may begin to equalize as nonstate actor terrorists employ more effective weapons, such as bioweapons, that have the capacity to kill mass quantities of individuals. However, to date, the state remains the undisputed top instigator of terror, and the body count attributable to state terror far exceeds that of any terrorism associated with nonstate actors.

In summary, states can sponsor terrorism (typically by directing a nonstate actor to perform a terrorist act on the state's behalf), or they engage in terror themselves (typically against their own populations), but it is generally understood that terrorism itself is an activity conducted exclusively by nonstate actors, outside of the purview or agency of the state.

Defining Terrorism—Why the Difficulty?

One of the great controversies and challenges in the study of terrorism is the issue of definition. It is a well-known fact that currently the international community does not subscribe to a single definition of terrorism, although many definitions currently exist that essentially and arguably speak to the same phenomenon. The U.S. Federal Bureau of Investigation defines terrorism as the "unlawful use of force or violence against persons or property to intimidate or coerce a government, the civilian population, or any segment thereof, in furtherance of political or social objectives."[52]

A second U.S. executive branch definition was contained in an executive order on terrorist financing. That order contained the following definition of terrorism: "(d) the term 'terrorism' means an activity that (i) involves a violent act or an act dangerous to human life, property, or infrastructure; and (ii) appears to be intended (A) to intimidate or coerce a civilian population; (B) to influence the policy of a government by intimidation or coercion; or (C) to affect the conduct of a government by mass destruction, assassination, kidnapping, or hostage-taking."[53] The United Nations has proposed a definition such that terrorism constitutes "criminal acts intended or calculated to provoke a state of terror in the general public."[54] Peter Chalk of the RAND Corporation argues that terrorism is the "use or threat of illegitimate violence that is employed by sub-state actors as a means to achieve specific political objectives."[55] Ayla Schbley offers up the following definition of terrorism: "Terrorism is any violent act upon symbolic civilians and their properties."[56] Christopher Harmon proposes the following succinct definition: "Terrorism is the deliberate and systematic murder, maiming, and menacing of the innocent to inspire fear for political ends."[57] Meanwhile, Jessica Stern defines terrorism as "an act or threat of violence against noncombatants with the objective of exacting revenge, intimidating, or otherwise influencing an audience."[58]

These varied definitions of terrorism have led to criticisms of the field of terrorism studies—if there is no internationally agreed-upon definition of terrorism, how can the subject be studied effectively? As one Australian analyst has written, "[t]he failure of the international community to define terrorism poses a difficult methodological problem for scholars who specialize in terrorism studies."[59] However, recent international treaties have provided greater guidance as to an internationally-accepted definition of terrorism. Specifically, the *International Convention for the Suppression of the Financing of Terrorism* (1999) provides a reasonably robust definition in Article 2, subpoint 1 (a) and (b). Section (a) states that any offense that is listed in the annex of the treaty (which lists previous terrorism conventions) would fall under the purview of this treaty. More significantly, section (b) provides a working definition of terrorism as follows: "Any other act intended to cause death or serious bodily injury to a civilian, or to any other person not taking an active part in the hostilities in a situation of armed conflict, when the purpose of such act, by its nature or context, is to intimidate a population, or to compel a government or an international organization to do or to abstain from doing any act."[60]

One way around the definition problem is to view terrorism in terms of its elements. Just as certain crimes in the American legal (or English common law) tradition are defined in terms of elements, terrorism can be viewed as an activity imbued with certain key elements, the sum of which is reflected in various definitions. In general, most terrorism will contain some or all of the following five elements: (1) political activity or purpose; (2) targeting of noncombatants (generally civilians); (3) communication; (4) psychological warfare; (5) which is conducted by nonstate actors.[61]

Political Nature of Terrorism

Terrorism must be recognized, at its very core, as being a form of political activity. Terrorists use criminal methods to pursue political objectives, not (usually) material gains.[62] Terrorist violence—propaganda of the deed—demonstrates "that the regime can be challenged and that illegal opposition is possible."[63] It may act as a catalyst for a larger revolt; it is, in the words of Martha Crenshaw, "a shortcut to revolution."[64] This description does not seek to legitimize terrorist activity, even to a slight degree; it simply seeks to distinguish terrorism from mere crime, which should be totally within the purview of law enforcement officials.

This analysis is important because it strikes at the heart of a debate within governments on whether to treat terrorism as a crime or as a form of warfare. Terrorism can of course be prosecuted on the basis of its constituent acts—murder, destruction of property, and so on—but the political nature of terrorism suggests that the activity must be given a higher priority than regular street crime or organized crime. Ambassador Ronald Spiers has proposed that terrorism be seen as a form of warfare. Just as states use war "as a method of carrying on politics by other means," terrorists use terrorism as politics by other means by using violence "to intimidate or instill fear for the purpose of advancing a political objective."[65] In addition, terrorists often view themselves as "combatants" or soldiers who are at war with the state or a particular regime.[66]

However, there is one major difference between war and terrorism—apart from tactics and tools—that relates to the legitimacy of the use of that particular type of force. War is considered legitimate, while terrorism is considered illegitimate. This is why the best analysis concedes that terrorism falls somewhere in the middle of the spectrum between war and crime. Clearly, terrorism encompasses elements of each and this is why, as is often the case, the response to terrorism will often involve law enforcement agencies, intelligence departments, and, when necessary, military forces.

Targeting of Noncombatants

Terrorism almost always involves the killing (or threat of killing) of noncombatant civilians. This goes to the heart of terrorism's illegitimacy. Terrorists make a "deliberate decision to abandon those restraints [adopted by states concerning warfare] or to refuse to accept as binding the prevailing moral distinctions between belligerents and neutrals, combatants and non-combatants, appropriate and inappropriate targets, legitimate and illegitimate methods."[67] This targeting of civilians (noncombatants) is also what distinguishes terrorism from guerilla war. Christopher Harmon singles out the killing of civilians as a key delegitimizing (as well as delegalizing) aspect of terrorism, and thus compares terrorism to the conduct of war crimes: "Many wars are legitimate but war crimes are never so; similarly, many forms of military violence may be justified, but not terrorism."[68]

Communication

At its heart, terrorism is about communication. Terrorism provides an opportunity, particularly when conducted in a media-rich environment, to achieve free advertising about a political cause or grievance. As noted earlier, terrorism capitalizes on fear, but this fear must be transmitted through the communication infrastructure, and thus, not surprisingly, terrorists tend to be savvy about how to reach and exploit this infrastructure. In the 1880s, anarchist terrorists benefited from the rise of the "new journalism" with its "sensational headlines in heavy black letters," which emphasized the sensational over the substantive.[69] Terrorists in the 1960s benefited from the advent of television, and particularly live broadcast television. For example, the Palestinian Black September Organization's attack at the Munich Olympics in 1972 was viewed by an estimated 800 million live-television viewers.

More recently, terrorists in the 1990s and 2000s have learned of the power of the Internet, which they use for propaganda, recruiting, and instruction, among other purposes. In addition, today's terrorists use a wide variety of new communication technologies to get their message out. Mohammad Sidique Khan, for instance, produced a martyrdom video prior to his execution of the London underground suicide attack in 2005; this video was posted on the Internet for all to see. Al-Qaeda and similar groups regularly issue video clips, posted on Internet Web sites, that show attacks on U.S. forces in Iraq or propaganda statements by their leaders.

Psychological Warfare

Closely related to the communication element, terrorists employ the tactics of terrorism because it enables them to achieve a level of influence or power beyond their actual numbers or strength. This is done through psychology and fear. Fear helps terrorists overcome the paradox that they face, that "their success depends on an appearance of strength that is sufficiently great to intimidate their enemies or mobilize their supporters."[70] Terrorists seek to cultivate fear by creating an atmosphere of "fear, anxiety, and collapse"[71] in an attempt to exploit the subsequent emotional reaction for political purposes. The cultivation of fear is related to other aspects of terrorism—striking noncombatant civilians in an indiscriminate and unpredictable manner. Terrorists are often hopeful that generation of massive and widespread fear will provoke a disproportionate and irrational response by the government being targeted. Terrorists believe that such overreaction will validate the grievances that motivated them in the first place. Moreover, the targeting of noncombatant civilians is a means to an end: "The real target is public opinion, and the success of a terrorist act can often be gauged by the amount of publicity received."[72]

The Centrality of Nonstate Actors to the Conduct of Terrorism

As noted earlier, terrorism is an activity conducted by nonstate actors. As Audrey Kurth Cronin has noted, "terrorism is distinguished by its nonstate character—even when terrorists receive military, political, economic, and other means of support from state sources. . . . Although states can terrorize, they cannot by definition be terrorists."[73]

Thus, combining all of the aforementioned elements, terrorism may be defined as indiscriminate violence committed by nonstate actors against noncombatant persons to instill or perpetuate fear within a wider audience for the ultimate purpose of achieving some political objective.

Final Observations Regarding Terrorism

Despite the all-encompassing term "terrorism," it is important to recognize that there is no single aspect of this phenomenon. Terrorism invariably arises within specific historical, social, or political contexts and thus each form of terrorism is unique. "Terrorism . . . involves many groups, many instruments, and, often, no central command. Terrorists are not a single foe, and no simple theory of deterrence can possibly apply to the spectrum that ranges from anti-U.S. or anti-Israeli 'martyrs' to members of American right wing militias."[74]

One useful way of thinking about terrorism is to categorize it into various types and subtypes, including ideological terrorism (including leftist and rightist terrorism), ethnoseparatist (nationalist) terrorism, religious terrorism, single issue terrorism, and so on. Historically, it may be reasonably argued that the most significant terrorism, at least in terms of its ability to influence the formation or evolution of states, is the ethnonationalist variety. It has been observed, for instance, that nationalist groups are better positioned to sustain protracted political campaigns and to maintain substantial financial and logistical support, particularly when compared with ideological groups.[75] The National Liberation Front in Algeria and the Jewish Irgun in Palestine are examples of two critically important ethnonationalist groups that employed terrorism as part of larger political campaigns, which ultimately had major consequences for subsequent formation of states.

Another important aspect in understanding terrorism is the delineation between international and domestic varieties. International terrorism is defined as terrorism that involves the government, citizens, or territory of more than one state.[76] Thomas Badey classifies international terrorism as the "repeated use of politically motivated violence with coercive intent, by nonstate actors, that affects more than one state."[77] According to the U.S. General Accounting Office, international terrorism simply is "terrorism involving citizens or the territory of more than one country."[78] By contrast, domestic terrorism is generally confined to a single country (origins of the perpetrators as well as the target of terrorism). In the context of the United States, domestic terrorism is defined as "the unlawful use, or threatened use, of force or violence by a terrorist group or individual based and operating entirely within the United States or its territories without foreign direction."[79]

Finally, perhaps the most difficult aspect of understanding the nature of terrorism is recognizing that the term is often prone to being misused or abused. The term is often used by "any individual or group for whatever displeases them in the behavior of others."[80] In some cases, ideological differences can result in charges of "terrorism" by one or more parties in a dispute. In early 2004, for instance, Education Secretary Rod Paige called the National Education Association, the largest teacher's union in the United States, a "terrorist organization" due to various ideological differences he had with the organization.[81] In another case in Canada, a legislator who opposed the behemoth American retailer Wal-Mart's plan to close down a unionized store in Quebec, accused the retailer of engaging in "economic terrorism."[82] The term is clearly intended as a delegitimizing tactic: "Those who seek to delegitimate the tactics and strategies of their opponents often describe them as terrorist acts."[83]

As Peter Chalk has noted: "The word terrorism is typically never used in a balanced, objective manner."[84] Martha Crenshaw echoes this by arguing that "the word [terrorism] has become a political label rather than an analytical concept, used to condemn one's enemies rather than to specify what terrorism is and what it is not."[85] Governments tend to label anyone who opposes their policies as a "terrorist," while antigovernment extremists will claim that they are the victims of state terror: "Use of the term [terrorism] usually implies a moral judgment: it is what the bad guys do."[86]

Conclusion

Terrorism is a phenomenon that has existed throughout history, and will continue far into the future. "Terrorism is, among other things, a weapon used by the weak against the strong."[87] It is a term fraught with controversy and emotion. Although there continue to be debates about precise definitions and parameters, a consensus appears to be emerging, particularly as the international community has adopted more than twelve key conventions and protocols since the 1960s that address various aspects of combating terrorism.[88]

These international measures, combined with international outrage over the events of September 11, 2001 (as well as other terrorist attacks around the world since that time), suggest that the issue of terrorism is regarded as a high-level security threat, one, it is hoped, that will be confronted with increasing levels of international cooperation in the years and decades ahead.

2

The Historical Evolution
of Modern Terrorism

When militant Islamists successfully launched suicide attacks against the United States Marine Corps compound and other targets in Beirut in 1983, Velupillai Prabhakaran of the Liberation Tigers of Tamil Eelam (LTTE) took notice. He recognized that "a small and little-known terrorist group . . . in a single attack, was able to offset its relative weakness and strike decisively against the world's leading superpower."[1] Prabhakaran became convinced that the LTTE should adopt the same tactics. Moreover, he believed that if his organization conducted suicide operations, then the goal of achieving Tamil Eelam (Tamil Homeland) could be reached much faster. Prabhakaran specifically argued that "if we conduct Black Tiger [suicide] operations, we can shorten the suffering of the people and achieve Tamil Eelam in a shorter period of time."[2]

The LTTE did in fact adopt suicide terrorism as a key tactic and, ultimately, it would become one of the most deadly organizations in the world. By the late 1990s, the LTTE had conducted more than 160 such attacks, and was responsible for roughly two-thirds of all suicide bombings conducted worldwide.[3] Moreover, prominent targets have included former Indian prime minister Rajiv Gandhi, who was killed by an LTTE suicide bomber in 1991, and the Sri Lankan Central Bank, which was bombed by a suicide truck bomber in January 1996. In October 1997, the LTTE staged a suicide attack against Colombo's World Trade Center, an attack that was modeled on the 1993 World Trade Center attack in the United States.[4]

But the larger lesson has to do with learning and the diffusion of terrorism tactics and doctrine. It should come as no surprise that terrorists tend to study other terrorists—they do it vertically (through the study of historical narratives and evidence) as well as horizontally (by studying the tactics and strategies of contemporaneous groups). Yitzhak Shamir of the Jewish nationalist group Lehi studied the tactics of Michael Collins of the Irish Republican Army (IRA) and even adopted "Michael" as his nom de guerre.[5] Similarly, Osama bin Laden was influenced by the ideas of Ibn Taymiyya, just as the Japanese Red Army Faction was influenced by the world revolution ideas of Che Guevara.[6] Meanwhile, Ilich Ramirez Sanchez, otherwise known as "Carlos the Jackal" was an admirer of the teachings of George Habash, leader of the Popular Front for the Liberation of Palestine (PFLP).[7]

Thus, as terrorists themselves demonstrate, the study (and awareness) of terrorism history can be useful when it comes to understanding contemporary events, or predicting future ones. Ironically, when faced with a sudden terrorism crisis, many governments today have a tendency to view the challenge as something new and unprecedented, often without realizing that many trends and patterns in terrorism have historical antecedents that may provide a useful guide for policy. At the very least, knowledge of terrorism's history may provide a roadmap that suggests or predicts the expected lifespan of a particular terrorism group or movement. Terrorism, after all, has existed throughout history; it could almost be described as a permanent feature of human civilization. This is because, as Ariel Merari asserts, "[t]errorism is a means, not goal. Because it is the simplest form of armed struggle, it appears whenever and wherever there is a conflict that is sufficiently acute to generate the will of some people to resort to violence."[8]

Analyzing terrorism from a historical perspective also reveals that terrorism generally does not occur in a vacuum. It often manifests as a reaction to certain political trends or social environments that exist at a particular stage in history. David Rapoport has proposed a very useful model for understanding modern terrorism that is premised on what he describes as historic "waves." A wave can be thought of as a "cycle of activity in a given time period—a cycle characterized by expansion and contraction phases."[9] Waves are international in character; "similar activities occur in several countries, driven by a common predominant energy that shapes the participating groups' characteristics and mutual relationships."[10] Essentially the theory suggests that modern terrorism, which began roughly in the middle of the nineteenth century, has tended to reflect larger tensions or broad sentiments in the international system within a particular period. Rapoport asserts that modern terrorism thus far has consisted of four major waves: anarchist (late nineteenth, early twentieth centuries), nationalist/anticolonial (post–World War I), ideological (1960s and 1970s), and religious (post-1979).[11]

Some of the Earliest Terrorists

Although modern terrorism (and its ideologies) is believed to have been around for about 150 years, the phenomenon of terrorism itself has been around much longer. Three groups in particular are representative of earlier terrorism experiences and are worthy of examination; they include the Sicarii, the Assassins, and the Thugs. These groups are notable because they serve as early precedents in which key tactics or themes in terrorism manifested or were developed, and some of these can be seen in terrorist groups operating today.

For example, the Jewish group Sicarii was premised on an ideology that man should not be ruled by laws of men, but by God, a notion that ironically parallels the ideas of the Muslim activist-writer Sayyid Qutb, considered a key intellectual influence on al-Qaeda.[12] The Assassins, moreover, provided humanity with a premodern example of suicide terrorism, suggesting that this common and increasingly popular tactic is not exclusively a modern phenomenon. Similarly, the Thugs, who were known to have killed tens of thousands of individuals, perhaps were an early example of mass casualty terrorists.

Of these three groups, the Sicarii is the oldest terrorist organization, having existed in Palestine in the first century C.E. The Sicarii, famous for their use of the sica (short dagger),[13] generally targeted fellow Jews and avoided targeting (at least directly) Roman soldiers or civilians. They hoped that by attacking Jewish ruling groups, through which the Romans implemented their authority throughout Jewish Palestine, they could ultimately undermine Roman governance.[14]

The Sicarii were also known for employing three sets of tactics against their targets: "selective, symbolic assassinations," more general assassinations that might be accompanied by the destruction or plundering of property, and, finally, kidnapping.[15] As Richard Horsley argues, "for the sacerdotal aristocracy and the Jewish notables the Sicarii probably intended the tactic of selective assassination as a punishment for previous exploitation of the people and collaboration with the Romans."[16] More important, however, the Sicarii understood that its attacks would not only demonstrate the vulnerability of the ruling regime but also instill widespread anxiety and fear—the classic strategy of terrorism.[17]

In contrast to the Sicarii, the Zealots, another Jewish rebellion group that was prominent from 66 C.E. to 72 C.E., were far more willing to attack Roman officials directly. The Zealots were known for their "ruthless campaign of both individual assassination and wholesale slaughter."[18] The Zealots employed an early version of chemical warfare by poisoning Roman wells and granaries and "even sabotaging Jerusalem's water supply."[19] "The Zealots hoped their actions would provoke Roman repression and Jewish rebellion."[20] Perhaps their most famous act—which some scholars attribute to the Sicarii[21]—was a mass suicide in 73 C.E. at the fortress of Masada, involving nearly 1,000 men, women, and children, following a three-year siege by the tenth Roman legion.[22]

The Sicarii and the Zealots are often confused as being the same group, although historical evidence suggests that the two were distinct and in fact "mutually hostile."[23] They did, however, share a common objective of seeking to design their particular actions specifically to provoke a mass uprising.[24] However, unlike the Zealots, the Sicarii were, as noted above, guided by a robust ideology that "there should be no lordship of man over man, that God is the only ruler."[25]

The Assassins (also known as Hashishiyah or Hashashin) were a second notable premodern terrorist organization that emerged roughly a thousand years later. Their name is derived from the word hashish,[26] although there is no indication in the Assassins' records that they actually smoked or consumed hashish.[27] The Assassins operated in Persia and Syria between 1090 and 1275.[28] Founded by Hassan Sabbah the Persian, they are described by Charles Nowell as "probably in their heyday, the fiercest of the fanatical sects that have terrorized the Islamic world."[29] Two branches eventually emerged in the organization, one Persian and the other Syrian, "though a connection still existed between them."[30]

Through acts of violence, they hoped to propagate a more purified form of Islam. The lowest ranking of the sect—known as fedayeen—were the actual attackers. "These [fedayeen] cared nothing for their own lives, and seemed to enjoy killing their victims in the most conspicuous places and under the most dramatic circumstances."[31] In other words, their attack methods were nearly suicidal in that they would stab their victims in broad daylight. As Bernard Lewis notes: "The Assassin went right up to his victim and normally made no attempt whatsoever to escape."[32] Some scholars see the techniques of the Assassins as an antecedent to contemporary suicide bombers. The Assassins consciously chose daggers as their weapon—as opposed to potentially more efficient weapons, such as poison or a missile—because daggers required close-in attack methods and thus increased the possibility that the assassin would be captured or killed.[33]

Like the Sicarii, the Assassins' objectives were rooted in both religion and politics. Among other things, they killed political leaders whom they deemed as corrupt in order to pave the way for a more pure and unblemished form of Islam. They also targeted the rich and powerful: "The Syrian Assassins followed the example of Hassan Sabbah and reserved their daggers for the rich and powerful, not stooping to attack the humble and poor."[34] Bernard Lewis argues that, ultimately, the Assassins did little more than terrorize: "The terrorism of the medieval Assassins lasted several centuries. It expressed the smoldering discontent and the continuing resentments of a society in which rapid changes were taking place. It made a tremendous impact. It terrorized a series of regimes. But it ended in total failure. The Assassins disappeared, having accomplished none of their purposes."[35]

A third notable example of premodern terrorists were the Thugs (also known as Thugees). They flourished for more than 600 years, from the thirteenth through the nineteenth centuries on the Indian subcontinent.[36] They attacked their victims on remote roads by using specific strangling techniques designed to avoid the spilling of human blood. It is estimated that the Thugs murdered more than 500,000 people, making them one of the most violent nonstate actor terrorist groups in history.[37] Unlike many terrorist organizations that seek to impress both an external and internal audience, it appears that the Thugs primarily focused on creating violence to impress their goddess, Kali. Indeed, Kali serves as the central character in the Thugs' narrative and motivation for actions. David Kinsley argues that "Kā-alī's association with the blood sacrifice (sometimes human), her position as patron goddess of the infamous Thugs, and her importance in Vāmācāra Tantric ritual have generally won for her a reputation as a creature born of a crazed, aboriginal mind."[38]

Unlike classic terrorists who seek to communicate their actions and ideology to a larger audience, the Thugs eschewed publicity; widespread fear was a by-product of their activities, not an objective.[39] Moreover, there is some controversy about whether they should be labeled terrorists at all, since it appears that they were driven less by political motives than by a cultish religion that relished human sacrifice,[40] although presumably the victims of the Thugs would have little intellectual hesitation in labeling Thugs as terrorists.

Modern Terrorism's First Wave: Revolutionary/Anarchist Terror

On September 6, 1901, Leon Czolgosz, a twenty-eight-year-old U.S. citizen who believed that "every King, Emperor, President or head of government [is] a tyrant"[41] shot and ultimately killed U.S. President William McKinley in Buffalo, New York. McKinley had been attending the Pan-American Exposition and had refused to be accompanied by a bodyguard. Although Czolgosz was suspected of having accomplices, later evidence revealed that he was the lone assassin; moreover, Czolgosz had publicly declared that "he alone is responsible for his crime."[42]

Notwithstanding Czolgosz's claims, U.S. authorities suspected that Czolgosz had indeed acted as part of a vast conspiracy involving other U.S.-based anarchists. On September 10, 1901, secret service agents fanned out throughout Paterson, New Jersey, to investigate "whether or not there was an Anarchist plot [there] to take the life of the President."[43] Simultaneously, authorities in Chicago arrested nine anarchists who were suspected of being linked to the assassination plot.[44] Of particular interest to authorities was Emma Goldman, whom Czolgosz had allegedly met prior to the McKinley assassination. Gold-man was described by one media source as the person "whose Anarchistic harangues are alleged to have 'fired the brain' of Leon Czolgosz."[45] She was quickly arrested and charged with "conspiracy to assassinate President McKinley."[46] In subsequent days, however, many of those arrested (including Goldman) would be released due to lack of evidence.[47]

The assassination of President McKinley was one in a series of anarchist murders spanning the end of the nineteenth century to the early twentieth century, and primarily targeting world leaders or members of European royal families. It was one of the key events in the first wave of terrorism, known as the anarchist wave, which generated profound fear throughout Europe and North America. In the context of modern terrorism, David Rapoport asserts that this anarchist/revolutionary wave had its genesis in Russia. Norman Naimark confirms this Russian connection by stating that: "[b]etween 1866, when a demented ex-student named Dmitrii Karakozov fired an errant shot at the Tsar Alexander II, and 1911, when Dmitrii Bogrov fatally wounded Prime Minister Petr Stolypin, Russia was absorbed by terrorism."[48]

As the industrial revolution progressed throughout Europe, terrorism began to reflect the broader tensions in international society at the time. The rise of universalist ideologies—such as Marxism and Communism—also shaped the foundations and evolution of terrorism: "From this milieu a new era of terrorism emerged, in which the concept had gained many of the fa-miliar revolutionary, anti-state connotations of today."[49] Carlo Piscane and his "propaganda by deed" are associated with this transformation. Piscane believed that "ideas result from deeds, not the latter from the former, and the people will not be free when they are educated, but educated when they are free."[50] The ideology is believed to be the foundation for Narodnaya Volya (or People's Will), one of the most significant revolutionary terrorist organi-zations of the period.[51]

The Narodnaya Volya was a "secret organization which comprised thirty members; it was dedicated to fighting the Czarist regime using systematic terror in the hope of kindling the revolutionary energy of the peasants."[52] Nar-odnaya Volya claimed to speak "for the people," but as the group progressed "the people had become an abstract concept with no equivalent in the real world."[53] They focused their energy on assassinating Tzar Alexander II, a feat that they attempted three times with no success. Eventually, they prevailed in 1881, but the assassination would ultimately prove disappointing: "the assassination did not produce the desired political results: the peasantry did not rise; moderate urban public opinion was horrified; and the radical cause lost support."[54] What happened instead was a massive government roundup of Narodnaya Volya's members. Ultimately, all the original members of the group were suppressed or eliminated and this led to various splinter or successor organizations that emerged to continue the struggle.[55]

The Narodnaya Volya was influenced by the ideas of Sergei Nechaev, whose famous booklet *Catechism of the Revolutionist*, elucidated principles that could easily resonate with contemporary religious terrorists and suicide bombers. On the issue of death and martyrdom, Nechaev argued that "In cold blooded and tireless pursuit of this aim, [the revolutionary] must be prepared both to die himself and to destroy with his own hands everything that stands in the way of its achievement."[56] In addition, Nechaev describes the "binary worldview" that can often be found in most terrorist movements, the notion that the revolutionary was part of one category of persons, while the object of its terror was on the other side. Nechaev argued that "[an individual] is not a revolutionary if he feels pity for anything in this world. If he is able to, he must face the annihilation of a situation, of a relationship, or of any person who is part of this world—everything and everyone must be equally odious to him."[57]

The Narodnaya Volya organization can also trace its intellectual foundations to Mikhail Bakunin, a Russian national who, until his death in 1876, played a central role in the anarchist movement in Switzerland, France, and Italy.[58] Born to an aristocratic family and heavily influenced by the writings of G.W.F. Hegel and French anarchist Pierre J. Proudhon, Bakunin advocated a comprehensive anarchism. Bakunin basically believed that all idea systems or means of governance, whether monarchic or parliamentary, forced people to become slaves. He believed that the state, and its inherent power of coercion, was the source of all evil.[59] To free the slaves of these systems (including states), he argued, "existing society had to be overturned."[60] Bakunin urged his followers to engage in all-out revolt against the established ruling class: "The present generation must in its turn produce an inexorable brute force and relentlessly tread the path of destruction."[61]

From an international perspective, Narodnaya Volya's most important contribution to terrorism was the template it provided for the anarchist movement, although some scholars are adamant about separating Russian revolutionary terrorists from anarchist terrorists.[62] Four months following Tsar Alexander II's assassination, a group of radicals convened an "anarchist conference" in London. To promote and encourage worldwide anarchist activities, the conferees decided to establish an "Anarchist International" (or "Black International").[63] It was during this conference that the doctrine of "propaganda by the deed" was officially recognized.[64] Although the anarchist conference had no real power, the participants were able to "create a myth of global revolutionary pretensions and thereby stimulate fears and suspicions disproportionate to its actual impact or political achievements."[65]

Overall, the anarchists reigned during the period encompassing the 1880s up to the first decade of the twentieth century. Between 1892 and 1901 (known as the Decade of Regicide), anarchists in Europe and the United States murdered about sixty individuals and injured an additional 200 with attacks involving bombs, pistols and daggers.[66] In Europe, the anarchists killed French President Sadi Carnot in 1894 and Antonio Cánovas, the Spanish prime minister, in 1897. Empress Elizabeth (Zita) of Austria and King Umberto of Italy were killed in 1898 and 1900, respectively. Responding to the wave of assassinations, Prince Bismarck of Germany noted that "anarchist crime was an infectious disease, in which vanity and the lust of fame often played a part."[67]

In addition, the anarchists killed many second-tier leaders; consequently, it should come as no surprise that the general public was both horrified and fascinated by the mysterious nature of the assassins and their motives.[68] In one instance, a bomb was thrown into the Chamber of Deputies, and in another, an anarchist fired shots from his gun in the Paris stock exchange. These anarchists shared a common goal. They wanted to "destabilize bourgeois society, [avenge] the suffering of the oppressed and that of earlier, martyred terrorists."[69]

In the United States, the anarchist movement had combined with latent xenophobia associated with rising immigration and tensions over organized labor to create a pervasive climate of fear that led to, among other things, the Haymarket Affair in Chicago in 1886, in which police were bombed by dynamite when they attempted to break up a crowd of angry labor strikers. Shots were also fired at police, who then "returned the fire with deadly effect."[70]

After three more hours, the mob was finally dispersed. Subsequently, eight anarchists were either hanged or imprisoned for the death of a Chicago policeman, despite very scant and questionable evidence.[71] The Haymarket Affair marked a key turning point in how the public viewed anarchists and their rhetoric; what was once considered "loose and flamboyant talk" had transformed into a "terrifying ominousness in the eyes of the adversaries of labor."[72] Moreover, the "foreignness" of the anarchists intensified antipathy against them: "The fact that most of the anarchists were recent immigrants—Germans, Russian Jews, and Italians—tended to intensify the prejudice against them."[73]

The anarchists cultivated a widespread sense of fear, which was facilitated by developments in communication and media technology. Just as contemporary terrorists benefit from the Internet, anarchists benefited from the beginning of the Age of Mass Journalism, with pioneering editors such as Joseph Pulitzer and his *St. Louis Post-Dispatch* and W.T. Stead and his *Pall Mall Gazette*.[74] The "new journalism" focused on "sensational headlines in heavy black letters" and "churning out exciting news for mass consumption and entertainment."[75] Given such a communications environment, it is not surprising that anarchist-inspired fear gripped populations on both sides of the Atlantic Ocean.

In addition, terrorists could travel easily across borders; immigration patterns created a "diaspora" phenomenon, which played a major role (in some cases as a source for financial support) in terrorism. Many leaders called for international laws or treaties to address this growing terrorism menace. However, an international conference on terrorism was stymied by, among other things, the refusal of the American government to send a delegation because "it feared that extensive involvement in European politics might be required, and it had no federal police force."[76]

Thus, overall the period of anarchist terrorism roughly spanned the 1880s to the early 1900s. Although the anarchists cultivated widespread fear, they did not engineer large-scale political movements designed to fight or undermine state power; their threat was more psychological in nature. There was no anarchist central command that was directing the campaign. In fact, the following description demonstrates how haphazard the international organization really was: "The reality [of anarchist organization structure] was one of scattered small groups or isolated individuals who shared some measure of common ideology and in some cases shared readership of the same books or periodicals."[77]

Eventually the anarchist wave would dissipate. Paul Berman argues that the anarchists and the threats they posed were largely contained; they were not viewed as large socially transforming threats: "[The] terrorists and their bombs and guns seemed, to most people in those years, a marginal affair—a problem of crime prevention, a philosophical problem, a mystery, but nothing larger."[78] Although this analysis is reasonable, it tends to discount the one effect generated by the anarchists—widespread, pervasive, and irrational fear. This is a goal that many terrorists have aspired to throughout history, and which will mostly likely continue well into the future.

Modern Terrorism's Second Wave: Anticolonial/Nationalist Terror

On April 24, 1916, Irish nationalists staged what is now known as the Easter Rising, in which they took over key buildings in Dublin and declared an Irish Republic. The Easter Rising had been directed and engineered by the Supreme Council of the Irish Republican Brotherhood, an organization formed in 1858 as "an oath-based secret society with the uncompromising intention of overthrowing English government in Ireland by force of arms and of establishing an Irish Republic."[79] Within a week, the British deployed troops and crushed the rebellion. Subsequently, the British proceeded to execute 16 rebels for the insurrection that had killed more than 794 civilians and 521 soldiers.[80]

In the aftermath of the British crackdown, it appeared that the Irish political movement had been crushed. But in fact, the Easter Rising was the pivotal event that would lead to the rise of the IRA, particularly due to the efforts of Michael Collins and Cathal Brugha who "began quickly and effectively to reconstitute the Irish underground."[81] Collins, considered the key strategist for the IRA, had been released from prison as part of an English amnesty declared in 1917.[82] He immediately began to reconstitute the Irish Republican Brotherhood's Supreme Council and the national infrastructure that it once controlled. In 1917, plans were made to model the Republican Army along the lines of the British Army and to implement national coordination of the IRA.[83]

The IRA experience had a profound impact on the development of modern terrorism. "The legacies of the IRA's early struggles—the role of martyrs, symbols, spies, money, and smuggled arms; the blend of politics, terror, and propaganda; the appeal to legitimacy, the military techniques and tactics—have become hallmarks of modern terrorism worldwide."[84] From a historical perspective, the IRA is a classic example of what David Rapoport describes as the second wave of modern terrorism. According to Rapoport, this wave gained momentum particularly after the signing of the Peace Treaty of Versailles that concluded World War I.[85] This wave featured anticolonial struggle and a growing belief in the principle of self-determination. In addition, the rise of second-wave terrorism often coincided with a rise of ethnic identity and consciousness. In Ireland, for instance, rising militancy coincided with "a revival of Irishness and the assertion of a distinct national identity."[86]

After World War I, anticolonial terrorism spread throughout the world, reflecting pro-independence and anticolonial struggles. For example, in British-ruled India, insurgency groups increasingly challenged colonial rule and occasionally turned to terrorism tactics, with much of the terrorism taking place in Bengal. The promoters of the insurgency wanted Indian self-government, known as swaraj.[87] The insurgents established terrorist secret societies, or samitis.[88] These groups engaged in terrorist tactics, such as beatings and killings. They also engaged in armed robberies as a way to buy arms and ammunition. At first the British did not respond aggressively, but by 1914 the Raj slowly began to see this insurgency as an attack on its entire rule in India and subsequently cracked down hard.[89] By 1917, the British had established an effective intelligence network and introduced a policy of "preventive arrest."[90]

Rapoport argues that only after the end of World War II did the true successes of second-wave terrorism begin to emerge. This era was characterized by a growing sense of optimism (including a reaction against the former colonial system) and reordering of the international system: "The collapse of the great colonial empires in the wake of World War II engendered a vast and rapid reordering of global relations, carried out under the pressures of burgeoning nationalism in former colonies and protectorates."[91] Within this milieu, many anticolonial and nationalist terrorist organizations pursued a strategy of creating enough destruction and disruption as to convince the occupying power (its government and people) that the costs of maintaining its repressive rule would be intolerable and that such costs would certainly outweigh any benefits that might accrue from staying or continuing its colonization.[92]

Harassment of the occupying force was a key strategy pursued by Jewish militants operating in Palestine, then under the British Mandate. The most radical of the various Jewish militant groups was arguably the Lohamei Herut Yisrael (or Lehi). The British referred to the group as the "Stern Gang," after the group's leader, Avraham Stern. Lehi saw itself more as an underground revolutionary movement than simply a military organization. The Lehi organization belonged in the rightist "quasi-fascist" political category, with elements of xenophobia and national egotism.[93] The group had three strategic goals: (1) to unite those individuals interested in joining together to fight the British; (2) to become the primary Jewish military organization on the world stage; and (3) to use armed force to take over the "Land of Israel."[94] Eventually the group would meet its demise after attempting to assassinate the commander of the British secret police. As a result of this attack, mainstream Zionist groups teamed up with the British to destroy Lehi.[95]

Unlike Lehi, the Irgun Zvai Leumi (or Irgun), another Jewish militant group (from which Lehi split in 1940), was slightly more moderate, having broken off from the Haganah, considered the mainstream underground Jewish defense organization. Irgun was also considered rightist and nationalist and, among other things, the group was actively engaged in smuggling Jewish immigrants into Palestine in the 1930s.[96] In addition, from 1936 to 1939, the Irgun conducted terrorist activities "while methodically attempting to provide a rational justification for the violence by calling it retaliation for Arab attacks."[97] Eventually, the Irgun accomplished its most daring operation, the bombing of Jerusalem's King David Hotel in July 1946. On two floors of the hotel's southern wing were located the "nerve center of British rule in Palestine: the government secretariat and headquarters of British military forces in Palestine and Transjordan."[98] The attack, one of the most significant mass casualty terrorist events in the twentieth century—although apparently the planners did not intend this outcome[99]—killed eighty-two people, including civilians, and injured dozens more. Despite a subsequent British military crackdown,[100] the attack is viewed historically as having set into motion a course of events that would eventually lead to British withdrawal from Palestine and the subsequent creation of an Israeli state.[101]

In Algeria, another key nationalist struggle was being engineered by the Front de Libération Nationale (FLN), which from 1954 was engaged in a campaign to achieve Algeria's independence from France. Like many nationalist struggles, the FLN was the beneficiary of assistance from sympathizers in neighboring countries; more than 20,000 FLN—or FLN sympathizer—fighters were assembled outside of Algeria, usually in adjacent territory.[102] In 1956, after two years in which it could claim very few successes, the FLN deliberately changed its strategy and began focusing on the country's capital, Algiers.[103] The rationale for this strategy change was that urban attacks would attract greater media attention and thus the FLN could appeal "directly to international opinion."[104]

In Algiers, the FLN's operations officer was Saadi Yacef, who was well known for orchestrating terrorist attacks on cafés and other civilian establishments, often relying on young and attractive women to serve as bomb carriers and planters.[105] In July 1957, a French military court sentenced two young Muslim women to die by guillotine after they were convicted of conducting café bombings in Algiers. Six other Muslims, including Yacef, were sentenced in absentia.[106] Eventually French paratroopers would capture Saadi Yacef in 1957 after the rebel leader "had eluded capture in the crowded Casbah for more than two years."[107]

At his trial, Yacef praised President Charles de Gaulle by stating, in effect, that if General de Gaulle had remained in power after World War II "there would have been no rebellion and no war in Algeria."[108] Moreover, Yacef stated that in the event that de Gaulle had stayed in office, the "rights of the Moslems would have been recognized and our attitude would have been quite different."[109]

Overall, nationalist or anticolonial terror has traditionally been viewed as the most successful terrorism, in terms of political goals actually having been achieved. For instance, the Irgun (in Palestine) and the FLN in Algeria are often seen as two groups that used terrorism successfully to achieve their ultimate political goal, although, as Martha Crenshaw cautions, "it is impossible to be precise about the role played by terrorism in bringing about independence in these contexts."[110] Moreover, there are other examples of nationalist terrorism that were not so successful.

In the United States, for instance, four Puerto Rican nationalists opened fire from the visitors' gallery on the floor of the U.S. House of Representatives in 1954, screaming "Viva Puerto Rico Libre!" (Long live free Puerto Rico!). While firing weapons, Lolita Lebron, the group's leader, and her compatriots unfurled a Puerto Rican flag.[111] Several members of Congress were shot, although none died. While the attack generated a national sensation, the long-term political consequences of the attack were relatively minor.[112]

Modern Terrorism's Third Wave: New Left Terror

On September 5, 1972, eight Palestinian terrorists associated with the group Black September Organization broke into the Munich Olympic Village and headed to a dormitory occupied by Israeli athletes. Immediately, they shot two members of the Israeli team and took an additional nine hostages. With the hostages under their control, the Palestinians began to broadcast their grievances and demands: they wanted roughly 200 Arab prisoners held in Israel to be released, safe passage (for themselves) to Egypt, as well as the release of two German terrorists, Andreas Baader and Ulrike Meinhof (leaders of the Baader-Meinhof Gang), with whom they had an alliance.[113]

Within hours, the attackers and hostages were taken by helicopter to an airfield at Fürstenfeldbruck where they believed they would board a Lufthansa aircraft for Egypt.[114] Instead, the Germans opened fire on the hijackers and in the chaos, all nine remaining Israeli athletes were eventually killed.[115] Although the Germans are widely regarded as having bungled the law enforcement intervention, a committee of the West Germany Bundestag, or lower house, would later conclude that the authorities "did everything possible, handled the situation appropriately and took the right decisions."[116]

The Munich Olympics attack is one of the watershed events of the third wave of modern terrorism, which flourished primarily during the 1960s and 1970s. This particular wave was stimulated by the Vietnam War, the 1968 student protest movement, and the general tensions associated with the cold war. Many "new left" terrorist groups, such as the German Red Army Faction and the Italian Red Brigades, saw themselves as protectors of the working classes, as well as the third world masses.[117] Not only was the new terrorism heavily ideological, it was also international. Bruce Hoffman describes the date July 22, 1968, as marking the beginning of the day that "modern, international terrorism" emerged.[118] This was the date that three armed Palestinian terrorists hijacked an Israeli El Al commercial flight en route from Rome to Tel Aviv and diverted it to Algiers, a plot engineered by the Popular Front for the Liberation of Palestine's chief of foreign operations, Dr. Wadi Haddad.[119] Haddad would also later be credited with organizing the multiple hijacking of four planes in September 1970, in which three were blown up at Dawson's Field in Jordan.[120]

In Germany, the Red Army Faction (RAF) began its terrorism campaign in the late 1960s when it was known as the Baader-Meinhof Gang.[121] The group targeted a number of individuals it believed represented U.S. military power and German capitalism, all considered symbols of Western imperialism. In September 1977, RAF operatives kidnapped Hanns-Martin Schleyer, who led the

German employees association; his corpse was found a month later in France.[122] In May 1982, the group published its first strategic document, which specified the group's goal of developing "a new stage of revolutionary strategy in the metropolis, in which the struggle of the revolutionary front would complement the struggle of freedom fighters in Asia, Africa and Latin America."[123]

Throughout the 1970s and 1980s, RAF operatives meticulously assassinated German industry leaders often after long periods of surveillance. Victims included Ernst Zimmermann, head of a prominent German company that built engines for fighter jets and tanks, who was tied up in his home and shot in the head.[124] Karl Heinz Beckurts, head of the research organization of Siemens AG was bombed in his car as it passed an explosive device containing twenty-two pounds of TNT.[125] The RAF's assassination of Alfred Herrhausen, former chairman of Deutsche Bank AG, was accomplished when Herrhausen's car passed through a beam of light that in turn set off the bomb that destroyed his vehicle.[126]

As the RAF terrorized Germany, the Italian Red Brigades were busy terrorizing Italy. During the 1970s and 1980s, the Red Brigades were the most famous leftist terrorist group in Italy. In their first ten years of existence, they conducted roughly 14,000 terrorist attacks that nearly paralyzed the Italian judicial system.[127] The origins of the group can be found in universities in Trento and Milan. At the University of Trento, Renato Curcio, a former sociology student, led a band of communist students who gradually developed their own anticapitalist ideology.[128] "They saw multinational corporate capitalism as a monster preparing to devour the world."[129]

In response to this perceived oppression, the Red Brigades believed that violent pressure was necessary to produce social change and revolution. They were best known for their kidnapping of Prime Minister Aldo Moro in March 1978, an act accomplished with an ambush so violent that five of Moro's bodyguards were killed.[130] The kidnapping shocked the Italian public and even elicited a personal plea from Pope Paul VI, who wrote (in a public statement): "Men of the Red Brigades, leave me . . . the hope that in your souls there still is dwelling a victorious sentiment of humanity."[131]

This and other pleas could not save Aldo Moro from his ultimate fate after a fifty-five-day hostage standoff: execution. On May 9, 1978, former prime minister Moro's bullet-ridden body was discovered by Italian authorities "in a parked car in the historic center of Rome."[132] Overall, the kidnapping and execution of Moro—as well as the ineffectual government response—stunned and galvanized the Italian state. Among other effects, Italian public opinion began to turn strongly against the Red Brigades and its fellow leftists.[133]

Nevertheless, in 1981 the Red Brigades accomplished another prominent terrorist feat by kidnapping American General James Lee Dozier, who at the time was deputy chief of staff for logistics and administration at NATO's headquarters in southern Europe. Dozier's kidnappers had entered his home in Verona, Italy, dressed as plumbers. They hit Dozier on his head "presumably with a pistol butt" and then tied up his wife and sealed her eyes and mouth with adhesive tape.[134] After the kidnappers searched Dozier's apartment, they put him into the trunk of a car.[135] Later they took him to an apartment in the ground unit of a "drab modern building on the outskirts of Padua."[136] For roughly six weeks, Dozier's right wrist and left ankle were chained to a steel cot, which was situated under a small tent. He was subjected to a "never-extinguished glare of an electric bulb."[137] He was also forced to wear earphones and listen to loud music.[138]

During Dozier's captivity, the Red Brigades issued various communiqués to the government and the public generally, detailing their demands or complaints. The first communiqué, issued only days after the kidnapping, was striking for its lack of any ransom demand. Instead it focused on international matters of interest to the Red Brigades, including a tribute to the German Red Army Faction.[139] Other communiqués were also notable for their lack of ransom demands as well as absence of concrete references to Dozier.[140] The fifth communiqué, found in a trash can in downtown Rome, contained a number of anti-NATO and anti-American statements, but no specific demands for Dozier's release.[141]

Shortly after the fifth communiqué was issued, however, the Italian government got its big break. With information gained from an informant, who had been tracked down after an unauthorized visit to his girlfriend,[142] the Italian authorities were able to mount a successful rescue of General Dozier. Dozier, who had been held for forty-two days, would later report that as police stormed the apartment, a Red Brigade operative was "leveling a gun at his head."[143] After this rescue, the Red Brigade experienced further defections of its members, who in turn acted as informants for the government.[144]

Despite the Dozier kidnapping debacle, the Red Brigades continued their terrorist campaign. In one antiterrorism raid, Italian police discovered plans by a key Red Brigade leader to launch a mass casualty attack on a meeting of the Italian Christian Democratic party.[145] Despite intense police pressure, the Red Brigades continued their killing spree well into the late 1990s. One of their most recent attacks involved the assassination of Massimo D'Antona, a labor adviser to the government. The Red Brigades justified the assassination on the basis that their victim had been an agent of "neocorporate policy."[146]

France's "new left" experience was much milder than that of Germany and Italy. The most prominent group, Action Directe, "was founded in early 1978 by a group of young people experienced in revolutionary or armed activity."[147] It partially comprised recruited members from other defunct organizations, including the Proletarian Left—New Popular Resistance (Gauche Prolétarienne—Nouvelle Résistance Populaire—GN-NRP), the Internationalist Revolutionary Action Groups (Groupes d'Action Révolutionnaire Internationaliste—GARI), among others.[148]

The Action Directe conducted its first attack on May 1, 1979, against the headquarters of the Association of French Industrialists.[149] Subsequently, the group attacked a number of French government agencies in response to their perceived oppressive or neocolonial activities.[150] These included the Direction de la Surveillance du Territoire (Directorate of Territorial Security—DST) and the Ministry of Cooperation.[151] During the height of the Lebanese War (in 1982), Action Directe conducted eight attacks on Israeli or Jewish targets in Paris.[152]

Coinciding with the activities of the European groups was the Palestinian movement (and its associated terrorist activities), which can probably best be described as a hybrid phenomenon, possessing both elements of second-wave (nationalist) terrorism and third-wave (ideological) terrorism. Yasser Arafat, leader of the Palestine Liberation Organization (PLO), proposed in 1967 that the Palestinians adopt terrorist tactics against Israeli unfortified civilian targets, instead of striking the Israel Defense Force directly since it was overwhelmingly superior in force and training. Eventually, Palestinians would establish an infrastructure that would involve multiple countries. Several splinter organizations, such as the Abu Nidal group, which eventually set up offices in Iraq, had assets in the Middle East and Europe.

Moreover, many of these Palestinian groups would link up with their European counterparts. Alliances with European leftist groups facilitated an expansion of operational space throughout Western Europe. European radicals were known to provide Arab (including Palestinian) militants "with help on lodging, travel and the like."[153] In addition, Arab embassies in Europe were accused of providing sanctuary and diplomatic passports to Palestinian operatives, including members of Black September, the group responsible for the Munich Olympics attack.[154] In 1972, terrorists sought by Dutch and Belgian police were "thought to be hiding in various Arab embassies in Europe."[155]

Moreover, Europe was more than just a convenient hideout; it was a location where Palestinians were quite willing to conduct violent operations. One analyst wrote that "a great deal of international terrorist incidents in Western Europe [was] caused by a spill-over from the Middle East."[156] In fact, by 1985, Middle Eastern terrorism had spread to five West European countries, resulting—in total—in 109 deaths (most victims were of Middle Eastern origin) and 540 injuries.[157] In some instances European terrorist groups would cooperate with their Middle Eastern counterparts, as was the case with the alliance between the Germany Red Army Faction and the PLO Black September

Organization. In return for their cooperation, the Palestinians offered training (in the Middle East), arms, and instruction. In one typical case, Italian police intercepted a consignment of surface-to-air missiles, antitank rockets, machine guns, and other weapons from the Popular Front for the Liberation of Palestine that was intended for the Red Brigades.[158]

Perhaps no alliance better illustrates the cooperation between Palestinian and "new left" groups than that involving the Japanese Red Army. Following a notorious hijacking in March 1970, George Habash of the Popular Front for the Liberation of Palestine (PFLP) approached the Japanese Red Army (JRA) and an alliance was subsequently formed. Following this, many JRA members began training in PLO camps situated inside Lebanon.

JRA operations also became more international; for instance, in 1972, the group boarded an Air France flight in Rome that was headed for Lod International Airport in Tel Aviv. Once they had landed and retrieved their baggage, the Japanese Red Army militants "stood and opened fire indiscriminately on the crowd before throwing several grenades."[159] Over twenty-six people were murdered in this incident, and more than seventy individuals were wounded.[160] Subsequent interrogations of one of the JRA survivors (two of the three had been killed in the incident) revealed clear operational links between the PFLP and the JRA.[161] The survivor, Kozo Okamoto, admitted to an Israeli military tribunal that "the attack was carried out in partnership" between the Red Army of Japan and the PFLP.[162]

In addition, Okamoto, in a defiant tone, would later tell the Israeli court that he had "no regrets about the people he killed."[163] He also publicly declared that he was "a soldier of the [Japanese] Red Army" and he "would like to warn the entire world the Red Army will slay anyone who stands on the side of the bourgeoisie."[164] Okamoto was subsequently sentenced to a life term in an Israeli prison; however, he was released about thirteen years later as part of a "prisoners for hostages" deal that the Israeli government struck with the Palestinians.[165] The Japanese government formally expressed regret for the Israeli decision to release Okamoto, a sentiment that partly reflected Japan's belief that the Lod Airport massacre had brought "national shame" to the country.[166] Japan had earlier apologized to Israel and the United States (many of the victims were Puerto Ricans) for the actions of the Japanese Red Army at Lod Airport.[167] In 1997, Lebanese officials would arrest Okamoto after he and other members of the Japanese Red Army were found to be operating in the Bekaa region.[168] However, after serving three years in prison, Okamoto was released and was later granted political asylum in Lebanon.

At first, it might seem odd that Palestinian groups, whose nationalist struggle would appear to be more suited to second-wave movements and ideologies, would be willing to cooperate so readily with young Western (or Japanese) students who populated "new left" groups. However, during the 1960s and 1970s, the Palestinian cause and movement reflected the ideological zeitgeist at the time—leftist, anti-imperialist, and Marxist.

Black September members, for instance, were characterized as "leftists"[169] and this facilitated "friendly ties with radical leftists in Western Germany and several more countries who sympathize with the Palestinian cause."[170] Similarly, the Popular Front for the Liberation of Palestine was distinguished by its Marxist ideology: "the group viewed the push for Palestinian independence as part of a class struggle against global imperialism, including those Western powers that backed Israel."[171]

The other incongruity in Palestinian–"new left" cooperation related to the latter's idealism and social background. In contrast to battle weary Palestinians, who had borne the brunt of military action by traditional military forces (namely, Israel and Jordan, for example), European and other "new left" terrorists were remarkably well-educated, well-connected, and well-heeled. The presence of privileged and politically connected terrorists was especially apparent in the radical American group, the Weathermen, "[m]ade up mostly of college-educated white women and men, many . . . [of whom] had parents who were wealthy or [had political power]."[172]

Many of the new left terrorist members attempted to downplay their privileged backgrounds. As one writer notes: "They tried to compensate for the absence of a proletarian background by the frequent use of four-letter words."[173] In Japan, the Japanese Red Army (Sekigunha) attracted "the bright sons and daughters of regional elites from all over Japan."[174] Had these young people not joined the Japanese Red Army, they would have likely "passed uneventfully into the elite bureaucracies of contemporary Japan."[175]

What the "new left" Europeans, Americans, and Japanese did bring—and a defining characteristic of much third-wave terrorism (if not of most terrorist movements in history)—was extreme idealism. Paul Wilkinson argues that these groups "created their own 'transcendental' rationality."[176] Specifically he notes:

> The chiliastic utopianism of groups like the Baader-Meinhof gang, the Weathermen and the Japanese Red Army totally rejected the existing order as being vile and beyond redemption. There was no ground for negotiating any compromise between their ends and those of the rest of society.[177]

Third wave "new left" terrorists sincerely believed that their struggles could transform society. One Italian Brigadist, Enrico Fenzi, wrote an autobiography detailing his rationale for becoming a terrorist. Among other things, he wrote that capitalism was a "dying dinosaur" and thus the Red Brigadists "were clearing the way for the communist fulfillment of history."[178]

Third-wave terrorism, like first-wave terrorism, which saw the rise of the "new [print] journalism," benefited extensively from the rise of mass media, and particularly television. "Modern communications have done more than anything else to promote terrorism as an effective way of waging war."[179] Even operations that would have been deemed tactical failures might be seen as strategic victories "provided that the operation is sufficiently dramatic to capture the media's attention."[180] The Palestinians' hijacking campaign beginning in the late 1960s was driven almost exclusively by the rise of electronic mass media, and particularly television.

Notwithstanding the power of an emerging electronic media, the overall impact of the European and other "new left" groups was rather fleeting. Paul Wilkinson has compared these groups "to tiny gangs of bandits" rather than to "serious political movements."[181] Consequently, they posed much less danger to Western states and societies than the fear they created seemed to imply, although the fact that some groups were supported by the Soviet Union added a sinister geopolitical dimension to their operations.[182] A major factor that probably accounts for their short, transitory existence is the absence of a strong, sustainable ideology. In the case of the Palestinians, their movement would eventually transform from secular nationalism to religious nationalism.

Modern Terrorism's Fourth Wave: Religious Terrorism

On October 12, 2002, operatives representing the Indonesian-based group Jemaah Islamiyah (JI) launched three bomb attacks against Western targets in Bali. Two of the bomb attacks were directed at night clubs in the Kuta district, and a third was detonated near the U.S. consular office in Denpasar. Overall, the attacks led to the death of 202 people, 164 of whom were foreign nationals (including 89 Australians).[183] More than 200 were injured.

The decision to attack tourist and resort locations in Bali was the product of a senior command decision made in Thailand in early 2002, in which senior JI leadership decided to attack softer targets in Asia.[184] The attack also reflected the mass casualty tactics of al-Qaeda, with whom JI had long had a relationship. According to an International Crisis Group report published in 2003: "JI has elements in common with al-Qaeda, particularly its jihadist ideology and a long period of shared experience in Afghanistan."[185] JI operatives also played a major role in facilitating the 9/11 attacks in the United States, and were slated to play a major role in the "second wave" attacks that were planned shortly afterward.[186] However, facts also suggest that JI has its own agenda, separate from al-Qaeda, which is to establish an Islamic state in Indonesia and a Southeast Asian region-wide caliphate.[187]

The attack is also considered a clear example of fourth-wave terrorism in that it was rooted in religious ideology, featured a suicide attack, and was not state-supported. According to David Rapoport and others, the rise of fourth-wave terrorism can be generally tied to the 1980s with the decline of the cold war and the increasing importance of globalization. The fourth wave also has its roots in the Iranian revolution of 1979, the Soviet invasion of Afghanistan in 1979, and other key events—such as the rise of Hezbollah in the early 1980s.[188]

In many respects, fourth-wave terrorism is an analogue of premodern terrorism (particularly as represented by the Sicarii and the Assassins)—both ideologies are rooted in religious identity and both are largely divorced from the state or its ideologies. Although the beginning of the fourth-wave era is linked to key events in Islamic (or Muslim-majority) countries, the trend can be found in all major religions. However, as David Rapoport notes, it is Islam that is at the heart of this religious wave: "Islamic groups have conducted the most significant, deadly, and profoundly international attacks."[189]

Fourth-wave terrorism, which some analysts describe as the "new" terrorism, is distinguished from traditional (modern) terrorism by its emphasis on unconstrained violence. In other words, instead of being constrained by a lateral (support) community, the fourth-wave terrorist is constrained only by his terrorist abilities. The traditional view that "terrorists want a lot of people watching, not a lot of people dead"[190] has been replaced by an arguably more accurate adage: terrorists want a lot of people watching and a lot of people dead.

However, fourth-wave terrorism does share certain characteristics with its antecedents, notably revolutionary-anarchist terrorism and "new left" terrorism. Like their anarchist or "new left" counterparts, fourth-wave terrorists such as al-Qaeda and Aum Shinrikyo view the world in binary terms—the division between good and evil, the world of the pure versus impure, or in the case of al-Qaeda, the world of Islam versus the world of infidels. Islamic militants are, in particular, motivated by the notion of jihad, which literally means "struggle."

Jihad has a wide range of meaning—from peaceful self-improvement to defensive violence—that forms the backbone of the Islamist or Salafist movement. One prominent intellectual tradition in Islam interprets Jihad as a complete and universal struggle. Taqi al-Din Ahmad Ibn Taymiyya, a prominent Islamic legal scholar who lived in the thirteenth century, wrote that anyone who stands in the way of the word of Allah must be fought, particularly as "lawful warfare is essentially jihad and since its aim is that the religion is

Allah's entirely."[191] Women, children, monks, old people, the handicapped, and the like may be spared death, but not if they "fight with words" or other supportive acts (such as spying).

Mawlana Abul A'la Mawdudi expanded on many of Ibn Taymiyya's ideas, including his notion of tawhid (unity of God) and its subpart: "unity of worship" model.[192] This model held that human-made laws were tantamount to apostasy because they competed with God's laws. Mawdudi also introduced the notion of the "modern jahiliyya" (which referred to the "period of ignorance" or paganism that existed in the world prior to the advent of Islam).[193] Mawdudi would also argue that "Islam does not intend to confine this revolution [against the rule of a non-Islamic system] to a single State or a few countries; the aim of Islam is to bring about a universal revolution."[194] Mawdudi explained that it was first necessary that Islamic activists carry out the revolution within the state system "but their ultimate objective is no other than to effect a world revolution."[195]

Sayyid Qutb, an Egyptian member of the Muslim Brotherhood who died as a political prisoner in the 1960s, expanded on Mawdudi's ideas. Qutb is often seen as the "godfather of revolutionary Sunni Islam."[196] Having read Mawdudi's most influential books, Qutb took the notion of jihad a step further, arguing that it is the true nature of Islam that it be spread universally until all men are liberated. Specifically, he wrote that jihad was essentially a struggle for "the freedom of man from servitude to other men, the establishment of the sovereignty of God and His Lordship throughout the world, the end of man's arrogance and selfishness, and the implementation of the rule of the Divine Shari'ah in human affairs."[197]

Moreover, Qutb departed from Mawdudi, who sought to form a political party and work within the system for reform, and instead advocated force.[198] In his own brand of "Islamic liberation theology"[199] Qutb argued that "force was necessary to remove the chains of oppression"[200] so that Islamic truth could prevail. Moreover, this struggle can never cease. "This struggle is not a temporary phase but an eternal state—an eternal state, as truth and falsehood cannot co-exist on this earth."[201] Qutb is considered one of the most influential leaders of the modern revolutionary Sunni Islamic movement; he inspired, among others, groups such as the Islamic Liberation Organization, Takfir wal-Hijra, Salvation from Hell, the Gamiyya Islamiyya, and Islamic Jihad.[202]

Abdullah Azzam, another important figure who resurrected "active participation in defensive jihad,"[203] also wrote of this universal aim. According to a biographer, "the Sheikh's [Azzam's] life revolved around a single goal, namely the establishment of Allah's rule on earth, this being the clear responsibility of each and every Muslim."[204] Moreover, the struggle could not end until "the Khilafah is established so the light of Islam may shine on the whole world."[205] Later, the manual used by al-Qaeda terrorists would recapitulate many of these themes, and expand on the martial nature of Islam's spread. Specifically, it states that "Islamic governments have never and will never be established through peaceful solutions and cooperative councils. They are established as they [always] have been: by pen and gun; by word and bullet; and by tongue and teeth."[206]

Thus, certain themes prominent among fourth-wave religious terrorists can be found in anarchism and in the "new left"—such as the view of the world as fundamentally corrupt. Another common theme is the prevalence of oppression that must be fought so that human society may be liberated. The difference may be that the religious terrorists have a plan on who or what would replace the "human government" once it was overthrown—anarchists and the "new left" were conspicuously vague about what would transpire following the destruction of the current order. Nevertheless, the themes that flow through these different eras of terrorism share remarkable commonalities, although their methods and ideologies have differed significantly.

In addition to its religious elements, fourth-wave terrorism has a number of critical characteristics that distinguish it from third-wave terrorism. First, fourth-wave terrorism, as mentioned earlier, is notable in that it thrives generally outside of the realm of the state or state control. This has implications with respect to structure as well as financial support. A recent U.S. congressional report summarized this trend as follows: "A modern trend in terrorism is toward loosely organized, self-financed, international networks of terrorists."[207] The loosely organized aspect refers to network structures that span the globe and yet remain operationally coherent. The trend of self-financing typically refers to reliance on charitable contributions, criminal activities, or self-made (or inherited) wealth. According to the same U.S. government report: "Terrorists increasingly have been able to develop their own sources of financing, which range from NGOs [nongovernmental organizations] and charities to illegal enterprises such as narcotics, extortion, and kidnapping."[208]

Second, fourth-wave terrorism is geared—arguably more than any other wave—toward mass casualty violence and outcomes. As earlier referenced, Brian Jenkins is famous for his quote that "terrorists want a lot of people watching, not a lot of people dead."[209] Fourth-wave terrorists are less constrained, compared to their antecedents. For this reason, governments are fearful that fourth-wave terrorists will resort to attacks involving chemical, biological, radiological, or nuclear (CBRN) weapons.

According to a U.S. government report on this subject, the one trend that looms over the entire issue of international terrorism is the proliferation of weapons of mass destruction (WMD).[210] CBRN weapons have the potential to create mass casualties: "This ability to inflict great numbers of casualties may cause terrorists to view chemical or biological weapons as a viable means for promoting an agenda of terror and destruction."[211]

Third, fourth-wave terrorism appears to be distinguished by its overwhelming reliance on suicide attackers. Indeed, David Rapoport argues that suicide terrorism "was the most deadly tactical innovation" of fourth-wave terrorism.[212] However, a reasonable argument could be made that fourth-wave suicide terrorists—who invariably refer to themselves as martyrs—are not that different from martyrs in other terrorism waves. IRA hunger strikers in the 1980s committed suicide for their cause, as did the founding members of the German Baader-Meinhof Gang. Nevertheless, it cannot be disputed that fourth-wave terrorism has ushered in an era of qualitatively unique (and quantitatively unprecedented) suicide terrorism.

Today, suicide bombings occur on an almost monthly, or even weekly, basis throughout the world. "About 400 suicide attacks committed by over thirty terrorist groups have taken place since the early 1980s and the beginning of the contemporary wave with Hezbollah in Lebanon."[213] Analysts such as Lee Harris note that the suicide tactics appear to be an end unto themselves: "[I]n the fantasy ideology of radical Islam, suicide is not a means to an end but an end in itself. Seen through the distorting prism of radical Islam, the act of suicide is transformed into that of martyrdom—martyrdom in all its transcendent glory."[214]

Conclusion

The earliest terrorists were nonstate actors driven by religious and ethnic motives. With the rise of the state and state system, terrorism was practiced by both state and nonstate actors. Within the nonstate category, terrorism manifested generally as part of revolutionary or anarchist movements, anticolonial movements, Marxist or "new left" movements, and finally religious terrorism. As noted above, certain common themes can be found in at least three of the types—anarchist, "new left," and religious. However, in the long term, the one terrorism that stands out in terms of its efficacy is ethnonationalist (or anticolonial) terrorism. Paul Wilkinson has written that history demonstrates that this category of terrorism has the greatest chance of success, in terms of achieving a reasonable political settlement.[215] Nevertheless, the more idealistic terrorist movements—the anarchists, the "new left," and the religious-motivated—are potentially more dangerous.

Fourth-wave terrorism is a label that specifically addresses the rise of religious-based terrorism and the emergence of a no-restraint ethos. Although it has many common links with premodern and modern terrorism, it is imbued with an ethic that favors unconstrained violence: "Indeed, the terrorist who possesses radical, religious beliefs seems 'primed' to commit acts of unconstrained violence believing that such acts are not only sacred, but also necessary to guarantee him or her a blessed existence in the afterlife."[216]

Consequently, fourth-wave terrorism has the potential to alter the course of terrorism history. Instead of creating generally sporadic but rather limited destruction—which was seen in premodern terrorism and waves one through three—terrorism now is potentially poised to generate the sort of violence and destruction once attributable only to states.

3

Terrorism in the Context
of Global Politics

On December 13, 2001, a five-man suicide squad drove a car onto the grounds of the Indian Parliament in New Delhi in one of the most daring terrorist attacks in India's recent history. Armed with AK-47 automatic weapons and an array of bombs and other light arms, the attackers rushed inside the building, tossed grenades, and gunned down anyone who opposed them. At least one of the attackers detonated explosives he had strapped to his body in an apparent suicide attack. Overall, the attackers killed at least seven people who were mostly police or security personnel.

Fortunately for India, the attackers did not succeed in carrying out their ultimate objective, which was to massacre as many parliamentarians as possible, including possibly India's prime minister. India reacted angrily to the attack, demanding that Pakistan take immediate action against the two groups believed to be responsible, namely, Lashkar-i-Taiba and Jaish-e-Mohammed (the latter group had been linked to a previous suicide bombing attack in October 2001 at the legislature of the Indian state of Jammu and Kashmir, which killed thirty-eight people).[1] In addition, on December 22, India recalled its top envoy to Islamabad "for the first time in thirty years" and also suspended transportation services between the two countries.[2]

Indian Home Minister L.K. Advani told reporters that the terrorist attack "was not an attack only on the building but at the very heart of our governance and symbol of democracy."[3] Another senior Indian politician accused Pakistan of attempting to "wipe out" India's political leadership.[4] Still another senior Indian official reportedly stated that the December 13 attack demonstrated that "Pakistan is still the epicenter of terrorism in the region."[5]

By December 19, Indian and Pakistani troops were massing on their respective borders and exchanging rounds of gunfire. Moreover, military and political leaders from each side hinted at the use of nuclear weapons, partly by boasting how they would respond effectively to a first strike by the opposing party.[6] India's army chief later warned that if India suffered a nuclear attack, "the perpetrator of that particular outrage shall be punished so severely that their continuance in any fray will be doubtful."[7]

By December 27, India had deployed ballistic missile batteries and increased patrols of jet fighters along its border with Pakistan.[8] Pakistan intelligence alleged that India had moved twenty-three army divisions into "strike positions along the border."[9] Intense shelling between Pakistan and India on December 28 along the border that separates the disputed territory of Kashmir prompted President George Bush to appeal for calm.[10]

Eventually, Pakistan, under pressure from India, announced at the end of December that it had "rounded up more than two dozen Islamic militants"[11] and detained one of the group's leaders. Yet this did little to ameliorate the security situation between the two countries. On January 12, 2002, the head of India's army, General Sunderajan Padmanabhan, stated that his forces were "fully ready" for a war with Pakistan. "What I'm doing is for real," the General contended, "I have not gone to do an exercise. I have to be ready for war to defend my country."[12] Indeed, military analysts estimated that India had massed more than a half-million soldiers along its border with Pakistan, which extended for 1,800 miles.[13] This mobilization would be the largest since 1971, the last time that the countries fought a full-scale war.[14]

By January 2002, relations had deteriorated between India and Pakistan to such a degree that various world leaders felt they had no other choice but to intervene. British Prime Minister Tony Blair warned that the growing conflict between India and Pakistan risked spiraling out of control, which could have "far-reaching and damaging consequences" for South Asia as well as the entire world.[15] Blair also met with Indian and Pakistani leaders in early January, just as U.S. Secretary of State Colin Powell announced that he would make a detour from an international conference in Afghanistan to visit both India and Pakistan, in hopes of defusing the crisis.[16]

In mid-January 2002, tensions began to recede slightly, particularly after General Pervez Musharraf of Pakistan delivered a speech in which he denounced "all forms of terrorism—including groups that operate under the 'pretext of Kashmir.'"[17] Musharraf appeared to be signaling a cessation of Pakistan's long-standing policy of sponsoring militant jihadi groups in Pakistan's proxy struggle with India over Kashmir.[18] Shortly after Musharraf's speech, Secretary of State Powell visited both Pakistan and India with the purpose of reducing tensions between the two countries. He had earlier compared the crisis to "an ocean liner or a car that's in forward gear."[19]

As a result of diplomatic efforts and domestic decisions in both India and Pakistan, a major war was ultimately averted. However, the December 13, 2001, attack on India's Parliament reminded the world that terrorists, despite their weak status vis-à-vis state power, potentially have the ability to trigger far greater traditional conflict—possibly including nuclear war—than their nominal capability might presume.

Conventional wisdom regarding terrorism has suggested that, while dramatic, violent, and disruptive, terrorism is nevertheless relatively inconsequential in terms of its larger effects on global politics and the international system. One study found that terrorists achieved their political goals only 7 percent of the time.[20] Notwithstanding this view, the Indian Parliament attack of 2001 suggests that terrorism, when placed within specific contexts, has the potential to stimulate profound political and military effects. At the very least, the December 2001 events in South Asia suggest that the question of terrorism's effect on the international system is more complicated than what is often presumed.

Terrorism and the International System

As a political activity or phenomenon, terrorism—and particularly international terrorism—occurs within the context of larger trends and shifts in the international system. In the aftermath of the September 11 attacks on New York City and Washington, DC, many U.S. commentators, scholars, and analysts claimed, in essence, that the devastating attacks had profoundly changed the world, and, by implication, the international system, in fundamental ways.

Moreover, since 9/11, the U.S. government has grounded its foreign policy on the notion that it should conduct a global "war" on terrorism, a move that resembles, in some respects, Theodore Roosevelt's reactions to the horrors perpetrated by the anarchist terrorists of the late nineteenth and early twentieth centuries. During that period, President Roosevelt called for an international campaign against anarchist terror. Specifically, he stated that the "crimes [of the anarchist] should be made a crime against the law of nations . . . declared by treaties among all civilized powers."[21] Unfortunately for President Roosevelt, a lack of political will during that period (both inside and outside of the United States) as well as the lack of a robust federal police force in the United States prevented the establishment of a viable regime to confront terrorism effectively.[22]

Terrorism is inherently a violent, dramatic, and shocking phenomenon. The effects of terrorism will be felt among its targets as well as among those who directly or indirectly observe the attacks. If the terrorist attack is large enough, it can have international effects as well, such as was seen following the 9/11 attacks in the United States. However, despite the horror of terrorism, the historical record is less than clear regarding its impact on international relations (and the international system generally), despite what many intuitively presume; some have even argued that the impact has been minimal.[23]

In the U.S. context, the irony is that as horrible as 9/11 was, few Americans have been victims of terrorism during the past two decades. From an actuarial point of view, in fact, Americans would be justified in having a greater fear of the effects of cigarette smoking, car driving, and recreational boating than terrorism. During the 1980s and 1990s, 871 Americans died worldwide from terrorism, which works out to be an average of roughly 44 per year.[24] In contrast, as noted in this book's preface, more than 42,000 Americans die yearly in automobile accidents and another 225,000 die annually from medical and pharmaceutical mishaps.

Notwithstanding these caveats, fear of terrorism pervades much of the world, particularly in the current historical era, and it is thus almost inevitable that this fear will entail certain political consequences, including effects on the international system. Audrey Kurth Cronin has argued that terrorism cannot be completely understood through the prism of any one academic discipline—it often entails elements of political science, psychology, anthropology, law, history, theology, economics, and forensic science, among others.

What political science contributes is a model for analysis known as the international system, which simply refers to the larger international conglomerate or web of interacting units (i.e., states, international organizations, and nonstate actors) that has no system above it.[25] Cronin argues that this level of analysis (with regard to the study of terrorism) is the least understood and least developed in political science—perhaps, she suggests, because of its difficulty.[26]

Martha Crenshaw suggests more practical reasons why the international system has not generally been relied upon as a decipher mechanism for terrorism. One problem is that the emphasis of "realists" on states has tended to neglect or overlook the role of transnational nonstate actors: "In such a [realist] framework, threats emanate from states, not non-states, and the most powerful states are the most important for American interests. Weak or failed states and shadowy underground conspiracies do not constitute challenges to the American position in the world. From this perspective, threats are simple to interpret. They stem from rival states that can challenge one's power now or in the future."[27]

Analyzing the international system first requires defining it. One reasonable description of the international system suggests that it consists of "patterns of interaction [in an international context] that exist among those actors that formulate and conduct a policy designed to further their foreign goals and interests."[28] Another definition holds that the international system is "the authority structure of a system for making and enforcing rules, for allocating assets, and for conducting other authoritative tasks."[29] The international system is inherently anarchic; it has no overarching or supreme authority to make rules, settle conflicts or disputes, and provide protection.[30] States must rely on their own efforts, or alliances with other states, in order to survive and protect themselves. There is no international "911" number to call in the event that states encounter trouble. Thus the authority structure of the international system is mostly horizontal, meaning that states gain legitimacy via the peer recognition of other states, instead of via a vertical power structure.[31]

Former secretary of state George Shultz described the international system as being premised on the state: "We live in an international system of states, a system that originated more than 300 years ago. The idea of the state won out over other ideas about how to organize political life because the state gave people a sense of identity, because it provided a framework for individual freedom and economic progress, and because states over time proved able to cooperate with each other for peace and mutual benefit."[32]

It is undeniable that the sovereign state system remains the lynchpin of the international system: "States have been, and continue to be, the most powerful political agents in international affairs."[33] Among other things, states have at least one characteristic unique to them that is unavailable to other actors in the international system, the ability to act militarily and to engage in legitimate and legally sanctioned violence.

However, states are not the only actors within the international system. They are joined by two other broad categories of actors: (1) intergovernmental organizations (IGOs) and (2) transnational nonstate actors. Intergovernmental actors are international organizations that consist of states (or their agents) who act as members—a good example is the United Nations. IGOs have played an increasingly important role in the international system, evidenced by their increasing numbers. "In 1900 there were thirty IGOs. That number has increased some 900 percent: there are now 272."[34]

The third category of actors is loosely defined as nonstate actors. Nonstate actors include private actors that have economic, political, social, or criminal roles and objectives. Two good examples include nongovernmental organizations (NGOs) such as Amnesty International and transnational corporations such as British Petroleum. Terrorist groups and transnational crime groups also fall within this category, although they have traditionally been assigned a marginal status within the traditional view of the international system. Once again, like IGOs, the prominence of transnational nonstate actors—and particularly NGOs—has increased dramatically during the past century. "In 1900, there were sixty-nine NGOs. Since then the number of NGOs has expanded seventy fold to approximately 5,000."[35]

Moreover, nonstate actors have assumed a much greater prominence in the international system. According to Muhittin Ataman, "[N]on-state actors have become essential instruments within the international system. Today, it is difficult to analyze international politics and behaviors of nation-states without attaching great importance to them."[36]

One way of categorizing nonstate actors is to delineate between "complementary" nonstate actors and "competitor" nonstate actors. Complementary nonstate actors, as the label implies, seek to work within the state system to advance some social, political, or economic goal. They may have political objectives, opinions, or motives that are antagonistic to states or a particular government, but they nevertheless seek to bring about change by working within the system. Nongovernmental organizations and international media organizations are considered complementary nonstate actors that seek to influence the state system, instead of destroying it.

In contrast, competitor nonstate actors seek to compete with the state for power, or replace the state altogether. As their label suggests, competitor nonstate actors seek to compete with the state by advocating for or actually creating alternative power (or governance) structures. For example, terrorist groups that seek to undermine a government for the purpose of establishing an alternative government system would be considered competitor nonstate actors. Similarly, certain transnational criminal organizations may be deemed competitors as they seek power to influence or control the state (or parts of its apparatus) or limit the state's sovereignty.

In addition to its constituent actors, the international system is also composed of a basic power structure. The primary currency of international relations is power and power is always shifting within the international system, sometimes slowly and, at other times, more quickly: "Powerful countries rise and fall in their relative power to one another."[37] With regard to power structure, typical analysis tends to focus on the relationships between the major actors, and this has traditionally meant states. Some scholars posit that the first half of the twentieth century witnessed the decline of a multipolar international system that had existed during the last third of the nineteenth century. Following the end of World War II in 1945, a new bipolar era began, and lasted until the late 1980s.

Since the end of the cold war, however, a new international system power structure has evolved; some would argue that it is now a unipolar system with the United States at the apex. Christopher Layne has argued that the current unipolar structure in the international system is unprecedented: "For the first time since the Roman Empire at its zenith, the international system is dominated by an *extant* hegemon."[38] Moreover, because of the overwhelming power enjoyed by the United States, particularly against other potential competitor states, "other states find it difficult—and possibly dangerous—to engage in traditional counterbalancing (hard balancing) against the reigning hegemon."[39]

How Terrorism Influences (and Is Influenced by) the International System

Terrorism's relationship with the international system can be viewed from two general angles. The first focuses on how terrorism has influenced or affected the international system. In this analysis, terrorists are similar to states in that both entities seek power, particularly if one views international relations through the lens of classical realism.[40] Power, according to Joseph Nye of Harvard University, "is the ability to effect the outcomes you want and, if necessary, to change the behavior of others to make this happen."[41] In the terrorism context, the desire for power can be viewed as a central thread running through all terrorist movements since the rise of the modern state system. "Modern terrorism can best be seen as a power struggle: central power versus local power, big power versus small power, modern power versus traditional power."[42]

Even today's religious terrorists are, in Audrey Kurth Cronin's view, engaged in an "ongoing modern power struggle between those with power and those without it."[43] Nevertheless, historical evidence suggests that, notwithstanding their power motives, terrorists have had—at least until recently—only a marginal impact on the international system. As Walter Laqueur has stated, "[Terrorism] has been a tragedy for the victims, but seen in historical perspective it seldom has been more than a nuisance."[44]

Moreover, most terrorism analysts and scholars will agree that, although terrorist attacks are horrific, they rarely have any sort of lasting political impact or effect on the international system. John Lewis Gaddis argues that anarchists, assassins, and saboteurs have operated throughout history; however, they have rarely destabilized states or societies and "the amount of physical damage they've caused [has] been relatively small."[45] Alex Schmid confirms this view by contrasting terrorism with more conventional war and genocide: "Compared to the fatality figures of contemporary wars and genocide, the losses due to acts of terrorism, while tragic and traumatic on an individual scale, are modest."[46] This is not to suggest that terrorism has had a minimal impact in terms of its local consequences—in many cases, the impact has been quite significant. Moreover, a terrorist attack, such as the bombing by the Irgun of the King David Hotel in Palestine in 1946, can be seen as a critical event that leads to a long series of effects that ultimately result in significant political transition (in that instance, the ultimate transition was the withdrawal of the British and the subsequent founding of the state of Israel).

An important exception to the argument that terrorism has had a minimal impact on the international system is when terrorists hit a critical node, or "geopolitical faultline." This often occurs in an environment when two or more belligerent or antagonistic powers are poised for conflict. In their strategic calculation, terrorists sometimes seek to exploit these situations and are hopeful that their violent actions may act as the precipitating event—or tipping point—that leads to much greater conflict.

One possible example of this phenomenon is the 1914 assassination of Archduke Franz Ferdinand, the heir apparent of the Austro-Hungarian throne, by a group led by Gavrilo Princip. This assassination is viewed historically as a trigger event for World War I, although it is important to note that the assassination did not cause World War I; instead, it was the subsequent Austro-Hungarian government's response that led down that perilous road.

In a recent study, Paul Schroeder makes this point succinctly: "Though Princip deliberately tried to start a great war, his terrorist action, which succeeded only by luck, could not in itself produce that war. Only Austria-Hungary could do that by its response, and it did."[47] Some argue that Austro-Hungarian rulers were "bent on exploiting even the [assassination] event itself and on squeezing the utmost profit out of it."[48] This involved, among other things, shaping public opinion as is often the case for government operations in contemporary contexts, to include using the Vienna Press Bureau to influence the media throughout Europe.[49]

Moreover, this case is complicated by allegations that the Serbian military intelligence apparatus had actually trained, supported, and armed these terrorists. The Austro-Hungarian government apparently knew about (or suspected) Serbian government links to the terrorists and thus "it considered the assassination the final outrage in a series of Serbian provocations and attacks directed against the monarchy."[50] The Serbian government's "hidden" role—as perceived by the Austro-Hungarian government—may have played the critical role in sparking the subsequent war, although it has also been stated that Austro-Hungarian leaders believed that an attack on Serbia would be contained and that "nobody else would interfere."[51] History of course proved otherwise.

In a more recent case, the ability of terrorism to significantly aggravate a preexisting conflict between two belligerent states was demonstrated in the 1987 bombing of a South Korean jetliner over the Indian Ocean by agents of North Korea, an attack that killed 115 people. The two North Korean agents had placed a bomb concealed in a radio on the doomed aircraft. Subsequently, they disembarked from the aircraft in Abu Dhabi and were later captured in Bahrain (one of the captured terrorists killed himself by biting into a poison capsule).[52] The attack was largely viewed as an attempt by North Korea to disrupt the hosting by South Korea of the Olympic Games in 1988.[53]

Although the attack did not ultimately interfere with the Olympic Games, it did raise tensions on the Korean Peninsula significantly. South Korea, for example, "put its 600,000 troops on top alert"[54] two months after the attack, once it had determined that North Korea had deliberately sponsored the attack. In the next month, the administration of U.S. President Ronald Reagan announced that it would deploy a "full-scale show of military force in and around South Korea" to deter a possible attack on the Olympic Games in Seoul.[55] In January 1988, Japan announced, in response to the South Korean airliner attack, that it would impose diplomatic sanctions on North Korea, which in effect meant that "all normal contact with the North Korean Government in Pyongyang" would be terminated.[56] Clearly, the terrorist attack had a major political impact in Northeast Asia; however, it is extremely doubtful that North Korea was actually seeking to bring about a war on the Korean Peninsula. What this case does demonstrate, however, is terrorism's ability to significantly exacerbate tensions that already exist and, in a worst-case scenario, possibly set into motion events that could lead to actual military conflict.

The most recent example of terrorism's ability to trigger international conflict, as mentioned in the opening section of this chapter, is the December 2001 attack on India's Parliament. The quick escalation of tensions stemmed from the fact that the Indian authorities accused Pakistan of supporting the terrorists who were alleged to have carried out the attack. India has accused Pakistan of supporting insurgency organizations as part of its proxy war against India in Kashmir.[57] Significant diplomatic intervention from outside powers—including both Britain and the United States—probably contributed to the reduction in conflict. In addition, the presence of nuclear weapons on both sides most likely influenced the strategic calculation of both Pakistan and India, and thus raised the stakes of military conflict significantly.

Thus, as can be seen from the India–Pakistan example, it appears that the power of terrorism in the international system can also depend on whether the terrorist groups are perceived as state-supported, or as pure nonstate actors. In the case of state-supported terrorist attacks, the impact on the international system—and on international relations between states in general—is likely to be much larger (even if war does not result, it can lead to a serious ratcheting up of tensions that takes many years to attenuate).

Thus, historical evidence suggests that when states are directly tied to terrorism (through evidence of funding or other forms of logistical or ideological support), the political potency of the specific terrorist incident rises considerably. When it was determined, for example, that Libya had sponsored a series of attacks in Western Europe, and particularly an attack on a Berlin discotheque that killed two U.S. servicemen on April 5, 1986 (and injured 230 others, including 64 Americans), the United States responded by launching on Libya's territory a massive air bombing raid known as "Operation El Dorado Canyon."[58]

The U.S. attack on Libya, including the capital of Tripoli and the port of Benghazi, killed 15, including the adopted daughter of Libyan leader Moammar Gadhafi, and injured more than 100.[59] In addition, the attack increased cold war tensions between the United States and Soviet Union, with the latter accusing Washington of promoting a "cynical lie" about claims that the Soviet Union ignored U.S. requests to stop Libya from bombing the Berlin disco.[60] In addition, days after the U.S. raids on Libya, the Soviet Union asserted its "full rights to use the Mediterranean for movements of its merchant and warships."[61]

Although the Libyan and North Korean cases are clear examples of state-supported terrorism, even in those cases that are presumably nonstate-actor–directed terrorist attacks, the bias among some policymakers has been to presume a state sponsor nonetheless. Henry Kissinger recently summed up this view in his testimony in 2002 before the U.S. Senate Foreign Relations committee: "Global terrorism cannot flourish except with the support of states that either sympathize or acquiesce in its actions."[62] States may not actually conduct overt acts to support the terrorists, but they can support terrorism by merely tolerating the presence or activities of terrorists within their territory.

However, this state-centric view in many ways ignores the potency and agility of network-based terrorist organizations such as al-Qaeda and similar groups. Moreover, the Kissinger view tends to dismiss or overlook the challenge of failed (or quasi) states that simply do not have the capacity to restrict activities on their territory—in other words, states with incomplete sovereignty—or failed states that do not, for all practical purposes, have a functioning government. This is one of the major challenges in fighting network-based transnational terrorism.

In contrast to terrorism clearly directed by states, nonstate-actor terrorists, who do not appear to be directly linked to states, have arguably had less influence on global politics or the international system, at least until the 1960s. The era of the 1960s arguably marks the true ascendancy of international nonstate-actor terrorism, although, of course, terrorists of previous eras (e.g., the anarchists) also had an international character. Nevertheless, terrorists in the 1960s, propelled by the rise of international television media and air transportation, seemed to gain a "front and center" quality on the international political stage.

For example, the year 1968 marked the beginning of the Palestinians' air piracy campaign, conducted "in part as an alternative strategy to the conventional battle which had brought disaster to the Arab coalition that in 1967 made war on Israel."[63] Bruce Hoffman argues that during this period, the nature and character of terrorism began to change: "For the first time, terrorists began to travel regularly from one country to another to carry out attacks. In addition, they also began to target innocent civilians from other countries who often had little if anything to do with the terrorists' cause or grievance. . . . Their intent was to shock and, by shocking, to stimulate worldwide fear and alarm."[64]

This view is supported by other scholars as well who view the 1960s as the critical "pivot" point where terrorism became a force in the international system. Peter Chalk notes that "by the late 1960s and early 1970s, extremist political violence had become a truly prominent feature of the international system."[65] Similarly, Aldo Borgu asserts that terrorism "has been a feature of international policies and security since at least the late 1960s."[66] This view is also shared by former Israeli prime minister Benjamin Netanyahu who makes the point that terrorism began its rapid growth in the 1960s primarily because of the early successes of two groups of terrorists—the PLO, which introduced hijacking as a tool for international terrorism, and the European leftist groups, which were known for carrying out daring bombing, kidnapping and assassination attacks throughout Europe. These various terrorist groups, which seemed to be independent from one another, "soon proliferated throughout Europe, Japan, North and South America, and the Middle East."[67]

Terrorism as a Reflection of Changes in the International System

A second way of analyzing terrorism's relationship with the international system is to view the problem of terrorism as an indicator—either leading or lagging—of larger trends and tensions in the international system. As noted above, the international system is a web that reflects multiple competitions for power. Within this view, terrorists are no different than states or other nonstate actors that seek power, but are nevertheless constrained by forces within the international system.

David Rapoport's "four waves" model of international terrorism—described in Chapter 2—captures the basic notion that it is the larger tensions in the international system at any one time in history that give rise to—or enable—terrorism. Rapoport's definition of a wave as "a cycle of activity in a given time period—a cycle characterized by expansion and contraction phases"[68] —suggests profound exogenous influences imposed by the international system that shape the character of terrorism within a particular era.

The September 11, 2001, attacks in the United States provide a good example of a case that shows how the international system has shaped terrorism. Some have argued that the 9/11 attacks, and more important the "fourth wave terrorism"[69] that it appeared to represent, reflected dramatic and fundamental changes in the international system, particularly with the end of the cold war in the 1980s. The 9/11 attacks occurred within a milieu of shifting social, economic, and political alignments in the international system. The attack itself was deemed a "massive intelligence failure"[70] by the United States, although in many respects it could be viewed as a massive paradigm failure in the sense that the dominant paradigm in international relations—realism—which posits the state as the primary referent actor, from which the most serious security threats emanate, simply could not explain or predict the dynamics of the 9/11 attack.

In fact, it could reasonably be argued that contemporary terrorism reflects at least four broad trends in the international system: the emergence of nonstate actors in the international system; the trifurcation of the international system; the rise of a unipolar power structure (and responses to such structure); and the rise of religion in the international system.

Rise of Nonstate Actors in the International System

The 9/11 attacks were perpetrated by nonstate actors. The convergence of various trends in the international system—communications, technology transfers, and networked societies—has bestowed on nonstate actors the ability (or, in some cases, the perceived ability) to influence global politics in innovative and unprecedented ways. Globalization privileges the rise of nonstate actors, which perhaps explains, at least partially, why their numbers have exploded in the past two decades. Nonstate actors are particularly adept at promoting or exerting what Joseph Nye calls "soft power," which is defined as the "ability to achieve desired outcomes through attraction rather than coercion, because others want what you want."[71] One reason for nonstate actors' influence is the fact that they—and their networks—are skillful at "penetrating states without regard to borders and using domestic constituencies for agenda setting."[72]

But not all nonstate actors are kind and "soft"—as described previously in terms of "complementary" vs. "competitor" labels; some nonstate actors (namely, the competitor variety) are quite willing to employ violence to obtain the power they desire. Amanda DiPaolo argues that violent nonstate actors, like their nonviolent counterparts, seek to achieve "an ability to establish or reinforce international structures of authority that express their point of view."[73] Violent nonstate actors will often imitate states: "they maintain a professional governance structure to simulate order and authority. They create independent research capabilities to act as intelligence."[74] Thus, to the extent that globalization empowers nonstate actors, it also empowers violent nonstate actors, and this creates a challenge for states. When terrorists were tied to states, pressure could be applied against those "sponsor" states to deter or mitigate the terrorist threat. The deterrence of terrorists who are tied to transnational nonstate actor networks, however, is much more difficult, if not impossible.[75]

Trifurcation of the International System

With the end of the cold war and rise in globalization, the international system
has become more complex. Joseph Nye argues that power in the international
system is distributed like a three-dimensional chess game. The top of the game
is state-to-state military relations, and the power structure is largely unipolar in favor of the United States. By comparison, the second level involves
economic relations; on this level, power is more evenly distributed, although
it is generally concentrated in developed regions, such as North America,
Europe, and Japan.[76]

The third level is perhaps the most relevant in terms of nonstate-actor terrorism. On this level, power is much more dispersed, to include developed
and developing countries alike. This level features "transnational relations
that cross borders and lie outside the control of governments."[77] The various
layers of this model are not impermeable. For example, economic activities
of corporate nonstate actors (presumably at play on the third level) would
definitely have an impact on the second level. Similarly, an attack on a particular state's critical infrastructure, emanating from the third level, would
likely have some effect on the first level (in terms of state-to-state relations).
Despite limitations of this model, it provides a useful framework in which
the power of nonstate actors can be understood, particularly in their relationship with states.

Rise of a Unipolar Power System

In reference to the first level of Joseph Nye's three-level model, the 9/11 attacks in the United States occurred during an era in which the international
system had transformed from a bipolar system to a unipolar system. The United
States has enjoyed a premier status in this unipolar system because it holds
"a preponderance across the spectrum of capabilities, including economic,
military, political, geopolitical, and technological."[78] However, a unipolar
system does not arise without costs. For instance, a unipolar structure has
arguably created an environment in which terrorists are tempted or motivated
to target the United States directly, as has been seen among Islamist groups
such as al-Qaeda. This is, as Randall Woods suggests, a normal process when
a country rises to world power status.[79]

Richard Betts argues that "American global primacy is one of the causes of
this war. . . . To groups like al-Qaeda, the United States is the enemy because
American military power dominates their world, supports corrupt governments
in their countries, and backs Israelis against Muslims."[80] The overwhelming
military superiority of the United States has created a situation where the only

way an enemy can strike at the United States is to employ terrorism, or other "irregular" forms of warfare. Terrorists may realize they cannot defeat the predominant power, but that does not stop them from trying. Moreover, the threshold for victory—at least in the eyes of the terrorists—may simply be "gaining international exposure and opening up new perspectives in relevant political debates to a broader audience."[81]

Michael Hudson argues that the world is witnessing the rise of a larger tension positing Westphalian states vs. transnational networks in which terrorism acts as the "equalizer weapon" because of its accessibility and low expense.[82] In contrast to a country like the United States, Japan—which, ironically, many viewed as an economic threat in the early 1990s—is not considered a terrorist target because "Japan's economic power does not make it a political, military, and cultural behemoth that penetrates their societies."[83]

Rise of Religion as a Force in the International System

A fourth key trend in global politics since the late twentieth century has been the increasing importance of religion—or at least the perception or awareness of such importance—in the international system. Samuel Huntington wrote a controversial essay in the early 1990s that described a post–cold war political environment in which cultural and "civilizational" identity would play an increasingly important role in determining the parameters of conflict. "Nation states will remain the most powerful actors in world affairs," Huntington wrote, "but the principal conflicts of global politics will occur between nations and groups of different civilizations. The clash of civilizations will dominate global politics. The fault lines between civilizations will be the battle lines of the future."[84] One of those fault lines, argued Huntington, would be between the West and Islam: "This centuries-old military interaction between the West and Islam is unlikely to decline."[85]

The tradition in Western social science has been to downplay or minimize the role of religion in international relations, including international terrorism. Robert Jervis recently wrote that "terrorism grounded in religion poses special problems for modern social science, which has paid little attention to religion, perhaps because most social scientists find this subject uninteresting if not embarrassing."[86] Jonathan Fox asserts that religion in international politics is overlooked because "social sciences, including international relations, have their origin in the rejection of religion."[87]

One could argue, however, that this attitude has begun to shift. Recently, for instance, a Harvard University faculty committee recommended that the university "should again require all undergraduates to study religion."[88] The rationale was based on the notion that as academics in a university, students who are not religious do not need to confront (or worry about) religion. However, when students are "in the world, they will have to" confront religious questions.[89] The decision by Harvard suggests a growing awareness among some American intellectuals that religion is indeed a major force in domestic and international politics and thus requires greater attention and understanding.

The Impact of September 11, 2001: A Transformation?

When terrorists struck New York and Washington, DC, on September 11, 2001, they arguably wrote a new chapter in the history of terrorism and its role in the larger context of political violence. Not only did the attack—and the underlying movement that it represented—reflect changes in the international system, it also shaped and perhaps even transformed the international system itself. Partially, this occurred because of the dramatic military response by the United States, the world's dominant superpower since the end of the cold war.

Just as the assassination of Archduke Ferdinand gave the Austro-Hungarian empire a license to attack Serbia, the 9/11 attacks gave President George W. Bush the critical opening to assert American military dominance first by attacking the regime of Afghanistan, a state that had harbored al-Qaeda, and subsequently by attacking Iraq, a state allegedly linked to the larger problem of proliferation of weapons of mass destruction (WMD).

In addition, the attacks on Afghanistan and Iraq reflected a policy within the U.S. administration of reordering the world in a way that would, among other things, make terrorism less attractive as a political strategy. According to this view, the United States sought to transform a dangerous world comprised of terrorists and rogue states. Describing this new foreign policy, Michael Hudson quotes Richard Haass of the Department of State as saying: "in the twenty-first century the principal aim of American foreign policy is to integrate other countries and organizations into arrangements that will sustain a world consistent with U.S. interests and values, and thereby promote peace, prosperity, and justice as widely as possible."[90]

Part of this process of reordering the world involved the doctrine of preemption, which is predicated on the notion that sovereignty is not complete, that "sovereignty does not grant governments a blank check to do whatever they like within their own borders."[91] David Hendrickson has argued that despite use of the term "preemption," what is really being justified is preventive war. While preemptive war is used when an enemy is on the verge of striking, "preventive war is the first use of force to avert a more remote though still ostensibly formidable danger."[92]

President George W. Bush established the foundation for preventive war in his 2002 State of the Union Address in which he listed North Korea, Iran, and Iraq as being part of an "axis of evil": "States like these [North Korea, Iran, Iraq], and their terrorist allies, constitute an axis of evil, arming to threaten the peace of the world. By seeking weapons of mass destruction, these regimes pose a grave and growing danger. They could provide these arms to terrorists, giving them the means to match their hatred. They could attack our allies or attempt to blackmail the United States. In any of these cases, the price of indifference would be catastrophic."[93] Thus, advocates for preventive war argue that since war or conflict is inevitable anyway, then we should "fight it under circumstances of our own choosing."[94]

From a terrorism perspective, the fact that a major power such as the United States would strike out militarily—exercising what Michael Cox refers to as "muscular globalism"[95]—is actually not surprising. A recent study argued that when states suffer mass casualty attacks, which exceed the bounds of what might be considered rational political conduct, such states tend to view the terrorists who conducted the attacks as a threat to their very existence.[96] Under these circumstances, a robust military response by such a state is probably more likely. For example, when 229 Russian civilians were killed in a 1999 attack on three apartment buildings near Moscow, an act that was linked to Chechen terrorists, Russian views on the Chechen conflict began to shift dramatically. Prior to that incident, Russians generally perceived that Chechens merely wanted to create a separate and independent state. However, after the apartment bombings, many Russians began to believe that the true objective of Chechen militants was to destroy Russia itself.[97]

Notwithstanding its own existential fears regarding Iraq's WMD ambitions (and possible links to al-Qaeda), the United States currently faces more complications as a result of its military presence in Iraq than were probably anticipated prior to the invasion. For example, a recent National Intelligence Estimate report described the U.S. military presence in Iraq as a "cause célèbre" for contemporary terrorists. Insurgent attacks—featuring improvised explosive devices and suicide bombers—are a daily way of life. In Afghanistan, moreover, a resurgent Taliban threat (also featuring suicide bombing attacks) suggests that the strategic victory in that country is far from complete.

The "9/11 Effect": An Emboldening of Terrorists?

Another consequence of the 9/11 attack is its impact on terrorists and their self-confidence. The 9/11 attacks arguably emboldened terrorists and generated within them the perception that they have state-like power not only to influence the international system but also perhaps even to transform it in accordance with their vision. As noted earlier, John Lewis Gaddis has written that terrorism has traditionally had a minimal impact on the international system, but 9/11 was something qualitatively different because it "showed that terrorists can now inflict levels of destruction that only states wielding military power used to be able to accomplish."[98] Thus, 9/11 obscured the dichotomy between states and nonstate actors in terms of the latter's ability to exert power and influence the international system. Nonstate actors, it could be argued, are potentially as influential as states.

Consequently, according to this post–9/11 view of terrorism, the world community now faces terrorist threats that, unlike past terrorist trends, "have the potential to fundamentally threaten the international system."[99] U.S. Defense Department officials have bolstered this view by regularly describing the terrorist challenge as a threat against the sovereign state system, and not merely an attack against a specific nation.[100] This contrasts with the traditional view, aired as late as 2000, when U.S. security analysts were downplaying the terrorist threat: "Today's terrorism does not constitute military power. Terrorism is assessed as posing only a small direct threat to our national survival, but its impact over time on U.S. foreign policy interests and U.S. national security may be far greater."[101]

The general emboldening of terrorists may explain why terrorist leaders such as Osama bin Laden apparently believe that they have state-like power to injure or even destroy another state, including a superpower such as the United States. In recent speeches, for instance, bin Laden has remarked about the economic effects of the 9/11 attacks. Moreover, a close examination of his statements suggests an al-Qaeda strategy to weaken the United States not by focusing on the first level (where raw military power is most effective), but on the second level, the realm of economic interdependence. In an interview with the Internet-based Jihad Online News Network, Osama bin Laden described what he understood as the economic consequences of the 9/11 attacks:

> The daily U.S. income is $20 billion. There was no business during the first week [following the September 11 attack] due to the psychological shock. And, no one has gone to work to this day due to the big shock. If you multiply $20 billion by seven days, the answer is $140 billion. But, it is actually more than that. You have to add it to the $640 billion. So what is the result? It is more than $800 billion. The loss of buildings is more than $30 billion. The number of employees dismissed by aviation companies to this day, or until two days ago, was over 170,000.[102]

Moreover, in an interview, bin Laden reveals that the World Trade Center was chosen as a target not merely because of its symbolic value—its towering presence and representation of strength—but also because it clearly represented the American economy: "Those who were killed in the World Trade Center towers were an economic power, not a school for children or a house. Those who were in the [World Trade] center backed the biggest economic power in that world that sows corruption on earth."[103] In another speech delivered by audiotape, bin Laden once again focuses on the economic consequences of 9/11:

> Their losses following the strike and its repercussions have reached more than a trillion dollars. They also witnessed a budget deficit for the third consecutive year. This year's deficit reached a record number estimated at $450 billion. Therefore, we thank God.[104]

Moreover, in November 2004, Osama bin Laden mentioned a "policy" implemented by his organization to economically damage the United States: "So we are continuing this policy in bleeding America to the point of bankruptcy."[105]

Regarding the question of whether or not Osama bin Laden (or the al-Qaeda organization) weakened American power, there is little doubt that the 9/11 attacks resulted in substantial economic loss for the United States, at least in the short term. An estimated 130,000 individuals lost their jobs in 462 mass layoffs attributable to the 9/11 attacks.[106] According to the comptroller of New York, the 9/11 attacks cost New York City $30.5 billion.[107]

The U.S. airline industry posted losses of approximately $17 billion from 2001 to 2003, due to the effects of 9/11 (but also including the effects of the SARS [severe acute respiratory syndrome] epidemic as well as the Iraq war).[108] On the insurance front, the loss of life and property resulted in the largest property/casualty claim in history (an estimated $40 billion).[109] In a report issued by the Organization for Economic Cooperation and Development (OECD), it described the amount of destruction in similar terms:

> The September 11 attacks inflicted casualties and material damages on a far greater scale than any terrorist aggression in recent history. The destruction of physical assets was estimated in the national accounts to amount to $14 billion for private businesses, $1.5 billion for State and local government enterprises and $0.7 billion for Federal government.[110]

However, it could be argued—as some reports have stated—that the economic losses, while devastating, were largely temporary. The U.S. economy has rebounded and has absorbed these losses. But this more positive analysis should be tempered by acknowledging certain permanent structural changes (and costs) that are related to 9/11. For example, around the world, governments have proposed and implemented thousands of new laws, regulations, and rules designed to diminish the chance of another major terrorist attack. Moreover, some estimates place the total cost of the U.S.-led "War on Terrorism" at more than US$400 billion, a number that grows by the week. In fact, one report recently noted that the "War on Terrorism" (which includes American military involvement in Iraq and Afghanistan) is "about to become the second-most-expensive conflict in U.S. history, after World War II."[111]

In the maritime realm, new regulations pertaining to additional security staff and equipment are expected to cost $1.3 billion, with annual costs of $730 million after that.[112] In the United States, the USA PATRIOT Act (Title 3) has expanded reporting requirements of the Bank Secrecy Act for financial transactions to other "nontraditional" industries, such as insurance companies, travel agencies, automobile dealerships, and jewelry shops, among others. The expansion of Bank Secrecy Act reporting requirements has created a structural change resulting in increased costs, which are now permanently embedded in the cost of doing business.[113]

Moreover, the more permanent impact has been a reorientation of money directed toward security, and away from more productive applications. As one recent U.S. congressional research report stated: "Resources that could have been used to enhance productive capacity of the country will now be used for security. Since it will take more labor and capital to produce a largely unchanged amount of goods and services, this will result in a slower rate of growth in national productivity, a price that will be borne by every American in the form of a slower rate of growth of per capita real income."[114]

However, after reviewing bin Laden's statements, and taking into account his organization's interest in chemical, biological, radiological, and nuclear (CBRN) weapons, there is growing concern that a major CBRN attack could bring about the economic harm that bin Laden envisages. According to an OECD study, an RDD—radiological dispersal device or "dirty bomb"—packed into a container and loaded onto a ship, and then clandestinely transported to a particular port, could, upon detonation, cause damages amounting to tens of billions of dollars.[115] "The very things that have allowed maritime transport to contribute to economic prosperity also render it uniquely vulnerable to exploitation by terrorist groups," according to the report.[116]

A nuclear attack would be even more devastating. Apart from the enormous loss of human life that can be expected, the long-lasting effect is likely to be in the economic realm. For instance, a nuclear device detonated in lower Manhattan would likely result in economic damage in excess of US$1 trillion.[117] According to an OECD report that assessed the economic effects of the 9/11 attacks, "an attack against, for instance, New York City using a nuclear weapon could leave most of the metropolitan area uninhabitable for years. The direct impact would reduce the country's production potential by about three percent."[118] One could argue that these are short-term effects that, like the aftermath of 9/11, would be absorbed and ameliorated in due course. However, the report points to more ominous structural changes that could weaken the United States permanently. The following assessment assumes a nuclear attack on New York City:

> Nationwide, both household and business confidence would be badly shaken, as well as the trust in the Government's capacity to protect the country. The displacement of the surviving population to non-contaminated areas would create the need for new housing. As standard insurance policies exclude nuclear attacks, the cost of reconstruction would fall on the budget, and the fiscal outlook would deteriorate markedly. The recent shrinkage of coverage for terrorism-related risks . . . would also leave most businesses dangerously exposed. Over the long term, such an attack would sharply reduce the readiness of persons and businesses to agglomerate in metropolitan areas. The trend would therefore be to disseminate in less populated areas, which may have a negative impact on innovation and productivity growth.[119]

The report concludes on an ominous note by noting that a second terrorist attack could have deeper and longer-lasting effects, especially if it involved weapons of mass destruction.[120] Such an attack would likely result in systemic changes in how societies (not just the United States) are ordered, how business is conducted, and how governance is conducted. Although the United States would likely rebound, or embark upon a military assault on the source country of the nuclear weapon, or its constituent materials, the longer-term effects, geopolitically, would likely be profound. The shifts in the international system would be visible, structural, and, most likely, permanent.

Conclusion

This chapter has examined the relationship between terrorism and the international system. In general, it is accepted that terrorism is more often shaped by the international system, rather than the other way around. However, 9/11 arguably changed this relationship, or at least elevated the significance of terrorism in terms of its effects on the international system. The 9/11 attacks were the product of an unprecedented convergence in the international system of religious, social, and technological trends.

In addition, the 9/11 attacks demonstrated al-Qaeda's ability to operate relatively freely in the third level of the Joseph Nye three-level model of the international system. Some states did not take the threat of terrorism seriously prior to 9/11, because traditionally only threats existing in or emanating from the first level—that is, state-based threats—were seen as true security threats. In addition, al-Qaeda was the product of a convergence of a number of functional and ideological trends, including globalization and its various processes, as well as the rise of radical religious ideologies that have, in many respects, emerged as a palliative against state failure and economic malaise.

The end result is a transformation of the power structure of the international system. Commenting on the systemic-change aspect of the post–9/11 view of terrorism, Audrey Kurth Cronin argues that "the age of terrorism is a new era in international relations, where the traditional tools of power politics will be less important than in the past."[121] Instead of merely being the product of trends in the international system, 9/11 brought about a situation in which terrorism significantly shaped the international system in a direct (not merely a proximate) manner.

Regarding the impact of terrorism on the international system, John Ikenberry and Charles Kupchan propose that "policymakers and scholars alike must continue to address whether the events of 9/11 fundamentally altered the international system, requiring not just adjustments to national strategy, but complete transformation."[122] For the Bush administration, the answer is clear, as evidenced by the fact that this administration has embraced "the effort to combat terrorism as America's defining mission for the foreseeable future."[123]

4

Globalization and the Information Revolution

The Impact on Terrorism

In February 2000, an Egyptian merchant living in Guangzhou, China, sought assistance from a local Internet firm to set up an Internet Web site. After a fee was negotiated, the Egyptian, Sami Ali, set up his Web site with the address "maalemaljihad.com."[1] With technical assistance from militants in Afghanistan, Pakistan, and the United Kingdom, Ali's Web site was open for business. The home page welcomed visitors to the site of Egyptian Islamic Jihad, a militant group closely associated with al-Qaeda. What was surprising about the Web site was not its content, but rather its location—hosted in a country with a centralized, nominally Communist government—far from the Middle East where such militant ideologies are rooted.

Four years later, in another case, an Internet company in Malaysia, Acme Commerce, claimed that it had unwittingly hosted a Web site that showed the May 2004 beheading of U.S. national Nick Berg, who was killed by Islamic extremists in Iraq. Malaysian leaders were embarrassed by the revelation and later Prime Minister Abdullah Ahmad Badawi vowed not to "allow any kind of Web page or any company operating on behalf of terrorists."[2] Acme Commerce denied any linkages to or sympathies for al-Qaeda or other similar groups. Later the company searched other sites that it hosted and discovered at least five more sites linked to al-Qaeda or other terrorist organizations, which were subsequently shut down.[3] The incident followed embarrassing revelations that Malaysia had been linked to Pakistani scientist Abdul Qadeer Khan's nuclear network.

Although these cases may appear unusual, they should be viewed within the context of transnational terrorist groups' increasing reliance on the Internet and other new communication technologies to plan and conduct their operations. Al-Qaeda in particular has masterfully exploited the Internet to advance its particular political agenda. For example, after enduring an onslaught of criticism in the Middle East regarding its operations and ideology, al-Qaeda reportedly launched an Internet offensive, relying on Web sites, such as the now defunct www.alneda.com, to promote its message and spread its propaganda. According to one analyst, "al-Qaeda attaches great importance to waging psychological warfare, and has used the Internet as its medium."[4]

Indeed, the information revolution has empowered militant Islamic groups in their campaign against the West. Information technology is used when planning attacks—information is passed via e-mail or chat rooms to operatives in the field—and it is used when justifying or explaining attacks. The information revolution has created opportunities for nonstate actors, such as al-Qaeda, that simply were unavailable before. With minimal costs, nonstate actors can establish a presence on the international stage and transform their asymmetry into a symbolic symmetry, as al-Qaeda has done in its "David versus Goliath" confrontation with the United States. These information revolution tools have, as one writer notes, "led to enhanced efficiency in many terrorist-related activities, including administrative tasks, coordination of operations, recruitment of potential members, communication among adherents, and attraction of sympathizers."[5]

But the larger enabler is not only information technology and the information revolution in which it is embedded, it is the process of globalization itself, of which the information revolution is one part. Terrorism always occurs within a larger political context. During the anticolonial struggles and movements of the early twentieth century, nationalist terrorism was prominent. During the cold war, leftist or Marxist terrorism was ascendant. Today, the prominent and most powerful trend is globalization and it is within this enabling environment that contemporary transnational terrorism continues to thrive.

Around the world, there is a growing sense that globalization and all of its disruptive processes are linked in some way to rising terrorism. Former South Korean president Kim Dae-Jung recently stated that globalization has generated great wealth, but it has also brought injustice in its wake, including human rights abuses, racial discrimination, and human trafficking.[6] Solomon Pasi, while serving as Bulgaria's Foreign Minister, drew the link between globalization and terrorism more closely in 2002 by stating that: "Terrorism is poisonous fruit of globalization and it will be destroyed also by globalization."[7] Audrey Kurth Cronin has argued that "globalization and terrorism are intricately intertwined forces characterizing international security in the twenty-first century."[8] Al-Qaeda—with its extensive transnational linkages, reliance on modern communications technology, and deft manipulation of international financial pathways—is one example of this trend.

Defining Globalization

Globalization has become the popular catchphrase used to describe the vast network of international interdependence—transnational cultural, economic, and military flows—that characterizes global society today. Defining what globalization actually is requires more precision. One definition posits that globalization represents "the growth of worldwide networks of interdependence."[9] R.J. Barry Jones asserts that globalization can be seen as an enhanced stage of internationalization: "Globalization can be understood as a higher stage of internationalization, which itself may be interpreted as an increase in the inter-societal flows of finance, trade, social patterns and human mobility."[10] Joseph Nye asserts that modern globalization in many ways reflects previous eras of globalization; however, what distinguishes contemporary globalization from the past is that the "networks are thicker and more complex, involving people from more regions and social classes."[11] Nye and his colleague Robert Keohane argue that three key elements facilitate the increased interdependence inherent in contemporary globalization.[12]

First, globalization is characterized by density of networks, which refers to the fact that as interdependence has grown, international networks have become thicker and more important. Second, globalization can be measured via institutional velocity, which refers to speed and magnitude of information exchange; it is within this element that the information revolution plays such an important role. The third element is transnational participation and complex interdependence.[13] This refers to the multiple channels between societies—not just at the elite level, but at the common level as well. Complex interdependence also implies the absence of a hierarchy of issues; all issues are important, depending on the particular network.[14]

Keohane and Nye also propose slightly different language to analyze the processes of globalization. First, they draw a distinction between interdependence and globalization. "Globalization" is, in many respects, an analogue of the 1970s phrase "interdependence." Both of these words, according to Keohane and Nye, "[express] a poorly understood but widespread feeling that the very nature of world politics is changing."[15] However, interdependence "refers to a condition, a state of affairs."[16] Interdependence can increase as it has done since the end of World War II, or it can decrease, as it did during the Great Depression of the 1930s. Globalization, on the other hand, "implies that something is increasing: there is more of it."[17] Globalization is the process of expanding "globalism"—the opposite would be "deglobalization" which would refer to the idea that globalism is decreasing.

Globalism is described as "a state of the world involving networks of interdependence at multicontinental distances."[18] These linkages can occur in terms of information flows, capital flows, international migration, or any other transnational flows (including diseases or environmental phenomena, such as acid rain). Interdependence is far less dynamic than globalization; interdependence simply refers to single transaction linkages. Globalism is a type of interdependence, except that it features two characteristics: multi-nodal networks (not simply single linkages) and multicontinental distances (not simply regional networks or linkages). Keohane and Nye point to the spread of Islam versus Hinduism to illustrate the basic differences between the concepts: "Islam's rapid diffusion from Arabia across Asia to what is now Indonesia was a clear instance of globalization, but the initial movement of Hinduism across the Indian subcontinent was not."[19]

An alternative way of viewing globalization is proposed by Stanley Hoffman who argues that globalization can be differentiated into three key parts: economic globalization, cultural globalization, and political globalization. Economic globalization, according to Hoffman, affects countries and societies directly because it encompasses international trade, foreign investment flows, and transnational technology transfers. Cultural globalization, on the other hand, refers to the "flow of cultural goods" that travel across borders, and can include artwork, movies, and other media that collectively transmit ideas. Political globalization is a product of both the economic and cultural varieties; it is characterized by the "preponderance of the United States and its political institutions and by a vast array of international and regional organizations and transgovernmental networks."[20]

As a predominant trend within the contemporary international system, globalization underpins transactions between states and private (nonstate) actors. In fact, one could argue that nonstate actors are privileged by the processes of globalization, a fact that is increasingly appreciated among security professionals. In his 2002 annual report to Congress regarding global threats to the United States, for example, Vice Admiral Thomas Wilson, director of the Defense Intelligence Agency, argued that traditional approaches to security have almost always focused on the "state-oriented threat model"—however, this state-centric model is no longer adequate, especially as nonstate actors have become empowered by the forces of globalization. He stated specifically that "non-state adversaries are not likely to be deterred by our overwhelming military superiority, and will often present challenges that do not lend themselves to a predominantly military solution."[21]

As an international economic and political phenomenon, globalization is expected to expand substantially in the future. A 2004 report by the National Intelligence Council stated that "we see globalization—growing interconnectedness reflected in the expanded flows of information, technology, capital, goods, service, and people throughout the world—as an overarching 'mega-trend,' a force so ubiquitous that it will substantially shape all the other major trends in the world of 2020."[22] Moreover, the report states that there will be winners and losers, and that the most successful countries will be those that "access and adopt new technologies."[23] Ultimately, globalization will profoundly shake up the political and economic status quo in many countries and will generate "enormous economic, cultural, and consequently political convulsions."[24]

The Global Militant Salafist Campaign:
An Antiglobalization Movement?

When Indonesia prosecuted one of the main perpetrators of the October 2002 Bali terrorist attack, which killed more than 200 people, it revealed just how globalization is perceived. When asked how he felt about the impact of the Bali attack, Amrozi bin Nurhasyim, a key operator in the plot who supplied the chemicals to make the bomb, told the court: "There's some pride in my heart. For the white people, it serves them right."[25] He said foreigners introduced moral decadence to Indonesia through television and Western lifestyles. "They know how to destroy religions using the most subtle ways through bars, gambling dens. And you must realize the debauchery of their television," he told the court.[26]

Although it may be tempting to dismiss or downplay Amrozi's comments, it should be recognized that these sentiments—the idea that globalization represents an invasion of unwanted social values—can be found throughout the developing world. In many developing countries, globalization is viewed as a threat, or as a type of insidious cultural invasion. "Modern-day globalization—the opening of borders to the greater movement of ideas, people and money—has stirred familiar anxieties about ill-defined 'outside forces.'"[27] Michael Mazarr takes the matter a step further: "In countries around the world, many consider globalization a threat to their values, jobs, and ways of life. They view globalization as U.S.-led, U.S.-directed, and most beneficial to U.S. interests and companies."[28]

Globalization, and particularly "cultural globalization," is perceived as bringing in decadent values, such as television with sexual images, widespread alcohol use, and violent music, that have the potential to undermine local, and typically conservative, social values. Moreover, resistance to cultural globalization is not limited to conservative Muslims or militant Salafis. According to Charles Selengut, even traditional Christians detest the values associated with cultural globalization: "They [traditionalist Christians] see individualism, secularism, and the radically pluralistic ethic of modernity as entirely destructive of the human condition."[29] Similarly, Pope Benedict XVI, while visiting Brazil in May 2007, warned of unfettered capitalism and globalization which, he argued, could give "rise to a worrying degradation of personal dignity through drugs, alcohol and deceptive illusions of happiness."[30]

Moreover, not only is globalization associated with permissive, immoral, or decadent values, it is almost invariably linked with Westernization, and in many eyes this means Americanization. Equating globalization with increased American influence, the *New York Times* columnist Thomas Friedman has argued that American power became so dominant in the 1990s that no country could remain immune to its cultural or social influences. "The net effect was that U.S. power, culture, and economic ideas about how society should be organized became so dominant (a dominance magnified through globalization) that America began to touch people's lives around the planet."[31]

Like an elephant walking nonchalantly across a grassy field, unaware of the insects being crushed under its weight, the United States—including its citizens, corporations, and culture—travels around the world, often not realizing the consequences of its vast and raw power. This power often translates into an altering of local values. Audrey Kurth Cronin asserts that "globalization, in forms including Westernization, secularization, democratization, consumerism, and the growth of market capitalism, represents an onslaught to less privileged people in conservative cultures"[32] who are then forced to contend with the dismantling of their traditional societies and value systems.

In many parts of the world, globalization is perceived as a new form of imperialism—an absolutist ideology that the West seeks to foist upon the world. Roger Scruton echoes this "invasion by globalization" theme by arguing that globalization lends an "in your face" quality to Western values and mores, particularly as they are thrust into Muslim-majority countries.[33] "In the days when East was East and West was West, it was possible for Muslims to devote their lives to pious observances and to ignore the evil that prevailed in the *dar al-harb* [Realm of War]. But when that evil spreads around the globe, cheerfully offering freedoms and permissions in place of the austere requirements of a religious code, so that the *dar al-Islam* [Realm of Islam] is invaded by it, old antagonisms are awakened, and with them the old need for allies against the infidel."[34]

Thus, it can be reasonably posited that terrorism is at least partially a response to what is often viewed as metastasizing globalization. According to one Hamas leader, Ismail Abu Shanab (who was assassinated in 2003 in an Israeli raid), globalization is just another means of American economic and cultural domination of the world: "Globalization is just a new colonial system," Abu Shanab argued. "It is America's attempt to dominate the rest of the world economically rather than militarily. It will worsen the gap between rich and poor. America is trying to spread its consumer culture. These values are not good for human beings."[35]

Viewed from an even harsher perspective, globalization is sometimes viewed as an encroachment on sovereignty. In the Middle East, according to Mark Strauss, "Islamists and secular nationalists alike portray globalization as the latest in a series of U.S.-Zionist plots to subjugate the Arab world under Western economic control and erase its cultural borders."[36] Within this perspective, globalization is viewed not just as a cultural menace, but a threat to the very soul of the host state. Sonja Hegasy argues that "a majority of Arab intellectuals have depicted globalization as pure cultural and economic imperialism, and their position has trickled down into daily newspapers and public opinion."[37] Daniel Benjamin and Steven Simon argue that the United States is resented in the Islamic world because "its cultural reach threatens traditional values, including the organization of societies that privilege males and religious authority."[38] In addition, American culture "offers temptation, blurs social, ethical, and behavioral boundaries, and presages moral disorder."[39]

Al-Qaeda has sought to capitalize on rising antiglobalization sentiment in developing and Muslim-majority countries, although it may not actually frame the conflict in those terms. For instance, al-Qaeda portrays itself as the vanguard against Western-led military and political globalization, and specifically Western (and particularly American) military campaigns in the Muslim world. Resistance to invasion by American and Western forces is a common theme for bin Laden. In one speech, he describes terrorist actions as being a response to particular "invasions" by specific Western or global powers. For instance, "The killing of Russians was after their invasion of Afghanistan and Chechnya; the killing of Europeans was after their invasion of Iraq and Afghanistan."[40] Bin Laden further states that the United States was targeted because of its invasions of various countries as well as its support for Israel: "[T]he killing of Americans on the day of New York [reference to September 11] was after their support of the Jews in Palestine and their invasion of the Arabian Peninsula. Also, killing them in Somalia was after their invasion of it in Operation Restore Hope."[41]

With regard to U.S. application of military force in Iraq and Afghanistan, Osama bin Laden has described such campaigns as being part of "a new crusader campaign against the Muslim world. . . . Only God knows the extent of its serious repercussions and negative effects on Islam and Muslims."[42] In addition, bin Laden compares the United States and its military operations in Muslim countries with the Roman Empire: "I also tell you that the Romans have gathered under the banner of the cross to fight the nation of beloved Muhammad, may God's peace and blessings be upon him."[43] This antimilitary globalization theme is consistent with a National Intelligence Report, portions of which were released in April 2006, that listed the war in Iraq as one of four key factors that are spreading the jihadist movement.[44]

Developing the Roman analogy further, bin Laden exhorts Muslims to be confident in the fact that, as with the decline of Rome, the decline of the United States and its global power is also imminent: "God has aborted their plots and weakened their might; so do not be scared of their great numbers. Their hearts are full of sin and they have begun to weaken militarily and economically, particularly in the aftermath of the New York day."[45]

The notion of "invasion" embedded within conceptualizations of globalization—and the need to repel the invasion—strikes a deep chord among many Islamic militants. Taqi al-Din Ahmad Ibn Taymiyya, considered an intellectual father to contemporary Islamic militant ideology, grew up within the milieu of the collapse of the central caliphate to the Mongol invasion from the East in the thirteenth century: "His painful experience as a refugee colored his attitude toward the conqueror Mongols throughout his life."[46]

Meanwhile, Hassan al-Banna, founder of the Muslim Brotherhood, spent his early days in the shadows of British colonialism. Similarly, Sayyid Qutb, considered an intellectual guide to Osama bin Laden and author of the influential book *Milestones,* also grew up under the shadow of growing Western cultural influence over the modernizing Egyptian state. Many of these early thinkers, whose ideas have directly or indirectly influenced al-Qaeda and other similar groups, have wrestled with the problem of confronting or managing an influx of powerful exogenous social or economic forces beyond their control.

Globalization, the Information Revolution, and "Television Terrorism"

If the al-Qaeda phenomenon can be characterized as an antiglobalization movement, ironically, the al-Qaeda organization has cleverly and deftly exploited the technologies of globalization and the information revolution to pursue its political campaign.[47] The information revolution—and particularly instantaneous satellite-based television—helps to catapult terrorist groups, or individuals, onto the world stage as symbolic equivalents to (or at least co-players with) states. For example, just weeks after the 9/11 attacks in the United States, al-Qaeda released a video depicting Osama bin Laden triumphantly declaring victory over the United States. He stated: "There is America, hit by God in one of its softest spots. Its greatest buildings were destroyed, thank God for that."[48] He then continued with a phrase that many Americans would remember because it captured much of the anxiety and paranoia being felt across the nation: "There is America, full of fear from its north to its south, from its west to its east. Thank God for that."[49] The words penetrated homes, businesses, and transportation terminals across the country.

What was remarkable about bin Laden's statement was not merely the content, but the manner in which this content was expressed, namely, via modern satellite and cable-based television. The rise of cable and satellite television networks today marks a new chapter in the evolving relationship between television and terrorism, which arguably had its genesis in the 1960s, a period that saw the advent of live, instantaneous, transnational televised communication. Prior to that period, terrorists simply could not reach huge audiences. Moreover, in the pretelevision era there was often a significant time lapse between the actual terrorist attack and the point at which it was noticed or recognized. This technological limitation could be seen with the assassination of President John F. Kennedy; although the president's assassination was filmed, only a few people beyond the United States saw the footage because so few owned television sets.[50]

Access to television grew, however, in the late 1960s. By September 1970, when the Popular Front for the Liberation of Palestine (PFLP) hijacked three New York-bound airliners and flew them to Dawson's Field in Jordan, television had emerged as a key tool to be exploited by terrorists. At one point in the hostage episode, after the ranks of news reporters had swelled, the PFLP decided to conduct a news conference. One reporter asked about the sanitary conditions on the TWA aircraft. Facing television cameras, the PFLP spokesman replied "Would you like to smell? What do you think—they don't have water. What do you think, asking this kind of questions [sic]?"[51] The PFLP believed that the hostage operation at Dawson's Field was important to show "how dire the situation was" in terms of their own political plight.[52] One of the Palestinian guerrillas, explaining the rationale for the hijackings, would later tell a British television interviewer that "we wanted to put the Palestinian question in front of international opinion."[53]

Future years would see advances in television broadcast technology that would result in more dramatic terrorist events with correspondingly far-reaching effects. At the 1972 Olympic Games in Munich, Germany, for instance, the Palestinian group Black September attacked and killed members of the Israeli Olympics team while over 800 million people around the world watched the tragedy unfold in front of their eyes.[54] Perhaps because of this vast televised publicity, the Munich Olympics attack was considered a symbolic victory for the Palestinians. Media analysis generated only days after the Munich attack recognized that, from a publicity angle, the Black September operatives had achieved at least some of their objectives. According to a *Wall Street Journal* report, "The mysterious Black September terrorists who introduced violent death to the Olympic Games on Tuesday probably gained some of their narrower political objectives . . . the terrorists once again focused world attention on the Palestinian cause."[55] Similarly, Bruce Hoffman notes that in terms "of the publicity and exposure accorded to the Palestinian cause, Munich was an unequivocal success—a point conceded by even the most senior PLO [Palestine Liberation Organization] officials."[56] Similarly, the September 11, 2001, attacks in New York City and Washington, DC, attracted even greater numbers of viewers—perhaps 2 billion or more (either via live television or delayed video)—around the world, with corresponding increases in publicity impact.

The significance of televised terrorism lies in the fact that the violent terrorist images become seared onto the minds of millions as they watch ubiquitous video images aired in twenty-four-hour news formats, hour after hour. Perceptions are thus created—often raw, unfiltered, and devoid of government interpretation—and these perceptions are distributed throughout vast viewer networks (whether via cable television, satellite television, the Internet, or other outlets). Television accentuates and perhaps even creates the "theatrical" nature of specific terrorist actions. Writing in 1977, Michael Flood argued that "television . . . has increased the visibility of violence and done more for terrorism than perhaps any other single factor."[57]

Mark Juergensmeyer refers to terrorist acts as constructed events. "At center stage are the acts themselves—stunning, abnormal, and outrageous murders carried out in . . . grand scenarios of conflict and proclamation."[58] Video depiction only magnifies this effect, and creates a historical record so that the image can be viewed over and over again. According to Brigitte Nacos, television shapes terrorism by emphasizing its spectacular qualities: "In the past, terrorism has often been compared to theatre because political violence is staged to get the attention of the audience. Although the theatre metaphor remains instructive, it has given way to that of terrorism as a global television spectacular, as breaking news that is watched by international audiences and transcends by far the boundaries of theatrical events."[59]

More significantly, R.D. Crelinsten argues that terrorists normally have an asymmetric standing with a state with which they have an adversarial relationship.[60] However, television has helped to break down this typically imbalanced, asymmetric relationship in favor of a more symmetric relationship between the two parties and, hence, has helped terrorist groups attain symbolic power symmetry with states. For example, if al-Qaeda engaged the United States (or any other adversarial country) in private discussions or clandestine communications, the relationship would likely be vertical, with the United States, as the more powerful actor (in military or "hard power"[61] terms), in the commanding position.

However, as long as al-Qaeda maintains its dialogue via private television networks, Internet video uplinks, and other new communication technologies, it maintains its status as a symbolic parity actor.[62] As Crelinsten has asserted,

"Access to the communication structure is intimately related to power."[63] As the communication structure becomes more diffused and more democratic, as a result of globalization and its attendant processes, then access to this structure becomes much easier in both technical and financial terms and thus the power of the terrorist group is increased.

An example of this "symbolic parity" between states and terrorist nonstate actors occurred in the days prior to the 2004 U.S. presidential election. During this period, Osama bin Laden suddenly appeared on American network television, as if he—not Ralph Nader—were the third-party spoiler candidate. Bin Laden presumably hoped that his pronouncements and warnings would sway the American electorate in a certain direction. But more important, the video imagery—and the distribution through private satellite cable companies such as the Middle Eastern-based al-Jazeera—allowed bin Laden to achieve symbolic parity with the United States. The video image anchored bin Laden's image inside the U.S. political process, transforming him, at least symbolically, into a major player, as significant as any other political actor.

In addition, Osama bin Laden's periodic appearance on television demonstrates the power of this medium in contemporary terrorism. Instantaneous nonfiltered television—CNN, al-Jazeera, and others—provides the oxygen of publicity for terrorist groups such as al-Qaeda. "Television in particular is no longer a medium which simply responds to terrorist events, it is an integral part of them."[64] Because television allows for huge, transnational audiences, "terrorists have learned to stage-manage their spectaculars for maximum audience impact."[65] Live television is crucial for terrorism because it quickly distributes the oxygen of terrorism, which is publicity—the very essence of terrorism: "Terrorists strive for attention, for recognition, and for respectability and legitimacy in their various target publics"[66] and terrorism acts as a convenient medium to promote and sustain this attention.

The Internet and the "Grand Narrative"

On June 2, 2006, Canadian police launched simultaneous raids in Toronto and other cities to disrupt one of the largest terrorist attacks being planned on Canadian soil. The men arrested or detained in the sweep were Canadian Muslims who had planned a series of dramatic terrorist attacks on Canadian soil, including the storming of the Canadian Parliament, the taking of hostages (primarily politicians, including the prime minister who was threatened with beheading), the bombing of power plants in Ontario, and the invasion of the studios of the Canadian Broadcasting Corporation.[67] Subsequent reports suggested that the CN Tower complex and the Toronto Stock Exchange were also targets.[68]

Investigators would later learn that many of the arrested men had used the

Internet—and particularly chat rooms contained within the Internet—to plan the operations. The would-be terrorists were very careful about their Internet use; most of the dialogue was encrypted and they judiciously relied on passwords. Nevertheless, Canadian intelligence officials managed to break through these security barriers and had monitored the communication since at least 2004.[69]

The Internet also provided a link to two Americans from Atlanta, Georgia: Syed Haris Ahmed and Ehsanul Islam Sadequee. Ahmed was a twenty-one-year-old Georgia Tech mechanical engineering student who had "become increasingly religious and was concerned about U.S. policy toward Muslims."[70] E-mail communications ultimately led to an actual trip to Toronto in March 2005 by the two Americans, where they intended to meet "like-minded Islamists."[71]

The Canadian case reflects the fact that since the 1990s, the Internet has increasingly become a key component of the information revolution, and terrorists have naturally exploited it to achieve their objectives. The Internet has allowed terrorists to reach a new level in terms of communications capability. As Bruce Hoffman recently told a U.S. congressional hearing "terrorist communications have now evolved to where terrorists can control the entire communications process . . . they [terrorists] can now determine the content, the context and the medium through which they broadcast and conceptualize their message."[72] Particularly impressive is the use of multimedia products on terrorism Web sites. As Hoffman has stated "weapons of terrorism today are no longer only the gun and the bomb, but now also include the mini-cam and video tape, the editing suite and attendant production facilities."[73]

The Internet's value to contemporary terrorists can be divided into two broad areas: ideational and functional. In the first case, ideational refers to the ability of the Internet to get out the message, story, or "narrative" of particular terrorist groups. Terrorists are very keen to tell their story and get their side of the conflict out to the public. Many terrorist organizations rely on a vast, globally connected array of Web sites and other private outlets to publish or air their particular views, to justify their actions, or to seek international sympathy for their cause. In the case of al-Qaeda, the narrative that is presented in the international media is one of a grand conflict between the United States and other Western countries and the world of Islam, not merely a conflict involving one country and a single terrorist organization.

In one tape, Osama bin Laden describes the jihad against Americans in Iraq as "a war of destiny between infidelity and Islam."[74] Moreover, according to this grand narrative, all Muslims "should view themselves as a single nation and unite to resist anti-Islamic aggression on the basis of obligatory defensive jihad."[75] Other aspects of the grand narrative, which are distributed to private Internet sites around the world, include assertions that the United States has committed crimes against Islam and that these crimes were part of a "Zionist-

Crusader" plot intended to annihilate Muslims around the world.[76] Such crimes justify al-Qaeda's declaration of war against the United States.[77]

By taking advantage of this networked, communications infrastructure, al-Qaeda and its affiliates have defined the terms and boundaries of the conflict. Moreover, by targeting and crafting messages to specific media outlets, al-Qaeda is able to tailor its message to fit particular audiences. For example, messages intended for European or American audiences tend to be much more moderate, and portray Osama bin Laden and other allied leaders in a more statesman-like manner.[78]

In the November 2004 address detailed above, Osama bin Laden directly made reference to arguments put forth by the Bush administration regarding the nature of terrorism. For instance, bin Laden directly addressed the assertion that terrorists "hate freedom," a phrase used by President Bush on numerous occasions. Bin Laden's response was: "I say to you that security is an indispensable pillar of human life and that free men do not forfeit their security, contrary to Bush's claim that we hate freedom. If so, then let him explain to us why we don't strike for example—Sweden?"[79] In this address, he also criticized the USA PATRIOT Act in language that almost resembled many U.S. domestic critics of this antiterrorism law: "So he [President Bush Sr.] took dictatorship and suppression of freedoms to his son and they named it the Patriot Act, under the pretense of fighting terrorism."[80]

In addition to ideational utility, the Internet also provides functional benefits to al-Qaeda. For example, the Internet provides a forum for militants around the world seeking information on weaponry, tactics, or other related topics. In one case, the discovery of al-Qaeda computers in Afghanistan revealed that the organization's decision to launch a chemical and biological weapons program was at least partly driven by the organization's access to communications—televised discussions, newspaper articles, and other open information available from the Internet—in the United States that highlighted a number of experts' fears about the possible imminent use of such weapons.[81] In Iraq, the Internet and the vast array of Islamist Web sites have played a "central role" in al-Qaeda operations in Iraq, according to a report by the London-based Arabic newspaper *Al-Sharq al-Awsat*.[82] The report elaborates: "Today the worldwide web has become a medium that is used by fundamentalists to transmit their messages and an outlet for their sympathizers to express their feelings of hatred towards the Western world."[83] As al-Qaeda has come under increasing U.S. military and other pressure, it has turned to networks (including the Internet) in an attempt to regain some command and control over the ideological and operational direction of the organization.[84]

Shyam Tekwani argues that the Internet and other new communication technologies are key foundations for current terrorist organizations, including al-

Qaeda. Not only do such media allow for the dissemination of propaganda, they also allow planning of operations. He contends, moreover, that the information revolution has contributed to the ability of like-minded terrorist groups to form transnational networks that can aid in disseminating propaganda, fund-raising, and recruitment. Such information infrastructure also helps terrorists plan and execute attacks across international borders more easily.[85] Consequently, the ability to use computers effectively is increasingly becoming a job requirement for contemporary terrorists. Tekwani notes that in Southeast Asia, "authorities . . . routinely find computers and diskettes on raids on terrorist hideouts across Asia, from Ramzi Yousef's Manila lair to LTTE [Liberation Tigers of Tamil Eelam] hideouts and JI [Jemaah Islamiyah] cells in Singapore."[86]

The Internet arguably has helped shape contemporary terrorism as profoundly as the rise of television in the 1960s. Grant Wardlaw argues that changes in communication, including the transmission of information, are the key distinguishing features of contemporary terrorism when contrasted with past forms of terrorism: "[A] very plausible case can be made that the most important differences between past and present terrorism may be traced to the modern, transnational flow of information."[87]

In the modern context, the Internet is allowing international Islamist groups, such as al-Qaeda, to create what David Martin Jones describes as an international "cybercaliphate." Jones argues that the modern Islamist seeks "a globalization of Islam's pre-modern scriptural injunctions that can leap over the bureaucratically-centralizing post-colonial arrangements into the transnational network of the cybercaliphate."[88] The advantage of such an Internet-based caliphate is that the ideas are divorced from the constraints and restrictions of the local community—the caliphate is, in a sense, dislodged from reality. These Internet-based associations become "abstract communities" that tend to be "more extreme examples of neo-orthodoxy among those deracinated from communities and tradition."[89]

On a more practical level, al-Qaeda has also turned to the Internet to create an online university—an "Al-Qa'ida University for jihad sciences" on the Internet.[90] The new online university will consist of separate colleges, each specializing in a certain "jihad science" including practicing with arms, car bombs, and the use of ammunition.[91] Students can also specialize in "electronic jihad" or "media jihad."[92] Admission to the online university requires that a candidate exhibit zeal and sincerity. "Without zeal neither jihad nor anything else would be of use," according to the university.[93] In another practical application of the Internet, the local al-Qaeda branch in Yemen opened a chat room in 2003 called "You ask and the jihad base in Yemen answers."[94] The Web site and chat room are designed to answer any question that members or supporters might have, regarding jihad or related matters.[95]

International Migration and the New Diaspora Order

In August 2006, officials in the United Kingdom uncovered a terrorist plot to blow up multiple passenger airliners as they transited the Atlantic Ocean. Officials reported that the plot "would have caused even greater casualties than 9/11."[96] Some compared it to the 1995 Philippines "Bojinka" plot in which eleven U.S. airliners were to be bombed as they crossed various routes within the Pacific Ocean.[97] As part of their roundup, British police reported that they had conducted sixty-nine raids on houses, apartments, offices, and vehicles.[98] Moreover, when they made their initial arrests of eleven British nationals implicated in the plot, they also discovered "bomb-making chemicals and equipment, suicide notes and so-called martyrdom videos of the would-be bombers.[99]

Perhaps the most alarming aspect of the plot was the fact that most of the plotters were British born. Three months later, the public would learn that this was among numerous plots being designed within the UK, apparently by UK nationals. In a surprise admission in November 2006, the director-general of Britain's MI5, Dame Eliza Manningham-Buller, disclosed that her agency was tracking "thirty alleged 'mass casualty' terror plots in operation in Britain."[100] In addition, she stated that MI5 was monitoring "200 groups or networks totaling more than 1,600 identified individuals in the UK."[101] Perhaps most surprising was her admission that "hundreds of young British Muslims [are] on a path to radicalization."[102]

What British officials discovered—or at least publicly revealed—in late 2006 reflects the fact that throughout Europe, radical Islamic ideologies have grown and have become more entrenched. This trend partly reflects the disorientation and alienation felt among many Muslim migrants who have not been embraced by nor culturally integrated into their host countries. More than 15 million Muslims live in Western Europe; they are the products of waves of immigration during the past half-century.[103] The largest recent wave occurred from the 1950s to the early 1970s.[104] Approximately 5 million Muslims live in France, and 2.5 million each live in Germany and the United Kingdom. Overall, Muslims constitute approximately 4 percent of the European Union's population. Some estimate that the Muslim population in Europe, based on current trends, could reach about 30 million by 2025 (which does not include EU-applicant Turkey).[105]

However, the integration of these migrants into larger West European society has been incomplete. The unemployment rate among Muslims is often double that of non-Muslims. In some cases, Muslims are simply not accepted (or are disliked) by the local population. In September 2006, the Open Source Center, a U.S. government research agency, published a media survey of the

European press that focused on European attitudes toward Muslim immigrants or residents. The report noted that the press "suggests significant resentment between Muslims and non-Muslims in the United Kingdom, France, Germany, and the Netherlands."[106]

Many of the press reports dealt with the issue of integration. One center-right French newspaper (*L'Express*) noted that the controversial "high-profile Muslim academic Tariq Ramadan [had suggested] that Muslim integration may not be necessary because France will eventually become a Muslim country."[107] According to a poll conducted by a German public television station "seventy percent of German respondents blame Muslim immigrants for making few efforts to integrate."[108] According to a Pew Research Center poll conducted in 2005, more than 80 percent of Dutch respondents stated that they believed that the country's Muslim community, numbering nearly 1 million, has "at least a fairly strong sense of Islamic identity," which they viewed as a "bad thing" for their country.[109]

Many young Muslim migrants who experience discrimination or exclusion in such places as Germany or France look to fundamentalist or militant ideologies as a way of overcoming their sense of alienation. Alternatively, they might discover such ideologies as a consequence of their own search for religious identity. According to Olivier Roy, "Radicalization is a peripheral result of the Westernization of Muslims born and living in Europe. It is linked with a generation gap and a depressed social status, and it perpetuates a pre-existent tradition of leftist, anti-imperialist protest in those communities."[110]

What was once considered a social problem for Western Europe is increasingly being viewed by European officials as a security challenge. For example, in the wake of the U.S. campaign in Iraq, intelligence officials in Europe are detecting rising militancy among Muslim immigrant communities. Intelligence officials report that "on working-class streets of old industrial towns like Crawley, Luton, Birmingham, and Manchester, and in the Arab enclaves of Germany, France, Switzerland, and other parts of Europe" militant ideologies are growing and, moreover, their proponents are becoming more open and aggressive in their advocacy.[111] European counterterrorism officials estimate that roughly 1 or 2 percent of the continent's Muslims—somewhere between 250,000 and 500,000 individuals—are involved in some sort of extremist activity.[112] In Germany, it is estimated that roughly 400,000 Muslims living in the country are "followers and supporters" of radical Islam and are actively seeking the establishment of an Islamic state.[113]

Many experts attribute this to a culture shock phenomenon, which occurs among Muslim immigrants, who then become "born-again Islamists." According to Timothy Savage: "Not accepted as an integral part of European society and at the same time repulsed by its secularism and materialism, a few individuals with a Muslim background, especially when confronted with a significant personal crisis, apparently find solidarity, meaning, and direction in radical Islamist groups that are actively looking for such recruits."[114]

Evidence suggests that, as mentioned above, the Iraq war may be fueling the trend. According to French intelligence reports, of the 15,000 prisoners taken in Iraq, between 200 and 300 were foreign fighters, including Europeans. European officials fear that these few fighters—imbued with new fervor and practical military experience—will return to Europe to pursue a militant agenda, much in the same way that their counterparts in the Afghanistan conflict did two decades earlier. In June 2005, a French newspaper reported that "Islamist militants linked to Iraq have been arrested in Italy, the Netherlands, Germany, and Spain in recent weeks."[115]

Rising Islamic militancy in Europe may also reflect a broader historical trend in which allegiance to transnational ideologies overshadows traditional loyalty to the state. Combined with the diaspora/overseas migrant phenomenon, globalization and the information revolution have allowed transnational ideologies—such as militant Islam or Salafism—to grow and spread. Moreover, these ideologies are typically rooted in (or are currently shaped by) a transnational interpretation of religion and, moreover, they are often divorced from states, or modern secularism. These ideologies allow an individual, faced with discrimination, alienation or hopelessness, to aspire to a status far and beyond what his or her local circumstances will permit.

In the al-Qaeda context, Afghanistan (and the anti-Soviet campaign of the 1980s) provided the international bonding experience among disparate individuals from around the world who sought a common cause in a shared religious tradition. The Afghanistan experience—and its resulting "Afghan alumni"—has helped facilitate the growth of this transnational ideology that, ironically, can be found quite prominently in the immigrant communities of North America and Western Europe.

For many Western countries, multiculturalism and liberalism present a dilemma. Western governments provide greater freedom and individual rights, but at the same time, by allowing immigrants to practice their own religion or to be attracted to radical ideologies, they endanger themselves, or unwittingly become bases for transnational violence elsewhere. Many Muslim migrants in Western Europe have fled more repressive regimes in Egypt, Saudi Arabia, or other countries that exert more control over potential Islamist activities. Thus, an ironic situation develops when European states advocate and campaign for strong counterterrorism measures abroad, and yet tolerate the same militant ideologies at home.

David Martin Jones has observed that "the British Home Office permits self-styled sheikhs Abu Hamza and Omar Bhakri Mohamed to recruit for al-

Qaeda from their state-subsidized mosque in Finsbury Park, North London, within half a dozen tube stops of Westminster."[116] In addition, he describes leading figures in the Saudi-funded Islamic Council of Britain who advocate the establishment of a united Islamic world that would include as a member state the Islamic Republic of the United Kingdom.[117] Many of the 9/11 pilots became radicalized in Western Europe—partly as a response to the freedoms they found around them, but also because of the general climate of religious tolerance and the lack of government scrutiny.

Jones argues that secularism, tolerance, and liberal values found in Western countries that harbor large Muslim minority communities actually encourage the spread of radical ideologies. Some Islamists, according to Jones, believe that "Western tolerance is weakness, and secularism a form of spiritual death requiring Islamic salvation."[118] Sayyid Qutb perceived Western "tolerance" as a form of weakness and immorality. Qutb described the time when he lived in the United States as a continual confrontation with Jahiliyyah (roughly defined as corruption, falsehood and ignorance). In chapter 10 of *Milestones,* Qutb asserts that he "took the position of attacking the Western Jahiliyyah, its shaky religious beliefs, its social and economic modes, and its immoralities."[119] He was also appalled by American "individual freedom, devoid of human sympathy and responsibility for relatives except under the force of law; at this materialistic attitude which deadens the spirit."[120]

From Qutb's point of view, living within the state of Jahiliyyah and being a good Muslim are simply incompatible. Qutb argues that "Islam cannot accept any mixing with Jahiliyyah. . . . Either Islam will remain, or Jahiliyyah: Islam cannot accept or agree to a situation which is half-Islam and half-Jahiliyyah."[121] From this perspective, migrants living in nominally non-Muslim countries could conceivably adopt the position that they must struggle against the host country, ultimately leading to its religious conversion. At the very least, this particular way of thinking sets the stage for potential conflict with the host state, which ultimately could lead to violence.

Globalization and Marginalization: Is There a Way Forward?

In 1997, an economic crisis swept through Southeast Asia, beginning in Thailand but soon spreading elsewhere in the region. One country in particular, Indonesia, endured especially harsh consequences and later near political collapse. The 1997 economic crisis demonstrated the power of what some economists term as "contagion"—the phenomenon in which ideas and panic can spread throughout an information-wired global community and thus create profound and sometimes disastrous financial and social consequences. The effects of this contagion in Southeast Asia were devastating on the state level as well as the individual level. Thousands of people endured layoffs or massive cuts in wages. The social and economic devastation eventually spread to South Korea, Russia, and other countries.

In an era of globalization, both positive and negative influences can race around the world with unprecedented speed. Countries connected by extensive communication networks become susceptible to sudden changes or disruptions caused by unexpected events. Thomas Homer-Dixon argues that this vulnerability is particularly acute in modern countries that rely "on intricate networks and [concentrate] vital assets in small geographic clusters."[122]

The economic, social, and cultural forces of globalization can be compared to a wildfire and just as a wildfire leaves charred remains and trails of destruction, so can the forces of globalization. Financial dislocation caused by contagion—or mass panics such as the 1997 economic crisis—can generate deep resentment within populations. Moreover, such dislocations and the poverty that results can create an enabling environment for nonstate-actor–driven terrorism. Ironically, it was during this period of state weakness in Southeast Asia, and particularly in Indonesia, that Jemaah Islamiyah began to strengthen and plan bold strikes, including the October 2002 attack in Bali.[123] The fall of Indonesian president Suharto in May 1998 (partially the result of the 1997 economic crisis and its various effects) transformed Indonesia into a weak democracy that featured intense political competition coming from various sectors. Most importantly, Indonesia's weakness allowed "hundreds of radical Muslim exiles [to return] to Indonesia" where they demanded political space.[124]

The 1997 economic crisis demonstrated how powerful and unconstrained transnational economic forces could actually be. The crisis also revealed the degree of marginalization experienced by much of the world's population, despite the promises of open trade and economic liberalization. In many parts of the world, globalization—or perhaps lack of it—has led not only to economic marginalization but also to social and cultural marginalization. Weakened states and corrupt governance, often the product of (or exacerbated by) economic crisis, contagion, or abrupt transitions from centrally planned to market-driven systems, leave millions stranded in a milieu of chaos, and, in some cases, outright anarchy.

Dislodged from social or economic certainties, some people are then attracted to religious fundamentalist ideas that offer clear guidance and comfort. Michael Mousseau argues that globalization encourages terrorism indirectly because of the social anarchy that it causes. He argues that millions today turn to "ethnofacism," sectarian murder, and fundamentalist religions as a way of attaining "psychic comfort in the face of volatile social anarchy."[125]

Economic globalization is a powerful force, but ironically it has bypassed much of the world, where unemployment problems continue to grow. Theodore Cohn has argued that globalization has largely been confined to the world's developed economies: Western Europe, North America, and Japan/East Asia.[126] In terms of foreign direct investment (FDI), it is within this triad that most activity is occurring: "In 1995, for example, the developed market economies accounted for 92.1 percent of the outward stocks of FDI and for 72.1 percent of the inward stocks of FDI."[127] Additionally, most of the world's trade flows really affect only this triad—"In 1993, North America, Western Europe, and Asia accounted for 84.2 percent of global merchandise exports and for 90.2 percent of world exports of manufactures."[128]

Less developed countries have increased their share of FDI, but in general this is still relatively limited to certain countries, such as Singapore, Brazil, Mexico, Malaysia, Thailand, and others. The world's least developed countries, located mainly in sub-Saharan Africa, received only 1.5 percent of FDI inflows during the 1980–84 period.[129] Poorer countries have generally not benefited from increased world trade either: "The least developed countries, with about ten percent of the world's people, accounted for only 0.3 percent of world trade in 1997—which was about half of their share two decades earlier."[130]

Thus globalization's effects—most notably its positive effects of encouraging economic growth—have been much less apparent in the less developed regions of the world. This has led to a "core" vs. "gap" dichotomy, according to Thomas Barnett, with the core comprised of countries that have benefited from globalization and the gap comprised of countries that have not. "To live in the Gap is to be surrounded by significantly higher rates of poverty," according to Barnett.[131] Gap countries also are less free, more violent, less healthy, and more solitary.[132] Between "core" and "gap" countries are "seam states," which are reasonably functional states that "ring the Gap."[133] Barnett's solution of inadequate globalization is to close the disparity between "core" and "gap" states. "The Core's political case for integrating the Gap's regions cannot be defined by fear," Barnett argues, "but must reflect a system-level understanding of the increasingly symbiotic economic relationship that evolves between the two."[134]

Like Barnett, Clair Apodaca also makes the case for "more globalization not less." She asserts that economic globalization has probably done more than any other factor, including international aid, to actually improve people's lives. In particular, the author is most enthusiastic about foreign direct investment. "FDI is the only globalization variable," she asserts, "that promotes every aspect of human and economic development in Asia. Contrary to what many theorists and several well-publicized cases suggest, FDI benefits not only the state and elites but also the poor and underprivileged."[135] This is why she is more inclined to advocate a "trade not aid" policy. Among other things, she argues that "'trade not aid' ought to be given greater consideration among human rights scholars, activists, and politicians, as it is clearly a means of encouraging human welfare and economic growth."[136]

Conclusion

When al-Qaeda members launched the 9/11 attacks in the United States, they were, in many respects, lashing out at globalization, and the values that they associated with the phenomenon. Many of al-Qaeda's members were marginalized from their native societies, or at least they perceived that their values and way of life were being overwhelmed by vast and powerful external forces that they could not control. Ironically, however, by conducting that attack, al-Qaeda transformed itself into a major player on the global stage. It became a global actor that owed its newfound fame and power to elements of globalization—and particularly the information revolution—that it so despised.

The 9/11 attacks also confirmed to governments worldwide the power of globalization. The spread of technology via the globalization process had acted as an enabler of terrorism; it had allowed terrorists to acquire even more disproportionate power than they would have had otherwise. Transforming civilian airliners into suicide missiles is just one example. New technologies flowing into the hands of nonstate actors are allowing destructive and currently theoretical scenarios—such as a nuclear attack on a major city—to possibly become reality in the future. Globalization did not solely create the current wave of terrorism; it did, however, enable it.

Terrorism throughout history typically occurs within the context of broader tensions in the international system. Globalization has indeed become that new *tension* in the international system. "[C]ontemporary international terrorism is both a reaction to globalization—with new objectives defined as a result—and facilitated by globalization, with new avenues of coordinating and carrying out attacks."[137] Whether globalization is good or bad depends largely on where one stands. For a developing country, globalization may present opportunities for international participation and economic advancement, or, alternatively, it might foster the destruction of precious cultural values.

If globalization is the present reality and force dominating the world—as many currently believe—then it must be understood in a comprehensive sense. Moreover, the manner in which the processes of globalization facilitate terrorism—and particularly mass casualty terrorism—must be grasped as well. The passions generated by antiglobalization must be managed, lest they result in a continuation of the vicious cycle of terrorism and political violence.

5

Religious Foundations for Terrorism

"God Almighty hit the United States at its most vulnerable spot," Osama bin Laden declared triumphantly in the aftermath of the 9/11 attacks, "He destroyed its greatest buildings. Praise be to God."[1] The speech, which was aired by the al-Jazeera television network, was designed to explain the rationale and motives behind the most devastating terrorist attack in U.S. history.

Furthermore, bin Laden explained why the attacks in New York and Washington should be seen as a form of revenge against American transgressions against the Islamic world for the past eight decades: "Our nation has been tasting this humiliation and contempt [emanating from the United States] for more than eighty years. Its sons are being killed, its blood is being shed, its holy places are being attacked."[2]

Some have questioned or even doubted bin Laden's religious motives, arguing that he cloaked his political and strategic objectives cynically within a concocted and distorted religious narrative. But evidence from a variety of bin Laden's statements—both prior to and following the 9/11 attacks—suggests that religion was indeed a core and genuine motivation. Daniel Benjamin and Steven Simon have argued that religion was the very *essence* of the 9/11 attack: "The motivation for the attack was neither political calculation, strategic advantage, nor wanton bloodlust," they argue, "it was to humiliate and slaughter those who defied the hegemony of God; it was to please Him by reasserting His primacy. It was an act of cosmic war."[3]

Such an assessment is validated by Osama bin Laden himself, whose words were recorded onto a videotape that was smuggled to the West and subsequently translated. Referencing the 9/11 attacks, bin Laden praises the young hijackers for the actions that, according to his perception, have promoted the spread of Islam: [bin Laden]: "Those young men (. . . inaudible . . .) said in deeds, in New York and Washington, speeches that overshadowed all other speeches made everywhere else in the world. The speeches are understood by both Arabs and non-Arabs—even by Chinese. It is above all the media said. Some of them said that in Holland, at one of the centers, the number of people who accepted Islam during the days that followed the operations were more than the people who accepted Islam in the last eleven years."[4]

The 9/11 attacks were the culmination of an ongoing campaign by the al-Qaeda organization to bring about what it perceived as God's will in the way that it believed was appropriate and this was by attacking the United States. Religious conviction and zeal—however distorted or manipulated—provided the foundation for al-Qaeda's philosophy, its goals, and also its tactics. This is not to say that bin Laden was not also driven by more worldly tactical goals (for instance, withdrawal of U.S. forces from the Middle East, replacement of secular regimes in the Middle East with religious-based governance, etc.).

But the underlying motivation for 9/11 was arguably ensconced in a notion of religious clash, between believers and unbelievers, the world of good and evil. In his speech of October 7, 2001, bin Laden speaks of two regions—"one of faith where there is no hypocrisy and another of infidelity, from which we hope God will protect us."[5]

Rising Importance of Religion in the International System

In the West, and particularly among academics, there is a tendency to ignore or downplay the power of religion in global society.[6] However, in the post–cold war era, it is increasingly obvious that religion remains a powerful force in the international system. This was demonstrated in late 2005 when a Danish newspaper published a series of cartoons depicting the Prophet Mohammed. One of the cartoons "depicted the Prophet with a turban shaped like a bomb with a lit fuse."[7] Realizing that the cartoons had offended Muslims, the editor of *Jyllands-Posten* (the Danish newspaper that had originally published the cartoons) apologized for causing offense, but not for exercising the right of free expression.[8]

However, the controversy gained momentum in early 2006 when a Norwegian publication reprinted the cartoons.[9] This time, the controversy grew to the point of violence and loss of life. At first, the protests consisted of demonstrations, Arab boycotts of Danish (and other Nordic) products, and a decision by Saudi Arabia, Syria, and Libya to withdraw their ambassadors from Copenhagen.[10] However, in subsequent weeks and months, mass protests—particularly in some Muslim-majority countries or regions—took a violent turn.

In Gaza, marked gunmen "swarmed the European Union offices" to protest the cartoons, although they eventually left after forty-five minutes.[11] In Indonesia, 300 "militant Indonesian Muslims" reportedly "went on a rampage" in the lobby of the building housing the Danish embassy.[12] By early February 2006, the Danish government was urging its citizens to leave Indonesia.[13] In Syria, crowds set fire to the embassies of Denmark and Norway.[14] In Pakistan, 400 people attacked a church in Sindh province "after accusations that a local Christian had burned pages from the Qur'an."[15]

In Nigeria, protests against the cartoons led to some of the worst violence of the entire controversy, particularly as latent tensions between Christians and Muslims were reignited. Attacks by Muslims on Christians in the northern part of the country led to retaliatory attacks by Christians. According to one report: "The cycle of tit-for-tat sectarian violence has pushed the death toll in the last week well beyond 100, making Nigeria the hardest-hit country so far in the caricature controversy."[16]

This controversy was followed by a similar one a few months later that was generated by a speech Pope Benedict XVI delivered at the University of Regensburg in Germany. In that speech, the pope quoted the words of a Byzantine emperor, Manuel II Paleologus, who addressed the issue of violence in the spread of Islam. The emperor reportedly stated (which the pope repeated): "Show me just what Mohammed brought that was new, and there you will find things only evil and inhuman, such as his command to spread by the sword the faith he preached."[17]

The speech drew an immediate and angry reaction throughout much of the Islamic world. As with the Danish caricature experience, protestors organized mass rallies in a number of Muslim-majority countries. In the southern Iraqi city of Basra, for instance, between 500 and 1,000 protestors marched on the streets to protest the pope's comments.[18] In the Somali capital of Mogadishu, an Italian nun was shot dead in an attack believed to be linked to the pope's remarks.[19] Palestinian Muslims engaged in a weekend of violent protests that included torching six churches.[20] In India, an effigy of the pope was set on fire.[21]

The Organization of the Islamic Conference released a statement saying it "regrets the quotations cited by the pope on the Life of the Honorable Prophet Mohammed, and what he referred to as 'spreading' Islam 'by the sword.'"[22] Eventually the furor died down when the pope issued a letter in which he stated "I wish also to add that I am deeply sorry for the reactions in some countries to a few passages of my address at the University of Regensburg, which were considered offensive to the sensibility of Muslims."[23]

The Power of Religion

The role of religion in stimulating (or at least accelerating) the controversies associated with the Danish caricature affair and the speech by Pope Benedict XVI can be understood or defined in a number of ways. At its core, religion is a belief structure that addresses the sense of disorder that many people perceive in their lives: "[I]n providing its adherents with a sense of conceptual order, religion often deals with the fundamental problem of disorder."[24]

More important, perhaps, from a social point of view is the element of individual empowerment and comfort that religion brings to individuals: "Religious faith and spirituality are a great source of personal empowerment and psychological sustenance. Humans have long derived personal strength from their religious practices and beliefs."[25]

Mark Juergensmeyer argues that a common thread in religion is the emphasis on "a certain kind of experience that people share with others in particular communities."[26] Any discussion of religion, therefore, implies "communities that have a tradition of sharing a particular religious point of view, a world view in which there is an essential conflict between appearance and deeper reality."[27] Jonathan Fox argues that religion has four basic functions: "To provide a value-laden worldview; to supply rules and standards of behavior based on that worldview; to organize adherents through institutions; and to legitimate actors, actions, and institutions."[28]

The resurgence of religion and religious identity partly reflects profound changes since the end of the cold war. Societies around the world are contending with disruptive transitions, economic dislocation, and moral questioning. Magnus Ranstorp attributes rising religious consciousness to the surrounding disruptive processes associated with globalization: "The accelerated dissolution of traditional links of social and cultural cohesion within and between societies with the current globalization process, combined with the historical legacy and current conditions of political repression, economic inequality, and social upheaval common among disparate religious extremist movements, have all led to an increased sense of fragility, instability, and unpredictability for the present and the future."[29]

The post–cold war world has also witnessed an increase in religious, ethnic, and communal sentiments and movements. This trend partly reflects the failure in the eyes of many people of secular ideologies and the state systems that have been built upon such ideologies: "Inconclusive modernization efforts and the failure of much of the non-western world to end its dependence on the West have added to the grievances of religious movements."[30] In addition, the overall sense that values, traditions, and "the family" have broken down has generated growing alienation, dislocation and various other anxieties. In the United States, for instance, the rise of right-wing religious movements reflects public distrust of government and feeds "on the public's perception of the immorality of government."[31]

Around the world, the Western model of secular governance appears to be on the defensive, if not declining outright. Secularism and Islam, for example, are anathema in that secularism "segregates the role of religion from matters of society and state, limiting it only to individuals and places of worship."[32] Islam, by contrast, "has guidelines for all aspects of life and demands its believers' commitment to all of its teachings."[33]

In the Middle East, Islam is emerging as the new salve to address the pain of declining states and hollow Arab nationalism. As Michael Hudson observes, "[The] slogan 'Islam is the solution' resonates deeply with individuals mired in the tensions and contradictions of contemporary Arab societies."[34] Following years of Western-inspired secularization, the Muslim world is witnessing a revival in Islamic consciousness or identity as reflected in growing attendance at mosques, public displays of piety and the spread of Islamic networks, political parties and social movements.[35]

Also throughout the Middle East, one can witness a movement away from secular government, in favor of political systems with heavy religious and even radical influences. In many parts of the Middle East, radical Islam has "influenced gender roles, relations with local Christians . . . consumption habits and public mores."[36] In the case of Kuwait, for instance, one scholar has suggested that Islamist influence has grown over the past twenty-five years and liberal influence has eroded, and moreover, "the Islamists have succeeded in sinking roots into Kuwaiti society through social organizations and business networks."[37] In Iraq, growing religious fervor is also emerging, and has roots predating the fall of Saddam Hussein. Iraq was once viewed as one of the most secular states of the Middle East, but in recent years, religion —and particularly militant Islam—has become much more important. Moreover, tolerance toward minority religions, such as Christianity, has ebbed considerably.[38]

Religion and Its Capacity for Violence

Although religion often brings comfort and a sense of universal meaning to individuals and societies, it also features a darker, violent side. "Religion, ordinarily a wellspring of hope, life, and virtue, stirs such deep passions that it also sometimes leads to violent action, to war, and even to terrorism."[39] Magnus Ranstorp argues that religious ideology justifies ever greater levels of violence because the struggle "is one purely defined in dialectic and cosmic terms as believers against unbelievers, order against chaos, and justice against injustice."[40] Moreover, religious ideology—unlike most state or secular ideologies—inspires "total loyalties,"[41] which leads some to conclude that "religions are generally more durable than states."[42]

Violence can also manifest in the context of religion when a believer—or community of believers—is challenged from some outside source. "[A]nything that a religious believer perceives to be a challenge to the religious framework underlying his behavior constitutes an existential threat for the whole constituency."[43] Not surprisingly, such a challenge—perhaps one posed by the disruptive force of globalization—is likely to be met with "drastic, often even deadly, responses."[44]

Religious militants—including terrorists—often view their actions as a part of a defensive effort to protect their faith or tradition. "Islam's jihad, for example, is essentially a defensive doctrine, religiously sanctioned by leading Muslim theologians, and fought against perceived aggressors, tyrants, and 'wayward Muslims.'"[45] But Islam does not have a monopoly over the tendency to invoke martial images: "The ideas of a Salvation Army in Christianity and a Dal Khalsa (Army of the Faithful) in Sikhism, for instance, are used to characterize a disciplined religious organization."[46] Some Christian theologians have described the vigorous practice of their faith as a "war" that unfolds within the spiritual realm.[47]

Even within a single country, religious and sectarian conflicts can lead to shocking levels of violence. In India, for instance, religion acted as a significant contributing factor provoking mass violence between Hindus and Muslims in the western state of Gujarat. The cycle of violence began when a fire—allegedly started by Muslims—broke out on a train carrying Hindu worshippers. Fifty-seven people died. Angry and in the mood for revenge, Hindus launched a campaign of gang-style killings against Muslims, including women and children.

The brutality of the violence was almost beyond imagination: women were subjected to gang rape prior to being executed and children were burned alive.[48] Gravediggers working at mass burial sites reported that bodies were arriving "burned and butchered beyond recognition."[49] Over 1,000 people, mostly Muslims, were murdered during the five-month period from February 2002 to June 2002.

The Gujarat episode in 2002 was not the only instance of Hindu–Muslim clashes. In early 1993, riots flared up between Hindus and Muslims as a result of the destruction by Hindus of a mosque in the northern town of Ayodhya.[50] At least 1,700 people—mostly Muslim—died in these riots.[51] Although it is difficult to ascertain absolute culpability regarding these riots and massacres, it is clear that sectarian clashes (such as Gujarat) have occurred within the milieu of rising Hindu militancy. Although Hindu militants represent only a minority of the larger Hindu community, many advocate an anti-Muslim campaign against madrassas (Islamic schools) and "the more brutal assertion of state power in Kashmir."[52] Some would even like to see a nuclear attack on Pakistan.[53]

Until recently—and during the period of the Gujarat riots—India was governed by the Bharatiya Janata Party (BJP), known by its critics as the party of Hindu nationalism. The BJP is the political arm of a secretive organization known as the Rashtriya Swayamsevak Sangh (RSS), or Organization of National Volunteers, also known as India's "leading Hindu nationalist group."[54] The group reportedly told the Muslim population of India "that their future safety lay in the goodwill of the majority."[55] The head of one of the RSS "branches," the Vishwa Hindu Parishad, or World Council of Hindus, allegedly urged Muslims in India to have blood tests to prove they were not of "Arabian" descent. He also reportedly stated: "I advise all Muslims to get themselves genetically tested for their Hindu origin."[56]

On another level, religious violence is often associated with the concept of millennialism, which is deeply entrenched within many religious traditions. Millennialism can be described as the "belief that human suffering will soon be eliminated in an imminent apocalyptic scenario, ensuring that the collective salvation of humanity is accomplished."[57] Consequently, a millenarian (a term sometimes used interchangeably with millennial) movement is "any movement that anticipates collective, earthly, imminent, total, supernatural salvation."[58]

Cults and various religious movements have emphasized that on certain dates, their visions or certain prophecies will be fulfilled. Many of these groups believe that a final apocalyptic act will usher in a new era. This is why millennialism and terrorism fit together so conveniently. Terrorists motivated by religious millennialist ideologies may seek to bring about this event—in other words, to force the apocalypse. Millennialism is often associated with messianism, which is defined as "the belief that a cosmic figure will shortly appear to reestablish order and restore justice."[59] In addition, messianism stems from messianic beliefs, which are characterized as beliefs that visualize "a day in which history or life on this earth will be transformed totally and irreversibly from a condition of perpetual strife which we have all experienced to one of perfect harmony that many dream about."[60]

In the Islamic context, Max Taylor and John Horgan argue that Sayyid Qutb's beliefs and ideologies, which form the foundation of contemporary Islamic fundamentalist or Salafist thinking, reflect millennialist tendencies; for example, Sayyid Qutb, in his analysis of contemporary Islam, focused on the "catastrophic nature of contemporary life."[61] Qutb shaped the views of the assassins of Anwar Sadat who was killed in 1981. The plotters apparently believed that by assassinating Sadat, it would trigger the establishment of an Islamic state. "They adopted a frankly millenarian outlook where it was argued that Sadat represented the apostate, the representative of Jahiliyyah."[62] In the assassins' eyes, the death of Sadat itself would trigger God's intervention, which partly explains why they made little preparation for a takeover of the Egyptian state.[63]

Millennialism, combined with religious nationalism, may explain religious violence in the modern state of Israel. On February 25, 1994, for example, Dr. Baruch Goldstein, a U.S. physician, walked into a shrine in Hebron, known to Muslims as the Ibrahimi Mosque, and opened fire on Muslim worshippers.

After firing 108 bullets over a period of 90 seconds, Goldstein had succeeded in killing 29 Muslims and injuring an additional 125.[64] Despite allegations and suspicions that Goldstein was part of a larger conspiracy, an Israeli government inquiry would later "put the entire blame . . . on Dr. Baruch Goldstein."[65] Moreover, the commission characterized Goldstein's act as a "base and murderous act" that was "unforgivable."[66] In addition, it characterized the massacre as "one of the harshest expressions of the Jewish-Arab conflict."[67]

The Goldstein case was stark and dramatic, but it was by no means the only example of contemporary Jewish terrorism and religious violence. Only a few months later, in September 1994, Israeli authorities arrested eight or nine individuals who, according to Israeli authorities, were thought to be part of a "terrorist network of rabidly anti-Arab Jews . . . with roots in this militant settlement [Qiryat Arba, Israeli-occupied West Bank] on the outskirts of Hebron."[68] On November 4, 1995, a twenty-five-year-old religious nationalist, Yigal Amir, would assassinate Prime Minister Yitzhak Rabin, and later tell a press conference that "what pulled the trigger was not only my finger, but the finger of this whole nation, which for 2,000 years yearned for this land and dreamed of it."[69] Among various motives, Amir wanted to prevent a planned transfer of much of the West Bank to Palestinian control.[70]

In 2001, five Palestinians were killed in separate roadside shooting incidents attributed to Jewish extremists in Hebron.[71] In September 2002, Jewish extremists were accused of planting a bomb in the playground of a Palestinian school in the West Bank village of Yatta, which injured five Palestinian children.[72] In another case involving a school bombing attempt, in September 2003, the Jerusalem District Court convicted three Jewish settlers for attempting to blow up a Palestinian girls' elementary school a year earlier in eastern Jerusalem. Police only uncovered the plot by chance; the Jerusalem police chief was quoted as saying: "Had the bomb gone off as planned, it would have caused casualties and damage."[73] In August 2005, Eden Natan Zada, an AWOL Israel Defense Force soldier who was wearing his uniform, opened fire on a crowded bus and killed four Israeli Arabs and wounded an additional seventeen. He was subsequently beaten and killed by a mob.[74] Zada is believed to have been associated in some manner with the Jewish Legion, a group accused of advocating terrorism.[75]

Religion and Its Capacity for Separation

The road to violent religious expression is often the final step in a long process that can be characterized as "separation" from the outside world. The separation tendency is sometimes driven by the fact that the organization or its adherents perceive that there are no conventional pathways to address a world gone awry.[76] Thus they have no choice but to withdraw; they have essentially foreclosed the ordinary options for dealing with their grievances.[77] Such a separation process can be seen in the Southeast Asia-based terrorist organization, Jemaah Islamiyah (JI). In January 2003, the Singapore government published its white paper on Jemaah Islamiyah titled *The Jemaah Islamiyah Arrests and the Threat of Terrorism.*

The report was generated in response to a plot uncovered about a year earlier in which key transportation and infrastructure sites were targeted. Specifically, JI operatives were seeking to conduct multiple truck bombings against U.S. targets in Singapore, including attacks against U.S. servicemen at particular mass-transit stations, bombings of a U.S. school, and additional attacks against U.S. and Israeli companies, among other plans. The report also detailed how JI conducted its recruiting activities, which involved multiple stages.

The first stage of recruitment involved religious classes that were offered to the general public. Potential recruits were invited to attend classes that were structured so as to be nonthreatening and to give potential recruits a "sense of Muslim fraternity and companionship."[78] Certain recruits who lingered after classes to ask questions were subsequently invited to the second stage of JI recruitment.

Second-stage recruits would be invited to listen to more intense lectures and to engage in deeper study, and would be encouraged to "find out more about the plight of Muslims in other regions, such as the Malukus, Bosnia, and Mindanao."[79] Ibrahim Maidin, the spiritual leader of JI-Singapore would engage "those [second-stage] students' interest and compassion further and finally [invite] those he deemed suitable to join JI."[80] Overall, it took about eighteen months to recruit a new JI member. During this period, the new recruit would be made to feel "a strong sense of exclusivity and self-esteem."[81]

The other subtle process employed in the recruitment process, particularly in the latter stages, involved separating the recruit from the outside world. "Secrecy, including secrecy over the true knowledge of jihad, helped create a sense of sharing and empowerment vis-à-vis outsiders."[82] Separating from the outside—including the use of an internal esoteric language, or "JI-speak"— helped solidify a JI identity within the new recruit.[83] Singapore officials also noted that after the induction of new Jemaah Islamiyah members, these new members tended to isolate themselves from mainstream religious communities or activities: "Keeping together as a closely-knit group reinforced the ideological purity of the group and kept them loyal to the teachings of their foreign teachers."[84] In addition, the need to separate from the outside world extended to choice of marriage partners: "The JI organization and the wider network is also held together by a complicated web of marriage alliances that at times makes JI seem like one large extended family."[85]

Anyone who dared leave the JI organization would be declared an infidel. New recruits were encouraged to take the *bai'ah* and thereby affirm "their allegiance to the JI leader or amir."[86] In addition, new recruits would sign a paper to indicate their choice of responsibilities—which might include dying for the group—that could not be altered or revoked later. All of these measures were designed to segregate the recruit from the outside world. Having signed documents, made public declarations, and performed various rituals, the new recruits felt that they "could not withdraw as they were already 'in too deep'"[87] On the positive side, however, new JI members could be assured of martyrdom "if they died in cause of *jihad*."[88]

As can be seen in the Singapore government report description, JI thrived on its ability to generate the image or fear of being under siege from the outside. The "narrative" that it promoted to future recruits was based on the notion that a cosmic struggle between Muslims and non-Muslims (and particularly Christians and Jews) was unfolding throughout the world. In addition, JI based much of its ideology on what Kumar Ramakrishna has described as a binary worldview—the clean versus the unclean, "us" versus "them."[89] This separation provides some convenience to terrorists; it allows them to justify "elimination" of the "other" because of their unworthiness or other imperfection.

Paul Pillar argues that the notion of a cosmic struggle is particularly powerful within militant Islamic groups. Islamists believe that they are engaged in a cosmic struggle with the non-Islamic world, a worldview that is fostered by the Islamic division of the world into *dar al-Islam* (Realm of Islam) and the *dar al-Harb* (Realm of War).[90] As a result, in a cosmic war the parameters of battle are widened; in other words, all things and all people are fair game. "It is a common trait of all extremists that they deem the lives of individuals who may die in the course of battling a cosmic enemy (including ones who die in terrorist attacks) to be of little importance."[91]

Casting a conflict in terms of cosmic struggle, moreover, allows for unconstrained violence and an appeal to a higher power. In the case of Aum Shinrikyo, the Japanese cult-like religious organization responsible for the 1995 Tokyo subway attack, the "separation" from the outside world was so complete that "escapees" were subject to being tracked down and murdered. In one case, Aum members abducted the brother of a woman who had escaped from the group. Aum members had hoped that the brother would reveal the whereabouts of the woman. Subsequently, he was given general anesthesia and died from heart failure.[92] In another case, Aum members killed a twenty-nine-year-old male after he helped a female member escape the group. Later, Aum members burned his body in a microwave heating device.[93]

Aum Shinrikyo's separation from the larger Japanese society was established when members joined, cut off contact with their families, and subjected themselves to the absolute rule of Shoko Asahara.[94] Aum saw its struggle with the outside world in increasingly apocalyptic terms. By the late 1980s, Shoko Asahara, the group's leader, became extremely fascinated with the notion that the world would soon be destroyed. He published a major religious treatise titled *The Destruction of the World*. In a subsequent book, Asahara claimed that "from now until the year 2000, a series of violent phenomena filled with fear that are too difficult to describe will occur. Japan will turn into a wasteland as a result of a nuclear weapons' attack. This will occur from 1996 through January 1998. An alliance centering on the United States will attack Japan. In large cities in Japan, only one-tenth of the population will be able to survive. Nine out of ten people will die."[95]

Having declared the outside world as corrupt and impure, Asahara increasingly sought to create an ideal society under the aegis of Aum Shinrikyo. Asahara dreamed of building the kingdom of Shambhala, an "ideal society consisting of people who have achieved psychic power."[96] The religious orientation of Aum Shinrikyo (and its successor organization, Aleph) was grounded in Buddhism "but with a strong mixture of assorted Eastern and Western mystic beliefs including the works of the sixteenth century French astronomer, Nostradamus."[97] Aum leaders taught that human beings can reach a number of levels of consciousness and enlightenment. In addition, the group was fascinated with the Hindu god Shiva—"This was significant since Shiva is the 'god of destruction' thereby explaining in part the violent nature of the cult and its particular emphasis on 'Armageddon.'"[98]

In another example, certain antiabortion activists in the United States have engaged in what might be called cosmic war. On September 3, 2003, Reverend Paul Hill was put to death in Florida by lethal injection. He was executed for the crime of murder, which he committed when he shot an abortion doctor and several other individuals. At a news conference held just prior to his execution, Hill stated that he expected a great reward in heaven and "looked forward to being in the presence of God."[99] The murders by Paul Hill prompted New York Representative (now Senator) Charles Schumer to declare such antiabortion activists as terrorists. He stated that the Pensacola killings were "not a form of protest against abortion, it is murder by terrorists, no different from the murders resulting from the [1993] World Trade Center bombing."[100]

Many of the most extreme antiabortion activists have also been Christian priests. Reverend David Trosch has reportedly stated that "killing an abortion doctor is meting out God's justice."[101] Don Spitz, a Virginia-based pastor who runs the Army of God Web page reacted to the execution of Paul Hill by asserting "what Paul Hill did was the correct thing to do. He did what God called him to do."[102] Army of God was also linked to an October 2001 plot to mail letters allegedly containing anthrax to abortion clinics throughout the country. Overall, more than 130 abortion clinics (including private physicians' offices that perform abortions) were targeted by the campaign, although none of the "anthrax" contained in envelopes was found to be real.[103]

Some Christian extremists have hoped that the use of violence could achieve what a Supreme Court decision may never deliver—a complete cessation of abortion. "By terrifying clinic workers across the country, extremists are winning the war over abortion without ever having to pass legislation or sway the Supreme Court."[104] This was what apparently motivated Eric Rudolph, who is allegedly responsible for planting bombs at the 1996 Atlanta Olympics, two abortion clinics, and a gay nightclub. At least one consultant to the FBI has labeled Rudolph a "Christian terrorist."[105] Some speculate that Rudolph may have been an adherent of (or was influenced by the ideology of) the Christian Identity movement.[106]

In the militant Christian context, the rise of the Christian Identity movement parallels, in some respects, the ideology of militant Islam. The Christian Identity movement was established in the United States after World War II by a network of preachers and writers who feared racial mixing and a grand conspiracy engineered by Jews. Christian Identity adherents have as their main concern Jews, whom they see as "the literal biological offspring of Satan, the descendants of Satan's sexual seduction of Eve in the Garden of Eden."[107] The Christian Identity movement "provides motivation for many acts of terrorism [in the United States] today";[108] moreover, like al-Qaeda, the Christian Identity movement has learned to use the power of the Internet to propagate its message to the general public.[109]

Religious Violence and the Challenge to the State

Religious extremists and terrorists, it is generally assumed, are not constrained in the way their secular counterparts supposedly are. They see the enemy as something to be annihilated, not compromised with. "That terrorists motivated by a religious imperative can contemplate such massive acts of death and destruction is a reflection of their belief that violence is a sacramental act or a divine duty."[110] Thus, terrorism, to the religious terrorist, takes on transcendental qualities and assumes what Mark Juergensmeyer and others describe as "cosmic war" status.[111] David Rapoport associates such absence of restraint with messianic adherents who believe they must participate in a struggle to "force the end": "When the stakes of any struggle are perceived as being great, the conventional restraints on violence diminish accordingly."[112] Peter Chalk echoes these themes with the observation that religious terrorists' primary goal is to inflict as much pain and suffering on an enemy that is fundamentally evil and beyond all redemption.[113]

Another aspect of religious terrorism is that it poses a fundamental threat to the state system. For example, Samir Kumar Das has argued that religious terrorism represents a systemic threat to states because, unlike secular terrorism (or even premodern religious terrorism) of the past, religious terrorism seeks a systemic change in the system of governance; it questions the very foundation or rationale for the state. Religious radicalism—the foundation of religious terrorism—"does not propose to replace one nation-state by another. Rather, it proposes to do away with the very structure of nation-states."[114]

In 1998, Osama bin Laden, who at the time was residing in Afghanistan, took the "cosmic war" notion to an entirely new level by declaring war on the world's only superpower, the United States. At that time, al-Qaeda and other militant or terrorist groups had just agreed to establish the Al Jabbah al Islamiyah al Alamiyyah li Qital al Yahud wal Salibiyyin, or the International Islamic Front for Fighting the Jews and Crusaders.[115] Once the organization was formed, it issued a fatwa, or legal decree, that urged Muslims to kill Americans anywhere and everywhere. Moreover, the statement invoked God and pleaded for God's help: "We—with God's help—call on every Muslim who believes in God and wishes to be rewarded to comply with God's order to kill the Americans and plunder their money wherever and whenever they find it."[116]

The 1998 fatwa issued by al-Qaeda is remarkable for a number of reasons. First, it was, as indicated earlier, essentially a declaration of war by a nonstate actor against a state. Second, it invoked the power and legitimacy of Allah or God to advocate the murder of civilians and military members from a particular country. As the fatwa clearly indicates, the United States was unambiguously identified as the evil "other," consistent with the binary worldview within militant religious ideology that requires a demarcation between good and bad, clean and unclean, and saved and unsaved.

By identifying the United States and American citizens so clearly, al-Qaeda had focused its resolve. Although anti-American rhetoric can be found in statements prior to the creation of the International Islamic Front, the 1998 statement left no doubt who the evil party was. In a sense, al-Qaeda had declared a "cosmic war" against the United States; it was not merely a physical war that would take place on the earthly plane.[117] It would also entail the canvassing of cosmic forces against what al-Qaeda viewed as evil American power.

Al-Qaeda and the International Islamic Front were products of both historic and more contemporary trends that had shaped militant Islamic ideology. From a contemporary perspective, al-Qaeda was the beneficiary of two key events that both occurred in 1979. The first was the Islamic revolution in Iran, and the second was the invasion of Afghanistan by the Soviet Union. In the first case, a corrupt and tyrannical Shah, supported by the United States, was deposed by a revolution that saw the creation of an Islamic state and the rise of the Ayatollah Ruhollah Khomeini. Paul Berman argues that the strategic significance of the Iranian revolution was that it "reaffirmed the undeniable reality that immense revolutions could, in fact, be carried out in the Muslim countries, not just in the name of Baath Socialism or some other version of nationalist radicalism but in the name of the purest Islam."[118]

In the second case, following the invasion of Afghanistan by the Soviet Union, the United States joined forces with Pakistan and a number of Arab countries to fund a guerrilla resistance to the Soviet invasion. The cost of this resistance was approximately $1.2 billion per year, approximately half of which came from Arab countries and the other half from U.S. taxpayers.[119] Richard Clarke, a former terrorism adviser to several U.S. presidents, argues that the Iranian revolution and the Afghanistan invasion by the Soviet army dramatically increased the power and influence of militant ideologies. "Both events rekindled the radical movement in Islam and both drew America further into the realm of Islam."[120]

More significant perhaps was the fact that the Afghanistan experience produced thousands of newly radicalized militants who were now faced with the prospect of returning to their home country, where their newfound self-confidence and religious zeal were not necessarily welcomed. Many of these displaced "Afghan alumni," now dispersed from Morocco to the Philippines, would form the network core of the emerging international Salafi movement, known as the al-Salafiyya al-jihadiyya, from which the al-Qaeda organization derives.[121]

However, to understand al-Qaeda in greater depth, it is necessary to reach further back into history. The ideologies underpinning al-Qaeda and similar organizations reach back to the earliest days of the founding of Islam itself. One of the first movements that may be ideologically comparable to today's militant Salafists (in terms of extremist tendencies) was led by the Kharijites, who appeared shortly after the birth of Islam in the seventh century and were known for their strict, fundamentalist views.

In subsequent centuries, various scholars propelled the movement, such as Taqi al-Din Ahmad Ibn Taymiyya in the thirteenth century.[122] Scholars consider Ibn Taymiyya a "great Islamic thinker who, though he died in the early fourteenth century, laid the intellectual foundations for Islamic extremism in the twentieth."[123] Ibn Taymiyya's most significant contribution to the Salafi moment was his concept of *Tawhid*—the unity of God—which was divided into the "unity of lordship and "the unity of worship."[124] The latter concept proposed that God was the "only object of worship and obedience" and thus by implication, reliance on man-made laws "is tantamount to obeying or worshiping other than God and thus apostacy."[125] This concept would have a huge impact on Mawlana Abul A'la Mawdudi in the 1930s and Sayyid Qutb in the 1950s and 1960s.[126]

In 1268, Ibn Taymiyya fled his home country, Iraq, and sought refuge in Syria in order to escape the invasion of the Mongols. The Mongol threat played a major role in the evolution of Ibn Taymiyya's thinking—and has established a broad theme that is used by Islamic militants today: "The role that the Mongols played as the threat to Islamic civilization in the thirteenth and fourteenth centuries is, in the view of al-Qaeda and likeminded extremists, currently played by Western civilization."[127] In Ibn Taymiyya's view, the Mongols, some of whom converted to Islam, represented a false, or pseudo-Islam. In particular, Taymiyya reserved most of his disdain for the reigning Mongol Ilkhan, Ghazan, who had invaded Syria in 1300. Ghazan had converted to Islam in 1295, but this conversion did not convince Taymiyya, who "argued that, although Ghazan sported the appearance of being a Muslim [but] . . . then having failed to raise up Islamic law in his realm, Ghazan demonstrated that his conversion was a sham. On this basis, Ibn Taymiyya pronounced him an apostate."[128]

In Islam, apostasy (abandoning the true faith) is considered a grave sin. Thus, declaring someone an apostate (engaging in what is known as *Takfir*) is something that should not be taken lightly. The accused in an act of *Takfir* is considered *kufr* (a nonbeliever) and thus separated from Islam.[129] "*Takfir* is an act that has a serious consequence even to the accuser. If his accusation is false, the judgment will rebound on him instead."[130] When Ibn Taymiyya criticized Ghazan, he "thus established a boundary between the truly Islamic society and its pseudo-Muslim enemies, who in his view posed a grave threat not just to the Muslims of Syria but to religion itself."[131]

The notion of apostasy also plays a major role in the contemporary narrative of al-Qaeda; for example, al-Qaeda pronouncements often highlight the organization's disdain for fellow Muslims whom it considers apostate. In 2003, Osama bin Laden issued a videotaped message to Iraqis, in which he criticized Arab regimes or individuals that assisted the United States by declaring them apostate: "We also point out that whoever supported the United States, including the hypocrites of Iraq or the rulers of Arab countries . . . should know that they are apostates and outside the community of Muslims. It is permissible to spill their blood and take their property."[132]

In a separate statement, issued in October 2003, bin Laden once again echoed the apostate theme by urging Muslims to reject any Arab regimes or individuals who cooperate with the United States: "Those who cooperate with the United States or its off-shoots, regardless of names and titles, are infidels and so are those who support infidel parties such as the Arab Socialist Ba'th [sic] Party, and the democratic Kurdish parties and their like."[133]

In another speech, delivered in December 2004, bin Laden makes a similar distinction between proper Muslims and those who have departed from the Muslim faith (and thus have become apostate): "Supporting America or Allawi's renegade government [in Iraq], or Karzai's government [in Afghanistan], or Mahmud Abbas' government [in Palestine], or any other renegade governments in their fight against the Muslims is tantamount to infidelity and a cause for departure from the [Islamic] nation . . . Everyone who aids and supports them in any kind of way has defected from religion and must be fought."[134]

The Challenge of Naming the Ideology

In late October 2005, President George W. Bush delivered a speech at Bolling Air Force Base in Washington, DC, in which he described the progress of his global war on terrorism. In his speech, he directly referenced the ideology that had underpinned the September 11, 2001, attack on the United States, as well as more recent attacks. He stated that the terrorists' attacks "serve a clear and focused ideology, a set of beliefs and goals that are evil, but not insane."[135]

He went on to list the various adjectives that have been coined by policy analysts, scholars, and others to describe this ideology: "Some call this evil 'Islamic radicalism'; others, 'militant jihadism'; still others 'Islamo-fascism.'"[136] But then he stated something that drove at the heart of the dilemma of his administration: "Whatever it is called, this ideology is very different from the religion of Islam."[137] Moreover, Bush not only asserted that a separation existed (between radicalism and Islam) but also that this radical ideology "exploits Islam to serve a violent political vision: the establishment, by terrorism, subversion, and insurgency, of a totalitarian empire that denies all political and religious freedom."[138]

President Bush's speech reflects a dilemma that many analysts have faced—how to describe the ideology that governs al-Qaeda without impugning the larger Muslim community. Since the beginning of its war on terrorism, the U.S. government has tried to walk a delicate semantic tightrope, on one hand, condemning violent Islamic militants, while on the other, praising—or at least showing respect for—the larger community of Muslims. Moreover, scholars and analysts must face a similar dilemma in their negotiation of a semantic landmine in attempts to describe the problem—militant jihadi ideology that manifests as terrorism—without impugning the larger religious community of Muslim believers. This is a constant problem for terrorism analysts, particularly as the evidence suggests that the phenomenon of militant violence and more mainstream Islamic ideologies cannot be so easily untangled.

Marc Sageman has coined the phrase "global Salafi jihad" to capture the ideology underpinning al-Qaeda.[139] Such a jihad is an offshoot of a larger social and political movement in the Islamic world known as Islamism. Islamism is defined "in the broadest sense as [a movement] promoting the application of Islamic shari'a (Islamic principles) to modern governance."[140] It is a movement limited to a minority (although arguably growing) segment of the Muslim community. Moreover, there is no monolithic "Islamism": "Within the Islamist movement, there are many divisions regarding not only the structure and nature of the ideal Islamic government, but also the appropriate means for achieving it."[141] A report by the International Crisis Group posits that Islamism manifests in three broad categories: (1) political, (2) missionary, and (3) jihadi.[142]

Political Islamism is perhaps best exemplified by the group known as the Muslim Brotherhood. The Muslim Brotherhood was founded in 1928 by Hassan al-Banna; its ideology—primarily conservative and anti-Western—was predicated on the assumption that it provided an alternative to Western liberalism.[143] The Brotherhood is just one of many organizations or political parties through which the objectives of political Islamism are expressed. Political Islamist groups range from more moderate varieties to those with a much more radical orientation. In Egypt, for instance, Islamism manifests within two broad factions, a moderate wing that has "no wish to topple the state" and who "apply the shari'a as a way to share power," and a more radical wing composed of those who express themselves "in various acts of violence."[144]

Political Islamism has played a major role in national liberation movements in the Middle East and elsewhere; in Algeria, even after the withdrawal of the French and triumph of the Front de Libération Nationale, Islamism maintained its appeal as the state was unable to deliver on promises. As Ray Takeyh argues: "As the imported Western models failed to fulfill their promises, an increasingly disillusioned middle class turned to the Islamists and their devastating critique of the prevailing order."[145]

Missionary Islamism, the second broad category of Islamism, is exemplified by two movements, the Tablighi movement, which began in India in 1926, and the more diffused Salafi movement, which has origins that reach back to the last quarter of the nineteenth century.[146] Of the two, the Salafi is clearly more significant.[147] Its founders were Persian Shiite Jamal al-Din al-Afghani (1838–1897) and the Egyptian Sunni Mohammed Abduh (1849–1905) who were both "concerned above all to enable the Muslim world to rise to the challenge of Western power."[148]

At its essence, the Salafi movement seeks to return to an era in which the purest form of Islam existed, namely, the time of the Prophet Mohammed and the two generations that followed him.[149] Salafis are also united by a common adherence to the concept of *tawhid* (the oneness of God).[150] Nonviolent Salafis emphasize "propagation and advice (usually private) to incumbent rulers in the Muslim world" and emphatically reject violence.[151] Moreover, in contrast to the Muslim Brotherhood and other political Islamist groups, Salafis tend to shun organizations "because devotion to an organization and its cause can detract from one's devotion to Islam."[152]

Jihadi Islamism is the third variant, or manifestation, of the larger Islamist movement. Jihadi Islamists are the minority within the Islamist movement "who believe in a militant approach to social change."[153] This variant can also be described as violent jihadism.[154] Within this movement exist three categories: (a) internal (which refers to the need to struggle against regimes that are deemed non-Muslim, or excessively secular); (b) irredentist (struggling to liberate land that was formerly controlled by Muslims); and (c) global (combating Western hegemony or power).[155] Jihadis are distinguished from their political Islamist counterparts by their commitment to the goal of violently overthrowing the existing international system and replacing it with an all-encompassing Islamic state.[156] On the national level, jihadi Islamists seek to "transform Muslim societies from the top by fighting leaders who use political power to lead Muslims away from the path of righteousness."[157] Al-Qaeda and its ideology—and the ideology of many groups that consider themselves allied with al-Qaeda—are derived from this third variant of Islamism.

The vibrancy of this ideology—militant jihadi Islamism—calls into question certain fashionable explanations as to why terrorism exists today. Some scholars point to colonization, others to economic exploitation, and still others to widespread poverty. These explanations may play some role, perhaps as "enabling" factors. But they rarely provide a complete answer. On the issue of al-Qaeda as a reaction to Western colonization, Mary Habeck makes the incisive point that "one of the earliest jihadi thinkers, Muhammad ibn 'Abd-al-Wahhab, developed his version of radical and violent Islam long before the West colonized Islamic lands, indeed at a time when Islam seemed triumphant."[158] She suggests that the material explanations for militant jihadis (i.e., poverty, privation, etc.) reflect a need among Western analysts to search for explanations that are not religious. In essence, she argues that "Western scholars have generally failed to take religion seriously."[159] Islamists, on the other hand, take religion quite seriously. They see the need to order society in a religious-based system, where religious rules and laws (not secular ones) are paramount. They reject modernist institutions and ideologies imported from the West—nationalism, capitalism, and socialism—because they "have largely failed to deliver either wealth or power or dignity to Muslim peoples."[160]

Nevertheless, within some quarters of the Muslim world, there persists a tendency toward denial. Just as many analysts and political leaders in the West attempt to achieve linguistic precision in how they describe the phenomenon of jihadi terrorism, they are met with another problem coming from certain Muslim-majority countries—an attempt by some political leaders to totally extricate terrorism from Islam, as if there were no relationship between the two phenomena.

For example, in the Chairman's Statement of the twelfth meeting of the ASEAN Regional Forum (ARF) held in Vientiane, Laos, on July 29, 2005, it is stated that: "Several Ministers emphasized the importance of addressing the root causes of terrorism and avoiding the identification of terrorism with any particular religion or ethnic group or nationality."[161] A month later, Pakistan's president, General Pervez Musharraf, addressed an international seminar on terrorism where he also attempted to decouple Islam from terrorism: "Firstly, terrorism must not, repeat must not, be linked with religion. There is nothing like Islamic terrorism, there is no terrorism in Islam."[162]

Finally, Malaysia's former prime minister, Mahathir Mohamad, made an incisive observation in his book *Terrorism and the Real Issues* regarding the relationship between Islam and terrorism: "Why is it that of late acts of terror seem to be more frequently committed by the followers of Islam, the Muslims. In the first place, only Muslim terrorists are linked to their religion. No one ever mentioned the religions of the terrorists of Northern Ireland, of Sri Lanka, of Japan, of Germany and of many other countries or people. But if they are Muslims they are always called Muslim terrorists."[163]

Although Mahathir's point is interesting and correct on many levels, it also discounts the fact that, with the exception of the Japanese group Aum Shinrikyo, most European or Sri Lankan terrorist groups have been ideological (Marxist, leftists, etc.) or nationalist in orientation. Their religious background or identity was a secondary identifier issue. Unlike al-Qaeda or Jemaah Islamiyah, whose very background, essence, and purpose are based in religion (al-Qaeda's appeal to God in its desire to avenge transgressions committed against Muslims, or Jemaah Islamiyah's goal of creating a pan-Islamic state in Southeast Asia, for instance), most terrorist groups in modern history have had largely secular or nationalist goals or orientations, with religion usually being an unimportant factor or goal.

Conclusion

Throughout history, religion has played an important role in orienting human beings toward peace and peaceful coexistence. Religion has also provided comfort, and an explanatory scheme in which individuals can attempt to understand their place in the larger cosmos. But religion has also had a dark side. The tendency toward universalist claims and absolute adherence has spawned a sinister alter-ideology that may be predisposed toward violence.

To understand trends in terrorism—and particularly the contemporary "fourth wave" of terrorism—one must understand religion's relationship with terrorism. More important, the conditions within various religious narratives that justify or even celebrate extreme violence must also be recognized, and to the extent possible, managed or mitigated. Although religious terrorism is not new, combined with new technology (such as chemical, biological, radiological, or nuclear weapons), its ultimate impact is likely to be far more profound than any of its secular antecedents.

6

Terrorism and Weapons
of Mass Destruction

The Ultimate Fear

In early 2003, officials of the newly created Department of Homeland Security issued a warning to residents of Washington, DC, in which they suggested that terrorists might be attempting to stage an attack in the area. American officials were cryptic in their comments, refusing to publicize the exact nature of the threat. They did, however, issue guidance on how residents could prepare for the attack. Officials urged families to create a "family emergency plan" which would involve selecting specific places to meet in the event of a disaster, as well as preparing a disaster kit, consisting of various emergency supplies.[1] Residents were also urged to install plastic sheeting over windows and to cover ventilation ducts with tape in order to maintain air purity. The Federal Emergency Management Agency urged families to maintain a food and water supply that would last at least three days.

The sense of alarm emanating from these official warnings was palpable throughout the Washington, DC, area; government leaders suggested that parents remain calm in front of their children in light of this threat. The unprecedented security precautions were a response to intelligence information that al-Qaeda was seeking to deploy nuclear, radiological, biological, or chemical weapons in a terrorist attack. Officials were most concerned about a radiological dispersal device (RDD), the so-called dirty bomb (a conventional bomb laced with radiological material). The deployment of an RDD was viewed by officials as not only feasible but also quite possible in light of intelligence discoveries and interrogations of al-Qaeda operatives. This Washington, DC, public warning incident, which turned out to be a false alarm, was followed by another nearly a year later. Shortly before January 1, 2004, officials in New York City issued similar warnings after intelligence suggested that al-Qaeda might conduct an RDD attack on the city during the New Year celebrations. However, in the end, no attack actually took place.

Overall, these warnings reflected a growing fear within the U.S. government that, in a post–9/11 world, terrorists would use any means to conduct a mass casualty attack and, moreover, would be quite willing to use chemical, biological, radiological, or nuclear (CBRN) weapons or materials—also referred to popularly as weapons of mass destruction (WMD)—to conduct such an attack. The horrific and catastrophic scale of al-Qaeda's attack on September 11, 2001, has led people to believe that in today's era of terrorism, there are no limits, no constraints—nothing that is "off the table." Moreover, these concerns have been reinforced by discoveries made by U.S. troops in Afghanistan of physical evidence and documents displaying an active effort on the part of al-Qaeda to develop a CBRN capacity.

The CBRN Element in Terrorism

Terrorism involving CBRN weapons has emerged as one of the key security concerns of the twenty-first century. Evidence derived from post–9/11 investigations, particularly in Afghanistan, supports the argument that terrorists are eager and willing to acquire and deploy such weapons. In addition, the decline of the Soviet Union after the cold war has unleashed massive amounts of CBRN technology and materials within the former Soviet Union and, as current evidence suggests, also onto the global stage. Such diffusion of technology is partially the result of government corruption, state breakdown, or the convergence of state technologies with organized crime. A number of intercepted smuggling attempts within the past decade, primarily of CBRN materials being smuggled to the West from the former Soviet Union, supports the case that a vast black market exists for CBRN materials. Globalization, moreover, is "at the heart of the danger of potential use of chemical, biological, nuclear, and radiological weapons."[2]

The notion that a lone rogue individual, or nonstate actor, would engage in acts of mass destruction has existed for over a century and has been the subject of popular novels and movies. After World War II, following the American atomic attacks on Japan, nuclear weapons emerged as the great concern, although most of the worry centered on nuclear weapons that were possessed by states. In fact, much of the cold war security structure rested on the doctrines of deterrence and mutually assured destruction, which were developed as a consequence of deployment of nuclear weapons by the United States, the Soviet Union, and their respective allies.

Since the 1970s, however, fears regarding nuclear weapons falling into the hands of nonstate actors—and particularly terrorists—have become more common. As Andrew O'Neil describes, policymakers and scientists, beginning in the 1970s, began to worry that terrorists might possibly gain access to nuclear weapons or other CBRN materials. "The specter of terrorist attacks involving WMD [CBRN] has preoccupied security analysts both within and outside official government circles since at least the early 1970s."[3]

Larry Collins argues that it was the 1972 Munich Olympics attack—and the accompanying international shock—that spurred the United States to seriously contemplate the possibility of nuclear terrorism (although of course nuclear materials were not involved in that attack), and, moreover, to create a special team, known as the Nuclear Emergency Support Team, to specifically counter such threats.[4] Until the 1972 Munich Olympics attack, he argues, "no one in the United States Government had thought seriously about the menace of organized, international terrorism, much less nuclear terrorism."[5] Similarly, in the late 1970s, Louis Rene Beres warned that nuclear conflict was no longer confined to the risk of war between the United States and the Soviet Union: "Today, with more than fifty major terrorist groups operating in the world, the most likely scenario of nuclear destruction has become one involving terrorist activity."[6]

The end of the cold war greatly magnified these fears for various reasons, including worries about the collapse of the Soviet Union and the potential security (and safeguarding) of CBRN materials and technology that were once part of the Soviet arsenal. What has worried many experts today is that traditional assumptions surrounding CBRN weapons, in which a limited number of states maintained control over such technologies and thus were in a position to limit their use, have given way to a more chaotic and unconstrained environment in which nonstate actors may have access to these same weapons. Alex Schmid has summarized the quandary in this way: "The post Cold War situation where weapons of mass destruction become within reach of non-territorial actors who cannot be deterred in the way that territorial actors can, creates an instability we have yet to learn to cope with."[7]

There is a growing sense of inevitability among security analysts and terrorism professionals regarding the role of CBRN weapons in terrorism. In the Israeli–Palestinian context, two analysts recently assessed whether CBRN weapons are likely to be used in terrorism in that setting. They generally concluded that although the possibility was still small, "at the very least, Israeli civilians and security planners should factor in the possibility that these weapons may eventually be used in their conflict with the Palestinians."[8] In a similar vein, Amy Sands of the Center for Nonproliferation Studies, argued in her testimony to the U.S. Senate Foreign Relations Committee that "it is clear that we are living in a new security era in which the possibility that terrorists could acquire and use WMD, including chemical and biological weapons, must be seen as real."[9]

These fears notwithstanding, to date there has been no terrorist-directed nuclear attack. Other CBRN (such as chemical or biological weapons) have been deployed, but their results have been rather limited, especially when compared with more devastating attacks involving traditional conventional bombs. This has led some to argue that the CBRN threat has been overstated. Representing this line of thinking, Ehud Sprinzak has written that "despite all the lurid rhetoric, a massive terrorist attack with nuclear, chemical, or biological weapons is hardly inevitable. It is not even likely."[10] He argues that most terrorists realize that such an attack would be extremely counterproductive: "Neither crazy nor stupid, most terrorists strive to gain sympathy from a large audience and wish to live after any terrorist act in order to benefit from it politically."[11] Similarly, Ariel Merari argues that terrorists are conservative and not particularly innovative in terms of their choice of weaponry: "[A]t the end of the [twentieth] century, terrorists still use the same weapons that they used in its beginning, namely: pistols, rifles, and improvised explosive devices."[12]

Undue attention to unconventional (CBRN) terrorism, argues John Parachini, is diverting attention away from more conventional (and more likely) modes of attack, such as deployment of high explosives and suicide terrorists. Parachini points to only three completed or attempted terrorist mass casualty attacks involving unconventional weapons material. The first involved the case of the Rajneeshee religious cult that attempted to influence a local election by poisoning local residents with *Salmonella typhimurium*. The second example involved the use of chlorine gas by the Liberation Tigers of Tamil Eelam against Sri Lankan armed forces, which injured approximately sixty government soldiers. And the third case involved the use of sarin gas by the Aum Shinrikyo group against passengers in a Tokyo subway in 1995.[13]

This small number of CBRN terrorist attacks reflects what Parachini and others call terrorists' natural inclination to employ "tried and true" conventional methods, rather than venturing into the unknown world of exotic or technically challenging weapons. Moreover, Parachini counsels policymakers that they should "guard against inordinate attention to unconventional weapons so as not to hamper attention to a clear and present danger: terrorist attacks with conventional explosives."[14] He argues, moreover, that conventional explosives have caused far more damage and destruction than deployment of unconventional weapons.[15]

This line of reasoning is consistent with another commonly accepted view of terrorism—that terrorists, in the words of Brian Jenkins, "want a lot of people watching, not a lot of people dead."[16] In other words, the traditional view of terrorism was that terrorists did not want to go too far: "Real terrorists—that is to say, those pursuing political aims—are more interested in publicity than in a great number of victims."[17] Moreover, the difficulty in actually conducting a successful CBRN attack would act as a natural constraint. According to Juliette Kayyem, former commissioner of the National Commission on Terrorism, "What we need to remember, however, is that despite popular portrayals, a WMD [CBRN] attack by a terrorist group is very difficult. Today, we know that terrorist groups in the Middle East are seeking the ability to use such agents, but their ability to do so is much less easy than their desire."[18]

An Emerging Anxiety

Nevertheless, the argument suggesting a minimal likelihood of actual CBRN use by terrorists has begun to change, particularly as a result of the 9/11 terrorist attacks in the United States. Indeed, these attacks revived a current of thinking that had gained prominence in the late 1990s in the United States and was reflected in a wave of literature during that period that began to seriously contemplate the possibility of CBRN weapons being used outside the context of normal interstate warfare. In 1998, in an essay appearing in the influential journal *Foreign Affairs,* Richard Betts argued that CBRN weapons, once considered "the technological frontier of warfare" and also key weapons for strong states, would now become "weapons of the weak—states or groups that militarily are at best second class."[19]

In other words, these weapons, which had been traditionally associated with strength, were now instruments that fostered vulnerability and weakness. CBRN weapons "have become the only hope for so-called rogue states or terrorists who want to contest American power."[20] As a result, for the United States and other developed countries, the real strategic worry had more to do with civil defense than with any offensive military utility that such weapons afforded. Moreover, confronting the specter of a massive terrorist attack involving CBRN weapons would now have to become the priority for powerful states in the international system. As Betts argued, "the response that should now be the highest priority is one long ignored, opposed, or ridiculed: a serious civil defense program to blunt the effects of WMD [CBRN] if they are unleashed within the United States."[21]

Among the various CBRN weapons, nuclear weapons are undoubtedly the category that provokes the most fear. Since the 1970s (and some would argue much earlier), U.S. officials have worried about the possibility that terrorists might gain access to a nuclear weapon. Stanley Jacobs proposes four key pathways that terrorists could use to access, develop, and deploy nuclear weapons or attack methodologies.[22] First, terrorists could steal an intact nuclear weapon and perhaps smuggle it into the target country. Second, they could attempt to construct a nuclear device based on information gleaned from unclassified sources. Jacobs concedes that although this is a theoretical possibility, "the conversion of that information into a functioning device is a task of a far different magnitude."[23] Third, they could seek to construct a radiological dispersal device, which is simply defined as a bomb that "combines conventional explosives, such as dynamite, with radioactive material, using explosive force to disperse the radioactive material over a large area, such as multiple city blocks."[24] Fourth, they could simply attack a nuclear reactor.[25] This last scenario is considered particularly serious because, as one U.S. government report stated, "operating nuclear reactors contain large amounts of radioactive fission products which, if dispersed, could pose a direct radiation hazard, contaminate soil and vegetation and be ingested by humans and animals."[26]

However, there are practical barriers to each of these various access pathways. Regarding terrorists stealing or otherwise illegally acquiring a nuclear weapon, Thomas Badey argues that it is unlikely that a nonstate actor could successfully steal or acquire a finished nuclear device.[27] Countries often invest tens of millions of dollars to develop nuclear weapons—as can be seen in the recent examples of Pakistan, Iran, and North Korea—and they would almost never, assuming logical reasoning, simply hand an intact nuclear device over to a nonstate actor, particularly given the long-term political and military ramifications (especially because such nuclear devices would likely contain a "signature" allowing it to be traced back to the source country).

This analysis, however, does not consider nuclear weapons that are unaccounted for (i.e., lost or misplaced). Currently, there are fears that some nuclear weapons in the former Soviet Union have disappeared, or are simply unaccounted for. For example, in 1997, former Russian Security Council secretary Alexander Lebed claimed that the Russian government was unable to account for roughly eighty atomic demolition munitions—popularly known as "nuclear suitcase bombs."[28] The devices weigh between thirty and forty-five kilograms and can fit into a backpack.

The second element of Jacobs's first pathway—smuggling a device into the target country—is probably more realistic. A report by the CIA once warned that the clandestine shipment of a nuclear device into the United States would likely be the primary pathway by which such a weapon would be used.[29] This would likely be the preferred method of delivery because, as a U.S. Department of Energy official recently testified: "Detecting a clandestinely-transported nuclear weapon or the materials to build one is inherently difficult. The radiation signatures [emitted] by fissile materials are relatively weak and can be further attenuated by shielding."[30]

Moreover, the structural trade environment inherent in globalization—vast global trade routes, economic pressures to minimize inspection, and a relentless emphasis on speed—make the smuggling scenario more likely. In the case of the United States, for instance, terrorists would likely not find it challenging to smuggle a nuclear device (or nuclear fissile materials) into the country via shipping containers, trucks, ships or aircraft.[31] The magnitude of cross-border traffic supports this assertion; every year, roughly 500 million individuals, 11 million trucks, and 2 million rail cars cross U.S. borders and the inspection rate is believed to be roughly 10 percent.[32] The United States has over 300 sea, land, and air ports of entry, any one of which could be used to smuggle in a nuclear weapon.[33]

In addition, seaports are considered particularly vulnerable in the United States. A recent U.S. government study suggested that an attractive possibility for terrorists would be the smuggling of a nuclear device aboard a ship container. Since many seaports are located near major population cities, the resulting detonation would likely kill up to a million people and inflict several billion dollars worth of economic damage.[34] The report named two cities, New York and Philadelphia, as being particularly vulnerable due to the close proximity of civilian populations.[35] On a more optimistic note, however, one barrier to the smuggling/detonation scenario in the post September 11 environment is that many states have significantly enhanced their radioactive (and other CBRN) detection capabilities inside their ports. However, it is the pre-inspection phase (the time that a ship enters a port, or an airplane flies over target airspace, prior to inspection) that remains a critical vulnerability.[36]

Regarding the second pathway described by Jacobs concerning the construction of a nuclear weapon, many experts are divided on the likelihood of this scenario. However, constructing an "improvised nuclear device" (IND)—as opposed to a flawless state-constructed weapon—may be more possible.[37] An IND can be thought of simply as a "crude nuclear bomb made with highly enriched uranium or plutonium."[38] A successful IND is believed to have the potential for yields in the ten- to twenty-kiloton range.[39] One possible scenario would be that terrorists construct a kind of IND called a "gun-type" weapon. In this type of weapon, "a mass of uranium highly enriched in the fissile isotope 235 (highly enriched uranium, or HEU) is shot down a tube (resembling an artillery tube) into another HEU mass, creating a supercritical mass and a nuclear explosion."[40] This model of a nuclear weapon was used in the Hiroshima, Japan, bombing in 1945. According to an official European government report, based on the May 2004 exercise Black Dawn, which simulated a nuclear detonation in a European city, the "gun-type" weapons could be constructed relatively easily:

> There is broad consensus among nuclear weapons experts that widely available plans could be used to build a "gun type" nuclear device, similar in design to the Hiroshima bomb, which was detonated without previous

testing. This device could be built with readily available machining tools. A simple gun-type improvised nuclear device using forty to sixty kilograms of ninety percent HEU could produce the explosive equivalent of ten kilotons or 10,000 tons of TNT.[41]

In addition, according to the U.S. government report, simple improvements in the design of a "gun-type" weapon could make it very versatile and mobile. In short, a gun-type weapon could easily be concealed inside a car, boat, or airplane; or it could occupy a small area within a shipping container.[42] More-over, the only true barrier to creating an effective gun-type nuclear device is to acquire a suitable quantity of HEU, the stockpiles of which are believed to be substantially unguarded in some parts of the world.[43] The second type of weapon, an implosion weapon, is considered more complicated, and would most likely require assistance from a state. This particular weapon relies on weapons-grade plutonium (WGPU, composed mainly of the isotope 239).[44] In this case, "a shell of WGPU is surrounded by chemical explosives arrayed to produce a symmetrical inward-moving (implosion) shock wave that com-presses the plutonium enough to be supercritical."[45] This particular nuclear weapon model was used in the explosion in Nagasaki, Japan, in 1945.

One of the big structural changes within terrorism that possibly makes the improvised nuclear weapon scenario more likely is that many of today's terror-ists are extremely educated; a great proportion have advanced degrees—includ-ing doctorates—in chemistry, engineering, and physics. In the case of Hamas, "members tend to be well-educated, and many senior members have graduate degrees in engineering, chemistry, physics, and medicine."[46] Globalization, ironically, creates an enabling environment—including increased educational opportunities—that could make CBRN attacks more likely. According to a U.S. Congressional Research Service study, "the rising level of education worldwide means that more people have the requisite training in chemical engineering, and the Internet has simplified communications, training, and cooperation within geographically dispersed terrorist groups."[47]

Fortunately, a significant barrier to the IND scenario would be difficulty in accessing weapons-grade uranium or plutonium. Groups such as Aum Shinrikyo (now known as Aleph) have attempted to acquire these materials, but there is little evidence that this nonstate actor, or any other, has succeeded thus far. Moreover, the ability to acquire such materials, on the black market or otherwise, would require substantial financial resources, more than most nonstate actors would be able to accumulate or maintain (with the obvious exceptions of Aleph and al-Qaeda). As Andrew O'Neil observes: "Despite some claims to the contrary, the core ingredients of weapons grade fissile material—highly enriched uranium and plutonium—are scarce internationally and very expensive to produce in sufficient quantities to manufacture even the crudest of nuclear devices."[48]

Given the difficulties that nonstate actors would likely encounter in their attempt to acquire, assemble, deploy, and/or detonate a nuclear device in a terrorist attack, Jacobs's third scenario—that terrorists may construct a radiological dispersal device—is probably much more realistic. Such a "dirty bomb" is considered technically much simpler than the alternatives and it is more likely that a terrorist could gain access to the required quantities of nuclear material that would make this bomb effective.[49] Many experts believe that unguarded nuclear waste facilities could become a source of materials to be used in a radiological bomb. Such waste could come from nuclear-medicine technology waste, dismantled tactical or strategic nuclear weapons, or expended nuclear power fuel rods.[50]

Moreover, the growing use of nuclear technology in medical and civilian sectors and the rise of the nuclear industry in general are increasing the possibility that radioactive materials will fall into the hands of terrorists.[51] Consequently, an RDD is viewed as the most likely radiological event. A recent U.S. study completed by the National Defense University stated that a successful "dirty bomb" attack on an American city could "expose hundreds of people to potentially lethal amounts of radiation."[52] The Federation of American Scientists determined that if a small amount of cesium-137 (an amount that could be found in a medical gauge) was detonated in an RDD at the National Gallery of Art in Washington, DC, the resulting radiation would cover forty city blocks and exceed Environmental Protection Agency contamination limits.[53]

A dirty-bomb attack would not likely cause immediate mass casualties—except for those individuals caught within the radius of the conventional blast—but could potentially kill hundreds or thousands over a long period of time because of exposure to radiation. Moreover, the economic consequences would likely be even more dramatic. According to the National Defense University study, even a small or moderate-size device could contaminate a large area—such as the central district of a large city—and require years of cleanup effort.[54]

The study's publication coincided with revelations that the U.S. government had conducted a secret dirty-bomb test near the Washington Monument on September 11, 2003, two years after the 9/11 attacks on New York City and Washington, DC. The fake bomb was placed on the Monument grounds by the Department of Interior, Office of Inspector General. The bomb test was designed to determine whether local authorities were adept at spotting the potential bomb. The police failed to spot the device; one police officer, who was in sight of the fake bomb, fell asleep in his patrol car.[55] Apparently, due to the belief within the U.S. government that the risk of a dirty bomb attack is high, the Department of Homeland Security decided to raise the threshold for acceptable levels of radiation. The rationale was that the current threshold, considered "ridiculously low" by some experts, would require the government to evacuate a targeted city for up to a century, or longer.[56]

The fourth pathway—attacking a nuclear reactor—is considered far more realistic in a post–9/11 world. In August 2003, for instance, Canadian authorities arrested nineteen individuals "on charges of conspiring to destroy a nuclear power plant on the shore of Lake Ontario."[57] In addition, *The 9/11 Commission Report* noted that Khalid Sheikh Mohammed's original 9/11 plot was much more ambitious than what actually transpired, and involved, among other things, attacking nuclear power plants with suicide aircraft.[58] Eventually, Osama bin Laden rejected this more ambitious attack plan in favor of the scaled-down version. Nevertheless, in an era of aerial suicide attacks, it is clear that this scenario is not as unrealistic as it may once have seemed.

Post–Cold War Paradigm Shift

Although the theoretical possibility for terrorist groups to obtain a nuclear weapon has always existed, it is not known to have happened to date. Moreover, terrorists tend to be conservative in terms of their deployment of weapons; they prefer to use methods—such as conventional bombing—that have been tested before. Thus, in theory, the current trend (preference for conventional explosives over unconventional explosives) would likely continue, except for the fact, as James Campbell has argued, that in a post–cold war world, major transformations have occurred in terms of supply and demand.[59]

Supply Changes

The end of the cold war has ushered in an era in which worries about "loose nukes" around the world have grown. The Soviet Union, which developed one of the world's largest nuclear arsenals during the cold war period, has faced severe economic challenges in the post-Soviet period—and many of its nuclear devices have been unaccounted for. Most experts agree that post–cold war Russia—and the former Soviet Union generally—remains a key vulnerability whereby nuclear materials may leak from the state realm into the realm of nonstate actors: "Russia inherited a vast nuclear complex where hundreds of tons of 'fissile material' (plutonium and highly enriched uranium) exist under inadequate and even non-existent security measures."[60]

It is generally accepted within the scientific community that huge stockpiles of plutonium and highly enriched uranium still exist in Russia. According to Rose Gottemoeller, "approximately 1,500 metric tons of highly enriched uranium were produced for the Soviet Weapons program and approximately 150 metric tons of plutonium. . . . That's why we worry about the Russian Federation."[61] The role of Russia as a potential "seepage" point is especially critical in the sense that access to fissile materials has been considered the greatest barrier for any potential nuclear terrorist.

However, this barrier is much less robust with regard to Russia, which has the world's largest supply of unirradiated HEU, estimated unofficially at between 1,000 to 1,500 tons.[62] This is enough HEU to create thousands of bombs, and would facilitate nuclear terrorism: "If they could obtain HEU, terrorists would face few obstacles to building a crude nuclear device capable of delivering a multiple-kiloton yield; a sophisticated implosion design would be unnecessary. Depending on the degree of enrichment and the design of the device, tens of kilograms of weapon-grade uranium are sufficient for one nuclear warhead."[63]

One possible means by which terrorists could illegally access these materials is via organized crime. A few weeks after the 9/11 attacks in the United States, reports surfaced that Russian organized crime syndicates were potentially cooperating with al-Qaeda and other groups to facilitate the illicit transfer of nuclear materials to these nonstate actors. The reports generated alarm throughout the world, especially as they occurred within a context in which Russia and other former Soviet states had, according to numerous reports, become a sieve for nuclear materials because of failures in internal control mechanisms.

Since 9/11, there have been numerous but scattered reports of al-Qaeda cooperation (or attempts at cooperation) with Russian criminals or corrupt officials to acquire a nuclear device. A former U.S. FBI agent has claimed that al-Qaeda purchased twenty "suitcase" bombs from former KGB agents in 1998.[64] Another report suggested that al-Qaeda had entered into a deal with Russian organized crime representatives to purchase nuclear materials, but later al-Qaeda negotiators discovered they had been cheated.[65]

Still another report stated that al-Qaeda had long established links with "Russian mafia middlemen" who purchased weapons in Ukraine and then exported them to terrorist groups throughout the Middle East and to the Taliban in Afghanistan.[66] This report is similar to another that appeared in the Arabic-language *al-Hayat* newspaper (in London), which claimed that al-Qaeda "acquired a nuclear capability from the Ukraine in the late 1990s."[67] The group allegedly bought the weapons "in suitcases in a deal arranged when Ukrainian scientists visited the Afghan city of Kandahar in 1998."[68] Although the claim is shocking, it has not been verified, and, moreover, it is reasonably believed by some to be a fabrication.[69]

In addition, there have been periodic incidents of the stealing of nuclear materials from Russian nuclear sites. One such case occurred in 1998 in the Chelyabinsk administrative region. In that case, Russian officials reported that "quite sufficient material to produce an atomic bomb" was targeted for theft.[70] Russian nuclear materials are particularly vulnerable to theft in two specific situations. First, loose constituent nuclear materials outside of nuclear weapons are vulnerable to theft due to inadequate protection measures in storage facilities. Second, nuclear materials are also vulnerable to theft during the warhead manufacturing process.[71] In the Chelyabinsk case mentioned above, agents with the Russian Federal Security Service determined that inside employees had intended to steal 18.5 kg (40.7 lbs) of highly enriched uranium.[72] In another case in 2004, undercover officers in Kyrgyzstan arrested an individual attempting to sell weapons-grade plutonium that was believed to have been stolen from a state facility. Investigating officials discovered that the individual, whom they identified only as "B," had hidden 60 small lead containers of plutonium-239 in an abandoned sheepfold.[73]

In addition to theft, the smuggling of nuclear materials through the former Soviet Union has become a major threat since the early 1990s. In Moldova, for instance, much of the country is viewed as a "gunrunner's haven" where large numbers of "rocket mounted 'dirty bombs'" (or warheads, designed to distribute deadly radiation) are now considered missing.[74] In Eastern and Southeastern Europe, the smuggling of nuclear and radioactive materials is well documented. For example, in Turkey, police have identified at least two main routes that were used between 1993 and 1999: a maritime route to Turkey that passed through Romania and Bulgaria, and a northern route that crossed from northern Iraq into Turkey.[75] Authorities have listed Russia, Georgia, Iran, and Azerbaijan as starting points for the nuclear trafficking.[76] Most of the material seized in Turkey has been natural uranium, low-enriched, or depleted uranium, although many seizures also revealed fraudulent attempts by traffickers to pass off nonnuclear materials as nuclear.[77]

The nuclear seepage problem from Russia is so serious that some have observed that the threat of nuclear attack is greater now than it was during the cold war: "The implicit threat to the United States from Russia's nuclear edifice is more acute than it was during the Cold War," according to John Newhouse, a former senior policy adviser with the U.S. State Department.[78] According to a bipartisan task force led by former Senate majority leader Howard Baker and White House counsel Lloyd Cutler, "The most urgent unmet national security threat to the United States today is the danger that weapons of mass destruction or weapons-usable material in Russia could be stolen and sold to terrorists or hostile nation-states and used against American troops abroad or citizens at home."[79] Moreover, a recent U.S. Government Accountability

Office report noted that since the 9/11 attacks in the United States, "there is heightened concern that terrorists may try to smuggle nuclear or radiological materials into the United States."[80]

The illicit world of nuclear or radiological smuggling serves as the Achilles heel of American counterproliferation efforts. "Too long underappreciated, illicit nuclear trade is a scourge lying at the heart of all efforts by America's current enemies to build or expand a nuclear arsenal."[81] Greed and fanaticism are two key motivating factors allowing nuclear smuggling rings to "continue to find ready customers willing to pay exorbitant prices."[82] According to a prominent U.S. senator, the International Atomic Energy Agency reported that during the period 1993 to 2004, over 662 confirmed cases of smuggling of nuclear or radiological materials were documented worldwide.[83]

Alongside worries that al-Qaeda (or its affiliates) and Russian criminal syndicates may be cooperating on nuclear matters, reports have emerged in the past few years from Pakistan about possible collusion between Pakistani scientists and al-Qaeda leaders. Pakistan is considered one of three states outside Russia with significant quantities of possibly unsecured HEU (the other two being Iran and North Korea).[84] With regard to Pakistan's relationship with al-Qaeda, press reports have indicated that nuclear scientists were seeking to assist al-Qaeda in the latter's quest to develop an arsenal consisting of various CBRN weapons. These concerns and allegations would later provide the backdrop for a shocking revelation that occurred on February 4, 2004, when Pakistan's top nuclear weapons scientist and founder, Abdul Qadeer Khan, appeared on Pakistani national television and admitted that he had shared Pakistani nuclear technology with other countries around the world.

The public admission capped decades of investigation by intelligence agencies who believed that Khan had operated—with some degree of official Pakistani complicity and assistance—a one-man nuclear proliferation operation. Evidence uncovered by internal investigations in Pakistan revealed that Khan had specifically delivered nuclear technology to Libya, Iran, and North Korea. Moreover, there is strong evidence that he did this with the blessing of the Pakistani military establishment—ostensibly an ally of the United States in the latter's "global war on terrorism."

Khan has argued that he was partly motivated by a desire to spread nuclear technology to the Islamic world in an attempt to shield the *umma* (the Islamic community) from Western pressure.[85] He reportedly suggested the idea of an "Islamic bomb" to then–prime minister Zulfikar Ali Bhutto.[86] Moreover, it is not clear that the distribution of nuclear technology was limited to states. As noted earlier, prior to the 9/11 terrorist attacks in the United States, two nuclear scientists, under the direction of Khan, traveled to Kandahar, Afghanistan, to meet with Taliban leaders. This meeting emboldened Mullah Omar to declare that the United States would suffer a terrible event. When the United States sought to interview the two scientists, Suleiman Asad and Muhammad Ali Muktar, they were suddenly declared "unavailable" by the Pakistani government because of an urgent project in Myanmar (Burma). The scientists were described as "very motivated" in their desire to assist al-Qaeda and its leadership in the field of CBRN weapons, although there is little evidence that this resulted in any tangible acquisition of CBRN materials or technology for al-Qaeda.[87]

The linkage between Pakistan's nuclear establishment and al-Qaeda was allegedly engineered by the Pakistani intelligence service, the Inter-Services Intelligence Bureau (ISI). In particular, the Pakistani scientists, with the blessing of the ISI, are believed to have instructed al-Qaeda operatives on techniques of building a radiological dispersal device. The events surrounding Khan's revelations reveal just how likely it is that nuclear technology—believed to be safely stored within the realm of the state—has seeped into the hands of "rogue" states and nonstate actors seeking to obtain a nuclear capability. Experts on nuclear weapons and terrorism have generally assured themselves that such seepage was not likely, and, moreover, that no state would be willing to take responsibility for such actions.

Nevertheless, the Abdul Qadeer Khan affair has revived fears that nuclear experts have harbored for decades, that somehow a "rogue" state or individual might seek to sell a nuclear device to a terrorist or a state known to sponsor terrorism. North Korea's recent test of a nuclear device is generally thought to be the product of the Khan network. A.Q. Khan "is known to have made at least thirteen visits to North Korea, which probably included trade in missiles as well as nuclear technology since his laboratory was involved in the development of both technologies."[88] Moreover, there is also some evidence that A.Q. Khan sought to stimulate Iraq's nuclear weapons program. In the mid-1990s, Khan, relying on a middleman named "Malik," allegedly approached the Iraqi regime of Saddam Hussein and offered to sell a nuclear bomb design and centrifuge parts for US$5 million.[89] The Iraqis reportedly declined the deal because they suspected it was either a criminal scam or a trap set up by a foreign intelligence agency.[90] Khan also approached other countries, including Iran, which, according to recent reports, received significant technical assistance from the network.[91]

More significantly perhaps was the vast network of middlemen who traded in dual-use technology that could be used to build centrifuges for the purpose of enriching uranium. The A.Q. Khan affair highlights what many security analysts believe to be a potential conduit for nuclear weapons flowing from states to nonstate actors—the problem of failing or "quasi" states. Mohan Malik has argued that "the breakup of states creates the danger of WMD

[CBRN weapons] falling into the hands of separatists and religious fanatics."[92] Specifically in the context of Pakistan, there is substantial worry that the country could splinter "with one piece becoming a radical Muslim state in possession of a nuclear weapon."[93]

Despite official assurance that the A.Q. Khan network has been dismantled, many experts believe that it is alive and active. In fact, some officials believe that "parts of the organization are yet to be uncovered" and this may include officials much more senior in the Khan network than previously believed.[94] The fact that Pakistan is not planning any prosecutions of suspected individuals suggests that the government seeks to avoid disclosing information that may implicate higher officials or which may otherwise prove embarrassing to Pakistan.[95]

In addition to Pakistan, Iran poses another danger for seepage from the state realm to the nonstate realm. First, "Iran has been pursuing WMD since the 1980s, in contravention of its numerous nonproliferation treaty obligations."[96] Second, Iran remains one of the key countries in the world that has an active and overt relationship with terrorist organizations. In April 2001, for instance, Iran held an international meeting in Tehran known as the International Conference on the Palestinian Intifada, to which it invited leaders from Hamas, Hezbollah, and Islamic Jihad "presumably to encourage greater cooperation between these groups in their campaigns against Israel."[97] Iranian leaders reportedly used this meeting to urge the eradication of the Israeli state. Such an ambitious plan might presume reliance, at some future date, on CBRN weapons.

It is now known that Iran is actively developing a nuclear capacity primarily through the use of front companies in Europe and acquisition efforts in Russia. "Tehran has principally been seeking material from European and Russian firms and has included some of the Khan middlemen in the process."[98] In March 2006, German officials raided dozens of firms that were suspected of selling nuclear-related materials to Iran during 2004 and 2005.[99] At least in theory, and based on its past agency relationship with nonstate actors, Iran could play a vital role in acting as a portal through which CBRN technology could exit the state realm into the hands of nonstate actors.

Demand Changes

In addition to changes on the supply side, there are also important shifts on the demand side of the equation that must be considered. Much of this chapter has focused on the technological aspects of CBRN weaponry. But a critical part of the larger analysis requires an examination of motivations to use such weaponry. Indeed, for decades, conventional wisdom has always presumed that terrorists would not use CBRN. There were generally three planks to this reasoning: first, terrorists did not need a large number of casualties to convey a symbolic message as part of their political objective; second, terrorists would be unable to overcome the technical and resource difficulties inherent in deploying CBRN weapons;[100] and third, that "mass-casualty attacks could result in the loss of the much-sought after approval and support of the wider group that the terrorists claimed to represent."[101]

Terrorism in a religious context—what David Rapoport refers to as "fourth-wave terrorism"—has undermined many of these assumptions, however. James Foxell is among a group of scholars and analysts who argue that the world is witnessing the rise of a new type of violence in which "total annihilation of opposing cultural and economic systems has become the straight-out ambition of a new breed of terrorists."[102] Similarly, James Campbell argued before the U.S. Congress that this terrorism evolution reflects the decline of the so-called "constrained terrorist." He argued that "the change in the characterization of terrorism may be indicative of a new era, one in which the traditional 'constrained' terrorist of the twentieth century is supplanted by the ultraviolent 'postmodern terrorist' of the twenty-first century."[103] Campbell further argues that this change can be explained by two factors: the rise of religious ideologies within terrorism—"religion has played a part in legitimizing ultraviolent acts throughout history"—and the removal of the bipolar constraints imposed by the cold war–era international system.[104]

Today there is little doubt that certain terrorist groups would use CBRN weapons if they could effectively acquire and deploy them. Aum Shinrikyo, for instance, is an example of an "unconstrained" religious group that sought nuclear weapons capacity. Investigations would reveal that the organization had attempted to purchase equipment that could ultimately have applications in the development of nuclear weapons. In 1987, for instance, Aum Shinrikyo opened an office in New York City under the name of Aum USA Company, Ltd. Among the objectives of having a presence in the United States was the ability to acquire U.S. technology that could be used, directly or indirectly, in the development of CBRN weaponry. In August 1993, for instance, the organization sought to acquire a Mark Ivxp Interforometer from the Zygo Corporation in Middlefield, Connecticut. This technology is used for a variety of civilian and military purposes, including the measuring of plutonium. In addition, Aum requested a "vibration isolation table which with modest reconfiguration can be used to measure spherical surfaces including plutonium used in nuclear weapons."[105]

Like Aum Shinrikyo, al-Qaeda has also expressed great interest in acquiring and deploying a nuclear device in a terrorist attack. According to a report issued as part of the Black Dawn nuclear scenario-based exercise (described above) conducted in Brussels, Belgium, in May 2004: "Acquisition of weapons of mass destruction has been a priority since the earliest days of al-Qaeda. There is ample evidence of the group's sustained interest in chemical, biological, radiological, and nuclear weapons. Osama bin Laden has asserted a 'religious duty' for al-Qaeda to seek nuclear weapons. His position has been confirmed by others, including the Saudi radical cleric Naser bin Hamad al-Fahd, who issued a fatwa in 2003 endorsing the use of weapons of mass destruction."[106]

In a 1998 interview, Osama bin Laden responded to a question regarding his intent to purchase nuclear weapons. He evaded mentioning nuclear weapons specifically, and instead responded that "to seek to possess the weapons that could counter those of the infidels is a religious duty."[107] He further stated—in a manner that made no admission—that "if I have indeed acquired these weapons, then this is an obligation I carried out and I thank God for enabling us to do that."[108] Two years later, in a separate interview with a Pakistani newspaper, Osama bin Laden was asked by the interviewer if there was any truth to Western allegations that al-Qaeda was seeking to obtain chemical or nuclear weapons. Bin Laden replied: "I wish to declare that if America used chemical or nuclear weapons against us, then we may retort with chemical and nuclear weapons. We have the weapons as deterrent."[109]

When pressed about the origins of these weapons, bin Laden subsequently refused to answer the question. However, according to Matthew Bunn, "The extensive downloaded materials on nuclear weapons (and crude bomb design drawings) found in Al Qaida camps in Afghanistan make it clear the group's continuing desire for a nuclear capability."[110] More ominous, as Daniel Benjamin and Steven Simon have noted, is the fact that al-Qaeda is among the first terrorist groups to actively seek a nuclear weapon for the purpose of destroying its enemy—in this case the United States—rather than simply using the device (or its constituent materials) for blackmail.

Another incentive for use of CBRN weapons—and particularly nuclear or biological weapons—is the functional likelihood that such weapons could achieve "kill parity" between al-Qaeda and the West (and especially the United States). Examining statements by al-Qaeda and its affiliates reveals a keen mathematical sense of justice. For instance, Sulaiman Abu Ghaith, nominal spokesman for al-Qaeda, wrote in an article in 2002 that the number of people killed in the 9/11 attacks on New York and Washington, DC, "were no more than fair exchange for the ones killed in the al-'Amiriya shelter in Iraq, and are but a tiny part of the exchange for those killed in Palestine, Somalia, Sudan, the Philippines, Bosnia, Kashmir, Chechnya, and Afghanistan."[111] In the same article, he continued with this chilling assessment: "We have not reached parity with them. We have the right to kill four million Americans—two million of them children—and to exile twice as many and wound and cripple hundreds of thousands."[112]

In the next sentence, Abu Ghaith specifically mentions the use of biological and chemical weapons, which would most likely be necessary in order to reach the 4 million body count mark: "Furthermore," he continues, "it is our right to fight them with chemical and biological weapons, so as to afflict them with the fatal maladies that have afflicted the Muslims because of the [Americans'] chemical and biological weapons."[113] In October 2003, Osama bin Laden once again made reference to the notion of mathematical parity: "You should know that we count our killed ones, may God have mercy on their souls, particularly those killed in Palestine at the hands of your allies, the Jews. So, we will punish you for them, God willing, just as what happened during the New York day."[114] Al-Qaeda may believe that only a CBRN attack could achieve the level of mortality necessary to achieve some degree of "kill parity."

Chemical and Biological Terrorism

In addition to nuclear and radiological weapons, terrorists may employ chemical or biological weapons as well. In a 1995 report, the CIA estimated that terrorists would almost certainly seek to develop and deploy chemical and biological weapons. Gordon C. Oehler, testifying before a U.S. Senate committee, asserted that "terrorist interest in chemical and biological weapons is not surprising, given the relative ease with which some of these weapons can be produced in simple laboratories, the large number of casualties they can cause, and the residual disruption of infrastructure."[115] He argues that "popular fiction and national attention" have given undue emphasis to nuclear weapons, whereas "chemical and biological weapons are more likely choices for such groups."[116]

As with nuclear weapons, significant changes in both the "supply" and "demand" dimensions of this phenomenon are influencing current trends.

Chemical Weapons

On December 14, 1999, U.S. customs inspector Diana Dean intercepted Ahmed Ressam along the U.S.–Canadian border. Following a series of routine questions, Ressam became extremely nervous and eventually exited his vehicle and fled on foot (although he was subsequently apprehended). When authorities inspected the trunk of his car, they discovered "four timing devices, 118 pounds of urea crystals, fourteen pounds of sulfate powder and forty-eight ounces of nitroglycerin."[117] Ressam, facts would later reveal, was intercepted on his way to conduct a terrorist operation at Los Angeles International Airport. Moreover, at his trial, Ressam revealed that he had received training in Afghanistan on how to use and deploy chemical agents as part of larger terrorist operations. In one specific exchange with prosecutors, Ressam revealed his training with cyanide:

> Question: The reason you were trained in the use of cyanide at the camps in Afghanistan was because you were going to use cyanide in your urban warfare, correct?
>
> [Ressam]: We don't know. Possibly if I needed it, I would use it. Yes, because it is very difficult to use gases in the field.
>
> Question: You were trained to use cyanide by placing the cyanide near the air intake of a building, correct?
>
> [Ressam]: They gave us some examples, but we did not try them out actually.
>
> Question: The reason one of the examples was to put the cyanide right near the air intake of a building such as a government building, correct?
>
> [Ressam]: Yes, that's right.
>
> Question: And the reason that you would put the cyanide, you were trained, near the air intake would be to kill the most amount of people without endangering yourself and without being detected, correct?
>
> [Ressam]: Yes, that's how gas is used in killing.[118]

In addition, according to Ressam's testimony, it is clear that al-Qaeda experimented with other chemicals, including some that could easily penetrate the epidermis of a human hand. The following is taken from trial testimony:

> Question: One of the things you learned at the Deronta camp was how to mix poisons with other substances, put them together and smear them on doorknobs; do you remember that?
>
> [Ressam]: Yes, I did say that.
>
> Question: Any person who would touch that doorknob would soon have poison running through their bloodstream, correct?
>
> [Ressam]: Yes, that's true; the poison will infiltrate his body.
>
> Question: And kill him or her, correct?
>
> [Ressam]: Yes.
>
> Question: That procedure was designed to be used against intelligence officers and other VIPs, correct?
>
> [Ressam]: Yes, yes.[119]

Ressam's testimony is consistent with other reports regarding potential use of chemical or biological agents by militant terrorist organizations. As noted in Chapter 1, on April 20, 2004, a Jordanian special counterterrorism unit thwarted a terrorist plot, engineered by al-Qaeda and affiliated individuals, to bomb the Prime Minister's Office, the U.S. embassy, and the General Intelligence Department (GID) in Amman. In addition to conventional explosives, the plot involved the use of toxic chemicals that would enhance the effects of the explosives and create "a cloud of toxins that would disperse around the GID compound and out in the city, inducing mass casualties."[120] In April 2004, the British domestic security service, MI5, foiled a plot by terrorists in Britain that would have resulted in the release of the highly toxic chemical osmium tetroxide in a major public transportation or shopping venue.[121] Similarly, on June 26, 2006, a representative from the Fatah-affiliated Al-Aqsa Brigades "confirmed that the group had chemical weapons which it was prepared to use against Israel."[122] The report, which could not be verified, further elaborated on the claim by stating that the Brigades had produced or developed "Twenty kinds of chemical and biological weapons over three years."[123]

For years, authorities have worried that "rogue" states or nonstate actors may actively develop and deploy chemical weapons. In 1989, the Iraqi government deployed chemical weapons in what is considered the first modern instance of chemical terrorism, when it released sarin gas on the Kurdish inhabitants of the village of Halabja, which killed thousands of people in a matter of minutes.[124] This was followed approximately five years later when the Japanese group Aum Shinrikyo conducted an attack in June 1994, in Matsumoto, Japan, which killed seven people and injured hundreds. This attack was followed by the more well-known Tokyo subway attack that occurred on March 20, 1995—involving the chemical nerve agent sarin—killing twelve individuals and injuring 5,500.

Almost two months after this attack, on May 5, 1995, Aum Shinrikyo attacked Shinjuku Station (part of the Tokyo subway system). In this attack, the group relied on sodium cyanide, which was placed in a public restroom. According to the U.S. Senate report, "the chemical device was a rather simple binary weapon consisting of two plastic bags, one containing two liters of powdered sodium cyanide and the other containing about 1.5 liters of diluted sulfuric acid."[125] When the bags were discovered, they were on fire, but they had not yet broken open. Had the bags broken open, the probable result would have been the release of hydrogen cyanide gas, which could have killed between 10,000 and 20,000 people. Finally, on July 4, 1995, Japanese authorities thwarted another attempted chemical attack by Aum Shinrikyo. In this case, the bags (two separate bags containing sulfuric acid and sodium cyanide) were discovered at the Kayaba-cho, Tokyo, and Ginza subway stations, as well as the Japanese Railway suburban Shinjuku station.[126]

Subsequent law enforcement investigations revealed that Aum Shinrikyo, a nonstate actor, had developed a vast and robust chemical and biological weapons program. Among other things, Aum Shinrikyo had "actively recruited scientists and technical experts in Japan, Russia, and elsewhere in order to develop weapons of mass destruction."[127] The cult had more than US$1 billion in assets, and thus had no financial constraints with regard to this effort. The group owned a variety of facilities, including medical clinics and trading companies that were used for research and import/export of lethal substances. In addition, Aum Shinrikyo purchased a sheep farm in Banjawarn station in rural Australia (about 375 miles northeast of Perth in Western Australia). One of the motives for purchasing this farm was to conduct experiments on sheep with the chemical sarin. Australian officials would later confirm that "sarin residue had been found in and near a group of about twenty-nine dead sheep on the station."[128] Overall, according to the U.S. Senate assessment, the "Aum cult was aggressively involved in chemical and biological weapons production . . . the Staff found evidence that they successfully produced nerve agents such as Sarin, Tabun, Soman, and VX, biological agents such as botulism and anthrax and controlled substances such as LSD."[129]

Chemical weapons are generally classified into four general categories, in accordance with the symptoms they produce: nerve agents, blister or mustard agents, choking agents, and asphyxiants.[130] They have been deployed extensively by states, for example, Germany and Japan during World War II. In addition, as noted earlier, at least two nonstate actors, Aum Shinrikyo and al-Qaeda, have also had active chemical weapons programs. In the case of al-Qaeda, one Italian report noted that al-Qaeda "purchased three chemical and biological agent production facilities in the former Yugoslavia in early May 1998."[131] In addition, al-Qaeda operated several chemical weapons facilities in Afghanistan, one of them located in the small village of Derunta, near the city of Jalalabad. Furthermore, al-Qaeda operated a fertilizer plant in Mazar-e-Sharif that was "also suspected of playing a role in possible chemical weapons production."[132]

Biological Weapons

In January 2003, authorities in Britain discovered vials of ricin—a deadly toxin—in an apartment above a pharmacy in London. Four men were later charged under Britain's Chemical Weapons Act and Terrorism Act.[133] Police believed the men had trained in the Pankisi gorge, which links Georgia and Chechnya, and had learned techniques for developing ricin and other chemical and biological weapons. The arrests in the United Kingdom came a month after similar discoveries occurred in France. In particular, in December 2002, French authorities had arrested four suspected Islamic militants who had in their possession chemicals and anticontamination suits. The arrests in France followed a much longer-term pattern of Arab men engaged in production of ricin (which is a plant toxin produced from castor beans) and other chemicals that could be used as weapons.[134] Ricin is considered a potentially effective bioweapon (although it is also banned under the Chemical Weapons Convention). It was used in 1978 by Bulgarian agents to kill dissident Georgi Markov in London, with the use of a novel umbrella-based weapon that injected a pellet of ricin into the victim.[135] Ingestion of ricin "causes nausea, vomiting, diarrhea, gastric hemorrhaging, and shock."[136] Moreover, injection produces internal bleeding, tissue death, and collapse of entire major organ systems.[137] With a high enough dose, death will occur within three to five days.[138]

Ricin is just one of many possible bioweapons that terrorists may employ in future CBRN attacks. Biological weapons are defined as "viral or bacterial pathogens, or toxins that have been developed to cause disease in humans, animals, or plants or lead to the destruction of materials."[139] The U.S. considers such weapons to be "weapons of mass destruction," alongside nuclear, chemical, and radiological weapons. In the weeks following the 9/11 attacks, the United States experienced several weeks of panic as letters full of anthrax spores were distributed, first to Florida, and then to sites around the country, including U.S. Senate offices. Following the opening of one of the anthrax letters in the Hart Senate Office Building, more than thirty congressional employees tested positive for anthrax exposure.[140] Subsequent investigations into the origins of the anthrax revealed that it probably originated from a U.S. government laboratory. This reinforced the view held by many scientists that biological weapons have been secretly propelled by state-sponsored research programs and have, as Gregory Koblentz has argued, "become one of the key security issues of the twenty-first century."[141]

One of the reasons is that access to biological agents is relatively easy. As one Department of Defense analyst noted in 1998: "Access to biological agents never appears to have been a limiting factor in the misuse of pathogens and toxins, because acquiring biological agents is relatively easy."[142] Moreover, biological agents are often the by-product of state-run programs, such as that in the erstwhile Soviet Union. These agents can also be obtained legally or illegally in the course of normal commercial development, particularly as the larger biotechnology revolution continues to unfold in laboratories and research centers throughout the world.

As noted above, one of the main worries is the existence of state-run biological weapons programs that have now been shut down, or significantly downsized. The Soviet Union started a major, well-funded program during the cold war known as Biopreparat. The program was "a civilian pharmaceutical and biotechnology enterprise, which also served as the civilian focal point of the Soviet biological weapons program."[143] The program produced a range of bioweapons involving smallpox, anthrax, plague, and other pathogens.

In 1992, Russia's President Boris Yeltsin acknowledged the program (the United States had already halted its biological weapons program in 1969)[144] and began the process of phasing it out, including shutting down offensive bioweapons research in such facilities as Stepnogorsk, Obolensk, and Vector. However, a U.S. General Accounting Office report noted in 2000 that "[t]he former Soviet Union's biological weapons institutes continue to threaten U.S. national security because they have key assets that are both dangerous and vulnerable to misuse."[145]

Moreover, in the process of these downsizings by the former Soviet Union, "hundreds, perhaps thousands, of scientists, engineers, and technicians were fired or had their wages cut."[146] Many fear that these scientists will offer their services to the highest bidder—whether a state or nonstate actor. Iran, for instance, has attempted to recruit these scientists by offering salaries in excess of US$6,000 per month.[147] In addition, claims by one former KGB official, Alexander Kouzminov, who was a senior member of the KGB unit responsible for biological espionage, casts doubts on the notion that the Russian security establishment has actually completely shut down the country's bioweapons program.[148]

Other states with active chemical and biological weapons programs have included South Africa and Yugoslavia. In South Africa, the government funded Project Coast, which "became a highly secretive program that engaged in offensive research."[149] Project Coast had a relatively small staff, 200 individuals, and an annual budget of US$10 million. In 1993, the project was shut down and this left many weapons scientists and other technicians suddenly unemployed,[150] a fact that left open the possibility that they might go to work for foreign governments or nonstate actors.[151] In Yugoslavia prior to 1991, the Yugoslav National Army had four facilities dedicated to its chemical weapons program; three were located in Serbia and one in Bosnia.[152]

Deploying biological agents as weapons requires sophisticated planning and execution. In an ideal scenario, biological weapons "are designed to disseminate pathogens or toxins in an aerosol cloud of microscopic particles that can be readily inhaled and retained in the lungs of the exposed population."[153] Acquiring biological weapons is also made simple because of the "dual use" factor. This means that certain materials, equipment, or facilities that are used for peaceful activities can also be exploited for terrorist ends. Many of these resources are available on the open market. Moreover, nonstate actors can acquire these materials through a multitude of clandestine means, particularly given the weakness of current arms control and disarmament regimes: "Preventing the acquisition of biological weapons through arms control and disarmament is extremely difficult."[154]

As with chemical and nuclear weapons, biological weapons are most likely to appeal to frustrated states or nonstate actors in the international system. In particular, the terrorists that are most likely to be interested in these weapons are the "radical religious philosophy [adherents] or apocalyptic worldview [adherents] that could justify the use of these weapons."[155] This is because such extremist religious groups are interested in highly lethal (or mass casualty) attacks.

How CBRN Weapons Have Changed Terrorism

On June 1, 2002, in New York, President George W. Bush delivered a speech at the United States Military Academy at West Point in which he extensively referenced the terrorist attacks of September 11, 2001. He asserted that "the gravest danger to freedom lies at the perilous crossroads of radicalism and technology."[156] Then he referenced the ideas underlying catastrophic terrorism: "When the spread of chemical and biological and nuclear weapons . . . [occurs] . . . even weak states and small groups could attain a catastrophic power to strike great nations."[157] Given this new threat, the president declared that deterrence, which he described as "the promise of massive retaliation against nations," can no longer be applied effectively against "shadowy terrorist networks with no nation or citizens to defend."[158] Outlining what would later be described as his doctrine of preemption, the president urged that "we must take the battle to the enemy, disrupt his plans, and confront the worst threats before they emerge." The president argued that "the only path to safety is the path of action. And this nation will act."[159]

President Bush's speech revealed several transformations related to terrorism and CBRN weapons. First, the speech reflected the growing realization that CBRN was a reality that could no longer be ignored or denied. In other words, the question of CBRN (WMD) weapons being used by terrorists was now seen as inevitable. As Vice Admiral Thomas R. Wilson has argued: "Some twenty-five countries now possess or are actively pursuing WMD [CBRN] or missiles. Meanwhile, a variety of non-state actors, including al-Qaeda, have an increasing interest. New alliances have formed, providing pooled resources for developing these capabilities, while technological advances and global economic conditions have made it easier to transfer material and expertise. Most of the technology is readily available, and most raw materials are common. . . . All told, the global WMD [CBRN] and missile threat to U.S. and allied territory, interests, forces, and facilities will increase."[160]

The rise of CBRN terrorism challenges the traditional paradigm of deterrence, which President Bush referenced in his speech, that was a mainstay of the cold war era. Under the deterrence principle, states would be deterred from using nuclear weapons by the threat of retaliation. This deterrence structure has played a major role in fostering stability since the advent of nuclear weapons. However, deterrence as a working principle may not be as effective with the rise of nonstate actors such as al-Qaeda. Mohan Malik argues that "nuclear weapons were never meant to deter transnational terrorists. Religious zealots bent on martyrdom have turned on its head a nuclear doctrine that was based on the deterrent value of mutually assured destruction."[161]

Deterrence seemed to work best when it was applied against territorially based adversaries. However, a "non-state actor such as al-Qaeda has no population or territory held in thrall, and its cult of martyrdom sees death as unimportant."[162] Echoing these sentiments, Amy Sands, testifying before Congress, offered her critique regarding U.S. policy assumptions related to weapons of mass destruction: "The U.S. appears to be approaching the problem of mass-casualty transnational terrorism, and the possibility of terrorist use of WMD [CBRN], in a manner consistent with deeply entrenched Cold War assumptions about warfare and deterrence."[163]

In addition to undermining the doctrine of deterrence, the virtual certainty and inevitability of CBRN weapons in the hands of terrorists has changed post–cold war geopolitical calculations about terrorists themselves—and their likely range of activities—as well as states that might be supportive of such organizations. According to Richard Ewing, a Nixon Center research fellow, the administration of George W. Bush couched its Iraq operations in the context of larger historic calculations. The administration had already accepted that CBRN weapons would spread to states in the Persian Gulf, as well as to nonstate actors: "In 1950, only the U.S. and the Soviet Union had atomic bombs. By 2000, poverty-stricken Pakistan and autarkic North Korea had acquired nuclear capabilities. With the threshold clearly dropping, what's to stop Micronesia or Sudan from getting the bomb in 2050?"[164]

Globalization has provided the framework in which the diffusion of CBRN technologies has proceeded in the Middle East and elsewhere. Thus, the reasoning goes, there is no practical way to stop the spread of these weapons, certainly not in the long term. Moreover, well-intentioned international treaties have clearly failed. Ewing argues that the administration reasoned that since the Middle East region "is going nuclear down the road, it must be as benign as possible,"[165] which, in the eyes of this administration, means a democratic system of governance. Thus, the Iraq campaign was not simply conducted because of fears of an imminent CBRN attack; rather, it was part of a much larger transformative campaign stemming from a recognition that illicit CBRN diffusion is an imminent threat. In other words, the emphasis was on changing—in a strategic sense—the system in which the diffusion would likely take place.

The irony is that this reasoning is not necessarily related to the events of September 11, 2001. Throughout the 1990s, a growing chorus of writers has warned of the inevitability of CBRN terrorism. In 1998, Ashton Carter, John Deutch, and Philip Zelikow published an influential essay in *Foreign Affairs* warning of a rise in catastrophic terrorism.[166] They argued that although the U.S. government was geared to address conventional terrorism, as represented by the twin bombings of the U.S. embassies in Kenya and Tanzania that year, it should instead focus on the new threat of catastrophic terrorism, which would involve CBRN weapons. They specifically reasoned that if the device that exploded in 1993 under the World Trade Center had been nuclear, or had dispersed a deadly biological weapon, "the resulting horror and chaos would have exceeded our ability to describe it."[167] They describe a scenario in which civil liberties would be scaled back, "allowing wider surveillance of citizens, detention of suspects, and use of deadly force."[168] They also argued that "the danger of weapons of mass destruction being used against America and its allies is greater now than at any time since the Cuban missile crisis of 1962."[169]

Conclusion

Historically, terrorists have been a nuisance in the international system, and, at times, have played a pivotal role in sparking or accelerating an already-brewing conflict. Nevertheless, terrorism usually did not result in state destruction, and, moreover, in the modern era "individual acts of 'modern' terrorism do not generally constitute a serious threat to national survival."[170] However, terrorism embedded with CBRN weaponry presents an entirely different scenario.

Within the security establishments of many countries, the notion that terrorists will not only acquire but also deploy CBRN in their attacks is increasingly seen as plausible, if not inevitable. The CBRN element has thus changed the way that certain states—particularly in the West, which has direct knowledge and experience with CBRN—view terrorism. Terrorists are potentially in a position to blackmail states in ways they could only have imagined in past eras, and as a result, they are positioned to threaten international security in unprecedented ways. Clearly, in light of this trend, the nature and threat of terrorism have changed dramatically.

7

Suicide Bombers

The New Face of Terrorism

On December 15, 1981, a suicide bomber in Beirut ushered in the modern era of suicide terrorism when he plowed his explosives-laden car into the Iraqi embassy, killing 26 people and injuring 110.[1] This attack was followed one and a half years later by another suicide attack conducted by the religious militant group Hezbollah in April 1983 against the U.S. embassy in Beirut, which killed 62 people and wounded 50. In October 1983, suicide car bombers would simultaneously blow up the U.S. Marine base in Beirut as well as the French paratroopers headquarters in the same city. Over 241 U.S. servicemen and 58 French troops died in these attacks. Both the United States and France subsequently withdrew their forces from the area. Although not completely understood at the time, these suicide attacks in Lebanon in the early 1980s signaled a major transformation in terrorism tactics, a transformation that continues to this day.

Suicide terrorism is generally defined as "the readiness to sacrifice one's life in the process of destroying or attempting to destroy a target to advance a political goal."[2] It is a phenomenon that is closely associated with fourth-wave—or religious—terrorism, although it is practiced among secular groups as well.[3] Suicide terrorism is distinguished from "classic" terrorism in that the terrorist intends to kill himself or herself in the process of conducting an operation. Suicide bombings may be used in military operations (targeting military personnel, infrastructure, etc.) or they may be directed against civilian targets. In the latter case, suicide attacks become "ends in themselves, designed to terrorize the civilian population and provoke some political change."[4]

As the Lebanon attacks described above imply, the decade of the 1980s was a major transition point for the modern era of suicide terrorism. However, antecedents for young Hezbollah bombers in Lebanon can be found in the Iran–Iraq war (1980–88) when young Iranians were encouraged to clear minefields "with 'keys of Paradise' hanging on their innocent necks."[5] Hezbollah was inspired and strongly influenced by "Iranian children, the so-called

'*Basij*' or 'mobilized,' who walked through mine fields ahead of the regular Iranian military forces during the early stages of the Iran-Iraq war. . . . The children deliberately set off the mines, thereby killing themselves, in order to ease the army's advance."[6] Afterward, the parents would be congratulated by family and friends for the martyrdom of their children. These sacrifices are celebrated in a memorial for the martyrs in Tehran, "a water fountain colored blood-red, symbolizing the endless flow of suffering and blood."[7]

Following Hezbollah's effective use of suicide operations in its attacks against American, French, and Israeli interests, the tactics eventually spread south.[8] By the end of the 1980s, other Muslim militant groups, namely Sunni organizations in Palestine such as Hamas and Palestinian Islamic Jihad (PIJ), were learning and deploying the tactic. One key reason for this was the forced expulsion by Israel of 415 Hamas and an additional number of PIJ members to southern Lebanon in 1989.[9] Hamas and PIJ members were subsequently welcomed and trained by Hezbollah, which by this time had integrated suicide bombing fully into its repertoire of terror tactics. Not only did Hezbollah provide aid to the deportees, it also provided military training, including instruction on how to prepare explosive devices as well as how to execute certain attack methods.[10] The deportees were allowed to return to Gaza and the West Bank in 1993; from that point on, Hamas deployed a number of suicide bombing operations against Israel. In fact, by 1993, suicide bombings had become "the most dominant Hamas tactic . . . along with occasional shooting, grenade, and time bomb attacks."[11]

Suicide Terror: Historical Context
and Contemporary Dynamics

Suicide terrorism is used by terrorist organizations because, quite simply, it is perceived as being effective. For example, from 1980 to 2001 suicide attacks comprised only 3 percent of all terrorist attacks, but were responsible for over half of all deaths attributed to terrorism.[12] Another statistic reveals that from 2000 to 2003, more than 300 suicide attacks were conducted, which resulted in the deaths of over 5,300 people in 17 countries throughout the world.[13] Suicide terrorism has been a key feature of the Israeli–Palestinian conflict since 2000. Since September 2000, Palestinian terrorist organizations have launched 147 suicide bombing attacks (as of December 2005) against Israeli targets, resulting in the deaths of 525 Israeli citizens.[14]

Although suicide terrorism is commonly associated with religious terrorism, it is also found within secular, leftist, or nationalist organizations. A substantial number of suicide attacks have been conducted by the Kurdish Worker's Party (PKK) and the Liberation Tigers of Tamil Eelam (LTTE), both nominally secular or Marxist organizations, and thus these attacks are generally thought of as nonreligious (although in the case of the LTTE there is good evidence suggesting a mix of religious and nonreligious motives). The PKK, for instance, conducted twenty-one suicide attacks between June 1996 and July 1999 at a time "when it was facing heavy military setbacks in Southeast Turkey."[15] For its part, the LTTE, until recently, held the "honor" of having conducted most of the world's suicide attacks since the mid-1980s.

In the religious context, two prominent premodern groups, the Sicarri and the Assassins, used methods that are comparable with contemporary suicide tactics. Assassins, for example, understood that they would not survive an attack. Moreover, like their contemporary analogues, Assassins operated under the narrative that their act of "sacrifice would lead them to paradise."[16]

Suicide-like operations can also be found in the anarchist terrorism era. Writing about the underground terrorist movement in Russia, Serge Stepniak-Kravchinski wrote that "From the day when he swears in the depths of his heart to free the people and the country, [the terrorist] knows he is consecrated to death. He faces it at every step of his stormy life. He goes forth to meet it fearlessly, when necessary, and can die without flinching."[17] Walter Laqueur makes the point that prior to World War I, most terrorism was, in essence, suicide terrorism: "The weapons used (the dagger, the short-range pistol, the unstable, primitive bomb) compelled the assassin to approach the victim very closely. As such, early terrorists were likely to be apprehended, and since capital punishment was still the rule, the prospect of returning alive from such missions was minimal—a fact well-known to the terrorists."[18]

Suicide terrorism also flourished in the eighteenth, nineteenth, and early twentieth centuries, particularly in South and Southeast Asia. In one study, Stephen Dale documents the existence and evolution of Islamic-based suicide terrorism from the 1700s to the early twentieth century, on the Malabar coast of southwestern India, Atjeh (Aceh) in northern Sumatra, and Mindanao and Sulu in the southern Philippines. Dale argues that these earlier instances of suicide terrorism presented "protests against Western hegemony or colonial rule by Muslims who felt that they had no other means of fighting against superior European or American power."[19] Moreover, in the view of those against whom suicide attacks were being conducted, such tactics, deployed in the eighteenth century, had "the same quality of irrationality and indiscriminate brutality that most Westerners feel to be characteristic of modern Middle Eastern terrorist attacks."[20]

Moreover, like its modern analogue, suicide terrorism conducted in the eighteenth and nineteenth centuries had its own version of pre-attack ceremonies and videotaped confessions. In the Philippine context, a would-be suicide terrorist "would usually signal his commitment to martyrdom by first divorcing his wife . . . by dressing himself in fresh, white, uncut cloth . . . and finally participating in a religious ceremony in which passages from the Qur'an or other texts, such as the *Hikayat Prang Sabi,* would be read aloud."[21] Moreover, similar to modern suicide terrorism, the nineteenth-century suicide attacker's commitment was generally viewed as irreversible; if he later backed out of the mission, he would be derided by friends and family as a "half-martyr," which would often provoke him to conduct the attack at some later point.[22]

As noted earlier, suicide terrorism in the late twentieth century began in Lebanon (Lebanon experienced roughly fifty suicide attacks between 1983 and 1999),[23] and then spread to other parts of the Middle East. In the Palestinian context, suicide terrorism played a major role during two key periods: 1994–96 and the period after November 2000. By 1995, suicide terrorism had already begun to be commonplace in Israel, at which time "Hamas and Palestinian Islamic Jihad used suicide attacks to derail the 1995 Oslo Interim Agreement" that was proposed to establish peace between Palestinians and Israelis.[24] Interestingly, just as the tactic spread from Lebanon to Palestine, it also jumped directly from Lebanon to Sri Lanka in the 1980s: "Prabhakaran [leader of the LTTE] . . . was inspired to experiment with this tactic in the wake of Hezbollah's stunning attack against the U.S. Marine barracks in Lebanon in 1983."[25]

In the 1990s, moreover, the method spread to other regions and continents, including Africa, South America, Europe, and South Asia. In Chechnya, the incorporation of suicide tactics greatly intensified the level of violence in the ongoing conflict between Chechen rebels and the Russian government. On December 27, 2002, for instance, suicide bombers used a truck bomb to blow up the headquarters of Chechnya's Moscow-backed government. On May 12, 2003, a suicide truck bomber attacked and killed at least sixty people in northern Chechnya. On May 14, 2003, a woman suicide bomber blew herself up, killing eighteen people in an apparent attack on the life of Akhmad Kadyrov, the Moscow-backed president at the time. In another dramatic attack on December 5, 2003, a suicide bomber attacked a commuter train in southern Russia, which killed forty-four people. Overall, at least eight of the major suicide bombing attacks perpetrated by Chechens occurred in 2003.[26]

In the following year, prominent suicide attacks included the simultaneous bombing of two airliners, which killed a total of ninety people. On August 31, a suicide bomber blew up a car outside of a Moscow subway stop, killing nine people. On September 1, 2004, more than twelve attackers, wearing suicide-bomb belts, seized a Russian school in Beslan, North Ossetia, taking hundreds of hostages (including schoolchildren).[27] A subsequent botched Russian counterterrorism assault on the school resulted in more than 300 deaths.

Suicide terrorism has also spread to South Asia. In Pakistan, the incidence of suicide terrorism has grown dramatically in the past three years, particularly in attacks between various Islamic sects. In the past, sectarian disputes between Sunnis and Shias would be settled with guns and bombs, but now suicide attacks have become more common.[28] The group that is attributed with bringing suicide terrorism to Pakistan in 2000 is Jaish-e-Mohammed. It conducted its first major suicide operation against India on December 25, 2000, when a twenty-four-year-old man named Bilal rammed an explosives-laden car into the Indian army headquarters in Srinagar.[29] In July 2003, one particularly gruesome attack involving suicide terrorism occurred within a Shi'ite mosque in Quetta, killing approximately fifty people and injuring sixty others.[30]

In recent years, suicide terrorism has also made a debut in Southeast Asia. On October 12, 2002, a suicide bomber detonated a van full of explosives near a nightclub in the Kuta resort district of Bali, an attack that killed over 200 people, mostly Western tourists. Nearly a year later, another suicide attacker bombed the J.W. Marriott hotel in Jakarta, and then a year after that a suicide terrorist bombed the Australian embassy. These attacks suggest that suicide terrorism is growing in Southeast Asia and may become a more common tactic in the years ahead.

Who Becomes a Suicide Terrorist?

The typical profile for a potential suicide bomber was once believed to be a young male who was usually poor, not particularly well-educated, unmarried, and hungry for revenge.[31] But recent cases have eroded this preconception, and thus made profiling more difficult. Today suicide bombers may be educated, have families, and own businesses. In the Palestinian context, although most suicide bombers have been young and male, an increasing number are educated. From 2000 to 2003, 22 percent of Palestinian suicide bombers were university graduates (from schools located in Palestinian Authority–administered territories) and 34 percent were high school graduates.[32]

One of the more recent developments has been the incorporation of women as suicide bombers, a trend that can be seen even among militant religious groups. In November 2005, a thirty-five-year-old Iraqi mother named Sajida al-Rishawi joined her husband in a joint suicide bombing of the Radisson Hotel in Amman, Jordan. The husband, Ali Hussein Ali al-Shamari, strolled into the ballroom of the Radisson Hotel with a suicide pack strapped to his chest, and then "mingled with wedding guests before detonating" his bomb.[33] Al-Rishawi, on the other hand, had been unable to detonate her belt. Having witnessed her husband blow himself up, she ran from the hotel with "her dress splattered in blood and still wearing the suicide belt" and quickly hailed a taxi in order to escape to the group's safe house.[34]

For those individuals targeted in the Radisson Hotel attack, the suicide bombing had devastating results. The newlyweds lost at least seventeen of their relatives.[35] Both groom and bride lost their respective fathers in the attack, although ironically they themselves were not harmed. A few days later, Jordanian officials apprehended al-Rishawi and subsequently aired her public confession on live television. Al-Rishawi explained how she conducted the operation, stating that on November 5, she had accompanied her husband to Jordan, carrying a fake Iraqi passport. They both continued on to the hotels, which had already been preselected for targeting.[36]

The case was remarkable for several reasons. First, this was among the first "spousal" suicide operations, in which a married couple would participate in an operation. Second, capturing a failed suicide bomber would provide Jordanian officials with unique insights into the terrorists' methodologies (including details such as who designed the suicide vest, who funded the operation, etc.). Al-Rishawi reported to Jordanian authorities how she and her husband, along with two Iraqis, had entered Jordan on forged Iraqi passports. She also reported that the group had rented a furnished apartment in Amman, and that her husband had instructed her on how to set off the explosives.[37]

A similar reliance on women suicide bombers can be seen with the Sri Lankan–based Liberation Tigers of Tamil Eelam. Of the more than 200 suicide operations that the group has conducted, the LTTE has used women in roughly 30–40 percent of their attacks.[38] Perhaps the most famous female suicide attack conducted by the LTTE was the assassination of Rajiv Gandhi in Sriperumbudur, India, on May 21, 1991, by the female bomber Dhanu. Female suicide bombers are included among the ranks of the Black Tigers, the elite suicide squad within the LTTE.[39] Moreover, they constitute "about twenty-four percent of the 316 who were killed and identified as being Black Tigers," which does not include Black Tiger cadres who were arrested or captured, or who otherwise died by ingesting cyanide capsules, which are issued as standard equipment for all LTTE cadres.[40]

In Chechnya, female suicide bombers are called Black Widows, a name that was created by the Russian and international press "when it became clear that many were acting in revenge for the deaths of their husbands, sons, and brothers."[41] Black Widows have been active since June 7, 2000, a date on which two female suicide bombers drove a truck filled with explosives into the Russian Special Forces detachment in the village of Alkhan Yurt in Chechnya. Since that date, Chechen female suicide bombers have been involved in twenty-two of the twenty-seven suicide attacks (or 81 percent of the total number) conducted by Chechen rebels. A key motivation—or enabler—for Chechen female bombers, according to one study, is "deep personal traumatization, and evidence of symptoms of post-traumatic stress disorder and dissociative phenomena"[42] which result from "direct personal traumatization."[43] In other words, many had witnessed the death or mistreatment of family members at the hands of Russian authorities and thus were motivated to conduct their suicide attacks.[44]

In the Palestinian context, the first (known) female suicide bomber was Wafa Idris, who detonated herself in January 2002 in downtown Jerusalem, killing an elderly man and wounding numerous others.[45] Press reports suggested that Wafa Idris lived a marginalized life in her society; her husband had divorced her, reportedly because of her inability to bear children. There were also suggestions that she acted partially out of revenge. Her career as a paramedic, some reasoned, exposed her to horrific scenes, such as strewn body parts, Israeli military abuses, beatings, and so on, and these factors may have motivated her action. Overall, the evidence suggests that Wafa Idris became a suicide bomber for personal—not religious or political—reasons.[46] Nevertheless, the bombing created a sensation in the Arab world, with newspapers describing her as a hero and a nationalist. One Egyptian writer expressed these laudatory words: "Wafa Idris elevated the value of the Arab woman and, in one moment, and with enviable courage, put an end to the unending debate about equality between men and women."[47]

Within Muslim culture, reliance on women as suicide bombers was traditionally viewed as less desirable due to the clash with some religious leaders' fundamentalist beliefs; however, this psychological barrier has broken down, probably because women exhibit certain key tactical advantages when they are used for suicide operations. For instance, they can achieve a greater degree of stealth and surprise, partly attributed to hesitancy among authorities in conservative countries to conduct body searches on women, or the general perception that women are not particularly violent. But some terrorist groups view women as ideal suicide bombers because they allow the terrorist organizations to field a greater number of combatants. In addition, women suicide bombers garner substantial publicity (which enables more recruiting), and thus they achieve a profound psychological effect.[48]

Root Causes of Suicide Terrorism

As suicide terrorism has spread throughout the world, policymakers and researchers have attempted to uncover the essential reasons for an act that seems to be so counter to the basic human impulse to survive. In essence, the question is posed: why do they do it? The tempting answer is that suicide bombers are insane, or otherwise mentally unbalanced (although this explanation has been largely rejected by psychologists who study the phenomenon). Others have suggested that religion explains it—that suicide bombers are making a grand bargain with their God such that if they proceed with the act, they will be rewarded in the heavenly realms with beautiful virgins and high honors.

Some scholars, however, downplay the link between religion and suicide terrorism. Robert Pape, for instance, argues that "the presumed connection between suicide terrorism and Islamic fundamentalism is misleading, and it may spur American policies that are likely to worsen the situation."[49] He asserts that religious justifications notwithstanding, nearly all suicide terrorists are focused on a "specific secular and strategic goal."[50] Religion may be used by terrorist organizations to recruit or seek aid from abroad, "but [it] is rarely the root cause."[51] Pape's thesis could be bolstered by the recent Singapore report suggesting that organizations use religious indoctrination techniques to "lure and lock" recruits into missions that perhaps, upon reconsideration, they may not have accepted otherwise.[52]

Others link suicide terrorism to the more traditional alleged causes of terrorism in general: poverty, unsettled conflicts such as Palestine, and general hatred of the West. Scott Atran, for instance, argues that U.S. foreign policy is the primary motivator. He cites a United Nations report that indicated "as soon as the United States began building up for the Iraq invasion, al-Qaeda recruitment picked up in thirty to forty countries."[53]

The remainder of this section will analyze the root causes of suicide terrorism from the perspectives of (a) organization factors, (b) individual factors, and (c) community (environmental) factors.

Organizational Factors

Suicide terrorism is almost never an individual enterprise. The suicide bomber is almost always "the product of an organizational process designed to transform otherwise normal individuals into agents of self-destruction."[54] The organization will identify potential suicide bombing candidates, indoctrinate them, train them, and assist them in their operation. The organization's involvement can extend even to providing the final disguise for the suicide bomber. For instance, when Bassem Jamal Darwish al-Takrouri blew himself up on the Number 6 urban bus near the French Hill in Jerusalem on May 18, 2003, he disguised himself as an "ultra-Orthodox Jew by wearing black pants, a white shirt, a skull-cap and ritual undergarment."[55] Hamas operatives prepared the disguise for him, and even helped dress him on the morning of the attack.[56] Similarly, Hamas operatives also helped Abd al-Basset Muhammad Odeh, who blew himself up at the Park Hotel in Netanya on March 27, 2002, to disguise himself as a woman, including shaving his beard, putting on makeup and a wig, wearing women's blue jeans, women's shoes, and so on.[57]

However, this raises an elemental question: why do terrorist organizations choose to use suicide terror methods? The simple answer, as noted earlier, is that it is perceived as effective. For example, in Hezbollah's suicide bombing of the U.S. Marine and French compounds in 1983, this act precipitated the total withdrawal of a Western military presence in Lebanon.[58] In the contemporary Iraq context, a U.S. military intelligence officer admitted the significant impact of suicide bombers in that country: "The effects of the suicide bombers, as you know, is huge. It is the enemy's precision-guided weapons. . . . It is the way the enemy creates great effects, devastating effects, on the Iraqi civilian population."[59]

This efficacy factor has also been well-known to Palestinian terrorist organizations. Assaf Moghadam asserts that "although suicide attacks accounted for less than one percent of all Palestinian attacks since September 2000, almost forty-four percent of all Israeli casualties that resulted from Palestinian attacks between September 2000 and August 2002 were killed in suicide terrorist attacks."[60] One leader of Hamas stated in 2002 that suicide bombing operations against the Israelis were allowing the Palestinians to gain "strategic parity" with Israel.[61]

Apart from its certain and profound lethality, suicide terrorism is also used by terrorist groups because of its ability to instill massive and disproportionate fear within the target population. Yoram Schweitzer has argued that suicide bombing is primarily geared at producing "a negative psychological effect on an entire population, rather than just the victims of the actual attack."[62] In July 2005, for example, insurgents in Iraq launched a simultaneous attack throughout Baghdad involving at least eight suicide car bombs that killed at least twenty-two people. The attacks "traumatized the capital on a day that is normally reserved for prayer and family."[63] In the Palestinian context, Adam Dolnik and Anjali Bhattacharjee describe the extreme fear that Hamas suicide operations against Israel brought about: "The panic and terror caused by suicide bombing is immense. The difficulty of detecting and stopping an attacker and the universality of the bomber's next target causes the general population to live in a constant state of fear."[64]

Like Hamas, al-Qaeda clearly understands the power of suicide terrorism to propagate fear among its enemies. Osama bin Laden has specifically cited the fear factor in his organization's decision to promote suicide terrorism. In an audio recording, obtained by a Pakistani newspaper, Osama bin Laden discussed the power of fear inherent in suicide operations against the United States: "There is no reason to feel frightened by U.S. power. U.S. tanks and troops are only cosmetic symbols of power. If you launch suicide attacks, I assure you, the U.S. citizens all over the world will be frightened. The United States will retreat in the face of your suicide missions."[65]

In a separate address delivered in December 2004, bin Laden, once again, emphasized the importance of suicide operations: "You should become diligent in carrying out martyrdom operations; these operations, praise be to God, have become a great source of terror for the enemy. They have perturbed its movement, frustrated its plans, and challenged its weapons and soldiers. These are the most important operations."[66]

In addition to the fear factor, organizations may choose to employ suicide operations as a matter of strategic choice so as to compel a response from the opposing (enemy) state. Robert Pape argues that "every suicide campaign from 1980 to 2001 has had as a major objective—or as its central objective—coercing a foreign government that has military forces in what they see as their homeland to take those forces out."[67] Mia Bloom, on the other hand, argues that terrorist groups turn to suicide bombing tactics under two circumstances: (1) when other terrorist or military tactics fail, and (2) when such terrorist groups are in competition with other groups "for popular or financial support."[68] Bruce Hoffman and Gordon McCormick argue that a suicide attack reflects a strategy of "signaling" on the part of the terrorist organization: "[S]uicide operations are a creative way of raising the expected costs of resisting its demands."[69] The suicide-sponsoring organizations thus seek to convince the state that it is better off negotiating a settlement—or striking some immediate bargain—now rather than holding out in the hope that the violence will dissipate or be contained in the future.[70]

In addition to the fact that they are effective, suicide operations are pursued by groups that seek to "outdo" rival groups. Suicide terrorism can beget more suicide terrorism among other groups who may feel left out, or who may feel pressure to join in on the practice and prove their terrorism credentials. Raphael Israeli makes this point with nonreligious Marxist-oriented Palestinian groups, such as the Popular Front for the Liberation of Palestine, that feel compelled to emulate their fundamentalist rivals: "It is quite extraordinary to watch members of the Marxist-oriented Popular Front talking of *jihad* and *istishhad* (martyrdom) when they set out for their operations. They realize the high status of the 'Islamikaze' in their society, and since they act against the same enemy, they have no compunction gaining popularity through using fundamentalist vocabulary and discourse."[71]

Similarly, the Al-Aqsa Martyrs Brigade was formed in November 2001, as a special suicide operations unit under the leadership of Fatah and its irregular militias, the Tanzim. As Bruce Hoffman and Gordon McCormick explain, the formation of this specialized group was Fatah's response to its need for a suicide capability to fend off the increased influence and power of its rivals: "The formation of the Al-Aqsa Martyrs was a clear challenge to Hamas and the PIJ and set in motion an almost macabre competition among them to see which group could execute the largest number of martyrdom operations."[72]

Organizations also rely on suicide bombings as a way of promoting internal group solidarity. Suicide attacks help reinforce "the group's sense of who they are, what they are about, why they are fighting, and where they are headed, all of which are essential for the long run survival and effectiveness of any underground political organization."[73]

However, one factor that terrorist organizations must take into account when opting to use suicide tactics is the likelihood that such attacks will provoke a massive response by the state. After the September 11, 2001, attacks, for instance, the American public readily acceded to the U.S. administration's plans to launch a war in Afghanistan, as well as to significantly curtail U.S. civil liberties (with passage of laws such as the USA PATRIOT Act), which was in major contrast to reactions after earlier attacks against the World Trade Center in 1993 or the Alfred P. Murrah Federal Building in Oklahoma City in 1995.

Similarly in World War II, the devastation brought about by Japanese kamikaze fighters (as well as intense resistance displayed by the Japanese on Okinawa) influenced President Harry S Truman in his decision to drop atomic bombs on Hiroshima and Nagasaki in 1945.[74] Suicide bombings directed against Israel in 2002 influenced Prime Minister Ariel Sharon's decision to reoccupy major towns in the West Bank.[75] Thus, terrorist organizations using suicide tactics must realize that the use of such tactics may cause them to be viewed as irrational and "beyond the bounds of negotiation" and thus states may feel they have no choice but to launch an extreme campaign of counterattack or eradication.

Individual Factors

Organizations may decide to employ suicide tactics as part of multiple strategic considerations; however, it is the individual who must actually go out to conduct the mission (and thus sacrifice his or her life under these extremely violent circumstances). This has raised many questions about what kinds of individuals would either choose or feel compelled to become a suicide bomber. A common reaction among many who hear of such attacks is that the attacker is mentally ill or insane. This perception is held not only by some segments of the general public but also among certain top world leaders. For example, when King Abdullah of Jordan gave his reaction to the CNN television network regarding the November 2005 bombing by Iraqi suicide bombers of the Grand Hyatt, Radisson, and Days Inn hotels, he specifically referenced the sanity of the bombers: "To walk into a lobby of a hotel, to see a wedding procession and to take your spouse with you into that wedding and blow yourself up—these people are insane."[76]

Most psychologists who study suicide terrorism reject insanity as an explanation for such activity. However, other psychological conditions may play a role in predisposing an individual to suicide terrorism. In the Palestinian context, for instance, one study has suggested that most suicide bombers have had previous experience in terrorism or violent operations of some sort. Thus these suicide bombers "have gone through an extended socialization process in the course of which they prepare to play their final roles."[77]

Reaction against persistent humiliation has been offered as another possible explanation. "Extreme shame, extreme humiliation, can be experienced as psychological death," argues Neil Altman, writing in the context of the Israeli–Palestinian conflict. According to this view, Palestinian suicide bombers believe that they have "already been killed by Israelis" (psychological death) and thus the "suicide bomber acts to throw his own death back at his oppressor in an act that is at once retributive and communicative."[78]

Although insanity or other forms of mental illness may be contributing factors for certain suicide bombers, it is clear that this is, at best, an inadequate answer to describe the phenomenon. In addition, it is also clear that there probably is no common explanation for all individual suicide bombers—some are motivated by certain factors operating in their social and educational backgrounds, while others are motivated by completely different factors. Nevertheless, this section will attempt to explore some of the factors that researchers and analysts believe to be at work.

Religious Motivations and Rewards

Suicide terrorism tends to be associated with religious terrorism, and not without justification. According to Bruce Hoffman, about 60 percent of the suicide attacks conducted since 1983 have been conducted by religious organizations. In many respects, the link between suicide terrorism and religion makes sense—many suicide terrorists view their act as a divine act, a gift to God and the larger religious struggle. Most Muslim suicide bombers, for example, believe deeply in the religious legitimacy of their act. They are not merely engaged in a war-making action; they are engaged in a religiously significant act, one that is imbued with a sense of redemption that centers on "saving oneself or loved ones from grave sin that could result in eternal damnation."[79]

Moreover, in the Islamic tradition, the religious narrative provides cosmic incentives for any potential suicide bomber. For example, suicide bombers gain a package of benefits from this act of self-sacrifice, including (1) extrications from the torments of the tomb; (2) exemption from the terrors of judgment day; (3) forgiveness for all sins committed during his lifetime; (4) privileges to recommend that relatives—up to seventy of them—enter paradise where the men will marry seventy-two black-eyed virgins (*hurriyyat*); (5) privileges to live "in the highest heaven with Allah, who will take care of all his needs, in the presence of the prophet Muhammad and righteous men."[80] Marriage to young virgins in the afterlife offers a particularly compelling draw to suicide terrorism, a concept that is supported by community efforts. This explains why the Palestinian press often reports suicide terror acts as "wedding announcements"—the significance being that the suicide bomber has married (in heaven) one of the "black-eyed virgins."[81]

In addition, suicide terrorism is intertwined with the notion of "martyrdom," which is, as mentioned earlier, a consistent theme throughout many historic terrorist movements (both religious and nonreligious). Many terrorist organizations that use suicide operations prefer to avoid use of the term suicide. In the Islamic context, particularly, use of the term "martyr" is preferred. As Bruce Hoffman and Gordon McCormick describe, "The difference [between the two terms] is more than semantic. Where the latter is considered to be a self-destructive and irrational act of desperation or mental pathology, the former is almost universally perceived to be a deliberate and ennobling act of self-sacrifice."[82] In the Palestinian context, the individual suicide bomber believes that he or she is engaging in an act of martyrdom (not suicide) and thus the term *istishhadi* is used. This special term is used in the Palestinian context to "give a special distinction to suicide bombers who have of their own free will chosen to become *shaheeds* and knowingly gone out on a mission from which they have no chance of returning alive."[83]

Martyrdom is not considered to be death, but rather a new beginning: "From the moment his first drop of blood spills, [the martyr] feels no pain and he is absolved of all his sins; he sees his seat in heaven; he is spared the tortures of the grave; he is spared the horrors of the Day of Judgment."[84] Characterizing a suicide bombing as a martyrdom operation, as opposed to a suicide operation, helps to overcome—at least in theory—the Islamic prohibition against suicide. Sudha Ramachandran describes the rationale in this way: "Islam frowns on suicide. Yet Islamic extremists have gotten around this problem by describing suicide attacks as acts of martyrdom. They have been justified as attacks on 'infidels' and therefore a part of jihad."[85] Thus, religious militants have carved out a "martyrdom exception" to the general rule within Islam, and many other religious traditions, that suicide is an unacceptable act.

In the context of the Sri Lankan–based LTTE, martyrs are celebrated as heroes. Moreover, they are treated with religious rituals and celebration and have shrines built in their honor: "The rituals and absolutions performed at these sites [shrines honoring martyrs] are similar to those reserved for deities and saints."[86] In addition, self-sacrifice has become the key principle for LTTE identity, and, ultimately, "self-martyrdom, for the greater good of the Tamil race."[87] This raises an issue with the LTTE, which has been characterized by some scholars as strictly a secular or a Marxist/Leninist-influenced organization.[88] Michael Roberts argues that suicide terrorism in the LTTE context relates to religion in much the same way that Tamil culture is rooted in key religious beliefs. Among other things, the act of suicide terrorism is an act of redemption. Interviews with female Tamil fighters have revealed that "the close bonding of combatants means that when one combatant is killed, her friends are all the more motivated to fight. In this way they redeem her."[89]

Audrey Kurth Cronin notes that although martyrdom is often associated with religion—and religious rewards—it can also occur in secular contexts: "The tradition of heroic martyrdom, where the hero sacrifices to save the life of his community, nation, or people, is a powerful element in many secular traditions."[90] In 1977, for example, following West Germany's successful commando raid in Mogadishu, Somalia (after the hijacking of a Lufthansa aircraft), Andreas Baader, the thirty-four-year-old leader of the Baader-Meinhof Gang, hanged himself in a German prison. West German officials feared that Baader was seeking to become a martyr and that the suicide would spark more violence against prominent Germans. Similarly, in 1981, members of the Irish Republican Army (IRA) launched a hunger strike to protest their treatment in British-run prisons. Bobby Sands, a twenty-seven-year-old convicted IRA terrorist who had won a seat in the British Parliament from Ulster was the first of the strikers to die.[91] After ten months, nine other convicted IRA terrorists would die as well. The IRA would later claim that the hunger strikes had "greatly increased its support among Ireland's Roman Catholics."[92]

Motivations of Personal Revenge or Hatred

Some evidence suggests that suicide bombers are motivated by an act of revenge, particularly in response to an event that affected them directly (such as the death of a loved one at the hands of security forces of the enemy power). Hiba Daragmeh, who blew herself up at the Amaqim shopping mall in Afula (near Haifa, Israel) on May 19, 2003, reportedly carried out her attack "to avenge her brother's imprisonment [in Israel]."[93] Audrey Kurth Cronin notes that revenge motives may be particularly operative in the case of women suicide bombers who are avenging the death or incarceration of siblings: "Suicide attackers are sometimes widows or bereaved siblings who wish to take vengeance for their loved one's violent death. In the case of widows, for example, the death of the spouse may cut the woman off from productive society and/or leave her with a sense of hopelessness, especially in very traditional societies."[94]

When Sajida al-Rishawi walked into the Radisson Hotel in Amman, Jordan, in November 2005, preparing to conduct a suicide attack at a Jordanian wedding party, she was aspiring to avenge the death of three of her brothers, who were killed during U.S. military operations in Al-Anbar Province.[95] "She did not do it because of some wish to restore a united caliphate stretching to Andalusia in Southern Spain. She did it for personal vengeance."[96] She was acting as part of a long Arab tradition of *tha'r,* which essentially translates as vendetta, revenge killing, or "blood feud."[97]

Revenge is also a common motive among LTTE suicide attackers. When the LTTE sought recruits for its suicide squads, it often focused on the families of those who the Sri Lankan authorities had victimized.[98] Similarly, revenge also appears to operate as a motive in the case of Chechen Black Widows (female suicide bombers). Having witnessed family members abused or killed by Russian officials, these women are driven by an ethos of revenge mandating "that when a loved one is harmed or killed, it is the responsibility of the family members to locate the evildoer and exact due recompense."[99]

Atoning for Past Sins

A desire to atone for past sins can also be a motivation. Alaa Ali Abdallah Karaki, who attempted to blow himself up in Jerusalem on December 28, 2002, admitted in a subsequent interrogation that "he had become more devoutly religious" and that he had decided to conduct the suicide attack "to atone for his years of infidel behavior."[100] Similarly, Andalib Khalil Muhammad Suliman reportedly carried out a suicide attack in Jerusalem on April 12, 2002, because "she was suspected of having an adulterous relationship with a Fatah operative."[101] Ayat Muhammad Lutfi al-Akhras, an eighteen-year-old Palestinian woman, blew herself up at a Jerusalem supermarket because "she apparently had an intimate relationship with [a Fatah/Tanzim operative]" and was possibly pregnant, a situation that would have been unacceptable in conservative Palestinian society.[102]

Related to the notion of atoning for past sins is the possible desire of the suicide bomber to redeem himself or herself to the larger community and its norms, from which his or her life path has diverged. For instance, Palestinian suicide bombing recruiters who focus on women recruits have often targeted "childless divorced or separated young women, or unwed and apparently 'unbetrothable' women"[103] because of a prevailing idea that these women would desire to redeem themselves for having chosen an "abnormal" path in life. Hanadi Garedat, a twenty-seven-year-old unmarried lawyer from a village in the Jenin area, was most likely attracted to the option of suicide bombing because of her "untenable position in a society that sanctifies marriage."[104] By conducting a suicide attack on a crowded restaurant in Haifa in October

2003, she may have perceived that she could rescue herself "from the lifelong spinsterhood dictated by her advanced age."[105]

Altruistic Motivations Toward Family

Suicide bombers may also be motivated by a desire to raise either their own status in society or that of their family. In the Palestinian context, this is fostered by the terrorist organization's practice of circulating posters and leaflets carrying the name and picture of the suicide bomber. In addition, the bomber's sacrifice often results in benefits to his or her family. "After the suicide attack, both the material and the social status of the shaheed's family improve significantly."[106] In some cases, families have received substantial financial payments from groups sponsoring the act, or from third parties (including foreign governments).

Community Factors

Community acceptance (and sometimes outright support) is nearly always essential for a sustained suicide terrorism strategy. Among other things, the community is the pool from which future recruits (and suicide bombers) will be drawn: "Popular acceptance of suicide tactics is clearly an essential prerequisite if a group expects to advance its position by killing off its membership and still find the follow-on volunteers needed to sustain its campaign over time."[107] A community-level analysis of suicide terrorism tends to place more emphasis on the social milieu in which the individual finds himself or herself, instead of attempting to assess psychological factors. From this perspective, suicide bombers "see themselves as embedded in a network of social relations to which they may be said to belong or want to belong. And, here sacrificial gift makes a triumphant return."[108] Thus, the bomber is acting on behalf of the group—essentially giving his or her life to the group or network.

Ariel Merari argues that social psychology factors and group dynamics play a major role in determining who becomes a suicide bomber. In other words, both organization and community factors are the main determinants. Once the organization recruits the individual, he or she undergoes indoctrination, then training, and then the final stage, which is the articulation of commitment. This often involves either a written declaration, or, more likely, a videotaping. Once the suicide bomber has articulated his intent in front of a video camera, the decision is essentially irreversible: "If he changes his mind he will suffer mockery and social contempt" and "loss of self-esteem."[109] The videotaping process serves as a form of "bridge burning"—essentially there is no going back; to retreat at this stage would be "a failure to meet one's commitment to the cause, to God, and to the nation."[110] Thus, the community and its values play a major role in determining the course of a suicide bomber. Public opinion about suicide bombing is thus a critical element. If the community supports the tactic, then it can flourish.

This can be seen particularly in the Palestinian context, where a plethora of videos exhorting people to become martyrs has become a potent, and, according to some analysts, destructive force in Palestinian society. Large segments of the Palestinian community laud and support—at least openly—the *istishhadi* (suicide bomber). The individual who chooses to become a suicide bomber "enjoys great popularity and is surrounded by an aura of respect stemming from his risk-taking, his bravery."[111]

According to Daphne Burdman, "the Palestinian belief that martyrs can solve problems in this conflict jeopardizes the possibility of a successful political solution."[112] The fact that children seem to be attracted to the ideal suggests a culture of martyrdom—suicide terrorism—is taking root. One study found that over 50 percent of one sample of children aged six to eleven "dream of becoming suicide bombers wearing explosive belts."[113]

Current Trends in Suicide Terrorism

In the early morning hours of July 7, 2005, terrorists attacked the London subway system in a series of nearly simultaneous suicide bombings. The first explosion occurred on the Northern Line; then at 8:50 a.m., there were three nearly simultaneous explosions, first, in the Circle Line tunnel between Liverpool Street and Aldgate stations, the second on the Circle Line near Edgware Road, and the third in the Piccadilly Line tunnel between King's Cross and Russell Square. At 9:47 a.m., another explosion occurred on the Number 30 bus in Tavistock Square.[114]

Overall, the attacks led to the deaths of 56 people (including the bombers); moreover, an additional 700 individuals were injured.[115] As the facts surrounding the attack became clearer, many British citizens were horrified to discover that the suicide bombers were fellow U.K. citizens. In fact, three of the bombers (Mohammad Sidique Khan, Shehzad Tanweer, and Hasib Hussain) were "British nationals of Pakistani origin, born and brought up in the U.K."[116] The fourth, Jermaine Lindsay, was a "British national of West Indian origin, born in Jamaica and based in Aylesbury prior to the attacks."[117]

Moreover, further details about the bombers would reveal that they led ordinary and uneventful lives. An official British government report would later remark: "The backgrounds of the four men appear largely unexceptional."[118] Khan was remembered as "quiet, studious and never in trouble"[119] and, moreover, "had a real talent and vocation for working with young people."[120]

Tanweer, meanwhile, "did well academically at school and was a gifted sportsman."[121] Hussain, not as talented in school, had nevertheless studied for a business degree in college.[122] Lindsay was seen by British investigators as "the outsider of the group" who had converted to Islam shortly after his mother had done so in 2000.[123]

The common thread uniting the four young men was increasing interest in religion. After his conversion to Islam, Lindsay, for example, began to study Arabic and memorize long passages of the Quran "showing unusual maturity and seriousness."[124] Hussain began wearing traditional Islamic clothing and a prayer cap after he and his family visited Saudi Arabia (as part of a Hajj visit) in early 2002. Tanweer left his university course early and subsequently began to focus on religious study and observance.[125] Khan, considered the leader of the group, had "turned to religion" after an incident in a nightclub.[126] Moreover, Khan, Tanweer, and Hussain were united by "the social life around the mosques, youth clubs, gyms, and Islamic bookshop in Beeston."[127]

Another common thread linking the men was their visits to Pakistan, a country that is associated with radical indoctrination, particularly of young Muslims residing in the West. First, the report noted that Khan may have visited Pakistan in the late 1990s, although this could not be confirmed. However, stronger evidence pointed to Khan's visit to Pakistan in 2003 during which he received training in a remote part of the country, close to the border with Afghanistan.[128] More significantly, Khan and Tanweer visited Pakistan from November 19, 2004, to February 8, 2005, supposedly to "identify a suitable school to study Islam."[129] During this trip, the two may have traveled to the border areas with Afghanistan and in that region "had some contact with al-Qaeda figures."[130]

The larger question, however, revolves around the trend of West Europeans—both immigrants and native residents—becoming radicalized and turning to suicide terrorism techniques. In the months following the subway attacks, British politicians and the media engaged in an introspective analysis concerning how suicide bombers could have been cultivated in British society. As one prestigious newspaper noted, "During the past four years, Britain is thought to have produced thirteen suicide bombers, palpable evidence that the country has developed a significant home-grown terrorist problem."[131] Perhaps the most disturbing realization coming out of the intelligence inquiries was the fact that the process of radicalization took very little time: "This means that the window of opportunity for identifying and disrupting potential threats could be very small."[132]

The experience in Britain would be followed months later by an incident in Belgium, where officials discovered that one of their citizens had become ensnared by the radicalization process. In this case, Muriel Degauque, a

Belgian national, traveled to Iraq and detonated her explosives vest near an American military patrol on November 9, 2005. Degauque, along with her husband, had entered Iraq through Syria in October 2005. Her detonation took six lives, including her own. Her husband was later killed by U.S. troops in a gun battle near Fallujah, after the Americans uncovered his hideout as a result of wiretaps conducted in Belgium.

Degauque surprised many analysts because she was European and a post-adolescent convert to Islam. Her parents described her as being "so nice" until she married an Algerian man and turned to Islamic fundamentalism.[133] But her second marriage to a Moroccan man appears to have stimulated her to work for a terror cell associated with al-Qaeda. For Degauque, the attraction to Islamic fundamentalism was possibly a response to delinquent activity as a youth, which, among other things, featured bouts of narcotics use. It is also clear that Degauque and her husband were not alone. After the attack, Belgian and French police conducted sweeps, arresting more than fourteen individuals in Belgium and one in France.[134] These arrests were partly possible because U.S. troops had found Degauque's passport and this allowed police to establish linkages throughout Belgium.

These two cases show that the phenomenon of suicide terrorism is not limited to the Middle East or Asia. It is a phenomenon that is attracting potential recruits from developed countries as well. What is disturbing is its suggestion that the recruits for suicide terrorism may be coming from the countries that are targeted by the terrorists themselves.

Conclusion

Suicide terrorism is a growing threat in the world today, and it can now be found on virtually every continent of the world. It is a phenomenon that was once believed to be transitory, but increasing evidence suggests that the tactic is being sustained by a momentum of its own, and thus it is likely to become a permanent feature of terrorism in the years and decades ahead.

As noted above, there are multiple explanations behind suicide bombings that stress organization, individual, and/or community level analysis. These explanations tend to weight one explanation significantly over the others. It is likely that most of these dimensions—individual, organization, and community—come into play, although the specific manner in which they manifest varies in accordance with specific ethnic or religious contexts. It remains notable, however, that although suicide terrorism is not a new phenomenon, its current role in contemporary terrorism and the scale of violence that it has brought are unprecedented.

8

Money and Violence

The Financial Foundations of Modern Terrorism

On June 23, 2006, the *New York Times* published an exposé regarding a key Bush administration counterterrorism program that was designed to monitor the records of the Belgian-based cooperative known as the Society for Worldwide Interbank Financial Telecommunication, or SWIFT. SWIFT has been described as "a crucial gatekeeper, providing electronic instructions on how to transfer money among 7,800 financial institutions worldwide."[1] Owned by more than 2,200 organizations, and used by virtually every major commercial bank, brokerage house, fund manager, and stock exchange in the world, SWIFT "routes more than 11 million transactions each day, most of them across borders."[2]

The revelations of U.S. monitoring of SWIFT data angered many administration officials, in addition to several members of Congress. At a hearing of the House Financial Services Committee, Subcommittee on Oversight and Investigations, Representative Geoff Davis (R-KY) stated: "I think it was extremely regrettable and frankly reprehensible that the *New York Times* published this information."[3] These sentiments were echoed at the same hearing by Representative Patrick McHenry (R-NC), who stated: "I do think it's horrible what the *New York Times* has done to this [monitoring of SWIFT data] program."[4] Eventually, the entire U.S. House of Representatives would vote (227 to 183, with 17 Democrats joining virtually all House Republicans) to condemn media organizations that "may have placed the lives of Americans in danger."[5]

Both President George W. Bush and Vice President Dick Cheney strongly defended the SWIFT monitoring program, which was being run out of the Central Intelligence Agency (CIA), but overseen by the U.S. Treasury Department. Vice President Cheney stated that he was disturbed by the fact that "some of the news media . . . disclose vital national security programs," thus making it difficult for the U.S. government to prevent future terrorist attacks.[6] A few key radio personalities and ex-politicians around the country even accused the *New York Times* of treason.[7] In its defense, a *Times* editorial, published one day after the SWIFT monitoring revelation, stated, among other things, that "if America is going to continue to be America, these [financial monitoring] efforts need to be done under a clear and coherent set of rules, with the oversight of Congress and the courts."[8]

Despite the emotive controversy surrounding disclosure of the SWIFT data monitoring program, a larger point was obscured; namely, since the 9/11 attacks on New York and Washington, DC, the U.S. government has been tracking, monitoring, and analyzing financial data in new and various ways.[9] Indeed, an open-source survey of congressional testimony, banking newsletters, and legal literature would reveal to any interested researcher that the U.S. government had launched an unprecedented effort—including both unclassified and classified programs—to monitor, track, and analyze virtually every financial transaction in the United States, and, increasingly, in other countries. This effort, of which monitoring of SWIFT data is just one part, is facilitated by the USA PATRIOT Act (Title 3) and other laws and directives (both domestic and international) and is partially a response to embarrassing revelations that emerged soon after the 9/11 attacks in the United States.

Indeed, media reports shortly after the 9/11 attacks had revealed that two key hijackers, Mohamed Atta and Marwan al-Shehhi, received wire transfers from an al-Qaeda operative based in the United Arab Emirates whom FBI officials had identified as Mustafa Ahmed al-Hisawi, also known as the "financial manager for Osama bin Laden."[10] Lawmakers were angered by the fact that the 9/11 plotters, who apparently spent "between $400,000 and $500,000 to plan and conduct their attack,"[11] had so blatantly and eloquently used the American financial system. As Representative Michael Oxley (R-OH), chairman of the Committee on Financial Services, stated a month after 9/11: "The terrorists used American freedoms and American dollars against us. They executed their plans with access to our financial system, including credit cards, ATMs, local checking accounts, and wiring money overseas."[12]

Consequently, a transformation has taken place regarding the role of money in fueling or sustaining international terrorism. As Juan Zarate, a senior U.S. Treasury Department official, stated before the House Committee on Financial Services: "The axiom now accepted around the world is that we must concentrate our national and collective power on breaking the financial ties that bind terrorist networks."[13] Following the money has become the new mantra; however, this has meant, among other things, that government police and spy agencies have amassed "unprecedented government databases of private transactions, most of them involving people who prove irrelevant to terrorism investigators."[14] Clearly, the challenge is for governments to strike a balance between the privacy interests of law-abiding individuals and the need to identify and curtail the "financial oxygen"[15] that sustains contemporary terrorism.

The Old Model: When States Supported International Terrorists

Terrorism, like many other forms of political activity, requires money to sustain itself. Terrorism finance typically involves two key processes: (1) the allocation or provisioning of funds necessary for carrying out a specific terrorist attack (including mundane expenditures for food, lodging, transportation, bomb precursor materials, and the like), and (2) long-term fund-raising that is required to "support terrorist operations, training, and propaganda."[16] Contemporary terrorists rely on an array of funding sources, ranging from contributions from individuals and charities, to criminal activities, to legitimate business activities and fund-raising drives. However, the existence of such a wide range of potential funding sources partially reflects the fact that since the end of the cold war, much state support for terrorism has declined (although it has not disappeared) and thus terrorists have had to become more resourceful and entrepreneurial.

After World War II, and particularly during the 1960s and 1970s, terrorist organizations could rely on the munificence of countries in the Soviet bloc, Asia, or certain parts of the Arab world to sustain their activities. It has long been understood that the Soviet Union "provided funding and support for terrorist operations via Eastern Europe and its client nations like Libya and Cuba."[17] The Reagan administration early on declared that the "Soviet Union was responsible for virtually all international terrorism, using it as a tool of surrogate warfare."[18] In 1981, President Ronald Reagan's secretary of state, Alexander Haig, also accused the Soviet Union of promoting "international terrorism."[19]

Regarding the Middle East, the Soviet Union's support for the Palestine Liberation Organization (PLO) began in a significant way in the early 1970s, after years of indifference.[20] Yet even this support was qualified and, at times, constrained. Later, the Soviet Union provided support to some of the Marxist groups, such as George Habash's Popular Front for the Liberation of Palestine (PFLP). Although Habash's relationship with Moscow had featured hostility and open criticism (primarily from George Habash), the relationship became much warmer when Habash supported the Soviet invasion of Afghanistan.[21] Subsequently, the Soviet Union provided "support and training for Habash's people, clearly including those engaged in terrorism."[22]

Not to be outdone, China pursued its own agenda with terrorist organizations, although in a much more cautious manner. Beijing's official position, articulated following the U.S. military raid on Libya in 1986, was that it "has always opposed and condemned all forms of terrorism and opposed the use of terrorist means in carrying out political struggle."[23] Nevertheless, this did not stop China from supporting various Palestinian causes in earlier years, particularly when such support would compete with or embarrass the Soviet Union. China was the first country outside the Arab world to recognize the PLO in 1965 and "give it material and political support."[24] Seven years later, when the issue of terrorism was placed on the UN General Assembly's agenda, China joined with some Arab states to block the move. Chen Chu, China's deputy permanent representative to the United Nations, stated that "it is perfectly just for the oppressed nations and peoples to use revolutionary violence against the violence of imperialism, colonialism, neocolonialism, racism, and Israeli Zionism."[25]

A month later, Chinese deputy foreign minister Chiao Kuan-hua told the UN General Assembly that "the Chinese people will always stand together with the Arab and Palestinian peoples in their just struggle against aggression."[26] As Lillian Craig Harris has observed, "Chinese support for the Palestinians has been considerably more significant and more consistent than is often realized. Until 1968, when limited Soviet support for the Palestinians began, the Chinese were the only major power to provide aid to the Palestinians."[27]

However, China also preferred the more moderate Palestinian groups—such as Yasser Arafat's Fatah organization—over those that were inclined to use terrorism: "China has consistently advised the Palestinians against international terrorism and has described such operations as PFLP airliner hijackings as 'impulsive acts' inconsistent with the goals of a war of national liberation."[28] Thus, China attempted to walk a fine line between supporting the Palestinian "cause" versus terrorism per se. Chinese officials, for example, characterized the 1972 Black September massacre of Israeli athletes in Munich as "unfortunate."[29] Moreover, a Chinese official told the UN, "We have never been in favor of such adventurist acts of terrorism."[30]

However, such restraint did not necessarily extend to other countries, including other members of the Soviet bloc. Media reports suggested that Bulgaria, for instance, was keen to aid and support terrorist organizations in the West. In 1982, Antonio Savasta of the Red Brigades disclosed that "communist Bulgaria offered to provide the group with arms and money after the NATO general [General James Dozier of the United States] was snatched."[31] However, the Red Brigades refused the aid. Similarly, in 1990, a defector from East Germany revealed how his country had been a "haven for terrorists of all kinds" during the cold war period. Carlos (Ilich Ramirez Sanchez) "the

Jackal," PFLP head George Habash, and Abu Nidal were regular visitors to East Berlin.[32] East Germany reportedly provided training to PLO operatives within its borders.[33]

By 1973, according to one report, the link between the Baader-Meinhof Gang and East Germany (and other states) was becoming clearer. According to one claim, Ulrike Meinhof's ex-husband disclosed that he and his former wife "were secret party members," and they had received $400,000 "in secret Communist funds through East Berlin and Prague."[34] The money supported various activities, including a leftist magazine and various student movements. In addition, Baader-Meinhof members and other terrorists "were constantly supported by the KGB-controlled East German secret police with houses in East Berlin, false papers and identity cards, money, arms, ammunition and terrorist training."[35] In September 1992, police in Athens, Greece, acting on a tip, arrested Helmut Voigt, who was alleged to have been the link between the Stasi (East Germany's State Security Service, also referred to as the secret police) and the Red Army Faction.[36]

Within the Middle East, states that have been most active—and overt—about their support of terrorist movements include Libya, Syria, and most recently, Iran. In the 1970s and 1980s, Libya was arguably the most blatant. Sustained by its oil wealth, Libya was suspected of donating millions to both European and Arab groups. In the mid-1970s, American, European, and Middle Eastern diplomats concluded that "a broad terrorist network, stretching from the Middle East to Africa and Europe, is being trained and armed and financed by Libya's leader, Col. Muammar el-Qaddafi."[37] One report suggested that Libya donated at least $100 million to Black September, Al Fatah's clandestine terrorist wing responsible for the 1972 Munich massacre, and "$40 million to other guerrilla groups."[38]

Today the phenomenon of state funding has diminished, although it has not disappeared. "State sponsorship of terrorism declined after the end of the cold war as outcasts such as Libya, Iran, Syria, and Sudan sought to reduce their international isolation."[39] As a result, terrorists have had to seek out other sources of funding, ranging from contributions from supporters, to proceeds from the international narcotics trade, kidnapping, extortion, and an array of other activities.

Terrorism Finance: The Role of Charities, Individuals, and Businesses

Many terrorists receive monetary support the old-fashioned way—as a gift. Terrorist groups may rely on co-ethnic diasporas in other parts of the world as a way to gain money for terrorism. The Sri Lankan–based Liberation

Tigers of Tamil Eelam (LTTE) has perfected the art of raising funds among diaspora Tamil communities spread throughout the world. The group regularly conducts pledge drives, distributes contribution cans next to cash registers in convenience stores, and directs door-to-door solicitation campaigns in various countries.

In Canada, the LTTE is estimated to have raised between $7 million and $22 million a year in direct and indirect support for the Tamil guerrillas, who are seeking an independent homeland in Sri Lanka.[40] In one case, a Tamil radio station in Canada conducted a fund-raising campaign over the airwaves, collecting pledges of more than $600,000.[41] Although Canada just recently officially designated the LTTE as a known terrorist organization (making it both illegal for the LTTE to raise money there as well as for Canadian residents to financially contribute to the LTTE), the organization still views Canada—with its large Tamil population—as a key source for funds. Moreover, future fund-raising efforts will likely go underground and involve the usual "intimidation, threats, extortion and violence," which is consistent with past LTTE practices.[42]

Reliance on diaspora donors extends to other ethnic groups as well. The Kosovo Liberation Army (KLA) "gathered substantial amounts of money from its large diaspora in countries such as Germany, Switzerland and Sweden before, and especially during, the war in 1998–99."[43] In 1998, a U.S. official confirmed that the KLA—known locally by its acronym UCK—had received increased support from outside sources, mostly the Albanian Diaspora; moreover, the UCK had become "emboldened in its operations and [had] been more aggressive in recent weeks."[44]

The United States is not immune to the co-ethnic diaspora effect. Historically, the United States has played a major role in supplying monetary support to the Irish Republican Army (IRA), a source of tension in U.S.-UK relations. The primary funding conduit was through an organization known as the Irish Northern Aid Committee, or Noraid, which has been described by American and Irish officials as the "IRA's best-organized and most fervent ally in the United States."[45] In 1975, UK prime minister Harold Wilson rebuked those whom he called "misguided Irish-American supporters" of the Irish Republican Army: "Those who subscribe to the Irish Northern Aid Committee are not financing the welfare of the Irish people," he contended, "as they might delude themselves. They are financing murder."[46]

Charities can provide another source of funds for terrorist groups. According to *The 9/11 Commission Report*, al-Qaeda regularly acquired cash from charities in two major ways: first by relying on "al-Qaeda sympathizers in specific foreign branch offices of large, international charities,"[47] and, also, by controlling certain charities completely. The 9/11 Commission discovered that "charities were a source of money and also provided significant cover, which enabled operatives to travel undetected under the guise of working for a humanitarian organization."[48]

In addition, the report highlighted the importance of individual donors who may act through charities or privately: "Al-Qaeda appears to have relied on a core group of financial facilitators who raised money from a variety of donors and other fundraisers, primarily in the Gulf countries and particularly in Saudi Arabia."[49] Many of these donors were responding to Islam's strong emphasis on charitable giving, known as *zakat*. "Some individual donors surely knew, and others did not, the ultimate destination of their donations."[50]

However, what the 9/11 Commission did not emphasize was the fact that the Arab charity terrorism-support infrastructure was well known prior to 9/11 and, in fact, was essentially condoned by the United States when it was directed against the Soviet occupation of Afghanistan. As fervent Muslims traveled to Afghanistan to engage in jihad (a holy struggle or campaign) against the Soviet army, which invaded in 1979, "wealthy Saudi business-men funneled millions of dollars to support the effort through assorted charities."[51] Thus, Arab money coalesced with CIA money to aid in the war effort against the Soviet Union.

At the time, the rising influence of the charities caused little concern for U.S. officials involved and, in fact, the trend was met "with approval."[52] However, as the Afghanistan war effort ended, the charity-based funding infrastructure remained. At this point, Osama bin Laden "tapped those fund-raising contacts to support his idea of a wider jihad, or holy war, against the West."[53] The Afghanistan experience thus laid the financial foundations for a much greater campaign on the part of al-Qaeda and affiliated groups. In 1996, some U.S. officials concluded that "businessmen in Saudi Arabia, Qatar and the United Arab Emirates helped finance the operations of Ramzi Ahmed Yousef," who was active in the 1993 plot to blow up the World Trade Center, as well as the Philippines-based Bojinka plot, which sought to bomb eleven U.S. airliners as they crossed the Pacific Ocean.[54]

In some cases, charities are exploited by the practice of "skimming." Gov-ernment investigators working in Bosnia, for instance, "found that [al-Qaeda] operatives skimmed money from relief charities and linked up with Bosnian crime bosses."[55] Bosnian "skimming" practices were apparently so successful that al-Qaeda decided to make this a model for similar skimming around the world.[56] In 1996, when President Bill Clinton sent letters to several Gulf Arab leaders seeking their assurance that charity funds were not being siphoned off to terrorists, he received a cool response from certain leaders. Kuwait's foreign minister, Sheikh Sabah al-Ahmed al-Jaber al-Sabah, stated that he "regretted" reading press reports about the Clinton initiative. "We have full confidence in [the charities] and all of [their] assistance and funds are not on the road to evil or terrorism," stated Sheikh Sabah.[57]

Occasionally, terrorists exhibit entrepreneurial flare by running their own businesses or enterprises, which then provide money for terrorism. In the 1980s, the PFLP reportedly "owned and operated a $2 million metal works factory in Sidon, Lebanon."[58] Similarly, the Japanese-based Aum Shinrikyo raised money with a number of legitimate businesses and enterprises, ranging from operating noodle shops to selling their spiritual leader's bath water.[59] Al-Qaeda has had mixed success with some of the businesses it established and managed. *The 9/11 Commission Report* concluded that when Osama bin Laden lived in Sudan, he owned a number of businesses and other assets. However, "these could not have provided significant income, as most were small or not economically viable."[60]

On the other hand, al-Qaeda or affiliated organizations (or individuals) made more effective use of the Malaysian-based firm of Konsojaya Trading Company, which listed its business as "exporting Malaysian palm oil to Afghanistan and Pakistan." In reality, it served as a key vehicle for funding the Philippines-based Bojinka plot. "Funds were cycled into the Philippines through Konsojaya, which also provided the financial support for paramilitary training of eight Singaporean Muslims in Pakistan and Afghanistan."[61]

The Criminal and Violent Side of Terrorism Finance

In December 1999, after a U.S. customs agent working on the U.S.-Canada border intercepted Ahmed Ressam, who was on his way to bomb the Los Angeles International Airport, authorities and the media began an inquiry into Ressam's background. Among other things, they learned that Ressam had lived for five years in Canada, supporting himself with petty crime and welfare fraud. He had arrived in Canada from France in 1994 with a fake passport, and promptly applied for political asylum. (His application was later rejected.) In the meantime, he supplemented his welfare payments "through shoplifting, pickpocketing, purse snatching and stealing tourists' suitcases."[62]

Ressam also sold fake passports, social security numbers, and driver's licenses. A friend—a fellow Algerian—paid Ressam between $60 and $200 apiece for stolen credit cards and passports.[63] In 1998, Ressam was convicted of stealing laptop computers from parked cars, and served a two-week sentence.[64] Overall, he was arrested four times and convicted twice. What the Ressam case reveals is the fact that many contemporary terrorists engage in criminal activities—sometimes in an amateurish fashion, while other times in a manner resembling a classic organized crime syndicate—to raise money, support themselves, or purchase key weapons or other materials that are needed to conduct terrorist attacks.[65]

Increasingly, it is recognized that terrorism and crime are closely linked. According to Antonio Maria Costa, executive director of the United Nations Office on Drugs and Crime (UNODC), "The basic funding of all terrorist organizations around the world has been criminal activity, not necessarily relating entirely to drugs. It could be kidnapping, it could be bank robbery, it could be other forms of violence. . . . The money by and large comes from criminal activities."[66] Confirming this point, a Spanish judge in April 2006 determined that the money used to fund the 2004 Madrid bombings was "obtained by illicit means, through drug trafficking or vehicle theft."[67]

The director of Europol, Max-Peter Ratzel, has also confirmed the link between terrorism and crime. He asserted that despite the lack of any "structural link" between terrorism and organized crime in Europe, investigators can still benefit by looking for matches between criminal databases and terrorism databases, since some individuals will show up in both: "What we have seen up to now is that there have been some terrorist organizations . . . that have financed themselves, inter alia, by criminal activities."[68] Similarly, Tamara Makarenko has observed that since state funding of terrorist groups has generally declined in the past one or two decades, many terrorist groups operating in the world today "are highly dependent on self-financing through criminal activity."[69]

Historically, one of the preferred ways of raising cash was to rob banks. Like Willie Sutton, the famous American bank robber who claimed he robbed banks "because that's where the money is,"[70] terrorists have also been attracted to banks for the same reason. Throughout history, bank robberies and terrorism movements have often been linked. In 1947, for instance, a "band of Zionist terrorists" in Palestine seized 150,000 Palestine pounds from an armored car as it was making deliveries to the British-owned Barclays Bank. However, following a gun battle that resulted in the deaths of four British policemen, the bandits were only able to abscond with 45,000 Palestine pounds (or $180,000). The raid of the armored car "came as the culmination of a series of robberies by which the dissident underground forces have been trying to replenish their coffers."[71]

The IRA was also known for stealing money from banks in Belfast, Northern Ireland. In 1973, British officials intercepted an internal memorandum, compiled by the Provisional wing of the IRA, which indicated that large sums of money stolen to finance IRA operations had been embezzled by top IRA officers and "at least £150,000 ($370,000) in cash taken from Belfast banks was involved."[72] In 1985, American law enforcement authorities arrested thirteen people in connection with the 1983 robbery of $7 million from a Wells Fargo depot in West Hartford, Connecticut: "Twelve of the 13 arrested were active in a Puerto Rico terrorist group, Los Macheteros,"[73] which took responsibility for the robbery. The Puerto Rican nationalist group also admitted responsibility for a number of acts in Hartford and Puerto Rico that had killed at least five people and wounded another sixteen since 1978.[74]

In Europe, both the Red Army Faction and the Red Brigades were known to raise cash by robbing banks.[75] East German authorities in 1990 arrested two former Red Army Faction members who were accused of robbing $120,000 from a West German bank in 1979.[76] Similarly, the Italian Red Brigades were so good at their craft that they could conduct a bank robbery with minimal violence. A Red Brigade representative would calmly approach a high-ranking bank manager and threaten his family (by revealing intimate details about the manager's life and family members); this pattern was followed, for instance, with the 1978 robbery of the Banco di Novaro in Genoa.[77]

In addition to robbing banks, terrorists have often engaged in kidnapping and extortion to raise needed funds. The Red Brigades conducted numerous kidnappings, leading to significant economic windfalls, which were often mistakenly attributed by Italian police to common criminals.[78] Similarly, in 1974, four Japanese Red Army (JRA) terrorists held the French ambassador and eleven other hostages at the French embassy in the Netherlands. Originally, the militants had demanded $1 million and the freedom of Yutaka Furuya, a fellow JRA member, who was being held in a French prison.[79] Following a four-day occupation of the embassy, after which the JRA terrorists had released nine hostages, the government of the Netherlands gave the terrorists $300,000 for the release of the remainder, including the French ambassador.[80] The JRA members were allowed to leave the country on an airplane provided by France. They eventually arrived in Syria, where they relinquished the funds to the PLO.

In the United States, one of the most notorious kidnapping cases involved the nineteen-year-old newspaper publishing heiress Patricia Hearst, who, on February 4, 1974, was kidnapped by the American-based Symbionese Liberation Army (SLA). The SLA, which had its origins in the California prison system, followed a "militant, loosely Marxist" ideology that opposed "racism, monogamy, the prison system and 'all other institutions that have made and sustained capitalism.'"[81] The kidnapping of Patricia Hearst was notable for a number of reasons, including the fact that Hearst "appeared to have become one of them [a Symbionese Liberation Army member]."[82] Hearst described herself as an "urban guerrilla" and a "soldier in the people's army."[83] Later, she participated in a robbery of a California bank, in which she carried an AK-47 rifle and subsequently drove a getaway car. She was arrested in September 1975, and later was found guilty of bank robbery.[84] After serving eighteen months in prison, President Jimmy Carter ordered her release, and in 2001, President Bill Clinton issued a presidential pardon.[85]

In some cases, the mere threat of violence by terrorist organizations could elicit payment, particularly if the payer was a large corporation. In the early 1970s, for instance, Ford Motor Company agreed to give the Argentine-based People's Revolutionary Army $1 million in medical supplies for Argentine hospitals. The group had "threatened to kill or kidnap Ford executives if its demands weren't met."[86] George Shultz, then secretary of the U.S. Treasury, stated that the $1 million payment was not "a particularly healthy thing to do," primarily because of concerns that it would stimulate similar demands on other U.S. companies abroad.[87]

In the contemporary context, kidnapping has emerged as a major internal security threat in many developing countries around the world, although in most cases it is an outgrowth of criminal rather than terrorist activities. In some cases, the criminal and terrorist motivations converge. In Colombia, for instance, local criminals engage in a practice of progressive kidnapping: an individual is first kidnapped, and then, after a ransom is paid, that person is simply transferred as a hostage to the Fuerzas Armadas Revolucionarias de Colombia (Revolutionary Armed Forces of Colombia, or FARC), which then extorts additional money from families and businesses, and thus earns substantial profits for itself.[88]

In Southeast Asia, one of the most dramatic and brazen kidnapping events occurred on April 23, 2000, when operatives from the Philippine-based Abu Sayyaf Group (ASG)—a semiterrorist, semicriminal organization—kidnapped more than twenty-one tourists from Malaysia, Germany, South Africa, Lebanon, Finland, and the Philippines at the Malaysian diving resort of Sipadan.[89] With hostages in their possession, the ASG operatives raced back into Philippine waters (via their two speedboats) and ultimately reached their jungle sanctuary. Subsequently, the ASG terrorists made exorbitant financial demands for release of the hostages—a ransom of $1 million per hostage. The drama became more bizarre when Libya offered to pay $25 million in exchange for most of the hostages. Such kidnappings are not rare in the Philippines and have been repeated often since 2000. In many cases, a complex nexus exists between criminal gangs and terrorist groups, often to the point of cooperation and mutual assistance.

Illegal narcotics provide yet another possible means through which terrorists can acquire money. In Afghanistan, the narcotics trade is playing a major role in funding terrorism and insurgency. According to Antonio Maria Costa, executive director of the United Nations Office on Drugs and Crime (UNODC), "drugs from Afghanistan [are trafficked] mainly to Europe and Russia across regions controlled by scores of warlords with multiple loyalties, insurgents affiliated with the Taliban, al-Qaeda, Hizb-e-Islami, and extremists from Central Asia and Pakistan. These groups impose transit and protection fees on drug cargoes."[90]

In the Western Hemisphere, the Colombian-based FARC, which was created in 1964 "as a left wing guerilla group dedicated to the violent overthrow of the Government of Colombia,"[91] provides the clearest linkages between terrorism and narcotics. On March 1, 2006, the U.S. Court for the District of Columbia issued a superseding indictment against more than forty individuals, primarily Colombian nationals, for violating various federal laws regarding narcotics trafficking and conspiracy. According to the indictment, "it was a part and an object of the conspiracy that All Defendants, and others known and unknown to the Grand Jury, would and did import into the United States . . . five kilograms and more of mixtures and substances containing a detectable amount of cocaine."[92]

In addition, the indictment alleges that the "FARC has evolved into the world's largest supplier of cocaine and cocaine paste."[93] The group is directly responsible for half of the world's supply of cocaine and "more than approximately 60% of the cocaine sent to the United States."[94] FARC has been designated by the U.S. secretary of state as a foreign terrorist organization (FTO). Initially, FARC's involvement in cocaine trafficking related to "taxes" that it imposed on non-FARC drug traffickers operating within territory it controlled; however, beginning in the 1990s, FARC took on a more direct role in the cocaine trade by transforming itself "into a broker between the cocaine paste producing campesinos and the cocaine transportation organizations that distributed the cocaine to the United States and elsewhere."[95] Having achieved a monopoly in cocaine paste purchases, FARC was then able to set the price of cocaine paste purchased from the campesinos.[96] The case of FARC and Colombian drug trafficking provides a direct example of a terrorist organization turning to narcotics to raise funds; narcotics have provided the organization with a sizable funding source of convenience and consistency.

Legal Measures Taken Against Terrorism Finance

As terrorism has increasingly become an international menace, many countries have begun targeting its financial foundations. One of the most significant initiatives against terrorist finance was introduced in 1999 and is known as the International Convention for the Suppression of the Financing of Terrorism. It entered into force on April 10, 2002. Among other things, the convention required states to "(1) take steps to prevent and counteract the financing of terrorists; (2) hold those who finance terrorism criminally, civilly or administratively liable, and (3) provide for the justification, freezing and seizure of funds allocated for terrorist activities."[97] By June 2005, the convention had been signed by 132 countries, and 117 were full parties to the agreement.[98]

The 1999 convention was a powerful step within the international community to stem terrorism financing. But the impact of 9/11 greatly enhanced the power of the convention, particularly with the passage of UN Security Council Resolution 1373. Passed only weeks after the September 11 attacks, Resolution 1373 "criminalized all activities falling within the ambit of terrorist financing [and] obliged states to freeze all funds or financial assets of persons and entities that are directly or indirectly used to commit terrorist acts."[99]

To implement the measures of Resolution 1373, the UN Security Council established a subsidiary organ known as the Counter-Terrorism Committee (CTC) "to monitor implementation and increase the capability of UN members to fight terrorism through the promotion and targeting of technical assistance."[100] Member states had to report to the committee within 90 days regarding the steps they had taken to implement the directives of the resolution.[101]

In addition to UN activities, the European-based Financial Action Task Force (FATF) has significantly expanded its mission to combat the financing of terrorism. In October 2001, the FATF specifically addressed terrorism finance by issuing eight special recommendations on the subject.[102] The first special recommendation, for example, urged countries to take immediate steps to ratify and implement fully the 1999 International Convention for the Suppression of the Financing of Terrorism, in addition to implementing UN resolutions related to the prevention and suppression of terrorism finance, particularly UN Security Council Resolution 1373.[103] In October 2004, the FATF included the ninth special recommendation, which addressed the growing problem of cash couriers. Additionally, the FATF has worked in close cooperation with the International Monetary Fund (IMF) and World Bank "to develop a common methodology to incorporate FATF's recommendations into the final sector reviews that all three entities undertake."[104]

In addition to international laws, resolutions, and other initiatives, the United States has a number of domestic laws that address terrorism finance. Under the International Emergency Economic Powers Act (IEEPA),[105] passed in 1977, as well as other statutes, the U.S. government has established "sanctions programs that prohibit named foreign terrorists, foreign drug kingpins, and their fronts and operatives from using their assets within U.S. jurisdiction or engaging in business or other financial activities with U.S. persons, including companies or individuals."[106]

The 1990 Anti-Terrorism Act made it illegal to provide material support, including funding and financial services, to foreign terrorist organizations.[107] Another law passed in 1996, which has been described as the "watershed legislative development of terrorist financing enforcement,"[108] is the Anti-Terrorism and Effective Death Penalty Act (AEDPA). This law gives the secretary of state authority to designate any group as a threat to U.S. national security, and thus makes it a crime for any person in the United States to provide funds or any material support to such group.[109] The AEDPA developed the concept of foreign terrorist organizations, or FTOs.[110] In addition, the AEDPA prevents U.S persons from "engaging in transactions with countries that support terrorism" and requires that financial institutions freeze financial accounts belonging to international terrorist organizations.[111]

In October 2001, President Bush signed into law the USA PATRIOT Act. Title 3 of the act is called the International Money Laundering Abatement and Anti-Terrorist Financing Act of 2001. In essence, Title 3 amended the various anti–money laundering provisions of the Bank Secrecy Act (BSA) and thus is intended to "promote the prevention, detection, and prosecution of international money laundering and the financing of terrorism."[112]

Among its more prominent features, Title 3 of the USA PATRIOT Act prohibits U.S. financial institutions from maintaining "correspondent accounts" for foreign shell banks.[113] In addition, Section 312 requires that U.S. financial institutions establish effective anti–money laundering procedures for accounts held by non-U.S. persons.[114] Title 3 also requires that other institutions—not simply banks—implement anti–money laundering programs, including institutions such as insurance companies, mutual funds, and hedge funds.

In addition, Title 3 expands the range of covered institutions that are required to file suspicious activity reports (SARs), which have been required for years under the BSA. SARs must be filed by financial institutions in the event that certain situational requirements or financial thresholds are met. For example, a person engaging in a financial transaction aggregating $5,000 or more, whom the bank determines "has no business or apparent lawful purpose or is not the sort in which the particular customer would normally be expected to engage," would likely be a candidate for a SAR filing.[115]

In 2002, the U.S. Treasury Department expanded the scope of institutions required to file SARs to include insurance companies, currency dealers and exchangers, mutual funds, casinos, card clubs, and broker-dealers.[116] The number of SARs filed has soared since the introduction of the USA PATRIOT Act. According to one Treasury Department assessment, in reference to SAR filings at depository institutions, "the volume of Suspicious Activity Report filings in the first six months of 2005 increased 45% over those filed in the same period in 2004."[117] In the case of money services businesses, casinos (and card clubs), and the securities and futures industry, SAR filings have increased 25 percent, 2 percent, and 27 percent, respectively, over the first six months of 2005 (compared to the year earlier).[118]

One of the most far-reaching provisions of Title 3 is Section 311, which authorizes the secretary of the Treasury Department to designate a foreign jurisdiction, institution, class of transactions, or type of account to be of "primary money laundering concern" and thus requires that U.S. financial institutions take certain "special measures" against this money laundering concern, which could range from enhanced recordkeeping to reporting requirements or total termination of correspondent banking relationships.[119] Section 311, grounded in the objective of preventing money laundering and protecting the U.S. financial system from the same, has become one of the most powerful foreign policy tools for the U.S. government as it combats terrorism finance and transnational crime.

Most recently the provision was used against a Macau-based bank known as Banco Delta Asia. This bank was allegedly used for years by the North Korean government to launder proceeds of crime and counterfeiting. North Korea, which has been designated by the U.S. Department of State as a state sponsor of terrorism, has actively engaged in state-sponsored crime as well: "Illicit activities have long been part of the North Korean economy, but they appear to have intensified in the 1990s, as the North Korean economy went into decline and central government control began to fray."[120]

Moreover, the state sponsorship extends into all facets of North Korea's government apparatus. In a statement to a U.S. Senate hearing, Peter Prahar of the State Department detailed how "foreign law enforcement cases have clearly established that North Korean diplomats, military officers, and other party and/or government officials have been involved in the smuggling of narcotics."[121] Moreover, according to Prahar, state-owned assets, such as ships and military patrol vessels, "have been used to facilitate and support international drug trafficking ventures."[122]

North Korea is not the only target of 311 sanctions. According to Daniel L. Glaser, the U.S. Treasury Department's acting assistant secretary at the Office of Terrorist Financing and Financial Crimes, Section 311 sanctions have been applied against jurisdictions or institutions located in Ukraine, Nauru, Burma (Myanmar), Syria, Latvia, and the Turkish Republic of Northern Cyprus.[123] Other targets of Section 311 include a bank in Belarus (known as "Infobank") widely reported to be "specializing in financial transactions related to arms exports because of the activities of its subsidiary corporation, Belmetalnergo."[124] Infobank and Belmetalnergo were accused of procuring and financing "weapons and military equipment for several countries deemed by the U.S. to be state sponsors of terrorism,"[125] including the Iraqi regime under Saddam Hussein.

Perhaps more significant is the designation of the Commercial Bank of Syria as a "primary money laundering concern" under Section 311. According to a prominent U.S. representative, "Evidence suggests that the CBS, the

Commercial Bank of Syria, was the recipient of the proceeds of more than $1.8 billion in oil sales from June 2000 to February 2003. These funds were deposited into accounts controlled by Iraq's state oil marketing organization at the Syrian bank, the CBS."[126] In addition, a U.S. Treasury Department report noted that Syria is a jurisdiction "with very limited money laundering controls."[127] However, from a terrorism-finance perspective, the report notes that Syria's money laundering vulnerabilities are exacerbated by its ongoing support for terrorist activity. Designated a state sponsor of terrorism since 1979, the Syrian government (as of 2006) "continued to provide material support to Lebanese Hizballah and Palestinian terrorist groups HAMAS, Palestinian Islamic Jihad (PIJ), and the Popular Front for the Liberation of Palestine (PFLP), among others."[128]

The Commercial Bank of Syria has also been linked to Iran's support of Hezbollah in Lebanon: "The Syrian Government also continues to permit Iran to use Damascus as a transshipment point for re-supplying Lebanese Hizballah in Lebanon."[129] The Iran connection was also highlighted in January 2006 when the Syrian government "facilitated a meeting in Damascus between Iranian government officials and several designated terrorist leaders, including Abdullah Ramadan Shallah, Ahmed Jibril, Hassan Nasrallah, and Khaled Mishal of Hamas."[130]

Because the Commercial Bank of Syria is a government-owned and controlled bank, it presents an "ongoing opportunity for the Syrian government to continue to support and finance terrorist activity."[131] In addition to pressuring Iran via Syria, current reports indicate that the U.S. government may be considering using Section 311 designations directly against Iran.[132] Overall, it is clear that the U.S. government views Section 311 of the USA PATRIOT Act as a critical tool to counter Iran and Syria's "financial infrastructure through which terrorists can move, store and launder their funds."[133]

Financial Regulations and Their Displacement Effects

As advanced, developed countries have increased their financial surveillance and legal infrastructures to counter terrorism finance, they have inadvertently pushed many activities into the realm of "less governed spaces" or have caused a reversion to more basic and less technical methods of conducting commercial transactions. As Anne Clunan argues, the lack of a robust international regime to counter terrorism finance is causing terrorist and other criminal finances to "flow to wherever the regulatory environment is loosest."[134]

One indicator of this trend is the rise in bulk cash smuggling, which can be seen as an indicator that terrorists are seeking to avoid formal banking channels.[135] For example, the Southeast Asian group Jemaah Islamiyah (JI) is known to rely on small-scale couriers who arrive with bags of cash. Personal couriers, often Indonesian migrants working in Malaysia who are not actual members of JI, helped transfer more than $15,000 in cash, which was used in the first Bali bombing of October 2002.[136] Indonesian police have confirmed that JI regularly uses cash couriers to smuggle cash into Indonesia to fund its operations.[137]

In the United States, bulk cash smuggling is traditionally associated with narcotics trafficking. As the United States has implemented stricter banking standards—resulting from requirements of the Bank Secrecy Act of 1970—narcotics traffickers have found it more difficult to achieve the initial "placement" stage of money laundering. (Placement refers to the first stage of money laundering; it involves the depositing of cash into a financial account, or transforming the cash into an electronic or bankable form; the other two stages of money laundering are "layering" and "integration.") As a result, a vibrant cash smuggling industry has grown, particularly along the U.S.-Mexican border. According to a U.S. Treasury official: "Cash associated with drugs typically flows out of the U.S. across the southwest border into Mexico, retracing the route that the drugs took entering the United States. Drugs and illicit proceeds also cross our northern and other borders."[138]

Bulk cash smuggling also plays an important role in funding the Iraq insurgency. "Richer jihadists and particularly suicide bombers [seeking to enter Iraq], are seen as trustworthy cash couriers if large shipments of money need to be delivered."[139] A Treasury Department official stated that cash couriers are the preferred means of delivering insurgency funds into Iraq for three key reasons: (1) the presence of porous borders with neighboring states; (2) the availability of long-established smuggling routes in the region; and (3) the lack of a formal and mature financial system in Iraq.[140] In addition to bags of cash, in some cases terrorists are physically transferring gold across borders. One report in 2002 described how Taliban and al-Qaeda operatives had "sent waves of couriers with bars of gold and bundles of dollars across the porous borders into Pakistan."[141]

In addition, terrorist organizations may rely increasingly on informal value transfer systems (IVTSs), such as Hawala or the Peso-Exchange system. Al-Qaeda began to rely on the Hawala system—"an informal and ancient trust-based system for transferring funds"[142]—for two basic reasons. First, once the organization transferred its operations to Afghanistan in 1996, it could not rely on a formal banking system since Afghanistan did not have one. Second, following the 1998 East Africa bombings, al-Qaeda recognized that its operations—to include all financial transactions—would be under intense scrutiny from that point onward.[143]

The problem for government regulators is that many global IVTSs have been developed, not for terrorism financing, but rather to address the banking needs of millions of poor, often migrant, workers throughout the world. In many parts of the world, these systems "represent the only financial system available."[144] An estimated $100 billion to $300 billion pass through the IVTS every year.[145] In certain cases, narcotics traffickers use such systems to move cash across international borders. The Colombian black market Peso Exchange, for instance, "is responsible for moving $5 billion worth of drug proceeds per year from the United States to Colombia."[146] The challenge emerges when such systems, originally created for purposes unrelated to terrorism, are then exploited by transnational terrorist organizations.

Conclusion

On September 24, 2001, the White House issued a press release describing the various actions that the U.S. government had taken against terrorism finance. The release stated that "the President has directed the first strike on the global terror network today by issuing an Executive Order to starve terrorists of their support funds."[147] The order listed an array of actions that the United States had taken—such as freezing assets of terrorist organizations, identifying charitable organizations that funnel money to al-Qaeda, and denying access to foreign banks that refuse to freeze terrorist assets—all of which were designed to undermine the global financial support structure that underpins terrorism.[148]

Nevertheless, terrorism has still continued. In October 2002, terrorists associated with the Indonesian-based Jemaah Islamiyah conducted attacks on nightclubs in Bali, Indonesia, killing 200 people. The attacks cost less than $50,000 to execute.[149] Attacks on British interests in Istanbul, Turkey, in 2003 cost less than $40,000 to execute.[150] The train bombings in Madrid, Spain, on March 11, 2004, may have cost only $10,000, while the July 7, 2005, subway attacks in London, England, cost just $1,000, and "were paid primarily out of one of the bomber's wages."[151] In September 2006, British officials reported that the plot to blow up multiple transatlantic airliners—described as "one of the most highly sophisticated terrorist operations ever organized"—would have cost less than 7,000 pounds (about US$13,300) to execute.[152]

In light of the rather minimal sums required to execute major terrorist attacks—sums that probably would not be noticed even under the most sensitive and invasive of financial surveillance structures—some may wonder whether international efforts against terrorism finance are meaningful at all. In addition, focusing on the "financial oxygen" of global terrorism, with an emphasis on technical approaches, more regulations, and greater coordination among financial intelligence units, may appeal to bureaucracies searching for tangible options to mitigate the terrorist threat, but the long-term efficacy is questionable.

Ultimately, if governments want to truly mitigate the causes of terrorism, they must focus on the "political oxygen"[153] that fuels terrorism. In the case of al-Qaeda (and related movements), this means addressing the meta-narrative that al-Qaeda thrives on, namely, that the international system—with the United States at its apex—is structurally positioned against Muslims around the world.[154] Long-festering conflicts and lingering perceptions of injustice (Palestine, Kashmir, Southern Philippines, and others) all play into this narrative. Thus, starving the "financial oxygen" that fuels terrorism must be pursued in tandem with an honest effort to mitigate the "political oxygen" that sustains many contemporary terrorist movements.

9

The Terrorism Ahead

Root Causes and Future Prospects

On October 23, 1983, a suicide bomber drove a five-ton capacity Mercedes truck loaded with 5,000 pounds of TNT into the lobby of the U.S. Marine Battalion Landing Team (BLT) Headquarters in Beirut, Lebanon. "The force of the explosion ripped the building from its foundation,"[1] a U.S. Department of Defense Commission report would later conclude; moreover, "The building then imploded upon itself. Almost all the occupants were crushed or trapped inside the wreckage."[2] The blast ultimately killed 241 U.S. military personnel and wounded an additional 100.[3]

Within days of the attack, General Paul Kelley, Commandant of the Marine Corps, was summoned (along with other officials) to testify before a frustrated and impatient U.S. Senate Armed Services Committee, which was investigating the incident. Kelley described in great detail the initial actions of the suicide truck bomber, including the fact that he had begun his assault by encircling the parking lot (thus gaining speed), then crashing through defensive wire emplacements, and then jumping over a sewer pipe "which had been placed as an obstacle to impede the movement of vehicles."[4] Finally, the truck plowed through a sandbag barrier before entering the lobby of the building with its explosive cargo.

General Kelley admitted that the Marine compound's security measures were "inadequate to counter this form of kamikaze attack"[5] but that "in all honesty, [he had yet] to find any shred of intelligence which would have alerted a reasonable and prudent commander to this new and very unique threat."[6] In the next paragraph, General Kelley sought to confirm this assertion by citing the views of the commander of the Lebanese Armed Forces, General Ibrahim Tannous, who reportedly stated that he could not recall "a terrorist attack of the type and magnitude which hit our headquarters on October 23."[7] Moreover, General Kelley concluded that "In his [General Tannous's] opinion, and in mine, this represents a new and unique terrorist threat, one which could not have reasonably been anticipated by any commander."[8]

In the subsequent question–answer session, General Kelley consistently emphasized the unprecedented nature of the attack and the fact that it could not have been anticipated. "What we saw this time was a dawn attack, an attack by a five-ton Mercedes truck that bowled over . . . all of our defenses. This kind of terrorist act is unprecedented. So it was a totally different type of act."[9] Later Kelley was asked by Senator Sam Nunn about a previous suicide attack on the U.S. embassy in April 1983, in which "a light truck detonated, killing over sixty people (including seventeen Americans) and destroying a sizable portion of the building."[10] Senator Nunn noted that "if someone was on a suicide mission in terms of the Embassy [then it might be reasonable] to assume . . . that someone else might go on a suicide mission."[11]

Kelley countered that the two attacks were different; the embassy attack involved a smaller truck while the marine headquarters attack involved a five-ton Mercedes truck. Senator Nunn then asked, since five-ton Mercedes trucks were common around the Beirut airport, why would it be unreasonable "to assume that a truck that was in common use around the airport might be utilized for this type of mission?"[12] General Kelley replied that "no one had ever experienced this kind of technique before—the technique of charging through defensive positions and forcing your way in."[13]

Kelley apparently believed that the U.S. embassy attack held few, if any, lessons for the Marine BLT in Beirut. Moreover, he was apparently unaware of a previous suicide car bombing directed against the Iraqi embassy in Beirut in 1981, considered the first major suicide attack in the region, which heralded the onset of this new and lethal terrorist methodology. Moreover, the marine leadership, including the commander on the ground, apparently did not adequately take into account the fact that "intelligence provided over 100 warnings of car bombings between May and October 23, 1983," although most of these threats failed to materialize.[14] But the larger problem was related to a lack of imagination. With respect to the October 23, 1983, marine headquarters attack, a Department of Defense commission would later conclude that "[f]rom a terrorist perspective, the true genius of this attack is that the objective and the means of attack were beyond the imagination of those responsible for Marine security."[15]

Fifteen years later, in February 1998, Dale Watson, former chief of the FBI's International Terrorism Operations Section, testified before a special terrorism subcommittee of the Senate Judiciary Committee. In this testimony, Watson described an array of threats posed by terrorists in the 1990s—and likely scenarios in the future. Among other things, he told lawmakers that "today's terrorists have learned from the successes and mistakes of terrorists that went before them. The terrorists of tomorrow will have an even more dizzying array of weapons and technologies available to them."[16]

In fact, Watson may not have realized it, but his focus on the "Bojinka" plot in the Philippines was a key example of the predicted "dizzying array" of weapons. The plot had a number of dimensions, one of which focused on destroying U.S. passenger aircraft en route over the Pacific Ocean. "By decrypting Yousef's computer files, investigators uncovered the details of a plot to destroy numerous U.S. air carriers in a simultaneous operation."[17] In addition, FBI interviews with Bojinka plot suspects in the Philippines had revealed a new dimension of airplane hijacking—the use of passenger aircraft as suicide bombs. The FBI largely dismissed this "third phase" of the Bojinka plot, mainly because it was still in the planning stages and did not appear to be particularly viable.

Ironically, the FBI assessment regarding "Bojinka"—especially concerning the suicide aircraft phase of the plot—was also shared by Osama bin Laden who was briefed in Afghanistan by Khalid Sheikh Mohammed, the designer of the 9/11 plot who would also eventually rise to become al-Qaeda's chief of external operations. In the meeting, held in 1996, Sheikh Mohammed pleaded with bin Laden "to give him money and operatives so that he could hijack ten planes in the U.S. to fly them into targets, with five targets on each coast of the United States."[18] Bin Laden was not convinced of the practicality of the plot. Three years later, however, he changed his mind and "summoned Sheikh Mohammed to meet him in Qandahar, Afghanistan."[19] At this meeting held in March or April 1999, bin Laden informed Sheikh Mohammed that al-Qaeda fully supported the plot and believed the idea would work.[20]

The question that arises in both of these cases centers on why, given the array of indicators suggesting that suicide bombing was becoming the preferred mode of attack, did officials not more vigorously prepare for this possibility? Why was the American public (or why were the servicemen, in the case of Lebanon) not put "on notice" that such a threat existed? In the case of Bojinka, why was civil aviation not required to implement key measures to counter aerial suicide tactics? Part of the answer is bureaucratic, and part cultural. As *The 9/11 Commission Report* stated, "Imagination is not a gift usually associated with bureaucracies."[21] In addition, the government lives within a world of secrecy—classified knowledge—that is kept far from public purview (for both bureaucratic and legal reasons), except in the case of planned or inadvertent leaks. Within this classified milieu, the clues for future plots or future trends in plots can sometimes be determined, but only if those with access privileges have the appropriate knowledge and imagination. More important, the classified "wall" prevents any prying eyes of the public who might seek to enforce accountability.

Terrorism, at its core, is a tactic of deception and surprise. When General Paul Kelley was asked by a U.S. senator what kind of vulnerabilities would remain at the U.S. Marine Headquarters following the October 1983 suicide attack, he answered: "The vulnerability is from all forms of terrorism. We just do not know from what direction they will come."[22] General Kelley obviously exhibited his own "tactical blindness" regarding potential terrorism threats. Such blindness exists in varying degrees at all levels of government, and in virtually every country around the world. But an even larger challenge is strategic blindness, particularly regarding the fundamental and global drivers of terrorism. After the 9/11 attacks—and similar attacks in London, Madrid, and Bali—governments around the world have spent billions of dollars on counterterrorism efforts. However, it is not clear that this money has been spent effectively or that terrorism, in any measure of the phenomenon, has actually diminished.

Root Causes: Searching for the "Holy Grail" of Modern Terrorism

Many governments believe that their ability to succeed against terrorism—to mitigate the terrorist threat or at least to make the option of terrorism less attractive to aggrieved individuals and groups in the long term—depends largely on their ability to identify and isolate key "root causes." Philip Wilcox, former coordinator for counterterrorism at the U.S. Department of State, made this point in his 2000 testimony before Congress when he argued that: "[W]e must recognize that terrorism, like other forms of political violence, is often an extreme symptom of conflict caused by political, ethnic, economic, or other factors. Effective counterterrorism cannot be a stand-alone policy that is limited only to diplomacy, law enforcement, intelligence, and other programs of counterterrorism per se. The programs are vital, but they are not enough unless we also address the root causes of terrorism."[23]

However, the search for the correct root causes is complicated because terrorism is not a monolithic threat—it is a complicated and protean phenomenon, reflecting the particular local circumstances or environment in which it is situated. Terrorists, as noted by Paul Davis and Brian Jenkins earlier in this book, are not a single enemy and thus they cannot be deterred or stopped by a single strategy or approach.[24] Moreover, terrorism is also difficult to counter because the terrorists themselves may perceive that they have little to lose, or they are motivated by religious or other ideologies that promote martyrdom.[25] Nevertheless, the root-causes argument is much more than an academic exercise. Governments often shape their national policies and spend enormous amounts of "counterterrorism money" on assumptions that reflect their perception of the root cause of a particular social problem, such as terrorism.[26]

In its 2006 National Security Strategy (NSS), the administration of George W. Bush stated that the "War on Terror" has been "both a battle of arms and a battle of ideas—a fight against the terrorists and against their murderous ideology."[27] The NSS goes on to delineate short-term versus long-term approaches to mitigating terrorism. Short-term responses include military forces and other "instruments of national power"[28] to kill, capture, deny operational space and access to weapons of mass destruction (WMD), and so on. The key to long-term success, however, requires "winning the battle of ideas, for it is ideas that can turn the disenchanted into murderers willing to kill innocent victims."[29]

What is particularly interesting about the NSS is that it outlines what the U.S. government believes are and are not root causes of international terrorism. The NSS specifically counsels that "we must be clear-eyed about what does and does not give rise to terrorism."[30] The following analysis and critique tracks the NSS structure and begins, as does the NSS document itself, with those factors that the U.S. government believes do not promote terrorism.

NSS: Factors That Do Not Cause Terrorism

Poverty Is Not Necessarily a "Root Cause" of Terrorism

The NSS discounts the role of poverty in promoting terrorism: "Terrorism is not the inevitable by-product of poverty. Many of the September 11 hijackers were from middle-class backgrounds, and many terrorists leaders, like bin Laden, are from privileged upbringings."[31] However, this assessment runs counter to a common notion among some terrorism analysts and media pundits who believe that terrorism is indeed rooted in poverty, at least in some manner.[32]

Moreover, this belief in a terrorism–poverty nexus has strong roots in history. For example, in the 1970s, conventional wisdom linked the rise of the Italian Red Brigades to a "disaffected mass" that was the product of "1.2 million unemployed young people between eighteen and twenty-nine."[33] In the contemporary context, Paul Pillar, former head of the CIA's counterterrorism center, argues that the majority of terrorists around the world are young adult males "unemployed or underemployed (except by terrorist groups), with weak social and familial support, and with poor prospects for economic improvement or advancement through legitimate work."[34] Jonathan Fox echoes this theme when he argues that in the long term "the best way to deal with fundamentalism is probably to mitigate the socio-economic dislocations and political-cultural disruptions caused by modernization."[35] Samuel M. Makinda also supports the notion that a relationship exists between poverty and terrorism; moreover, he proposes economic development as an antidote. "Development has the potential to reduce the chances of terrorism by eliminating or modifying the conditions that produce discontent."[36]

Complicating this analysis, however is the fact that there is no direct link between poverty or unemployment and the person who becomes a terrorist; otherwise solving or mitigating terrorism might be a more direct and straightforward matter: "It is not nearly as simple a matter as giving disgruntled people votes or a higher income."[37] Moreover, many of the world's wealthier Muslim-majority countries have paradoxically produced more terrorists than poor Muslim-majority countries. Fifteen of the nineteen hijackers in the September 11, 2001, attacks in the United States came from Saudi Arabia, one of the most affluent Muslim-majority countries in the world.[38]

Similarly, the twenty Jemaah Islamiyah operatives in Singapore, who were part of a planned attack against the United States and other targets in December 2001, lived in one of the most prosperous countries in Asia. Many of the young men, moreover, had good jobs and strong educational credentials.[39] This may explain the basis of the official U.S. government view, which questions the poverty–terrorism nexus.

However, simply because the world has witnessed "wealthy terrorists" in recent years does not mean that the poverty–terrorism nexus should be dismissed entirely. "Although bin Laden and many of his lieutenants and agents have not been the victims of poverty or deprivation, tens of millions of people in the region have been."[40]

In the Middle East, stagnant economies and rising unemployment are creating an enabling environment for terrorism. *The 9/11 Commission Report* noted that since the 1990s, high birthrates and declining infant mortality had produced a situation where there was "a large, steadily increasing population of young men without any reasonable expectation of suitable or steady employment."[41] Many of these men, frustrated by poor job prospects and lack of opportunities, were thus easy targets for radicalization, which is a precursor to terrorism. Overall, the evidence suggests that although the poverty–terrorism linkage is less than direct, such a nexus appears to be stronger in certain parts of the world than in others, and thus the role of poverty is potentially an important contributor to, or enabler of, terrorism.[42]

Hostility to U.S. Policy in Iraq Is Not Relevant to Terrorism

The NSS states that "terrorism is not simply a result of hostility to U.S. policy in Iraq. The United States was attacked on September 11 and earlier, well before we toppled the Saddam Hussein regime."[43] However, in recent years, most terrorism experts agree that the single issue that has spawned grievances—as well as helped fuel the militant "jihadi" cause—is the U.S. invasion of Iraq. Ironically, prior to the Iraq invasion, Vice President Dick Cheney drew direct linkages between al-Qaeda and Iraq. In one speech, he accused the Iraqi regime of aiding and protecting al-Qaeda: "His [Saddam Hussein's] regime aids and protects terrorists, including members of al-Qaeda."[44] In a subsequent speech, he discussed Iraq's hosting of an al-Qaeda camp in its northeastern area: "Al Qaeda had a base of operation there up in Northeastern Iraq where they ran a large poisons factory for attacks against Europeans and U.S. forces."[45]

Some scholars and government officials have suggested, however, that the more robust relationship between Iraq and terrorism has occurred since the American-led invasion. Moreover, some have suggested that Iraq may emerge as the "new Afghanistan"—a new epicenter of terrorism.[46] In Saudi Arabia, for example, where a major terrorist plot involving 172 men was disrupted in late April 2007, analysts there asserted that the chaos in Iraq "has fueled radical ideology among the region's youth, while providing an environment for militants to train."[47]

Barry Desker and Arabinda Acharya argue that: "Iraq has now emerged as the new epicenter of transnational terrorism, in much the same way as Afghanistan following the Soviet occupation in 1979."[48] Such an assessment was recently confirmed by a surprisingly candid admission in 2005 by Porter Goss, director of Central Intelligence, who stated: "Islamic extremists are exploiting the Iraqi conflict to recruit new anti-U.S. jihadists. . . . These jihadists who survive will leave Iraq experienced in and focused on acts of urban terrorism. They represent a potential pool of contacts to build transnational terrorist cells, groups, and networks in Saudi Arabia, Jordan and other countries."[49] These views were again confirmed in 2006 by the bipartisan Iraq Study Group, which concluded: "[Iraq] is now a base of operations for international terrorism, including al-Qaeda."[50]

Not only has the Iraq operation generated a new army of Islamic militants, it has diminished the standing of the United States, according to worldwide opinion polls. According to one analyst, "Never has the U.S. (according to international public opinion polls) been so resented, if not loathed, by so many people around the world. And this is exactly the kind of environment in which al-Qaeda terrorists—who represent a real and ongoing threat to the U.S. and others—thrive."[51] Across the globe, foreign observers increasingly view the United States, in its counterterrorism efforts, as "trigger happy," inclined to exercise poor judgment, and prone to violence.[52]

According to the Pew Global Attitudes Project, anti-American sentiment has risen dramatically since the terrorist attacks on September 11, 2001. In Muslim-majority countries, such as Turkey, Pakistan, Jordan, and Morocco, unfavorable views of the United States have held fairly consistently since

2002, although the downward descent appears to have stabilized between 2003 and 2004. Moreover, in several surveys of Muslim countries, substantial numbers of people "believe suicide attacks against Americans and other Westerners in Iraq are justifiable."[53] Muslim-majority countries have a low opinion of the U.S.-led "war on terrorism": in March 2004, only 28 percent of those surveyed in Morocco, 12 percent surveyed in Jordan, and 16 percent surveyed in Pakistan actually favored the U.S.-led war on terrorism.[54] Ironically, Osama bin Laden received a favorable rating in Pakistan (65 percent), Jordan (55 percent), and Morocco (45 percent).[55] Additionally, according to the survey, a substantial number of Muslims believe that the war on Iraq has not helped mitigate terrorism. A majority of respondents in Turkey, Pakistan, and Morocco, for instance, believe that the Iraq war has had a negative impact on the fight against terrorism.[56]

Not only is the United States held in low regard in Muslim-majority countries, it is also increasingly unpopular in many countries thought to be traditional allies, countries whose participation will be necessary for any sustained campaign against terrorism. In Britain, France, and Germany, for instance, there is rising support for an independent European foreign policy that would be decoupled from the United States.[57]

Israeli–Palestinian Conflict and Terrorism

The NSS states that "terrorism is not simply a result of Israeli-Palestinian issues. Al-Qaeda plotting for the September 11 attacks began in the 1990s, during an active period in the peace process."[58] However, despite the assertions of the NSS, many terrorism experts believe that the Palestinian issue does indeed play a major role in fueling terrorism. "The Israeli-Palestinian conflict is a boon to al-Qaeda," writes Stephen Van Evera. "[It] gives al-Qaeda a chance to pose in its propaganda as a defender of Arabs and Muslims against a predatory Israeli/American juggernaut."[59] Osama bin Laden has mentioned the Palestinian problem in a number of his speeches.[60] In fact, the Israeli–Palestinian conflict is arguably a cause célèbre for militant Salafist violence and has served in that role for decades. Writing in 1977, C.L. Sulzberger noted that "it is more than ever necessary to settle the Arab-Israeli question soon. If such is not done, unwise statesmen or terrorists connected with the confrontation may blow the earth up."[61] Ironically, more than thirty years later, conditions in the Israeli–Palestinian context—and the conflict generally—have arguably not changed appreciably.

Moreover, the Palestinian problem is one of a host of long-festering conflicts, such as those in Kashmir, Afghanistan, Chechnya, the southern Philippines, and Thailand, which are the products of unique local ethnic and religious dynamics, but which also feed into larger, international anti-Western narratives. These local conflicts help foster the "narrative" that Islam is under assault. Moreover, these issues are often "advertised" and documented on the Internet and have become powerful recruitment tools. In Germany, for instance, Salim Boukhari, whom German authorities described as the "driving force" behind a December 2000 plot to "bomb revelers at the Christmas marketplace outside the Notre-Dame Cathedral in Strasbourg,"[62] was recruited by friends who showed him videos of Muslims being persecuted throughout the world. Specifically, he saw movies showing Muslims being oppressed in Palestine and Chechnya and later revealed that these movies had "made a profound impression on him"[63] and in fact promoted him to become a mujahid in Chechnya. Moreover, many of these images become the basis of video-rich Web sites that promote jihadi ideology and boost recruitment.

U.S. Counterterrorism Policies and Root Causes

The NSS states that U.S. counterterrorism policies are not the root cause: The NSS states that "terrorism is not simply a response to our efforts to prevent terror attacks. . . . Indeed, the terrorists are emboldened more by perceptions of weakness than by demonstrations of resolve."[64] This would seem to be accurate at first glance; after all, in some cases a state may have no other choice but to resort to aggressive military actions to counter an immediate threat. Paul Davis and Brian Jenkins argue that the United States, in its battle with al-Qaeda, must pursue a dual strategy of militarily "crushing" al-Qaeda, and at the same time, implementing longer-term measures that address the root causes of terrorism in order to prevent the rise of the next generation of terrorists.[65]

Nevertheless, there appears to be evidence suggesting that as the United States has carried out its war on terrorism, the incidence of terrorism has paradoxically increased, or at least has not diminished appreciably. This was revealed in the U.S. State Department's 2003 *Patterns of Global Terrorism,* which supposedly showed the U.S. "turning the terrorist tide."[66] Embarrassingly, the report was found to be loaded with errors. It nevertheless catalogued 169 significant terrorist events in 2003, the "highest annual count in twenty years."[67] The report was subsequently revised.

NSS: Factors That Do Cause Terrorism

Political Alienation, Lack of Voice, and Terrorism

The NSS states that "transnational terrorists are recruited from people who have no voice in their own government and see no legitimate way to promote change in their own country."[68] As terrorism is often viewed as a violent form of political expression resulting from a particular grievance, some have suggested that the absence of democracy—or democratic institutions—contributes to terrorism, and correspondingly, the presence of oppressive political systems tends to spawn or cultivate militant proterrorism ideologies. This argument is particularly important for the United States, which has based some of its foreign policy—and particularly the notion of "transformational diplomacy"[69]—on this contention. The U.S. government asserts a strong inverse relationship between democracy and terrorism: "Democracy is the opposite of terrorist tyranny, which is why the terrorists denounce it. . . . The advance of freedom and human dignity through democracy is the long-term solution to the transnational terrorism of today."[70]

The link between oppressive governance and terrorism seems to be supported by the case of al-Qaeda's top two leaders, Osama bin Laden and Ayman al-Zawahiri, who come from countries, Saudi Arabia and Egypt, respectively, that are largely authoritarian and provide only scant public space—if any at all—for dissenting political views. Paul Pillar argues that political repression (including a general frustration with one's rulers or system of government) is one of the most important factors generating terrorism: "People who are angry over such issues are more likely to resort to extreme measures, including terrorism and other forms of violence, than ones who are not."[71]

A recent Harvard University study supports the notion that the type of political system within a particular country is more predictive than poverty per se of terrorist activity. The study recognizes that within the "root causes" controversy, "the widespread view that poverty creates terrorism has dominated much of this debate."[72] However, the study suggests that the type of political system and degree of political freedom determine whether a country is prone to terrorism. The study concludes that "countries with intermediate levels of political freedom are shown to be more prone to terrorism than countries with high levels of political freedom or countries with highly authoritarian regimes."[73] As countries transition from authoritarian regimes to more liberal (democratic) regimes, this phase "may be accompanied by temporary increases in terrorism."[74] This may explain why the problem of "quasi-states" can be just as problematic as failed states, in terms of their ability to host—purposely or inadvertently—terrorist organizations. Quasi-states, defined as states with semifunctional but incomplete governance, tend to lie in the intermediate range, between authoritarianism and high levels of political freedom.[75]

One major shortcoming of the oppressive political systems or lack of democracy thesis is that many of the adherents of al-Qaeda's—and similar Salafists'—ideology have been based in Western Europe, where democratic and free expression is regularly allowed and encouraged. The NSS acknowledges this anomaly but simply encourages "deepening the reach of democracy [in these particular countries] so that all citizens enjoy its benefits."[76] However, such a prescription may be inadequate for a variety of complex reasons. As Gerard Alexander asserts, "authoritarianism is not a sufficient condition for extremism. . . . Al-Qaeda-type beliefs have found support among at least some Muslims in democratic Turkey and western Europe."[77]

This is important because a key component of President Bush's counterterror strategy—and one of the key arguments put forth to justify the invasion of Iraq—is the desire to counter or undermine tyrannous regimes that breed "despair and anger."[78] Terrorism scholar Walter Laqueur has suggested the uncomfortable proposition that democratic systems of governance may be the most hospitable to terrorism and that "terrorism has never had a chance in an effective dictatorship."[79] According to Laqueur:

> [The] historical record shows that while, in the nineteenth century, terrorism frequently developed in response to repression, the correlation between grievance and terrorism in our day and age is far less obvious. The historical record shows that the more severe the repression, the less terrorism tends to occur. This is an uncomfortable shocking fact, and has, therefore, encountered much resistance. But it is still true that terrorism in Spain gathered strength only after Franco died, that the terrorist upsurge in West Germany, France, and Turkey took place under social democratic or left-of-center governments, that the same is true with regard to Peru and Colombia, and that more such examples could easily be adduced.[80]

Grievances and Terrorism

A second cause of terrorism, according to the NSS, is the presence of grievances that can be blamed on others. Some have argued that unpopular U.S. foreign policy choices—excessive support of Israel (at the expense of Palestinians), military action in Afghanistan or Iraq, or inaction on key global issues (e.g., climate change)—create "political oxygen" that fuels grievances that terrorists are later able to exploit.[81] In particular, the perceived inconsistency or lack of fairness in American foreign policy is sometimes listed as a key culprit in fueling grievances, particularly in the Muslim world. Some argue that the United States has a double standard in its foreign policy that is recognized and resented around the world. As the Pakistani scholar Egbal Ahmad asserts regarding U.S. foreign policy and terror: "Don't condone Israeli terror, Pakistani terror, Nicaraguan terror, El Salvadoran terror, on the one hand, and then complain about Afghan terror or Palestinian terror. It doesn't work."[82]

For his part, Osama bin Laden commonly cites lists of alleged U.S. injustices, which he then uses to justify his actions. As Stephen Zunes argues:

> [Osama bin Laden] is a businessman who—like any good businessman—knows how to take a popular fear or desire and use it to sell a product in this case anti-American terrorism. The grievances expressed in his manifestos—the ongoing U.S. military presence in the Gulf, the humanitarian consequences of the U.S.-led sanctions against Iraq, U.S. support for the Israeli government, and U.S. support for autocratic Arab regimes—have widespread appeal in that part of the world.[83]

Grievances are also created by what Thomas Friedman has described as the "poverty of dignity" that seems to exist in the Middle East. Specifically, Friedman argues: "What radicalized the September 11 terrorists was not that they suffered from a poverty of food, it was that they suffered from a poverty of dignity. Frustrated by the low standing of Muslim countries in the world, compared with Europe or the United States, and the low standing in which they were personally held where they were living, they were easy pickings for militant preachers who knew how to direct their rage."[84]

Dennis Ross, a former ambassador with extensive experience in the Middle East, also describes this region as one that is "characterized by a sense of indignity."[85] Part of this, Ross asserts, is related to a sense of loss over a glorious history. Another factor is the sense of betrayal regarding promises that were made after World War I. Ross notes that Osama bin Laden released a videotape following the September 11 attacks in the United States in which he referred to eighty years of humiliation in the Middle East, particularly after World War I when many Arabs were promised independence. "[N]ot only did they not get the independence," Ross asserts, "but their image of having one Arab state, which was going to be the key to reestablishing their glory, was also frustrated."[86]

Conspiracy, Misinformation, and Terrorism

A third contributing cause of terrorism is, according to the NSS, a pervasive environment of conspiracy and misinformation. The NSS states that "terrorists recruit more effectively from populations whose information about the world is contaminated by falsehoods and corrupted by conspiracy theories. The distortions keep alive grievances and filter out facts that would challenge popular prejudices and self-serving propaganda."[87] One of the most famous of these discredited conspiracy theories, which nevertheless continues to circulate around the world, relates to alleged action on the part of 4,000 Jewish employees who, it is claimed, failed to show up for work on September 11, 2001.[88]

In Indonesia, for instance, conspiracy theories related to terrorist attacks in the country (and outside) are rife. The U.S. government—and particularly the CIA—is often blamed as the "dark hand" behind various political developments, including the struggle in Aceh.[89] Sidney Jones of the International Crisis Group described another conspiracy theory related to Bali and other terrorist bombings: "The U.S. embassy issued a warning to its citizens to avoid public places in Indonesia twelve hours before the explosion. The CIA picked a place that few Americans frequented. It supplied the materials for the bomb. It then tried to blame al-Qaeda and radical Islam in an effort to win support for a war against Iraq, and offered to help with the investigation as a way of infiltrating American troops into Indonesia so they can eventually establish a new foothold in Southeast Asia."[90] In Europe, moreover, large numbers of Germans, French, and other Europeans (although still a minority) "believe in a secret American conspiracy surrounding 9/11."[91] The large number of conspiracy theories suggests that the U.S. government needs to increase the amount and quality of its information diplomacy—sometimes called "strategic communication"—around the world. However, such information must be credible and perceived as legitimate, not merely as propaganda.

Terrorism Ideology as a "Root Cause" of Terrorism

The NSS argues that terrorism partially springs from "an ideology that justifies murder."[92] It elaborates that "terrorism ultimately depends upon the appeal of an ideology that excuses or even glorifies the deliberate killing of innocents."[93] This is consistent with others who argue that ideology is the foundation of terrorism movements. Ideology here is simply meant as "a systematic body of concepts especially about human life or culture."[94] As Paul Davis and Brian Jenkins aptly state: "Although political, social, and economic factors are among the root causes of problems that foster terrorism, it should also be emphasized that [in the case of contemporary militant Islamist groups] the perverse extremist view of Islam that has been so prominently taught in some Islamist circles is another root cause."[95] For this reason, much of U.S. counterterrorism strategy is focused on addressing and countering extremist ideology because "[i]t is ideological belief, reinforced by propaganda operations, that convinces recruits and supporters that their actions are morally justifiable."[96]

In addition to terrorism ideology, the "profession" of terrorism itself—and its attractiveness—is another closely related root cause. Terrorism can almost be thought of as a "way of life" in which the terrorists themselves attain certain benefits including status and psychological rewards.[97] Terrorists may choose their particular vocation because it comes with opportunities to accumulate "power, prestige, privilege, and even wealth."[98] Moreover, it may be unrealistic to presume that terrorists will voluntarily cease being terrorists, or "retire." "Terrorists whose only sense of significance comes from being terrorists cannot be forced to give up terrorism, for to do so would be to lose their very reason for being."[99]

From this vantage point, desire for power, prestige, and status can thus be thought of as a root cause of terrorism. For example, Velupillai Prabhakaran, leader of the Liberation Tigers of Tamil Eelam, dropped out of school at age sixteen and began to associate with Tamil "activist gangs," with which he later participated in a kidnapping. In 1972, he helped form a militant group known as the New Tamil Tigers, and became its co-leader at age twenty-one.[100] Prabhakaran later assassinated Jaffna's newly elected mayor, an act that gained him national notoriety. Prabhakaran "won considerable power and prestige as a result of the deed, which he announced by putting up posters throughout Jaffna to claim responsibility."[101] Prabhakaran then consolidated control and power over his organization, which he later renamed the Liberation Tigers of Tamil Eelam (in 1976). In the case of Prabhakaran, individual motivation, ambition, and ruthlessness provide a glimpse into the "root cause" of terrorism.

The Past as Prologue: Wave Transitions and the Future of Terrorism

Apart from analyzing root causes, another means of gaining strategic insight into likely causes and trends in international terrorism is to incorporate a framework that emphasizes historic transitions. As noted in Chapter 2, the four-wave model of modern terrorism proposed by David Rapoport informs readers that terrorism unfolded or flourished within the context of larger shifts or tensions in the international community. Examination of these tensions (and the international environment generally) may yield clues regarding the likely course of terrorism, and thus may potentially provide policymakers with advance knowledge for purposes of prevention (or at least abatement) and, if that fails, preparation for the inevitable.

A cursory review of the four-waves framework reveals the following key transition points. First wave—anarchist—terrorism occurred within the context of a growing trend toward representative government. The second wave reflected the disintegration of empires and the rise of new, independent states.[102] The third wave occurred within the context of broader tensions in the international system, namely, the Vietnam War and, more broadly, the cold war itself.[103] Fourth-wave terrorism occurred within the context of rising religious values and certain precipitating events, such as the Soviet Union's invasion of Afghanistan and the Iranian revolution.

Moreover, analyzing the various objectives of each wave reveals certain interesting and persistent trends. The first and third waves appear similar in the sense that each had rather vague goals of undermining the extant system (including the system of governance within a particular country, or globally). Anarchists saw human government as a cause of human oppression: "In order for the masses to be free, the rulers must be killed."[104] Third-wave terrorists saw the capitalist-driven Western system as oppressive, particularly against third world populations.

By contrast, second-wave terrorists were perhaps the most practical—they had defined (politically and geographically) nationalist goals. However, second-wave terrorism did not exist in a vacuum. It was aided by the fact that "[b]oth colonialism and imperialism were no longer popular causes: jingoism had long since given way to guilt-ridden disillusion with any overseas military adventures."[105] In addition, the colonizers (such as Britain and France) were themselves financially strapped (after having undergone two world wars) and thus were not enthusiastic about maintaining their overseas possessions.

Fourth-wave terrorists arguably represent a hybrid between third- and second-wave terrorists. Some fourth-wave terrorists seek to take over key states, as part of a larger antisystemic ideological struggle, which is why some analysts have described the larger Salafist movement as a global insurgency. Jemaah Islamiyah, an al-Qaeda affiliate, sought to conduct multiple insurgencies in Southeast Asia to create a Daulah Islamiyah (Islamic state).[106] Simultaneously, some of the goals of fourth-wave terrorists have bordered on fantasy or operated on a cosmic level. Lee Harris argues that al-Qaeda is driven by a fantasy ideology and this has major implications for American counterterrorism efforts. "We are fighting an enemy who has no strategic purpose in anything he does—whose actions have significance only in terms of his own fantasy ideology. . . . It matters not how much stronger or more powerful we are than they—what matters is that God will bring them victory."[107] If al-Qaeda is pursuing vague political goals, then we must heed the warning issued by Walter Laqueur in 1977: "The less clear the political purpose in terrorism, the greater appeal to unbalanced persons."[108]

The wave model also provides insights into how tactical innovations transformed particular waves of terrorism. First-wave terrorism benefited from the invention of dynamite and incendiary bombs. Second-wave terrorists developed new tactics, such as guerrilla-like hit-and-run operations against government troops as well as assassination policies against police: "Second-wave strategy sought to eliminate the police—a government's eyes and ears—first, through systematic assassinations of officers and/or their families."[109] In third-wave terrorism, the rise of civil aviation provided new opportunities for terrorism: "the development of international civil aviation . . . created new vulnerabilities and lucrative targets for the terrorist to exploit."[110] Hijacking became a prominent tool, in addition to the invention and application of barometric pressure bombs on aircraft.[111] Similarly, advances in telecommunications also made their impact with third-wave terrorists. Hijackings would lead to negotiations with governments, which could in turn be aired on live television, thus creating the "high drama" necessary to advance a particular terrorist cause.

This use of communication tools becomes even more important in fourth-wave terrorism, particularly with the rise of the Internet, video-uplink technology, and computer-assisted manipulation of video and still images. Fourth-wave terrorism has also seen increased application of chemical, biological, radiological, and nuclear (CBRN) weapons, although some writers argue that the most likely scenario involves chemical and biological weapons, rather than nuclear. Chris Quillen argues that changes in human lifestyles—notably increased urbanization and the clustering of large populations in confined buildings—provides an invitation to use chemical or biological weapons.[112]

Finally, the wave model provides key insights about transitions and decline in terrorism trends. For instance, first-wave terrorism declined because of generational change and changing political moods, not to mention the onset of two world wars. Second-wave terrorism declined because of the success of the terrorist movements: "it is indisputable that, at the very least, the tactical 'successes' and political victories won through violence by groups like the Irgun, EOKA [Ethniki Organosis Kyprion Agoniston, or National Organization of Cypriot Fighters], and the FLN [Front de Libération Nationale, or National Liberation Front, Algeria] clearly demonstrated that—notwithstanding the repeated denials of the governments they confront—terrorism does 'work.'"[113]

Third-wave terrorism, like its first-wave antecedent, declined because of generational change—the ideology could not sustain beyond the first generation—and because of the decline of the cold war. Moreover, the ideology underpinning third-wave terrorism appeared rather ephemeral: "These movements [of the third wave], are more analogous to tiny gangs of bandits than to serious political movements."[114] Rapoport maintains that fourth-wave terrorism is scheduled to end in 2025; however, given the power of religion as a force in societies confronting disruptive and cataclysmic social and economic change, the 2025 date may be a bit optimistic. Religious terrorism could in fact lead to a double wave—a "super wave"—that could span 100 years or so. The first, second, and third waves were essentially secular waves. One could argue that terrorism infused with religious ideology has much greater sustainability.

Will fourth-wave terrorism continue throughout the twenty-first century? Or will it be replaced by a fifth wave that features another set of (perhaps nonreligious) grievances? As described above, the wave model and similar theories emphasize the environmental conditions in the international system that shape terrorism. "Terrorism is a by-product of broader historical shifts in the international distribution of power in all of its forms—political, economic, military, ideological, and cultural."[115] Thus, based on this framework, it is plausible that a major event—perhaps a world war or an environmental or health-related cataclysmic incident—could create the conditions that facilitate the rise of a new wave.

Alternatively, as suggested above, the fourth wave may simply continue, although its exact nature may evolve to a different form. Jessica Stern, for instance, has described the protean nature of al-Qaeda. "This capacity for change has consistently made [al-Qaeda] more appealing to recruits, attracted surprising new allies and—most worrisome from a Western perspective—made it harder to detect and destroy."[116] From this perspective, it is plausible that al-Qaeda could actually disappear and be replaced by new groups that carry on the militant Salafist struggle.

The Future Unveiled: Conditions That Will Shape Terrorism in the Years and Decades Ahead

Although specific terrorist acts and plots cannot be accurately predicted—without direct and actionable intelligence—the larger enabling or environmental conditions that will shape terrorism in the future are much more amenable to forecasting. This chapter asserts that seven key trends will define terrorism (and its evolution) in the decades ahead; moreover, these trends may perpetuate the current fourth wave of terrorism, or may precipitate the transition to a fifth or even sixth wave. Many of these trends are in motion today and are readily apparent; in fact, in some countries they are being experienced in their "acute" phase. However, the chapter maintains that these various trends will become even greater determinants of the larger terrorism-enabling environment in the decades to come.

The first of these trends is demographic—a major underlying trend that manifests in a number of ways. Historically, terrorists tend to be young adults, and, moreover, since the 1960s, many have come from the Middle East and North Africa. In light of these facts, the *World Development Report*'s demographic projections for this region may raise some concerns: "The MENA [Middle East and North Africa] region has about 100 million young people aged 12 to 24. The number of young people in these countries will peak in the next 25 years."[117] Viewed in isolation, large numbers of young people should not cause alarm; however, burgeoning numbers of youth without a corresponding increase in educational, and, most important, employment opportunities may present a different picture.

The *World Development Report* notes that while youth populations are growing, unemployment continues to be a challenge: "Average unemployment rates are highest among youth and adults in MENA, when compared to all other developing regions. The share of young people among the region's unemployed is higher than 50 percent in most countries."[118] The report notes that in Egypt, Qatar, and Syria, youth comprise more than 60 percent of the unemployed, while in Tunisia, the unemployment rate for young people between twenty and twenty-four years old is more than three times that of individuals over the age of forty.[119] According to the National Intelligence Council (NIC) 2020 report, "Alienation among unemployed youths will swell the ranks of those vulnerable to terrorist recruitment."[120]

Demographic trends will also manifest in other ways that will almost certainly have implications for terrorism and political violence. Urbanization must be counted as one of the most important of subtrends; today roughly 50 percent of the world's population currently lives in cities. This number is expected to rise to 60 percent in the next thirty years.[121] For terrorists and insurgents, the growth of urban areas presents a number of opportunities. As Frank Hoffman writes, "would-be insurgents and terrorists are going where the people and money are, and seek security by hiding among the population and the complexity of a modern metropolis."[122] Terrorists may be able to exploit the instability and lack of public security that will inevitably be present in certain urban areas, particularly in developing countries.[123]

Another opportunity for terrorists relates to the clustering of populations in finite geographical areas. "Advanced societies concentrate valuable things and people in order to achieve economies of scale."[124] But such clustering can provide an irresistible target for a mass casualty terrorist employing either conventional or CBRN weapons, a prospect that is particularly appealing since urban areas also feature another advantage that is critical to the success of a terrorist operation: extensive media presence and coverage.

The second key trend is globalization. To the extent that globalization underpins or exacerbates international terrorism in the contemporary context, this factor is likely to play an even more important role in the decades ahead (barring some major cataclysmic, international, systemic-altering event). Moreover, if poverty is linked to terrorism—as some believe—then this "root cause" is likely to become more severe in the wake of rising and unrestrained globalization in the years ahead. "Over the next fifteen years, gaps will widen between those countries benefiting from globalization—economically, technologically, and socially—and those underdeveloped nations or pockets within nations that are left behind."[125]

Global poverty—exacerbated by uneven globalization—may influence terrorism in a number of ways. Susan Rice, a former assistant secretary of state for African affairs, argues that terrorism often flourishes within a complex web of transnational security threats—disease, crime, environmental degradation—that often "emerge from impoverished, relatively remote regions of the world."[126] Poverty, joblessness and lack of hope within key populations—namely unemployed, educated youth—may render them vulnerable to recruitment by militant organizations. On a more strategic level, moreover, poverty "bears indirectly on terrorism by sparking conflict and eroding state capacity, both of which create conditions that can facilitate terrorist activity."[127]

International migration—a key process in globalization—may help ameliorate or soften the differences between richer and poorer countries, particularly as remittances help reduce poverty at the grassroots level.[128] In 2005, migrants remitted more than US$233 billion worldwide, with about US$167 billion flowing directly to developing countries.[129]

However, the migration "safety valve" will always be vulnerable to occasional backlash and xenophobia in migrant-receiving states. Developed countries are increasingly raising barriers to international migrants; some states are characterizing illegal migration as a security threat and are deploying military forces to guard land and maritime borders. As legal avenues for migration evaporate, potential migrants are turning to human smuggling and trafficking syndicates. It is estimated that global criminal syndicates smuggle or traffic roughly one million individuals per year, about half of whom are subjected to sexual exploitation.[130] The illegal trade in people is extremely lucrative; along the U.S.-Mexican border, for example, criminal gangs earn between US$6–9 billion annually smuggling people from Mexico to the United States.[131]

In addition, the process of globalization itself—a force that many believe can actually help reduce poverty—will likely be resisted if it is identified as "Americanization," which many see as "threatening to their cultural and religious values."[132] As globalization proceeds, some may view it as American hegemony in disguise; others may see globalization as a hegemonic cultural consolidation of diverse peoples into a single ideological "culture of liberalization, privatization, and marketization."[133] Such transformation will invariably stimulate resistance. As Jessica Stern has claimed, the "jihadi idea" is emerging as the "cool" and fashionable way to express dissatisfaction "with the status quo—with globalization, with America's dominant role in the world, with the power elite."[134] This is particularly true for Muslims living in Europe. Thus, the relentless power of globalization is likely to carry the seeds of its own destruction—or at least its opposition.

The third key trend, which is intimately related to globalization, is the spread of transnational crime. Globalization has emboldened ethnic-specific criminal organizations to set up operations far beyond their home operating zones. Mexican drug-trafficking cartels, for instance, have expanded their operations to Peru, even to the point that they have had "several members of the [Peruvian] police and army on their payroll."[135] Many newly independent former Soviet states have emerged as veritable exporters of transnational crime. In the former Soviet republic of Georgia, organized crime syndicates have moved abroad and "established new networks in Europe, Russia, and the U.S."[136] In Europe, Georgian organized crime groups are involved in an array of illegal activities including money laundering, smuggling (commodities, people, and narcotics), and bankruptcy fraud.[137] Moreover, criminal groups are forming alliances of convenience throughout the world. Georgian criminal groups have teamed up with Russian and Albanian organized crime to conduct criminal activities in Western Europe.[138]

Transnational crime helps to undermine states by infecting their apparatus and institutions. Phil Williams contends that this "infection" can occur on several levels. First, the criminal enterprise may simply take over "at least parts of the state apparatus, resulting in . . . a captured state."[139] Or the state itself could evolve into a virtual "continuing criminal enterprise."[140] Alternatively, the state may evolve in a way such that "personal enrichment and state survival become so bound that they are impossible to separate."[141] For these reasons, crime is emerging and transforming from a local law-enforcement problem to an international-security challenge. Criminal organizations are growing in power in many parts of the world.

The rise of crime has a number of key implications for terrorism. A state that is infected with transnational crime can also become vulnerable to terrorist organizations because of a nexus that may exist between criminal organizations—or criminal enterprises—and terrorist or insurgent organizations. Terrorism in Chechnya, for instance, is virtually sustained by organized crime. "Commonly referred to as a haven for organized crime, Chechnya has given terrorists the opportunity to profit from the illegal sale of oil, trafficking in illicit narcotics and weapons, and kidnapping."[142] In Iraq, according to the Iraq Study Group, "organized criminal rackets thrive . . . [and] some criminal gangs cooperate with, finance, or purport to be part of the Sunni insurgency or a Shiite militia in order to gain legitimacy."[143] Transnational crime can provide a stateless milieu in which terrorism can flourish without worries of strong state intervention.

In the wake of declining state support for terrorism, transnational crime provides a critical alternative platform. In Peru, for instance, areas that are used for coca cultivation "are in areas where the Shining Path (Sendero Luminoso: SL) has its strongest presence, namely the Upper Huallaga Valley and Apurimac-Ene River Valleys."[144] Tamara Makarenko asserts that globalization has intensified the evolution and symbiosis between transnational crime and terrorist organizations: Moreover, in some cases the relationship has evolved into "convergence" in which "criminal and terrorist organizations could converge into a single group simultaneously exhibiting characteristics of both."[145]

The fourth key trend, which is significantly related to the third, is the problem of weak, failed, or quasi-states. A number of factors can lead to weak states: poor governance, poor economic planning, demographic issues, health issues, environmental factors, and many others. Whatever the cause, failed states are seen as a key problem for the spread of terrorism in the twenty-first century, and, moreover, quasi-states (states that are reasonably functional, but not entirely so) are also dangerous. According to Jorg Rabb and H. Brinton Milward, "there is increasing evidence of a close connection between al-Qaeda and the failed states of Liberia, Sierra Leone, and Burkina Faso in West Africa."[146] They contend that terrorism, arms trafficking, commodities smuggling (diamonds, in particular, in West Africa), and failed states provide the basis for transnational violence.

Failing states may also contribute to the problem of ungoverned spaces, which could provide terrorists with safe havens. Alternatively, such spaces may emerge as the domain of criminal syndicates that "may take virtual control of regions within failing states to which the central government cannot extend its writ."[147] In the tri-border area of South America (which includes Argentina, Brazil, and Paraguay), a lack of "effective government controls, weak law enforcement, and open frontiers" provides an enabling environment for criminals and terrorists whose "relationship can at times be seen as symbiotic."[148]

A fifth key trend, related to the problem of weak or failing states, is the global challenge of climate change. In April 2007, a distinguished panel of retired U.S. military generals and admirals released a report describing the various security implications of global climate change. Among other things, they noted that climate change acts as a "threat multiplier for instability in some of the most volatile regions of the world."[149] Climate change—manifesting as extreme weather events, drought, flooding, sea level rise, increased cyclone activity, retreating glaciers, and rapidly spreading diseases—may foster the destabilization of weak or failing states and thus cultivate "the conditions for internal conflict, extremism, and movement toward increased authoritarianism and radical ideologies."[150]

Since early 2002, American counterterrorism policy has been grounded within a framework of creating or sustaining an international system comprised of healthy, well-governed states that have the capacity and willingness to cooperate with the United States. Climate change, however, is threatening to undermine this goal. Many Muslim-majority countries, with which the United States is hoping to forge long-term counterterrorism alliances—for example, countries such as Indonesia or Bangladesh—are geographically positioned within tropical zones that will likely face significant and devastating effects from climate change. The net result will be increased possibilities for terrorist organizations—or their precursor political organizations—to gain a foothold within those societies and acquire legitimacy.

Climate change not only poses a functional threat to state capacity (thus resulting in a reduced ability to counter potential terrorist threats), it also potentially threatens the United States from an ideational or strategic communication perspective. As residents of poor developing countries—whether Muslim-majority or not—see their livelihoods literally wash away, they may be reminded by firebrand jihadi or anti-globalization speakers or commentators that the source of their misery is ultimately the United States and the global economic system that it dominates. If the United States continues to be perceived as an obstacle to solving (or at least mitigating) the climate change threat, it may be particularly vulnerable to such accusations, whether they are properly grounded in science or not. Such charges may add to the global narrative that the international system, dominated by Western, Christian powers, is "rigged" in such a way so as to benefit only the rich, to the detriment of poorer—sometimes Muslim-majority—countries.

The sixth key trend is increasing ethnic and religious identity, from which conflicts are arising. As states decline in importance or power, many people revert to more basic ethnic or religious identity markers; thus, ethnicity and religious identity and affiliation will likely matter more in the twenty-first century. On the ethnic side, certain criteria are believed to be required before a group calls itself an ethnic community, including a common name, a belief in a common ancestry, shared historic experiences, shared culture (i.e., a bundle of factors including language, religion, customs, music, institutions, and possibly food), attachment to a specific piece of territory and a general sense of their common ethnicity.[151] As state identity diminishes, ethnic conflict may grow in those states comprised of multiethnic societies: "Groups will inevitably disagree about political, economic, and social issues, and in multiethnic countries the fault lines will often be defined in ethnic terms."[152]

Religious identity is also likely to grow stronger. The NIC report also notes that religion is likely to play an even more important role in the social and political life of countries than it does today. "Over the next fifteen years, religious identity is likely to become an increasingly important factor in how people define themselves."[153] Moreover, this identity is likely to be vigorous and passionate. The NIC report notes that many religious adherents are becoming "activists." "They have a worldview that advocates change of society, a tendency toward making sharp Manichaean distinctions between good and evil."[154]

Moreover, religious conflict and violence will be among the factors underpinning the future of warfare, according to Martin van Creveld.[155] Van Creveld argues that combatants in the future will not be armies but "groups whom we today call terrorists, guerillas, bandits, and robbers."[156] They will be motivated less by institutional norms and more by "fanatical, ideologically-based, loyalties."[157] This religious conflict may be centered as much on "intrareligious" disputes as on more traditional "interreligious" disputes. For example, what is unfolding in Iraq, according to Niall Ferguson, is not a clash between the West and Islam, but rather "increasingly, a clash within Islamic civilization itself."[158] This is consistent with the findings of the *Iraq Study Group Report*, which stated that al-Qaeda (and its affiliated movement) seeks to instigate "a wider sectarian war between Iraq's Sunni and Shia, [to thus drive] the United States out of Iraq."[159]

The seventh major trend will be the desire on the part of terrorists to achieve increasingly "spectacular" results in their planned attacks. The 9/11 operations in New York and Washington, DC, significantly raised the standards of what constitutes notable and prestigious—from a terrorist perspective—catastrophic terrorism. A high body-count—as evidenced, for instance, by the transatlantic airliner bombing plot disrupted by British authorities in August 2006—has become the new standard for contemporary terrorists. This is why the CBRN element, despite criticism that such concerns are overblown and alarmist, is still important and relevant from a counterterrorism planning perspective. Certain CBRN-based attacks, if properly executed, would allow terrorists to achieve a higher level of violence. Moreover, the successful deployment of a CBRN weapon—even without a significant increase in mortality, compared to using more conventional means—would instill new levels of fear and psychological effects within the target population (and the international community generally), presumably increasing the international prestige of the terrorist group that dared to deploy it.

Recent evidence uncovered from disrupted plots or seized intelligence suggests that these concerns are not merely speculative or theoretical. In Chapter 1, for instance, it was noted that the Jordan chemical weapons plot was significant because it signaled a growing interest in turning to chemical weapons. It should also be recalled that the Jordan chemical plot planners genuinely hoped—and believed—that they could destroy more than 80,000 lives. Moreover, this is not an isolated case for al-Qaeda. A scientist affiliated with Jemaah Islamiyah, for instance, owned a company in Malaysia "that provided cover for his laboratory that was dedicated to CB [chemical and biological] research for al-Qaeda."[160] Moreover, as part of its "second wave" attack strategy for the United States (which was planned following the 9/11 attacks), al-Qaeda had intended to conduct a suicide airplane attack on a nuclear power plant within the United States (this idea was originally conceived in the early 1990s, as part of the Bojinka plot).[161] Khalid Sheikh Mohammed admitted to investigators that Mohammed Atta (the chief pilot in the 9/11 attacks in the United States) had "used a computer program to locate a nuclear power generating plant in Pennsylvania, which Bin Laden agreed to add to the list."[162] Later, when the attack plan was scaled back, the nuclear plant target was removed; however, its initial inclusion may indicate future plans to conduct such an attack.

Conclusion

Terrorism has existed throughout history, and, in some cases, it has succeeded in bringing about the desired change envisaged by the terrorists; thus, to the extent that terrorism is viewed by nonstate actors as an effective tool, it is not likely to abate anytime soon. Moreover, one of the key challenges to deterring or countering terrorism is the fact that the phenomenon itself is so complex and multifaceted.

This chapter has examined the various challenges involved in both identifying "root causes" of terrorism and determining the proper (or most efficacious) strategies that should be implemented to mitigate terrorism. Clearly, there is no easy answer, especially because there is no single threat of terrorism, but rather a myriad of groups that are motivated and driven by various agendas. It could be reasonably argued that no matter how well a government may design its counterterrorism measures, it will never completely eliminate terrorism.

Just as humans must contend with infectious diseases, they may also have to contend with terrorism as part of the human condition. Aldo Borgu summarizes this view: "At best terrorism can only be contained to the point where it is considered manageable. Spreading democracy worldwide, eradicating poverty, improving the delivery of basic services in Iraq or solving the Israel-Palestine issue will not eliminate the threat of terrorism. Attacking the so-called root causes of terrorism is important to deny the terrorists the chance of wider strategic success but it will not eliminate the threat of terrorist attacks themselves."[163]

However, with appropriate policies and cooperation between states and other nonstate actors, the threat of terrorism can at least be managed or contained. Greater reliance on "soft power"—what Joseph S. Nye defines as "the ability to get what you want through attraction rather than coercion or payments"[164]—rather than hard (military) power will likely generate a more long-term, sustainable environment that is inhospitable to terrorism. In addition, wealthy, developed states must understand that one key to mitigating terrorism lies in eliminating the enabling environment, and one way that this can be done is to cultivate a more equitable and fair international system.

Notes

Preface

1. *National Strategy for Combating Terrorism* (Washington, DC: White House, September 2006), 1, www.whitehouse.gov/nsc/nsct/2006/nsct2006.pdf (accessed March 26, 2007).

2. James A. Lewis, senior fellow, Technology and Public Policy Program, Center for Strategic and International Studies, transcript of statement before the House Committee on Government Reform Subcommittee on National Security, Emerging Threats, and International Relations, *Federal Document Clearing House Congressional Testimony,* September 19, 2006.

3. Eric Lichtblau and Mark Mazzetti, "Military Is Expanding Its Intelligence Role," *New York Times,* January 14, 2007, www.nytimes.com/2007/01/14/washington/14spy.html?ex=1326430800&en=8a893fe46c8a8c1c&ei=5088 (accessed May 4, 2007).

4. Ibid.

5. Associated Press, "Cheney Defends Bank and Credit Searches," January 14, 2007.

6. The full name of the USA PATRIOT Act is "Uniting and Strengthening America by Providing Appropriate Tools Required to Intercept and Obstruct Terrorism."

7. Charles Doyle, "The USA PATRIOT Act: A Legal Analysis," *Congressional Research Service: Report for Congress,* April 15, 2002, CRS1, www.fas.org/irp/crs/RL31377.pdf (accessed January 15, 2007).

8. Ibid.

9. *A Review of the Federal Bureau of Investigation's Use of National Security Letters* (Washington, DC: U.S. Department of Justice, Office of the Inspector General, March 2007), 45.

10. Ibid., 59.

11. President George W. Bush, transcript of remarks following a meeting on the PATRIOT Act, *Weekly Compilation of Presidential Documents,* January 3, 2006, 4.

12. This was the number for 2002. See Shankuan Zhu et al., "Obesity and Risk of Death Due to Motor Vehicle Crashes," *American Journal of Public Health,* 96, no. 4 (April 2006): 734.

13. David Blumenstein, "A Fresh Approach to Managing the Cost of Health Coverage: The Link Between Quality and Cost," *Benefits and Compensation Digest,* March 2006, 28.

14. Osama bin Laden, transcript of speech originally aired by Al-Jazeera Television on December 27, 2004, translated by Foreign Broadcast Information Service, January 31, 2005.

15. David C. Rapoport, "The Four Waves of Modern Terrorism," in *Attacking Terrorism: Elements of a Grand Strategy,* ed. Audrey Kurth Cronin and James M. Ludes (Washington, DC: Georgetown University Press, 2004), 62.

16. Bruce Hoffman, "Change and Continuity in Terrorism," *Studies in Conflict & Terrorism,* 24 (2001): 424.

17. Senator Russ Feingold of Wisconsin, *Congressional Digest,* April 2006, 111.

Chapter 1

1. Sebestyen Gorka and Richard Sullivan, "Jordanian Counterterrorist Unit Thwarts Chemical Bomb Attack," *Jane's Intelligence Review,* 16, no. 10 (October 1, 2004): 23.

2. "'Confessions' of Group Planning Jordan Chemical Attack," *BBC Monitoring International Reports,* April 26, 2004.

3. Ibid.

4. Ibid.

5. Ibid.

6. Ibid.

7. "Part Three: Topics—The Attacks of September 11, 2001," *Congressional Reports: Joint Inquiry into Intelligence Activities Before and After the Terrorist Attacks of September 11, 2001,* 310, http://a257.g.akamaitech.net/7/257/2422/24ju120031400/www.gpoaccess.gov/serialset/creports/pdf/part3.pdf (accessed October 26, 2006).

8. *The 9/11 Commission Report: Final Report of the National Commission on Terrorist Attacks Upon the United States* (New York: Norton, 2004), 153.

9. "Part Two: Narrative—The Attacks of September 11, 2001," *Congressional Reports: Joint Inquiry into Intelligence Activities Before and After the Terrorist Attacks of September 11, 2001,* 209, http://a257.g.akamaitech.net/7/257/2422/24ju120031400/www.gpoaccess.gov/serialset/creports/pdf/part2.pdf (accessed October 26, 2006).

10. Ibid., 210.

11. Ibid.

12. Ibid.

13. Ibid.

14. Ibid., 211.

15. Ibid.

16. Ibid.

17. Ibid., 212.

18. "Truck Overturns en route to Chemical Attack," *Los Angeles Times,* April 17, 2007, A4.

19. Testimony of General W.E. Gaskin, U.S. Marine Corps, Commanding General, Pentagon Briefing Studio, Arlington, Virginia, *Federal News Service,* March 30, 2007.

20. Richard Evans, "Global Jihad's Chemical Aspirations," *Jane's Terrorism & Security Monitor,* July 12, 2006.

21. Ibid.

22. As stated by Senator Richard Shelby of Alabama on *Face the Nation,* CBS, September 16, 2001 (Lexis-Nexis database).

23. *The 9/11 Commission Report,* 348.

24. "'Confessions' of Group Planning Jordan Chemical Attack."

25. Matt Bai, "Kerry's Undeclared War," *New York Times Magazine,* October 10, 2004, 38.

26. Richard W. Stevenson, "Bush Faults Kerry on Terrorism Remarks," *New York Times,* October 12, 2004, 23.

27. Raphael F. Perl, "Terrorism and National Security: Issues and Trends," *Congressional Research Service: Issue Brief for Congress* (order code 1B10119), March 9, 2006, 8.

28. Ed Blanche, "Ayman al-Zawahiri: Attention Turns to the Other Prime Suspect," *Jane's Intelligence Review,* 13, no. 11 (November 1, 2001): 18.

29. Gabriel Weimann, "www.terror.net: How Modern Terrorism Uses the Internet," *United States Institute of Peace Special Report,* no. 116 (March 2004): 1.

30. Walter Laqueur, "Postmodern Terrorism," *Foreign Affairs,* September–October 1996.

31. Perl, "Terrorism and National Security," 7.

32. Christine Hauser, "Scores Are Killed in Attack on Sri Lankan Convoy," *New York Times,* October 16, 2006, www.iht.com/articles/2006/10/16/news/blast.php (accessed October 16, 2006).

33. Paul Wilkinson, *Terrorism Versus Democracy: The Liberal State Response* (London: Frank Cass, 2002), 13.

34. Paul Medhurst, *Global Terrorism: A Course Produced by the United Nations Institute for Training and Research* (New York: United Nations, 2002), 5.

35. "The Order of the Day: Robespierre's Reign of Terror in the French Revolution," in *Encyclopedia of World Terrorism,* vol. 2 (Armonk, NY: M.E. Sharpe, 2003), 629.

36. Grant Wardlaw, *Political Terrorism: Theory, Tactics, and Counter-Measures* (New York: Cambridge University Press, 1989), 15.

37. Ibid.

38. "The Order of the Day," 629.

39. Audrey Kurth Cronin, "Rethinking Sovereignty: American Strategy in the Age of Terrorism," *Survival,* 44, no. 2 (Summer 2002): 121.

40. R. Thackrah, "Terrorism: A Definitional Problem," in *Contemporary Research on Terrorism,* ed. Paul Wilkinson and Alasdair M. Stewart (Aberdeen, UK: Aberdeen University Press, 1987), 38.

41. Jerrold Post, transcript of prepared testimony before the House Committee on Government Reform Subcommittee on National Security, Veterans Affairs, and International Relations, *Federal News Service,* October 12, 2001.

42. Wardlaw, *Political Terrorism,* 10.

43. Ibid.

44. Raphael Cohen-Almagor, "Foundations of Violence, Terror and War in the Writings of Marx, Engels and Lenin," *Terrorism and Political Violence,* 3, no. 2 (Summer 1991): 18.

45. Richard Drake, "Ideology and Terrorism in Italy: An Autobiography as Historical Source," *Terrorism and Political Violence,* 4, no. 2 (Summer 1992): 49.

46. Irina Paperno, "Exhuming the Bodies of Soviet Terror," *Representations,* no. 75 (Summer 2001): 89.

47. Ibid., 109.

48. Andrew Silke, "Terrorism and the Blind Men's Elephant," *Terrorism and Political Violence,* 8, no. 3 (Autumn 1996): 22.

49. Guenter Lewy, "The First Genocide of the 20th Century?" *Commentary,* 120, no. 5 (December 2005): 48.

50. Stephen A. Hart, "The Holocaust," in *Encyclopedia of World Terrorism,* vol. 1 (Armonk, NY: M.E. Sharpe, 1997), 98.

51. Walter Laqueur, "Reflections on Terrorism," in *The Terrorism Reader: The Essential Source Book on Political Violence Both Past and Present,* ed. Walter Laqueur and Yonah Alexander (New York: NAL / Penguin, 1987), 382.

52. Chris Quillen, "A Historical Analysis of Mass Casualty Bombers," *Studies in Conflict & Terrorism,* 25, no. 5 (September–October 2002): 282.

53. Executive Order on Terrorist Financing, "Blocking Property and Prohibiting Transactions with Persons Who Commit, Threaten to Commit, or Support Terrorism" (September 24, 2001), www.whitehouse.gov/news/releases/2001/09/20010924-1.html (accessed March 26, 2007).

54. General Assembly Resolution 51/210 Measures to Eliminate International Terrorism, 1999, accessed on May 16, 2007 at www.un.org/documents/ga/res/51/a51r210.htm.

55. Peter Chalk, "The Nature of Contemporary Terrorism," paper presented to the Council on Security Cooperation Asia-Pacific (CSCAP) Transnational Working Group, Sydney Australia, May 2001, 8.

56. Ayla Schbley, "Defining Religious Terrorism: A Causal and Anthological Profile," *Studies in Conflict & Terrorism,* 26, no. 2 (March–April 2003): 107.

57. Christopher Harmon, *Terrorism Today* (London: Frank Cass, 2000), 1.

58. Jessica Stern, *Terror in the Name of God: Why Religious Militants Kill* (New York: HarperCollins, 2003), xx.

59. Carlyle A. Thayer, "Al-Qaeda and Political Terrorism in Southeast Asia," in *Terrorism and Violence in Southeast Asia: Transnational Challenges to States and Regional Stability,* ed. Paul J. Smith (Armonk, NY: M.E. Sharpe, 2005), 81.

60. United Nations, *International Convention for the Suppression of the Financing of Terrorism,* http://untreaty.un.org/English/Terrorism/Conv12.pdf (accessed May 5, 2007).

61. I am indebted to Peter Chalk for this section; this is a modified version of Chalk's seven elements of terrorism, which include (1) political activity; (2) criminal behavior; (3) psychological warfare; (4) indiscriminate application; (5) targeting of noncombatants; (6) centrality of communication; and (7) conducted by nonstate actors. See Chalk, "The Nature of Contemporary Terrorism."

62. Ahmed Galal Ezeldin, *Terrorism and Political Violence: An Egyptian Perspective* (Chicago: Office of International Criminal Justice, University of Illinois at Chicago, 1987), 37.

63. Martha Crenshaw, "The Logic of Terrorism: Terrorist Behavior as a Product of Strategic Choice," in *Origins of Terrorism: Psychologies, Ideologies, Theologies, States of Mind,* ed. Walter Reich (Cambridge: Cambridge University Press, 1990), 19.

64. Ibid.

65. Ronald Spiers, "The Anatomy of Terrorism," *Foreign Service Journal,* September 2004, 44.

66. Ariel Merari, "Israel Facing Terrorism," *Israel Affairs,* 11, no. 1 (January 2005): 223–24.

67. D.C. Rapoport, "Why Does Religious Messianism Produce Terror?" in Wilkinson and Stewart, *Contemporary Research on Terrorism,* 74.

68. Harmon, *Terrorism Today,* 2.

69. Richard Bach Jensen, "Daggers, Rifles and Dynamite: Anarchist Terrorism in Nineteenth Century Europe," *Terrorism and Political Violence,* 16, no. 1 (Spring 2004): 140–41.

70. Bruce Hoffman and Gordon H. McCormick, "Terrorism, Signaling, and Suicide Attack," *Studies in Conflict & Terrorism,* 27, no. 4 (July–August 2004): 247.

71. Chalk, "The Nature of Contemporary Terrorism," 3.

72. Everett L. Wheeler, "Terrorism and Military Theory: An Historical Perspective," *Terrorism and Political Violence,* 3, no. 1 (Spring 1991): 21.

73. Audrey Kurth Cronin, "Behind the Curve: Globalization and International Terrorism," *International Security,* 27, no. 3 (Winter 2002–3): 33.

74. Paul K. Davis and Brian Michael Jenkins, *Deterrence and Influence in Counterterrorism: A Component in the War on Al-Qaeda* (Santa Monica, CA: RAND, 2002), 7.

75. Wilkinson, *Terrorism Versus Democracy,* 19.

76. Chalk, "The Nature of Contemporary Terrorism," 8.

77. Thomas J. Badey, "Defining International Terrorism: A Pragmatic Approach," *Terrorism and Political Violence,* 10, no. 1 (Spring 1998): 92.

78. *Combating Terrorism: Interagency Framework and Agency Programs to Address the Overseas Threat* (Washington, DC: General Accounting Office, May 2003), 13.

79. Ibid.

80. Ezeldin, *Terrorism and Political Violence,* 14.

81. "NEA Called a 'Terrorist Organization,'" *St. Petersburg Times,* February 24, 2004, www.sptimes.com/2004/02/24/news_pf/Worldandnation/NEA_called_a_terrori .shtml (accessed February 12, 2005).

82. Kathleen Harris, "NDP Berates Wal-Mart," *Winnipeg Sun,* February 12, 2005, www.canoe.ca/NewsStand/WinnipegSun/Business/2005/02/12/pf-928752.html (accessed February 12, 2005).

83. Samuel M. Makinda, "Global Governance and Terrorism," *Global Change,* 15, no. 1 (February 2003): 48.

84. Chalk, "The Nature of Contemporary Terrorism," 1.

85. Martha Crenshaw, *Terrorism and International Cooperation* (New York: Institute for East-West Security Studies, 1989), 5.

86. Chalk, "The Nature of Contemporary Terrorism," 1.

87. Ian O. Lesser, "Countering the New Terrorism: Implication for Strategy," in *Countering the New Terrorism,* ed. Lesser et al. (Santa Monica, CA: RAND, 1999), 85, www.rand.org/pubs/monograph_reports/MR989/ (accessed January 31, 2007).

88. United Nations Office on Drugs and Crime, "Conventions Against Terrorism," www.odccp.org/odccp/terrorism_conventions.html (accessed March 26, 2007).

Chapter 2

1. Bruce Hoffman and Gordon H. McCormick, "Terrorism, Signaling, and Suicide Attack," *Studies in Conflict & Terrorism,* 27, no. 4 (July–August 2004): 259.

2. Ibid.

3. Rohan Gunaratna, "Organized Crime and International Terrorist Networks," in *The Global Threat of Terror: Ideological, Material and Political Linkages,* ed.

K.P.S. Gill and Ajai Sahni (New Delhi: Bulwark Books and Institute for Conflict Management, 2002), 257.

4. Ibid., 258.

5. Rory Miller, "Ireland and the Israeli-Palestinian Conflict," *Yale Israel Journal,* no. 8 (Winter 2006): 19.

6. Meredith Box and Gavan McCormack, "Terror in Japan: The Red Army (1969–2001) and Aum Supreme Truth (1987–2000)," *Critical Asian Studies,* 36, no. 1 (March 2004): 97.

7. Pamala L. Griset and Sue Mahan, *Terrorism in Perspective* (Thousand Oaks, CA: Sage, 2003), 51.

8. Ariel Merari, "Terrorism as a Strategy of Struggle: Past and Future," *Terrorism and Political Violence,* 11, no. 4 (Winter 1999): 59.

9. David C. Rapoport, "The Four Waves of Modern Terrorism," in *Attacking Terrorism: Elements of a Grand Strategy,* ed. Audrey Kurth Cronin and James M. Ludes (Washington, DC: Georgetown University Press, 2004), 47.

10. Ibid., 47.

11. Ibid.

12. Sayyid Qutb, *Milestones* (New Delhi: Islamic Book Service, 2002), 57.

13. Solomon Zeitlin, "Masada and the Sicarii," *Jewish Quarterly Review,* 55, no. 4 (April 1965): 302.

14. Richard A. Horsley, "The Sicarii: Ancient Jewish 'Terrorists,'" *Journal of Religion,* 59, no. 4 (October 1979): 444–45.

15. Ibid., 439.

16. Ibid., 440.

17. Ibid., 445.

18. Bruce Hoffman, "'Holy Terror': The Implications of Terrorism Motivated by a Religious Imperative," *Studies in Conflict & Terrorism,* 18, no. 4 (1995): 271.

19. Ibid.

20. Arie Perliger and Leonard Weinberg, "Jewish Self-Defense and Terrorist Groups Prior to the Establishment of the State of Israel: Roots and Traditions," *Totalitarian Movements and Political Religions,* 4, no. 3 (Winter 2003): 92.

21. Zeitlin, "Masada and the Sicarii," 304.

22. Ariel Merari, "The Readiness to Kill and Die: Suicide Terrorism in the Middle East," in *Origins of Terrorism: Psychologies, Ideologies, Theologies, and States of Mind,* ed. Walter Reich (Cambridge: Cambridge University Press, 1990), 201.

23. S. Zeitlin, "Zealots and Sicarri," *Journal of Biblical Literature,* 81, no. 4 (December 1962): 395.

24. Mia Bloom, *Dying to Kill: The Allure of Suicide Terror* (New York: Columbia University Press, 2005), 10.

25. Zeitlin, "Masada and the Sicarii," 302.

26. Bernard Lewis, "The Sources for the History of the Syrian Assassins," *Speculum,* 27, no. 4 (October 1952): 477.

27. Kevin M. McCarthy, "The Origin of Assassin," *American Speech,* 48, nos. 1/2 (Spring–Summer 1973): 78.

28. Jessica Stern, *The Ultimate Terrorists* (Cambridge: Harvard University Press, 1999), 15.

29. Charles E. Nowell, "The Old Man of the Mountain," *Speculum,* 22, no. 4 (October 1947): 497.

30. Ibid.

31. Ibid., 501–502.

32. Bernard Lewis, "Islamic Terrorism?" in *Terrorism: How the West Can Win,* ed. Benjamin Netanyahu (New York: Farrar, Straus, Giroux, 1986), 68.

33. David Rapoport, "Sacred Terror: A Contemporary Example from Islam," in Reich, *Origins of Terrorism,* 121.

34. Nowell, "The Old Man of the Mountain," 507.

35. Lewis, "Islamic Terrorism?" 69.

36. Stern, *The Ultimate Terrorists,* 15.

37. Ibid.

38. David Kinsley, "Freedom from Death in the Worship of Kali," *Numen,* 22, fasc. 3 (December 1975): 184.

39. David C. Rapoport, "Fear and Trembling: Terrorism in Three Religious Traditions," *American Political Science Review,* 78, no. 3 (September 1984): 660.

40. Ibid., 658–77.

41. "Czolgosz Guilty," *New York Times,* September 25, 1901, 1.

42. "No Partner in Crime," *Washington Post,* September 8, 1901, 5.

43. "After Paterson Anarchists," *New York Times,* September 11, 2001, 3.

44. "Chicago Anarchists Free," *Washington Post,* September 24, 1901, 2.

45. "Emma Goldman Is Arrested in Chicago," *New York Times,* September 11, 1901, 2.

46. Ibid.

47. "Chicago Anarchists Free," 2.

48. Norman M. Naimark, "Terrorism and the Fall of Imperial Russia," *Terrorism and Political Violence,* 2, no. 4 (Winter 1990): 171–72.

49. Bruce Hoffman, *Inside Terrorism* (New York: Columbia University Press, 1998), 17.

50. Ibid.

51. Ibid., 18.

52. Thomas G. Otte, "Russian Anarchist Terror," in *Encyclopedia of World Terrorism,* vol. 1 (Armonk, NY: M.E. Sharpe, 1997), 55.

53. Ibid.

54. Ibid.

55. Hoffman, *Inside Terrorism,* 19.

56. Sergey [Sergei] Nechaev, "Catechism of the Revolutionist (1869)," in *Voices of Terror: Manifestos, Writings and Manuals of Al-Qaeda, Hamas, and Other Terrorists from Around the World and Throughout the Ages,* ed. Walter Laqueur (New York: Reed Press, 2004), 72.

57. Ibid., 73.

58. Vladimir G. Simkhovitch, "Russia's Struggle with Autocracy," *Political Science Quarterly,* 20, no. 1 (March 1905): 118.

59. Samuel Rezneck, "The Political and Social Theory of Michael Bakunin," *American Political Science Review,* 21, no. 2 (May 1927): 275.

60. Otte, "Russian Anarchist Terror," 54.

61. Mikhail Bakunin, "Revolution, Terrorism, Banditry," in Laqueur, *Voices of Terror,* 70.

62. Vladimir Simkhovitch presents this case; he insists that Russian revolutionary terrorism was a very distinct phenomenon from anarchist terrorism. He states that "it seems utterly impossible to class even the Russian terrorists of a quarter of a century ago as anarchists." See Simkhovitch, "Russia's Struggle with Autocracy," 120–21.

63. Hoffman, *Inside Terrorism*, 19.

64. Marie Fleming, "Propaganda by the Deed: Terrorism and Anarchist Theory in Late Nineteenth Century Europe," in *Terrorism in Europe*, ed. Yonah Alexander and Kenneth A. Myers (New York: St. Martin's Press, 1982), 16.

65. Hoffman, *Inside Terrorism*, 19.

66. Richard Bach Jensen, "The United States, International Policing and the War Against Anarchist Terrorism, 1900–1914," *Terrorism and Political Violence*, 13, no. 1 (Spring 2001): 16.

67. "Prince Bismarck on Anarchists," *New York Times*, September 23, 1898, 10.

68. Walter Laqueur, *The New Terrorism: Fanaticism and the Arms of Mass Destruction* (New York: Oxford University Press, 1999), 20.

69. Chris Flood, "French Anarchist Terror," *Encyclopedia of World Terrorism* (New York: M.E. Sharpe, 1997), 57.

70. "Why They Were Hanged," *New York Times*, November 12, 1887, 1.

71. Everett Carter, "The Haymarket Affair in Literature," *American Quarterly*, 2, no. 3 (Autumn 1950): 270–71.

72. Charles A. Madison, "Anarchism in the United States," *Journal of the History of Ideas*, 6, no. 1 (January 1945): 59.

73. Ibid., 58.

74. Richard Bach Jensen, "Daggers, Rifles and Dynamite: Anarchist Terrorism in Nineteenth Century Europe," *Terrorism and Political Violence*, 16, no. 1 (Spring 2004): 140–41.

75. Ibid.

76. Rapoport, "The Four Waves of Modern Terrorism," 49.

77. Flood, "French Anarchist Terror," 57.

78. Paul Berman, *Terror and Liberalism* (New York: Norton, 2003), 37.

79. Tom Bowden, "The Irish Underground and the War of Independence 1919–21," *Journal of Contemporary History*, 8, no. 2 (April 1973): 13.

80. John Bowyer Bell, "Terror in Ireland 1916–1923," *Encyclopedia of World Terrorism*, vol. 1, 66.

81. Bowden, "The Irish Underground," 14.

82. "Irish Rebels Freed," *Washington Post*, June 16, 1917, 3.

83. Bowden, "The Irish Underground," 14.

84. Bell, "Terror in Ireland 1916–1923," 67.

85. Rapoport, "The Four Waves of Modern Terrorism," 52–53.

86. Bowden, "The Irish Underground," 10.

87. Tim Moreman, "Terror in Colonial India 1900–1947," in *Encyclopedia of World Terrorism*, vol. 1, 165.

88. Ibid.

89. Ibid.

90. Ibid., 166.

91. Robert H. Kupperman and Darrell M. Trent, *Terrorism: Threat, Reality, Response* (Stanford, CA: Hoover Institution Press, 1979), 19.

92. Horsley, "The Sicarii," 444.

93. Arie Perliger and Leonard Weinberg, "Jewish Self-Defence and Terrorist Groups Prior to the Establishment of the State of Israel: Roots and Traditions," *Totalitarian Movements and Political Religions*, 4, no. 3 (Winter 2003): 108.

94. Ibid., 109.

95. Ibid.

96. Ibid., 100.

97. Ibid.

98. Hoffman, *Inside Terrorism*, 51.

99. Menachem Begin, *The Revolt: Story of the Irgun* (New York: Henry Schuman, 1951), 220.

100. Ibid., 227.

101. Perliger and Weinberg, "Jewish Self-Defence and Terrorist Groups," 104.

102. Laqueur, *The New Terrorism*, 23.

103. Hoffman, *Inside Terrorism*, 61.

104. Ibid.

105. Ibid., 62.

106. Homer Bigart, "2 Moslem Women to Die," *New York Times*, July 16, 1957, 5.

107. Thomas F. Brady, "Rebel Chief Seized in Algiers Gunfight," *New York Times*, September 25, 1957, 1.

108. Henry Tanner, "Algerian on Trial Lauds de Gaulle," *New York Times*, June 24, 1958, 5.

109. Ibid.

110. Martha Crenshaw, *Terrorism and International Cooperation* (New York: Institute for East-West Security Studies, 1989), 22.

111. Manuel Roig-Franzia, "A Terrorist in the House," *Washington Post*, February 22, 2004, W12, www.washingtonpost.com/ac2/wp-dyn/A48918–2004Feb17?language =printer (accessed October 11, 2006).

112. William Henry Chamberlin, "Terrorism in America," *Wall Street Journal*, March 8, 1954, 12.

113. "1972 Munich Olympics Massacre," Background Information Summaries, 2006, 2, available at http://web.ebscohost.com/ehost/detail?vid=4&hid=104&sid=1ee db399-b1f0–437b-86ed-e1f078cfd4fc%40sessionmgr106 (accessed May 16, 2007).

114. Hoffman, *Inside Terrorism*, 71.

115. "1972 Munich Olympics Massacre," 2.

116. "Bonn Panel Praises Handling of Munich," *New York Times*, September 19, 1972, 5.

117. Rapoport, "The Four Waves of Modern Terrorism," 56.

118. Hoffman, *Inside Terrorism*, 67.

119. "Dr. Wadi Haddad, Palestinian Mastermind of Hijackings," *Washington Post*, April 2, 1978, B4.

120. Ibid.

121. "Terrorist Murder Stuns a Germany Euphoric over Rapprochement," *Wall Street Journal*, December 1, 1989, A1.

122. Ibid.

123. Ely Karmon, *Coalitions Between Terrorist Organizations: Revolutionaries, Nationalists and Islamists* (Leiden/Boston: Martinus Nijhoff, 2005), 78.

124. Roger Thurow and Peter Gumbel, "Blunt and Brutal, the Chill of Terrorism Again Descends Upon Western Europe," *Wall Street Journal*, February 4, 1985, 27.

125. Thomas F. O'Boyle and Peter Gumbel, "Bombing Death of Top Siemens Official Rekindles German Fears of Terrorism," *Wall Street Journal*, July 10, 1986, 29.

126. "Terrorist Murder Stuns," A1.

127. Laqueur, *The New Terrorism*, 29.

128. Gianni Statera, "Student Politics in Italy: From Utopia to Terrorism," *Higher Education,* 8, no. 6 (November 1979): 659.

129. Richard Drake, "Italy in the 1960s: A Legacy of Terrorism and Liberation," *South Central Review,* 16, no. 4 (Winter 1999–Spring 2000): 66.

130. R.W. Apple, Jr., "Kidnappers End Silence, Releasing a Photo of Moro and a Statement," *New York Times,* March 19, 1978, 3.

131. "Text of Pope's Plea to Kidnappers," *New York Times,* April 23, 1978, 10.

132. Henry Tanner, "Moro Slain, Body Found in Rome; West's Leaders Assail Terror," *New York Times,* May 10, 1978, 21.

133. Statera, "Student Politics in Italy," 660.

134. Sari Gilbert, "Red Brigades in Verona Seize U.S. General," *Washington Post,* December 18, 1981, A1.

135. Ibid.

136. David Fleming, "Italian Police Rescue Dozier After 42 Days," *Wall Street Journal,* January 29, 1982, 32.

137. Henry Kamm, "Dozier Tells of 42 Days in a Pup Tent," *New York Times,* February 3, 1982, A3.

138. Ibid.

139. Henry Tanner, "General's Captors Issue a Statement," *New York Times,* December 20, 1981, 1.

140. Sari Gilbert, "Red Brigades Release Message and Snapshot of Gen. Dozier," *Washington Post,* January 26, 1982, A1.

141. Ibid.

142. Alison Jamieson, "The Italian Experience," in *Combating the Terrorists: Democratic Responses to Political Violence,* ed. H.H. Tucker (New York: Facts on File, 1988), 136.

143. Sari Gilbert, "Raid in Padua Frees Gen. Dozier," *Washington Post,* January 29, 1982, A1.

144. Richard Drake, "Italy in the 1960s," 67.

145. Ibid.

146. Ibid., 68.

147. Karmon, *Coalitions Between Terrorist Organizations,* 134.

148. Ibid.

149. Ibid., 135.

150. Ibid.

151. Ibid., 135–36.

152. Ibid., 140.

153. Eric Pace, "Arab Guerrillas Are Reported to Get Direct Shipments of Soviet Weapons," *New York Times,* September 18, 1972, 53.

154. Raphael Rothstein, "Israel: Fighting Terror with Terror," *Washington Post and Times Herald,* October 15, 1972, B3.

155. Ibid.

156. A.J. Jongman, "Trends in International and Domestic Terrorism in Western Europe, 1968–1988," *Terrorism and Political Violence,* 4, no. 4 (Winter 1992): 49.

157. Ibid.

158. "Red Brigades Arms Cache," *Washington Post,* February 7, 1982, A28.

159. Barry Davies, *Terrorism: Inside a World Phenomenon* (London: Virgin Books, 2003), 79.

160. Yoshihiro Kuriyama, "Terrorism at Tel Aviv Airport and a 'New Left' Group in Japan," *Asian Survey,* 13, no. 3 (March 1973): 336.

161. Davies, *Terrorism,* 79.

162. Kuriyama, "Terrorism at Tel Aviv Airport," 336.

163. "Japanese Guerrilla: No Regrets," *Washington Post and Times Herald,* July 14, 1972, A19.

164. Ibid.

165. Paul Lewis, "Israel Frees 1,150 to Obtain Release of Last 3 Soldiers," *New York Times,* May 21, 1985, A1.

166. Clyde Haberman, "Japan Protested Convict's Release," *New York Times,* May 22, 1985, A16.

167. Ibid.

168. Douglas Jehl, "Lebanon Seizes Japanese Radicals Sought in Terror Attacks," *New York Times,* February 19, 1997, A5.

169. Eric Pace, "The Black September Guerrillas: Elusive Trail in Seven Countries," *New York Times,* October 12, 1972, 1.

170. Ibid.

171. "People and Events: The Popular Front for the Liberation of Palestine" (background information for documentary titled "Hijacked!"), *American Experience,* www. pbs.org/wgbh/amex/hijacked/peopleevents/p_pflp.html (accessed March 26, 2007).

172. Jay Robert Nash, *Terrorism in the 20th Century: A Narrative Encyclopedia from the Anarchists, Through the Weathermen, to the Unabomber* (New York: M. Evans, 1998), 181.

173. Laqueur, *The New Terrorism,* 27.

174. Patricia G. Steinhoff, "Hijackers, Bombers, and Bank Robbers: Managerial Style in the Japanese Red Army," *Journal of Asian Studies,* 48, no. 4 (November 1989): 725.

175. Ibid., 726.

176. Paul Wilkinson, *Terrorism Versus Democracy: The Liberal State Response* (London: Frank Cass, 2002), 27.

177. Ibid.

178. Richard Drake, "Ideology and Terrorism in Italy: An Autobiography as Historical Source," *Terrorism and Political Violence,* 4, no. 2 (Summer 1992): 48.

179. Davies, *Terrorism,* 25.

180. Hoffman, *Inside Terrorism,* 73.

181. Wilkinson, *Terrorism Versus Democracy,* 26.

182. Michael A. Ledeen, "Soviet Sponsorship: The Will to Disbelieve," in Netanyahu, *Terrorism,* 91.

183. "Bali: Death Toll Set at 202," BBC News, February 19, 2003, http://news.bbc. co.uk/2/hi/asia-pacific/2778923.stm (accessed March 26, 2007).

184. Bruce Vaughn et al., "Terrorism in Southeast Asia," *Congressional Research Service: Report for Congress* (order code RL31672), February 7, 2005, 11.

185. International Crisis Group, "Jemaah Islamiyah in South East Asia: Damaged but Still Dangerous," *ICG Asia Report,* no. 63 (August 26, 2003): 1, www.crisisgroup. org/library/documents/report_archive/A401104_26082003.pdf.

186. Substitution for the testimony of Khalid Sheikh Mohammed, Defendant's Exhibit 941, *United States v. Moussaoui* (Cr. No. 01–455-A), 38–39, www.rcfp. org/moussaoui/pdf/DX-0941.pdf (accessed May 10, 2007).

187. International Crisis Group, "Jemaah Islamiyah in South East Asia," 1.

188. Magnus Ranstorp, "Hizbollah's Command Leadership: Its Structure, Decision-Making and Relationship with Iranian Clergy and Institutions," *Terrorism and Political Violence,* 6, no. 3 (Autumn 1994): 303–4.

189. Rapoport, "The Four Waves of Modern Terrorism," 61.

190. Brian Michael Jenkins, "Terrorism in the 1990s," address to the 26th Annual Seminar of the American Society for Industrial Security, Miami Beach, Florida, September 25, 1980, 5.

191. Taqi ud-Deen Ahmad Ibn Taymiyyah, "The Religious and Moral Doctrine of Jihad," in Laqueur, *Voices of Terror,* 393.

192. Quintan Wiktorowicz, "A Genealogy of Radical Islam," *Studies in Conflict & Terrorism,* 28, no. 2 (March/April 2005): 78.

193. Ibid.

194. Syed Abul Ala Maududi, "Jihad in Islam," in Laqueur, *Voices of Terror,* 398.

195. Ibid.

196. Wiktorowicz, "A Genealogy of Radical Islam," 78.

197. Sayed Qutb, "Jihad in the Cause of God," in Laqueur, *Voices of Terror,* 394.

198. Wiktorowicz, "A Genealogy of Radical Islam," 79.

199. Ibid.

200. Ibid.

201. Qutb, "Jihad in the Cause of God," 396.

202. Wiktorowicz, "A Genealogy of Radical Islam," 80.

203. Ibid., 84.

204. "Sheikh Abdullah Yusuf Azzam: A Short Biography," in Laqueur, *Voices of Terror,* 423.

205. Ibid.

206. "Al-Qa'eda Manual," in Laqueur, *Voices of Terror,* 403.

207. Raphael Perl, "Terrorism, the Future, and U.S. Foreign Policy," *Congressional Research Service: Issue Brief for Congress* (order code IB95112), March 6, 2003, 1.

208. Ibid., 6.

209. Jenkins, "Terrorism in the 1990s," 5.

210. Perl, "Terrorism, the Future, and U.S. Foreign Policy," 1.

211. Dana A. Shea, "Terrorism: Background on Chemical, Biological, and Toxin Weapons and Options for Lessening Their Impact," *Congressional Research Service: Report for Congress* (order code RL31669), December 1, 2004, 5.

212. Rapoport, "The Four Waves of Modern Terrorism," 62.

213. Rohan Gunaratna and Graeme C.S. Steven, *Counter-Terrorism: A Reference Handbook* (Santa Barbara, CA: ABC-CLIO, 2004), 70.

214. Lee Harris, "Al-Qaeda's Fantasy Ideology," *Policy Review,* no. 114 (August 2002): 29.

215. Wilkinson, *Terrorism Versus Democracy,* 19.

216. James Campbell, "On Not Understanding the Problem," in *Hype or Reality? The "New Terrorism" and Mass Casualty Attacks,* ed. Brad Roberts (Alexandria, VA: The Chemical and Biological Arms Control Institute, 2000), 21.

Chapter 3

1. Rama Kakshmi, "Indians Blame Attacks on Pakistan-Based Group," *Washington Post,* December 15, 2001, A23.

2. Pamela Constable, "India Recalls Pakistani Envoy," *Washington Post,* December 22, 2001, A12.

3. Xinhua General News Service, "India to Liquidate Terrorists, Sponsors," December 13, 2001.

4. Peter Beaumont, "War in Afghanistan: Border Crisis," *Guardian* (London), December 19, 2001, 6.

5. "India Mulls Tactics in Clash with Pakistan," *Financial Times,* December 20, 2001, 10.

6. Rahul Bedi, "General Says India Is 'Ready for War,'" *Irish Times,* January 12, 2002, 12; see also "Pakistan to Retaliate if Necessary to Indian Threat," Agence France Presse, December 27, 2001.

7. Rajiv Chandrasekaran, "Head of Army Declares India Is Ready for War," *Washington Post,* January 12, 2002, A14.

8. Rajiv Chandrasekaran, "Indian Missiles Put 'in Position,'" *Washington Post,* December 27, 2001, A01.

9. John F. Burns and Celia W. Dugger, "India Builds Up Forces as Bush Urges Calm," *New York Times,* December 30, 2001, 1A.

10. Farhan Bokhari et al., "Bush Appeals for Calm After Night of Heavy Shelling," *Financial Times,* December 29, 2001, 10.

11. Craig Whitlock and Rajiv Chandrasekaran, "Pakistan Detains Islamic Militants," *Washington Post,* January 1, 2002, A01.

12. Chandrasekaran, "Head of Army Declares India Is Ready for War," A14.

13. Ibid.

14. Ibid.

15. Brian Groom, "Kashmir Conflict 'Could Spiral Out of Control,'" *Financial Times,* January 4, 2002, 3.

16. Todd S. Purdum, "Powell Will Visit India and Pakistan," *New York Times,* January 10, 2002, 12.

17. Farhan Bokhari and Edward Luce, "Pakistan President Walks a Political Tightrope," *Financial Times,* January 14, 2002, 7.

18. Ibid.

19. Todd S. Purdum and Erik Eckholm, "Powell Embarks on Mission to South Asian Powder Keg," *New York Times,* January 16, 2002, A8.

20. Max Abrahms, "Why Terrorism Does Not Work," *International Security,* 31, no. 2 (Fall 2006): 43.

21. David C. Rapoport, "The Four Waves of Modern Terrorism," in *Attacking Terrorism: Elements of a Grand Strategy,* ed. Audrey Kurth Cronin and James M. Ludes (Washington, DC: Georgetown University, 2004), 52.

22. Richard Bach Jensen, "The United States, International Policing and the War Against Anarchist Terrorism, 1900–1914," *Terrorism and Political Violence,* 13, no. 1 (Spring 2001): 20.

23. G. John Ikenberry and Charles A. Kupchan, "Liberal Realism: The Foundations of a Democratic Foreign Policy," *National Interest,* no. 77 (Fall 2004): 41.

24. Walter LaFeber, "The Post September 11 Debate over Empire, Globalization, and Fragmentation," *Political Science Quarterly,* 117, no. 1 (March 22, 2002): 1.

25. Barry Buzan, Ole Weaver, and Jaap de Wilde, *Security: A New Framework for Analysis* (Boulder, CO: Lynne Rienner, 1998), 5.

26. Audrey Kurth Cronin, "Introduction: Meeting and Managing the Threat," in Cronin and Ludes, *Attacking Terrorism,* 35, 39.

27. Martha Crenshaw, "Terrorism, Strategies, and Grand Strategies," in Cronin and Ludes, *Attacking Terrorism*, 77.

28. John M. Rothgeb, Jr., *Defining Power: Influence and Force in the Contemporary International System* (New York: St. Martin's Press, 1993), 52.

29. John T. Rourke and Mark A. Boyer, *World Politics: International Politics on the World Stage* (New York: McGraw-Hill/Dushkin, 1998), chapter 3, 49.

30. Ibid.

31. Ibid.

32. George P. Shultz, "Terror and the States," *Washington Post*, January 26, 2002, A23.

33. Anthony F. Lang, Jr., "Evaluating Middle East Foreign Policy Since 9/11," in "The Impact of 9/11 on the Middle East," *Middle East Policy*, 9, no. 4 (December 1, 2002): 75.

34. Rourke and Boyer, *World Politics*, 49.

35. Ibid., 51.

36. Muhittin Ataman, "The Impact of Non-State Actors on World Politics: A Challenge to Nation-States," *Alternatives: Turkish Journal of International Relations*, 2, no. 1 (Spring 2003), www.alternativesjournal.net/volume2/number1/ataman2.htm (accessed January 6, 2005).

37. Rourke and Boyer, *World Politics*, 56.

38. Christopher Layne, "The Unipolar Illusion Revisited: The Coming End of the United States' Unipolar Moment," *International Security*, 31, no. 2 (Fall 2006): 29.

39. Ibid.

40. In using the term "classical realism" I refer predominantly to realism as espoused by Hans J. Morgenthau; see Hans J. Morgenthau, "Political Power: A Realist Theory of International Politics," in *Classics of International Relations*, 3rd ed., ed. John A. Vasquez (Upper Saddle River, NJ: Prentice Hall, 1996), 24–27.

41. Joseph S. Nye, Jr., "Limits of American Power," *Political Science Quarterly*, 117, no. 4 (2002–3): 548.

42. Audrey Kurth Cronin, "Transnational Terrorism and Security," in *Grave New World: Security Challenges in the 21st Century*, ed. Michael E. Brown (Washington, DC: Georgetown University Press, 2003), 282.

43. Ibid., 284.

44. Walter Laqueur, *The New Terrorism: Fanaticism and the Arms of Mass Destruction* (New York: Oxford University Press, 1999), 3.

45. John Lewis Gaddis, "A Grand Strategy of Transformation," *Foreign Policy*, November 1, 2002, 50.

46. Alex P. Schmid, "Terrorism and the Use of Weapons of Mass Destruction: From Where the Risk?" *Terrorism and Political Violence*, 11, no. 4 (Winter 1999): 106.

47. Paul W. Schroeder, "The Risks of Victory: An Historian's Provocation," *National Interest*, no. 66 (Winter 2001–2): 24.

48. M. Ljuba Jovanovic, "The Murder of Sarajevo," *Journal of the British Institute of International Affairs*, 4, no. 2 (March 1925): 60.

49. Ibid.

50. Schroeder, "The Risks of Victory," 23.

51. H.R. Knickerbocker, "The Danger of War in Europe," *International Affairs*, 13, no. 4 (July–August 1934): 482.

52. William M. Carley, "How Asian Schoolgirl, Tutored in Espionage, Became Bomber of Jet," *Wall Street Journal*, October 12, 1989, A1.

53. Fred Hiatt, "North Korea's Isolation Seen Dangerous for Its Foes," *Washington Post,* February 23, 1988, A17.

54. "South Korean Troops on Alert After North Blamed for Jet Crash," *Toronto Star,* January 15, 1988, A3.

55. Richard Halloran, "U.S. Planning Show of Force for Seoul Games," *New York Times,* February 7, 1988, A1.

56. Clyde Haberman, "Japanese Imposing Sanctions on North Korea," *New York Times,* January 26, 1988, A8.

57. Somini Sengupta, "With Wrath and Wire, India Builds a Great Wall," *New York Times,* January 2, 2002.

58. Walter J. Boyne, "El Dorado Canyon," *Air Force Magazine Online,* 82, no. 3 (March 1999), www.afa.org/magazine/March1999/0399canyon.asp (accessed October 4, 2006).

59. Mary Williams Walsh, "5 Suspects to Face Trial in '86 German Disco Blast," *Chicago Sun-Times,* February 8, 1997, 13.

60. Celestine Bohlen, "Soviets Reject U.S. Charge on Disco Bombing," *Washington Post,* April 18, 1986, A26.

61. Ibid.

62. Henry A. Kissinger, transcript of testimony before the Senate Foreign Relations Committee, "U.S. Policy Towards Iraq," *Federal News Service,* September 26, 2002.

63. Christopher Harmon, *Terrorism Today* (London: Frank Cass, 2000), 2.

64. Bruce Hoffman, *Inside Terrorism* (New York: Columbia University Press, 1998), 67.

65. Peter Chalk, "The Evolving Dynamic of Terrorism in the 1990s," *Australian Journal of International Affairs,* 53, no. 2 (July 1999): 151.

66. Aldo Borgu, "Combating Terrorism in East Asia—A Framework for Regional Cooperation," *Asia-Pacific Review,* 11, no. 2 (November 2004): 49.

67. Benjamin Netanyahu, "Defining Terrorism" in *Terrorism: How the West Can Win,* ed. Netanyahu (New York: Farrar, Straus, Giroux, 1986), 11.

68. Rapoport, "The Four Waves of Modern Terrorism," 47.

69. Ibid., 61.

70. As stated by Senator Richard Shelby of Alabama on *Face the Nation,* CBS, September 16, 2001 (transcript file accessed through Lexis-Nexis).

71. Joseph S. Nye, Jr., "Soft Power and Conflict Management in the Information Age," in *Turbulent Peace: The Challenges of Managing International Conflict,* ed. Chester A. Crocker, Fen Osler Hampson, and Pamela Aall (Washington, DC: U.S. Institute of Peace Press, 2001), 354–55.

72. Ibid., 359.

73. Amanda DiPaolo, "Battle for State Control: Lessons from Violent Nonstate Actors Imitating the State: Colombia, Nicaragua, and Lessons for Iraq," *World Affairs,* 167, no. 4 (March 22, 2005): 167.

74. Ibid.

75. Bruce Hoffman, "Change and Continuity in Terrorism," *Studies in Conflict & Terrorism,* 24, no. 5 (2001): 425.

76. Joseph S. Nye, Jr., "Redefining the National Interest," *Foreign Affairs* (July–August 1999): 24.

77. Ibid.

78. James E. Dougherty and Robert L. Pfaltzgraff, Jr., *Contending Theories of International Relations* (New York: Longman, 2001), 133.

79. Woods argues that the Spanish-American War marked the arrival of the United States as a world power—moreover, once the U.S. attained this status, it started to become the target of overseas militant attacks. See Randall B. Woods, "Terrorism in the Age of Roosevelt: The Miss Stone Affair," *American Quarterly,* 31, no. 4 (Autumn 1979): 478–79.

80. Richard K. Betts, "The Soft Underbelly of American Primacy: Tactical Advantages of Terror," *Political Science Quarterly,* 117, no. 1 (2002): 20.

81. Oliver P. Richmond, "Realizing Hegemony? Symbolic Terrorism and the Roots of Conflict," *Studies in Conflict & Terrorism,* 26, no. 4 (July–August 2003): 299.

82. Michael C. Hudson, "Imperial Headaches: Managing Unruly Regions in an Age of Globalization," *Middle East Policy,* 9, no. 4 (December 1, 2002): 63.

83. Betts, "The Soft Underbelly of American Primacy," 20.

84. Samuel P. Huntington, "The Clash of Civilizations," *Foreign Affairs,* 72, no. 3 (Summer 1993): 22.

85. Ibid., 31–32.

86. Robert Jervis, "An Interim Assessment of September 11: What Has Changed and What Has Not?" *Political Science Quarterly,* 117, no. 1 (2002): 37.

87. Jonathan Fox, "Religion as an Overlooked Element of International Relations," *International Studies Review,* 3, no. 3 (Fall 2001): 54.

88. Justin Pope, "Harvard Prodded on Religion Courses," *Washington Post,* October 4, 2006, www.washingtonpost.com/wp-dyn/content/article/2006/10/04/AR2006100401445 (accessed October 5, 2006).

89. Ibid.

90. Hudson, "Imperial Headaches," 62.

91. Ibid.

92. David C. Hendrickson, "Toward Universal Empire: The Dangerous Quest for Absolute Security," *World Policy Journal,* 19, no. 3 (Fall 2002): 7.

93. President George W. Bush, transcript of annual State of the Union address, January 29, 2002, www.whitehouse.gov/news/releases/2002/01/20020129–11.html (accessed May 8, 2007).

94. Hendrickson, "Toward Universal Empire," 7.

95. Michael Cox, "Empire by Denial: The Strange Case of the United States," *International Affairs,* 81, no. 1 (2005): 17.

96. Abrahms, "Why Terrorism Does Not Work," 60.

97. Ibid.

98. Gaddis, "A Grand Strategy of Transformation," 50.

99. Audrey Kurth Cronin, "Behind the Curve: Globalization and International Terrorism," *International Security,* 27, no. 3 (Winter 2002/03): 31.

100. Ryan Henry, principal under secretary, Department of Defense, transcript of address to the Asia-Pacific Center for Security Studies, Honolulu, Hawaii, August 3, 2004.

101. Raphael Perl, specialist in international affairs, Congressional Research Service, transcript of prepared statement before the House Committee on Government Reform's Subcommittee on National Security, Veterans Affairs, and International Relations, *Federal News Service,* July 26, 2000.

102. Text of interview with Osama bin Laden, October 21, 2001, Jihad Online News Network, translated from Arabic by Foreign Broadcast Information Service, January 21, 2003.

103. Ibid.

104. "Al-Jazirah Carries Bin Laden's Audio Messages to Iraqis, Americans," Doha Al-Jazirah Satellite Channel Television, October 18, 2003, translated from Arabic by Foreign Broadcast Information Service.

105. "Al-Jazirah Site Posts 'Full Transcript' of Bin Ladin's Message," Doha Al-Jazirah Satellite Channel Television, November 1, 2004, translated from Arabic by Foreign Broadcast Information Service.

106. Gail Makinen, "The Economic Effects of 9/11: A Retrospective Assessment," *Congressional Research Service: Report for Congress* (order code RL31617), September 27, 2002, 6.

107. Brian Dunlap, "Thinking the Unthinkable—Businesses Prepare for the Worst," *New Jersey Business Magazine,* 50, no. 9 (September 10, 2004): 146, www.njbusinessforce. org/THNKNG_UNTHNKBLE-NJBF04.pdf (accessed May 9, 2007).

108. Hyunjoon Kim and Zheng Gu, "Impact of the 9/11 Terrorist Attacks on the Return and Risk of Airline Stocks," *Terrorism and Hospitality Research,* 5, no. 2 (August 1, 2004): 150.

109. Makinen, "The Economic Effects of 9/11," 4.

110. Patrick Lenain, Marcos Bonturi, and Vincent Koen, "The Economic Consequences of Terrorism" (working paper 334, Economics Department, Organization for Economic Cooperation and Development [OECD], July 17, 2002), 6.

111. Lori Montgomery, "The Cost of War, Unnoticed," *Washington Post,* May 8, 2007, D01.

112. "Open to Attack . . ." *Lloyd's List,* July 23, 2003, 7. See also OECD report, www.oecd.org/dataoecd/19/61/18521672.pdf (accessed May 8, 2007).

113. "Can Car Dealers Fight Terrorism? The White House Seems to Think So," *American Banker,* May 16, 2003, 6.

114. Makinen, "The Economic Effects of 9/11," 2.

115. "Open to Attack . . . ," 7.

116. Ibid.

117. Matthew C. Weinzierl, "The Cost of Living: The Economics of Preventing Nuclear Terrorism," *National Interest,* Spring 2004, accessed on 16 May 2007 from http://findarticles.com/p/articles/mi_m2751/is_75/ai_n6076390.

118. Lenain, Bonturi, and Koen, "The Economic Consequences of Terrorism," 7.

119. Ibid.

120. Ibid.

121. Audrey Kurth Cronin, "Rethinking Sovereignty: American Strategy in the Age of Terrorism," *Survival,* 44, no. 2 (Summer 2002): 134.

122. Ikenberry and Kupchan, "Liberal Realism," 41.

123. Ibid.

Chapter 4

1. Andrew Higgins, Karby Leggett, and Alan Cullison, "Uploading Terror: How Al-Qaeda Put Internet in Service of Global Jihad," *Wall Street Journal,* November 11, 2002, A1.

2. Sean Young, "Investigation Urged into Web Sites After American's Beheading Posted," Associated Press Worldstream, May 14, 2004.

3. Ibid.

4. Paul Eedle, "Al-Qaeda Takes Fight for 'Hearts and Minds' to the Web," *Jane's Intelligence Review,* 14, no. 8 (August 2002): 25.

5. Audrey Kurth Cronin, "Behind the Curve: Globalization and International Terrorism," *International Security,* 27, no. 3 (Winter 2002–3): 47.

6. "Korea's Kim Dae-Jung Sees Poverty as Root of Terrorism," *World News Connection,* October 25, 2002.

7. Anatolia News Agency, "Turkey: Bulgarian Minister Says Terrorism 'Poisonous Fruit of Globalization,'" *BBC Worldwide Monitoring,* April 12, 2002.

8. Cronin, "Behind the Curve," 47.

9. Joseph S. Nye, Jr., *The Paradox of American Power: Why the World's Only Superpower Can't Go It Alone* (New York: Oxford University Press, 2002), 78.

10. As cited by Petr Reimer (in his review essay of R.J. Barry Jones, *The World Turned Upside Down? Globalization and the Future of the State* [Manchester and New York: Manchester University Press, 2000], *Journal of International Relations and Development,* 6, no. 1 [March 2003]: 96).

11. Nye, *The Paradox of American Power,* 78.

12. Robert O. Keohane and Joseph S. Nye, Jr., "Globalization: What's New? What's Not? And So What?" *Foreign Policy,* no. 118 (Spring 2000): 108.

13. Ibid.

14. Ibid., 115.

15. Ibid., 104.

16. Ibid., 105.

17. Ibid.

18. Ibid.

19. Ibid., 106.

20. Stanley Hoffman, "Clash of Globalizations," *Foreign Affairs,* 81, no. 4 (July–August 2002): 108.

21. Vice Admiral Thomas R. Wilson, director, Defense Intelligence Agency, transcript of prepared testimony before the Senate Armed Services Committee, "Global Threats and Challenges," *Federal News Service,* March 19, 2002.

22. *Mapping the Global Future: Report of the National Intelligence Council's 2020 Project* (Washington, DC: Government Printing Office, December 2004), 10, www.dni.gov/nic/NIC_globaltrend2020.html (accessed May 9, 2007).

23. Ibid., 11.

24. Ibid., 14.

25. Reuters, http://asia.news.yahoo.com/030612/3/z939.html; accessed on May 16, 2007 at http://vic.apan-info.net/AsiaPacificDailyNews/2003/12June2003-DAILYPRESSSUMMARY-web.doc#_Toc43178504.

26. Ibid.

27. Mark Strauss, "Antiglobalism's Jewish Problem: Globalization at Work," *Foreign Policy,* no. 139 (November–December 2003): 61.

28. Michael J. Mazarr, "Saved from Ourselves?" *Washington Quarterly,* 25, no. 2 (Spring 2002): 224.

29. Charles Selengut, *Sacred Fury: Understanding Religious Violence* (Walnut Creek, CA: Altamira Press, 2003), 166.

30. Alan Clendenning, "Pope Assails Marxism, Capitalism at End of Brazil Tour," Associated Press, May 14, 2007.

31. Thomas L. Friedman, "A Theory of Everything," *New York Times,* June 1, 2003.

32. Cronin, "Behind the Curve," 30.

33. Roger Scruton, *The West and the Rest: Globalization and the Terrorist Threat*

(Wilmington, DE: Intercollegiate Studies Institute, 2002), as summarized in book review by C. Dale Walton, "The West and Its Antagonists: Culture, Globalization, and the War on Terrorism," *Comparative Strategy,* 23 (2004): 305.

34. Ibid.

35. Ismail Abu Shanab, interview with Jessica Stern, in *Terror in the Name of God: Why Religious Militants Kill,* ed. Stern (New York: HarperCollins, 2003), 40–41.

36. Strauss, "Antiglobalism's Jewish Problem," 62.

37. Sonja Hegasy, Centre for Modern Oriental Studies, Berlin, Germany, in Mustapha Kamel Al-Ayid et al., "The Impact of 9/11 on the Middle East," *Middle East Policy,* 9, no. 4 (December 1, 2002): 75.

38. Daniel Benjamin and Steven Simon, *The Age of Sacred Terror: Radical Islam's War Against America* (New York: Random House, 2003), 407.

39. Ibid.

40. "Bin Ladin Threatens Revenge on Israel, U.S., Offers Truce with Europeans," Dubai Al-Arabiya Television, April 15, 2004, translated from Arabic by World News Connection, http://why-war.com/news/2004/04/15/binladin.html (accessed May 10, 2007).

41. Ibid.

42. "Bin-Ladin Tapes Address Iraqis, Americans, Vow More Attacks—Full Text," *BBC Monitoring International Reports,* October 18, 2003.

43. Ibid.

44. Declassified Key Judgments of the National Intelligence Estimate, "Trends in Global Terrorism: Implications for the United States," April 2006, http://media. washingtonpost.com/wp-srv/nation/documents/Declassified_NIE_Key_Judgments_ 092606.pdf (accessed March 26, 2007).

45. "Bin-Ladin Tapes Address Iraqis, Americans, Vow More Attacks."

46. John L. Esposito, *Unholy War: Terror in the Name of Islam* (New York: Oxford University Press, 2002), 45.

47. Shyam Tekwani, "Media, Information Revolution, and Terrorism in Southeast Asia," in *Terrorism and Violence in Southeast Asia: Transnational Challenges to States and Regional Stability,* ed. Paul J. Smith (Armonk, NY: M.E. Sharpe, 2005), 240.

48. "I Bear Witness That There Is No . . ." *Washington Post,* October 28, 2001.

49. Ibid.

50. Brigitte L. Nacos, "Terrorism as Breaking News: Attack on America," *Political Science Quarterly,* 188, no. 1 (March 22, 2003): 23.

51. Transcript of "Hijacked!" *American Experience,* PBS, www.pbs.org/wgbh/ amex/hijacked/filmmore/pt.html (accessed October 25, 2005).

52. Ibid.

53. "Transcripts: The Guerrilla's Story (Interview of Leila Khaled)," *BBC News,* January 1, 2001, accessed May 10, 2007 at http://news.bbc.co.uk/1/hi/in_depth/ uk/2000/uk_confidential/1090986.stm.

54. Nacos, "Terrorism as Breaking News," 23.

55. Robert Keatley, "Olympic Outcome: Munich Killings Refocus Attention on Palestine Issue, Jar Peace Bids," *Wall Street Journal,* September 7, 1972, 2.

56. Bruce Hoffman, *Inside Terrorism* (New York: Columbia University Press, 1998), 73.

57. Michael Flood, "Nuclear Sabotage," *Washington Post,* January 9, 1977, 29.

58. Mark Juergensmeyer, *Terror in the Mind of God: The Global Rise of Religious Violence* (Berkeley: University of California Press, 2000), 122.

59. Brigitte L. Nacos, "The Terrorist Calculus Behind 9/11: A Model for Future Terrorism?" *Studies in Conflict & Terrorism,* 26, no. 1 (January–February 2003): 3.

60. R.D. Crelinsten, "Power and Meaning: Terrorism as a Struggle over Access to the Communication Structure," in *Contemporary Research on Terrorism,* ed. Paul Wilkinson and Alasdair M. Steward (Aberdeen, UK: Aberdeen University Press, 1987), 443.

61. Nye, "Limits of American Power," 552.

62. Tekwani, "Media, Information Revolution, and Terrorism in Southeast Asia," 227.

63. R.D. Crelinsten, "Power and Meaning: Terrorism as a Struggle over Access to the Communication Structure," in *Contemporary Research on Terrorism,* ed. Paul Wilkinson and Alasdair M. Stewart (Aberdeen, UK: Aberdeen University Press, 1987), 443.

64. Grant Wardlaw, *Political Terrorism: Theory, Tactics and Counter-Measures* (London: Cambridge University Press, 1982), 38.

65. Ibid.

66. Nacos, "Terrorism as Breaking News," 23.

67. Doug Struck, "Terrorism Allegations Detailed in Canada," *Washington Post,* June 7, 2006, A01.

68. Dan Darling, "No Terrorist Is an Island," *Weekly Standard,* June 19, 2006 [accessed via Lexis-Nexis database].

69. Michelle Shephard, "How Internet Monitoring Sparked a CSIS Probe," *Toronto Star,* June 3, 2006.

70. Bill Torpy, "Suspected Terrorists; Atlanta, Toronto Men Had Much in Common," *Atlanta Journal Constitution,* June 11, 2006, 1A.

71. Nicolaas van Rijn, "Plot Began in Chat Room," *Toronto Star,* June 5, 2006, B02.

72. Bruce Hoffman, corporate chairman, Counterterrorism and Counterinsurgency, and director, RAND Corporation, transcript of testimony before a hearing of the House Select Intelligence Committee, "Terrorist Use of the Internet for Communications," *Federal News Service,* May 4, 2006.

73. Ibid.

74. Christopher M. Blanchard, "Al-Qaeda: Statements and Evolving Ideology," *Congressional Research Service: Report for Congress* (order code RL32759), February 4, 2005, 9.

75. Ibid., 8.

76. Febe Armanios, "The Islamic Traditions of Wahhabism and Salafiyya," *Congressional Research Service: Report for Congress* (order code RS21695), December 22, 2003, 4.

77. Ibid.

78. Blanchard, "Al-Qaeda: Statements and Evolving Ideology," 8.

79. "Al-Jazirah Site Posts 'Full Transcript' of Bin Ladin's Message."

80. Ibid.

81. Alan Cullison and Andrew Higgins, "Files Found: A Computer in Kabul Yields a Chilling Array of Al-Qaeda Memos," *Wall Street Journal,* December 31, 2001, A1.

82. "Arabic Paper Examines al-Qa'idah, Islamist Use of Internet," *BBC Monitoring of International Reports,* May 16, 2005.

83. Ibid.

84. Chris Dishman, "The Leaderless Nexus: When Crime and Terror Converge," *Studies in Conflict & Terrorism,* 28, no. 3 (May–June 2005): 239.

85. Tekwani, "Media, Information Revolution, and Terrorism in Southeast Asia," 234.

86. Ibid.

87. Wardlaw, *Political Terrorism,* 31.

88. David Martin Jones, "Out of Bali: Cybercaliphate Rising," *National Interest,* no. 71 (Spring 2003): 81.

89. Ibid.

90. "Al-Qa'idah Establishes 'Internet University' for Recruitment-UK Arab Paper," *BBC Monitoring International Reports,* November 21, 2003.

91. Ibid.

92. Ibid.

93. Ibid.

94. "Al-Qa'ida Yemeni Branch Opens Chat Channel for Members," *BBC Monitoring International Reports,* October 27, 2003.

95. Ibid.

96. Mark Rice-Oxley et al., "Foiled Terror Plot on Scale of 9/11," *Christian Science Monitor,* August 11, 2006, 1.

97. David Hughes, "Ten Lockerbies in One Day," *Aviation Week and Space Technology,* 165, no. 8 (August 21, 2006).

98. "11 British Muslims Charged in Bomb Plot," *Washington Times,* August 22, 2006, A01.

99. Ibid.

100. Lee Glendinning, "MI5 Head Warns of Up to 30 Terror Plots at Work in Britain," *Independent,* November 10, 2006, http://news.independent.co.uk/uk/crime/article1963077.ece (accessed November 10, 2006).

101. Ibid.

102. Ibid.

103. Simon Kuper, "Political Muscle," *Financial Times,* September 27, 2003, 23, http://search.ft.com/ftArticle?page=1&queryText=%22Hakki+Keskin%22&id=030 927001087 (accessed May 9, 2007).

104. Ibid.

105. "Look out, Europe," *Economist,* June 24, 2006.

106. "Analysis: Resentment of Muslims Growing in Europe," Open Source Center, February 8, 2006.

107. Ibid.

108. Ibid.

109. Ibid.

110. Olivier Roy, "EuroIslam: The Jihad Within?" *National Interest,* no. 71 (Spring 2003): 72.

111. Patrick E. Tyler and Don Van Natta, Jr., "Militants in Europe Openly Call for Jihad and the Rule of Islam," *New York Times,* April 26, 2004, A1.

112. Timony M. Savage, "Europe and Islam: Crescent Waxing, Cultures Clashing," *Washington Quarterly,* 27, no. 3 (Summer 2004): 31–33.

113. Ibid., 46.

114. Ibid., 33.

115. "French Intelligence Identifies Threat from Jihadists Returning from Iraq," *Le Monde* (Paris), June 27, 2005. EUP200506270290003 (reported in Foreign Broadcast Information Service), Paris, *Le Monde* (Internet Version—WWW), in French June 27, 2005.

116. Jones, "Out of Bali," 83.

117. Ibid.

118. Ibid., 84.

119. Sayyid Qutb, *Milestones* (New Delhi: Islamic Book Service, 2002), 138.

120. Ibid., 139.

121. Ibid., 130.

122. Thomas Homer-Dixon, "The Rise of Complex Terrorism," *Foreign Policy,* no. 128 (January–February 2002): 52.

123. Zachary Abuza, *Militant Islam in Southeast Asia: Crucible of Terror* (Boulder, CO: Lynne Rienner, 2003), 140.

124. Ibid., 140–41.

125. Michael Mousseau, "Market Civilization and Its Clash with Terror," *International Security,* 27, no. 3 (Winter 2002–3): 27.

126. Theodore H. Cohn, *Global Political Economy: Theory and Practice* (New York: Addison Wesley Longman, 2000), 357.

127. Ibid.

128. Ibid.

129. Ibid.

130. Ibid.

131. Thomas P.M. Barnett, *The Pentagon's New Map: War and Peace in the Twenty-First Century* (New York: G.P. Putnam's Sons, 2004), 161.

132. Ibid., 161–65.

133. Ibid., 188.

134. Ibid., 190.

135. Clair Apodaca, "The Globalization of Capital in East and Southeast Asia," *Asian Survey,* 42, no. 6 (2002): 904.

136. Ibid., 905.

137. Audrey Kurth Cronin, "Sources of Contemporary Terrorism," in *Attacking Terrorism: Elements of a Grand Strategy,* ed. Cronin and James M. Ludes (Washington, DC: Georgetown University Press, 2004), 38.

Chapter 5

1. Open Source Center, "Al-Jazirah Carries Bin Ladin's Address on U.S. Strikes," GMP20011007000232 Doha Al-Jazirah Satellite Channel Television in Arabic 1825 GMT 07 October 2001.

2. Ibid.

3. Daniel Benjamin and Steven Simon, *The Age of Sacred Terror: Radical Islam's War Against America* (New York: Random House, 2003), 40.

4. Transcript, "Usama bin Laden Video Tape," December 13, 2001, translated from Arabic by George Michael and Kassem M. Wahba, http://news.findlaw.com/hdocs/docs/binladen/binladenvid121301rls.pdf (accessed February 6, 2005).

5. Open Source Center, "Al-Jazirah Carries Bin Ladin's Address on U.S. Strikes."

6. Robert Jervis, "An Interim Assessment of September 11: What Has Changed and What Has Not?" *Political Science Quarterly,* 117, no. 1 (Spring 2002): 37.

7. "Playing with Wildfire: Free Speech on Religion Is a Right but Common Sense Is a Duty," *Financial Times,* February 3, 2006, 16.

8. Ibid.

9. Ibid.

10. Ibid.

11. Craig S. Smith and Ian Fisher, "Temperatures Rise over Cartoons Mocking Muhammad," *New York Times,* February 3, 2006, A3.

12. Ibid.

13. Anne Penketh and Eric Silver, "Danes Are Urged to Leave Indonesia as Protests Grow," *Independent,* February 13, 2006, 20, http://news.independent.co.uk/europe/article345066.ece (accessed May 9, 2007).

14. Karl Vick, "Cartoons Spark Burning of Embassies," *Washington Post,* February 5, 2006, A15.

15. Declan Walsh and John Aglionby, "Church Ablaze as Cartoon Protests Continue Across Globe," *Guardian* (London), February 20, 2006, 18.

16. Lydia Polgreen, "Nigeria Counts 100 Deaths over Danish Caricatures," *New York Times,* February 24, 2006, 8.

17. "Pope's Islam Comments Condemned," CNN, September 15, 2006, www.cnn.com/2006/WORLD/europe/09/15/pope.islam/ (accessed May 9, 2007).

18. "Al Qaeda Threat over Pope Speech," CNN, September 18, 2006, www.cnn.com/2006/WORLD/europe/09/17/pope.islam/ (accessed May 9, 2007).

19. Malcolm Moore, "Security Around the Pope Is Stepped Up," *Daily Telegraph* (London), September 18, 2006, 4.

20. Ibid.

21. Ibid.

22. "Pope's Islam Comments Condemned."

23. Text of Pope Benedict XVI's Statement, BBC News, September 17, 2006, http://news.bbc.co.uk/2/hi/europe/5353774.stm (accessed March 26, 2007).

24. Mark Juergensmeyer, *The New Cold War? Religious Nationalism Confronts the Secular State* (Berkeley: University of California Press, 1993), 32.

25. Paul N. Anderson, "Religion and Violence: From Pawn to Scapegoat," in *The Destructive Power of Religion: Violence in Judaism, Christianity, and Islam,* ed. J. Harold Ellens (Westport, CT: Praeger, 2004), 268.

26. Mark Juergensmeyer, "The Logic of Religious Violence," in *Terrorism and Counterterrorism: Understanding the New Security Environment,* ed. Russell D. Howard and Reid L. Sawyer (Guilford, CT: McGraw-Hill/Dushkin, 2002), 145.

27. Ibid.

28. Jonathan Fox, "The Effects of Religion on Domestic Conflicts," *Terrorism and Political Violence,* 10, no. 4 (Winter 1998): 43.

29. Magnus Ranstorp, "Terrorism in the Name of Religion," *Journal of International Affairs,* 50, no. 2 (Summer 1996): 46.

30. Fox, "The Effects of Religion on Domestic Conflicts," 51.

31. Mark Juergensmeyer, "Terror Mandated by God," *Terrorism and Political Violence,* 9, no. 2 (Summer 1997): 20.

32. "Section 4: Our Response to the Perspective of Others," in *Moderation in Islam in the Context of Muslim Community in Singapore* (Singapore: Pergas, 2003), 108–9.

33. Ibid.

34. Michael C. Hudson, "Imperial Headaches: Managing Unruly Regions in an Age of Globalization," *Middle East Policy,* 9, no. 4 (December 1, 2002): 61.

35. Mohammed M. Hafez, *Manufacturing Human Bombs: The Making of Palestinian Suicide Bombers* (Washington, DC: U.S. Institute of Peace Press, 2006), 34–35.

36. Emmanuel Sivan, "The Clash Within Islam," *Survival,* 45, no. 1 (Spring 2003): 27.

37. Kristin Smith, "Kuwait: Islamist-Liberal Politics" (summary of paper presented at the annual meeting of the American Political Science Association, Boston, MA, August 31, 2002), in "The Impact of 9/11 on the Middle East," *Middle East Policy,* 9, no. 4 (December 1, 2002): 75.

38. "Iraq's Christian Minority Flees as Extremist Threat Worsens," *New York Times,* October 17, 2006, A1.

39. Christopher Harmon, *Terrorism Today* (London: Frank Cass, 2000), 27.

40. Ranstorp, "Terrorism in the Name of Religion," 52.

41. David Rapoport, "Some General Observations on Religion and Violence," *Terrorism and Political Violence,* 3, no. 3 (Autumn 1991): 120.

42. Ibid., 136.

43. Fox, "The Effects of Religion on Domestic Conflicts," 44–45.

44. Ibid.

45. Ranstorp, "Terrorism in the Name of Religion," 47.

46. Mark Juergensmeyer, "Sacrifice and Cosmic War," *Terrorism and Political Violence,* 3, no. 3 (Autumn 1991): 106–7.

47. Ibid.

48. Pankaj Mishra, "The Other Face of Fanaticism," *New York Times Magazine,* February 2, 2003, 43, www.sacw.net/DC/CommunalismCollection/ArticlesArchive/pmishraFeb2003 (accessed May 9, 2007).

49. Ibid.

50. Ibid.

51. Ibid.

52. Pankaj Mishra, "Holy Lies," *Guardian* (London), April 6, 2002, 24.

53. Ibid.

54. Edward Luce and Demetri Sevastopulo, "Blood and Money," *Financial Times,* February 21, 2003, 15.

55. Ibid.

56. Ibid.

57. "Doomsday Religious Movements," *Canadian Security Intelligence Service,* Report no. 2000/03, December 18, 1999, www.cesnur.org/testi/canada.htm (accessed May 9, 2007).

58. Michael Barkun, "Millenarian Aspects of 'White Supremacist' Movements," *Terrorism and Political Violence,* 1, no. 4 (October 1989): 410.

59. Juan R.I. Cole, "Millennialism in Modern Iranian History," in *Imagining the End: Visions of Apocalypse from the Ancient Middle East to Modern America,* ed. Abbas Amanat and Magnus Bernhardsson (London: I.B. Tauris, 2002), 282–311, www-personal.umich.edu/~jrcole/bahai/2003/millen2.htm (accessed May 9, 2007).

60. D.C. Rapoport, "Why Does Religious Messianism Produce Terror?" in *Contemporary Research on Terrorism,* ed. Paul Wilkinson and Alasdair M. Stewart (Aberdeen, UK: Aberdeen University Press, 1987), 74.

61. Max Taylor and John Horgan, "The Psychological and Behavioural Bases of Islamic Fundamentalism," *Terrorism and Political Violence,* 13, no. 4 (Winter 2001): 46.

62. Ibid., 47.

63. Ibid.

64. Clyde Haberman, "Israel Panel Says Killer at Hebron Was Acting Alone," *New York Times,* June 27, 1994, A1.

65. Clyde Haberman, "June 26–July 2: Hebron Massacre," *New York Times,* July 3, 1994, 2.

66. Haberman, "Israel Panel Says Killer at Hebron Was Acting Alone," A1.

67. Ibid.

68. Clyde Haberman, "Israel Asserts Group Plotted to Kill Arabs," *New York Times,* September 15, 1994, A1.

69. Joel Greenberg, "Rabin's Killer Says He Acted for Past Generations of Jews," *New York Times,* November 21, 1995, A1.

70. Ibid.

71. Charles A. Radin, "Hebron's Jewish Extremists Protected Despite Actions," *Boston Globe,* November 23, 2001, A15.

72. Eric Silver, "School Bomb Blast Blamed on Jewish Extremists," *Independent,* September 18, 2002, 13, www.palestinecampaign.org/archives.asp?xid=1003 (accessed May 9, 2007).

73. Margaret Coker, "Israel Convicts Jews in School Bomb Try," *Atlanta Journal-Constitution,* September 18, 2003, 7A.

74. Rebecca Anna Stoil, "Seven Arrested in Killing of Jewish Terrorist Zada," *Jerusalem Post,* June 14, 2006, 3.

75. Yaakov Katz et al., "Police Raid Jewish Legion Offices," *Jerusalem Post,* January 9, 2006, 5.

76. Juergensmeyer, *Terror in the Mind of God,* 184–86.

77. Ibid.

78. *White Paper: The Jemaah Islamiyah Arrests and the Threat of Terrorism* (Singapore: Ministry of Home Affairs, January 7, 2003), 15.

79. Ibid.

80. Ibid.

81. Ibid.

82. Ibid.

83. Ibid.

84. Ibid., 22.

85. International Crisis Group, "Jemaah Islamiyah in South East Asia: Damaged but Still Dangerous," *ICG Asia Report,* no. 63 (August 26, 2003): 27, www.crisisgroup. org/library/documents/report_archive/A401104_26082003.pdf.

86. *White Paper: The Jemaah Islamiyah Arrests,* 16.

87. Ibid.

88. Ibid.

89. Kumar Ramakrishna, "Countering Radical Islam in Southeast Asia: The Need to Confront the Functional and Ideological 'Enabling Environment,'" in *Terrorism and Violence in Southeast Asia: Transnational Challenges to States and Regional Stability,* ed. Paul J. Smith (Armonk, NY: M.E. Sharpe, 2005), 155.

90. Paul R. Pillar, *Terrorism and U.S. Foreign Policy* (Washington, DC: Brookings Institution Press, 2003), 65.

91. Ibid.

92. "List of Indictments Against Aum Shinrikyo Cult Founder Shoko Asahara," *BBC Monitoring International Reports,* April 24, 2003.

93. Ibid.

94. Tomoe Moriya, "Religious Violence in Contemporary Japan: The Case of Aum Shinrikyo" (book review), *Sociology of Religion,* 63, no. 4 (December 22, 2002): 545.

95. John F. Sopko and Alan Edleman, transcript of prepared statement before the Senate Government Affairs Committee, Permanent Subcommittee on Investigations, "Hearing on Global Proliferation of Weapons of Mass Destruction: A Case Study on the Aum Shinrikyo," *Federal News Service,* October 31, 1995.

96. Manabu Watanabe, "Religion and Violence in Japan Today: A Chronological and Doctrinal Analysis of Aum Shinrikyo," *Terrorism and Political Violence,* 10, no. 4 (Winter 1998): 83.

97. Sopko and Edleman, statement before the Senate Government Affairs Committee.

98. Ibid.

99. Joe Thoma, "Smiling, Unrepentant Anti-Abortion Extremist Is Executed in Florida," Agence France-Presse, September 4, 2003.

100. James Risen, "Abortion Clinic Slayings May Kill Operation Rescue," *Los Angeles Times,* August 10, 1994, A1.

101. Diane Hirth, "Abortion Extremists Justify Their Violence," *Sun-Sentinel* (Ft. Lauderdale, FL), July 24, 1995, 1A.

102. Thoma, "Smiling, Unrepentant Anti-Abortion Extremist Is Executed."

103. William Booth, "Bioterror Takes on Another Face," *Washington Post,* October 21, 2001, A08.

104. Jennifer Gonnerman, "The Terrorist Campaign Against Abortion," *Village Voice,* November 10, 1998, 36.

105. Alan Cooperman, "Is Terrorism Tied to Christian Sect?" *Washington Post,* June 2, 2003, A03.

106. Ibid.

107. Michael Barkun, *Religion and the Racist Right* (Chapel Hill: University of North Carolina Press, 1997), 4.

108. Tanya Telfair Sharpe, "The Identity Christian Movement: Ideology of Domestic Terrorism," *Journal of Black Studies,* 30, no. 4 (March 2000): 605.

109. Ibid., 615.

110. Bruce Hoffman, "Responding to Terrorism Across the Technological Spectrum," *Terrorism and Political Violence,* 6, no. 3 (Autumn 1994): 372.

111. Juergensmeyer, *Terror in the Mind of God,* 184–86.

112. Rapoport, "Why Does Religious Messianism Produce Terror?" 80.

113. Peter Chalk, "The Evolving Dynamic of Terrorism in the 1990s," *Australian Journal of International Affairs,* 53, no. 2 (1999): 159.

114. Samir Kumar Das, "Ethnicity and the Rise of Religious Radicalism: The Security Scenario in Contemporary Northeast India," in *Religious Radicalism and Security in South Asia,* ed. Satu Limaye, Robert Wirsing, and Mohan Malik (Honolulu: Asia-Pacific Center for Security Studies, 2004), 270.

115. Paul Medhurst, *Global Terrorism: A Course Produced by the United Nations Institute for Training and Research* (New York: United Nations Institute for Training and Research, 2002), 132.

116. www.globalterrorism101.com/BinLadenText.html (accessed November 12, 2004).

117. Juergensmeyer, *Terror in the Mind of God,* 145–50.

118. Paul Berman, *Terror and Liberalism* (New York: Norton, 2003), 107.

119. Gilles Kepel, Institute of Political Studies, Paris, France, transcript of testimony before the National Commission on Terrorist Attacks upon the United States, *Federal News Service,* July 9, 2003.

120. Richard A. Clarke, *Against All Enemies: Inside America's War on Terror* (New York: Free Press, 2004), 36.

121. International Crisis Group, *Understanding Islamism,* March 2, 2005, 16.

122. Quintan Wiktorowicz, "A Genealogy of Radical Islam," *Studies in Conflict & Terrorism,* 28, no. 2 (March–April 2005): 78.

123. Michael Doran, "The Pragmatic Fanaticism of Al-Qaeda: An Anatomy of Extremism in Middle Eastern Politics," *Political Science Quarterly,* 117, no. 2 (Summer 2002): 178.

124. Wiktorowicz, "A Genealogy of Radical Islam," 78.

125. Ibid.

126. Ibid.

127. Doran, "The Pragmatic Fanaticism of Al-Qaeda," 177.

128. Ibid., 179.

129. "Section 5: A Just and Balance Position on Selective Important Issues," in *Moderation in Islam in the Context of Muslim Community in Singapore* (Singapore: Pergas, 2003), 236–37.

130. Ibid.

131. Doran, "The Pragmatic Fanaticism of Al-Qaeda," 179.

132. Transcript, "Usama bin Laden's Message to Iraq (Urges Muslims to Overthrow Regimes)," Doha Al-Jazirah Satellite Channel Television, February 11, 2003, translated from Arabic by Foreign Broadcast Information Service.

133. "Al-Jazirah Carries Bin Laden's Audio Messages to Iraqis, Americans," Doha Al-Jazirah Satellite Channel Television, October 18, 2003, translated from Arabic by Foreign Broadcast Information Service.

134. Dan Darling, "Special Analysis: The 12/04 bin Laden Tapes," December 30, 2004, www.windsofchange.net/archives/006101.php (accessed on January 21, 2007).

135. President George W. Bush, remarks to a joint armed forces officers' wives luncheon, Bolling Air Force Base, Washington, DC, *Federal News Service,* October 25, 2005.

136. Ibid.

137. Ibid.

138. Ibid.

139. Marc Sageman, *Understanding Terror Networks* (Philadelphia: University of Pennsylvania Press, 2004), 1.

140. Ahmed Fekry and Sara Nimis, "Preface," in Montasser Al-Zayyat, *The Road to Al-Qaeda* (London: Pluto Press, 2004), xiii.

141. Ibid.

142. International Crisis Group, *Understanding Islamism,* 1.

143. Ibid., 7.

144. Gilles Kepel, "Islamists Versus the State in Egypt and Algeria: The Quest for World Order," *Daedalus,* 124, no. 3 (June 22, 1995): 109.

145. Ray Takeyh, "Islamism in Algeria: A Struggle Between Hope and Agony," *Middle East Policy,* 10, no. 2 (June 22, 2003): 62.

146. International Crisis Group, *Understanding Islamism,* 9.

147. Ibid., 4.

148. Ibid., 9.

149. International Crisis Group, *Indonesia Backgrounder: Why Salafism and Terrorism Mostly Don't Mix,* September 2004, 2.

150. Quintan Wiktorowicz, "Anatomy of the Salafi Movement," *Studies in Conflict & Terorrism,* 29, no. 3 (2006): 207.

151. Wiktorowicz, "A Genealogy of Radical Islam," 75.

152. International Crisis Group, *Indonesia Backgrounder,* 3.

153. Fekry and Nimis, "Preface," in *The Road to Al-Qaeda,* xv.

154. Greg Fealy of the Australian National University introduced me to this term.

155. International Crisis Group, *Understanding Islamism,* 1.

156. Mary R. Habeck, associate professor, Strategic Studies, School of Advanced International Studies, transcript of statement before the House Committee on Armed Services' Subcommittee on Defense, *Federal Document Clearing House Congressional Testimony,* November 3, 2005.

157. Fekry and Nimis, "Preface," in *The Road to Al-Qaeda,* xv.

158. Habeck, statement before the House Committee on Armed Services.

159. Ibid.

160. Mohammed Ayoob, "Deciphering Islam's Multiple Voices: Intellectual Luxury or Strategic Necessity?" *Middle East Policy,* 12, no. 3 (Fall 2005): 86.

161. Chairman's Statement, Twelfth Meeting of the ASEAN Regional Forum, Vientiane, Laos, July 29, 2005, www.aseansec.org/17642.htm (accessed February 3, 2006).

162. Text of the Pakistani president's address at the Seminar on Global Terrorism, *BBC Monitoring International Reports,* August 29, 2005.

163. Mahathir Mohamad, *Terrorism and the Real Issues* (Putrajaya, Malaysia: Pelanduk, 2003), 42–43.

Chapter 6

1. "What Steps to Take Before, After Attack," *Washington Post,* February 16, 2003, A14.

2. Audrey Kurth Cronin, "Transnational Terrorism and Security," in *Grave New World: Security Challenges in the 21st Century,* ed. Michael E. Brown (Washington, DC: Georgetown University Press, 2003), 295.

3. Andrew O'Neil, "Terrorist Use of Weapons of Mass Destruction: How Serious Is the Threat," *Australian Journal of International Affairs,* 57, no. 1, 2003, 99–112.

4. Larry Collins, "Nuclear Terrorism," *New York Times,* December 14, 1980, SM9.

5. Ibid.

6. Louis Rene Beres, "International Terrorism and World Order: The Nuclear Threat," in *Studies in Nuclear Terrorism,* ed. Augustus R. Norton and Martin H. Greenberg (Boston: G.K. Hall, 1979), 361.

7. Alex P. Schmid, "Terrorism and the Use of Weapons of Mass Destruction: From Where the Risk?" *Terrorism and Political Violence,* 11, no. 4 (Winter 1999): 112.

8. Gary L. Ackerman and Laura Snyder, "Would They If They Could? If the Israeli-

Palestinian Conflict Continues, Terrorist Groups Could Be Drawn to Far Deadlier Weapons," *Bulletin of the Atomic Scientists,* 58, no. 3 (May 1, 2002): 47.

9. Amy Sands, Ph.D., transcript of testimony before the U.S. Senate Foreign Relations Committee, "Deconstructing the Chem-Bio Threat," *Federal Document Clearing House Congressional Testimony,* March 19, 2002.

10. Ehud Sprinzak, "On Not Overstating the Problem," in *Hype or Reality: The "New Terrorism" and Mass Casualty Attacks,* ed. Brad Roberts (Alexandria, VA: Chemical and Biological Arms Control Institute, 2000), 5.

11. Ibid.

12. Ariel Merari, "Terrorism as a Strategy of Struggle: Past and Future," *Terrorism and Political Violence,* 11, no. 4 (Winter 1999): 54.

13. John V. Parachini, "Comparing Motives and Outcomes of Mass Casualty Terrorism Involving Conventional and Unconventional Weapons," *Studies in Conflict & Terrorism,* 24, no. 5 (September–October 2001): 390–91.

14. Ibid., 403.

15. Ibid., 400–401.

16. www.terrorismanswers.org/terrorism/media.html (accessed January 9, 2005).

17. Walter Laqueur, "Weapons of Mass Destruction," reprinted in *Terrorism in Perspective,* ed. Pamala L. Griset and Sue Mahan (London: Sage, 2003), 239–40.

18. Juliette N. Kayyem, former commissioner, National Commission on Terrorism, transcript of prepared testimony before the House Armed Services Committee, Special Oversight Panel on Terrorism, *Federal News Service,* July 13, 2000.

19. Richard K. Betts, "The New Threat of Mass Destruction," *Foreign Affairs,* January/February 1998, 27.

20. Ibid., 28.

21. Ibid., 27.

22. Stanley S. Jacobs, "The Nuclear Threat as Terrorist Option," *Terrorism and Political Violence,* 10, no. 4 (Winter 1998): 151–55.

23. Ibid., 152.

24. U.S. Government Accountability Office, "Combating Nuclear Terrorism: Federal Efforts to Respond to Nuclear and Radiological Threats and to Protect Emergency Response Capabilities Could Be Strengthened," September 2006, report GAO-06–1015, 8.

25. Jacobs, "The Nuclear Threat as Terrorist Option," 155.

26. Carl Behrens and Mark Holt, "Nuclear Power Plants: Vulnerability to Terrorist Attack," *Congressional Research Service: Report for Congress* (order code RS21131), February 4, 2005, 3.

27. Thomas J. Badey, "Nuclear Terrorism: Actor-based Threat Assessment," *Intelligence and National Security,* 16, no. 2 (Summer 2001): 44.

28. Kenneth Patchen, "The Nuclear Suitcase Bomb and Nuclear Terrorism: The Lebed Claims," *National Observer,* no. 41 (Winter 1999): 47.

29. *Foreign Missile Developments and the Ballistic Missile Threat to the United States Through 2015* (Washington, DC: Central Intelligence Agency, September 1999), www.iraqwatch.org/government/US/CIA/cia-nie99msl.htm (accessed May 9, 2007).

30. Steve Aoki, transcript of testimony before the Senate Judiciary Committee's Hearing of the Terrorism, Technology, and Homeland Security Subcommittee, "Detecting Smuggled Nuclear Weapons," *Federal News Service,* July 27, 2006.

31. Graham Allison and Andrei Kokoshin, "The New Containment: An Alliance Against Nuclear Terrorism," *National Interest,* no. 69 (Fall 2002): 40.

32. Ibid.

33. Jonathan Medalia, "Nuclear Terrorism: A Brief Review of Threats and Responses," *Congressional Research Service: Report for Congress* (order code RL32595), September 22, 2004, 4.

34. Jonathan Medalia, "Terrorist Nuclear Attacks on Seaports: Threat and Response," *Congressional Research Service Report for Congress* (order code RS21293), January 24, 2005, 1.

35. Ibid., 6.

36. Medalia, "Nuclear Terrorism," 6.

37. Charles D. Ferguson and William C. Potter, *The Four Faces of Nuclear Terrorism* (New York: Routledge, 2005), 3.

38. U.S. Government Accountability Office, "Combating Nuclear Terrorism," 7.

39. Ibid.

40. Medalia, "Nuclear Terrorism," 2.

41. *Black Dawn* final report, www.sgpproject.org/events/Black%20Dawn%20-Final%20Report.pdf (accessed February 20, 2005).

42. Medalia, "Nuclear Terrorism," 4.

43. Ibid., 9.

44. Ibid., 2.

45. Ibid.

46. Ackerman and Snyder, "Would They if They Could?" 43.

47. Linda-Jo Schierow, "Chemical Plant Security," *Congressional Research Service: Policy Papers,* January 20, 2004, 6.

48. O'Neil, "Terrorist Use of Weapons of Mass Destruction," 102.

49. Jacobs, "The Nuclear Threat as a Terrorist Option," 153–55.

50. Joseph W. Foxell, Jr., "The Prospect of Nuclear and Biological Terrorism," *Journal of Contingencies and Crisis Management,* 5, no. 2 (June 1997): 99–100.

51. Andrew Loehmer, "The Nuclear Dimension," *Terrorism and Political Violence,* 5, no. 2 (Summer 1993): 50.

52. Joby Warrick, "Study Raises Projection for 'Dirty Bomb' Toll," *Washington Post,* January 13, 2004, A02.

53. Jonathan Medalia, "Terrorist 'Dirty Bombs': A Brief Primer," *Congressional Research Service: Report for Congress* (order code RS21528), October 29, 2003, 3.

54. Warrick, "Study Raises Projection for 'Dirty Bomb' Toll," A02.

55. Richard Leiby, "Park Police Bomb Their Terrorism Test," *Washington Post,* January 13, 2004, C01.

56. Fred Ikle, transcript of testimony before the Senate Judiciary Committee's Hearing of the Terrorism, Technology, and Homeland Security Subcommittee, "Detecting Smuggled Nuclear Weapons," *Federal News Service,* July 27, 2006.

57. Ferguson and Potter, *The Four Faces of Nuclear Terrorism,* 2.

58. *The 9/11 Commission Report: Final Report of the National Commission on Terrorist Attacks upon the United States* (New York: Norton, 2004), 154.

59. James K. Campbell, "On Not Understanding the Problem," in Roberts, *Hype or Reality?* 17.

60. Jon B. Wolfsthal and Tom Z. Collina, "Nuclear Terrorism and Warhead Control in Russia," *Survival,* 44, no. 2 (Summer 2002): 71.

61. Rose Gottemoeller, senior associate, Carnegie Endowment for International Peace, *Federal News Service,* September 24, 2002.

62. Morten Bremer Maerli and Lars van Dassen, "Europe, Carry Your Weight," *Bulletin of the Atomic Scientists,* 60, no. 6 (November–December 2004): 19.

63. Ibid.

64. Jack Kelly, "Terrorists Shopping for Mass Casualty Weapons," Scripps Howard News Service, February 25, 2003.

65. Ibid.

66. "Russia, the CIS and Terrorism," *Jane's Intelligence Digest,* January 10, 2003.

67. Joe de Courcy, "Does Al-Qaida Have a Nuclear Capability?" *Stratint Special Bulletins,* February 12, 2004, www.courcyint.com/csb/CSB3240.asp (accessed November 9, 2006).

68. Ibid.

69. Ibid.

70. Wolfsthal and Collina, "Nuclear Terrorism and Warhead Control in Russia," 71.

71. Ibid., 76–77.

72. Allison and Kokoshin, "The New Containment," 39.

73. Carolynne Wheeler, "Smuggler Seized in Kyrgyzstan with Weapons-grade Plutonium," *The Guardian* (London), September 30, 2004, 17.

74. George Jahn, "AP Investigation: Soviet Weapons Cache, Arms Dealing and Dirty Bomb Cause Concern in Moldova's Separatist Enclave," Associated Press, January 9, 2004, www.publicinternationallaw.org/docs/PNW/PNW.12Jan_04.htm#Moldova (accessed May 9, 2007).

75. Lale Sabrihomuglu, "Turkey Detects Nuclear Material Trafficking," *Jane's Intelligence Review,* 14, no. 8 (August 2002): 30.

76. Ibid.

77. Ibid., 31.

78. John Newhouse, "The Threats America Faces," *World Policy Journal,* 19, no. 2 (June 22, 2002): 21.

79. Ibid., 21.

80. U.S. Government Accountability Office, "Combating Nuclear Terrorism," 7.

81. David Albright, transcript of testimony before the House International Relations Committee, *CQ Congressional Testimony,* May 25, 2006.

82. Ibid.

83. Senator Dianne Feinstein, transcript of testimony before the Senate Judiciary Committee's Hearing of the Terrorism, Technology and Homeland Security Subcommittee, "Detecting Smuggled Nuclear Weapons," *Federal News Service,* July 27, 2006.

84. Medalia, "Nuclear Terrorism," 3, 9.

85. Jasjit Singh, "The Secret Empire of Dr. Khan," *Indian Express,* February 4, 2004, www.hcindiatz.org/khan.htm (accessed May 9, 2007).

86. "A.Q. Khan: The Man Who Built Pakistan's Bomb," *Japan Economic Newswire,* May 26, 1998.

87. A. Oppenheimer, "Al-Zarqawi, al-Qaeda and WMD," *Jane's Terrorism and Security Monitor,* October 1, 2004.

88. Leonard Weiss, transcript of testimony before the Committee on House International Relations, Subcommittee on International Terrorism and Nonproliferation, *CQ Congressional Testimony,* May 25, 2006.

89. "Dr. Khan's Nuclear Supermarket," *Jane's Intelligence Digest,* February 13, 2004.

90. Ibid.

91. Douglas Jehl, "CIA Says Pakistani Network Aided Iran's Nuclear Program," *New York Times,* November 23, 2004.

92. Mohan Malik, "The Stability of Nuclear Deterrence in South Asia: The Clash Between State and Anti-State Actors," in *Religious Radicalism and Security in South Asia,* ed. Satu P. Limaye, Mohan Malik, and Robert G. Wirsing (Honolulu: Asia-Pacific Center for Security Studies, 2004), 349.

93. Ibid.

94. Andrew Koch, "Investigators Suspect Nuclear Smuggling Network Is Still Active," *Jane's Intelligence Review,* July 1, 2006.

95. Albright, testimony before the House International Relations Committee, May 25, 2006.

96. Greg Giles transcript of statement before the House Committee on Homeland Security's Subcommittee on Prevention of Nuclear and Biological Attacks, *Congressional Quarterly,* September 8, 2005.

97. Sands, testimony before the U.S. Senate Foreign Relations Committee, March 19, 2002.

98. Koch, "Investigators Suspect Nuclear Smuggling Network Is Still Active."

99. Ibid.

100. U.S. General Accounting Office, *Combating Terrorism: How Five Foreign Countries Are Organized to Combat Terrorism,* Report GAO/NSIAD-00–85 (Washington, DC: April 2000), 11.

101. Ackerman and Snyder, "Would They If They Could?" 46.

102. Joseph W. Foxell, Jr., "The Debate on the Potential for Mass-Casualty Terrorism: The Challenge to U.S. Security," *Terrorism and Political Violence,* 11, no. 1 (Spring 1999): 95.

103. Campbell, "On Not Understanding the Problem," 23.

104. Ibid.

105. John F. Sopko and Alan Edleman, transcript of prepared statement before the Senate Governmental Affairs Committee's Permanent Subcommittee on Investigations, "Hearings on the Global Proliferation of Weapons of Mass Destruction: A Case Study on the Aum Shinrikyo," *Federal News Service,* October 31, 1995.

106. *Black Dawn* final report.

107. Osama bin Laden, interview by Rahimullah Yusufzai, December 23, 1998, in Ben Venzke and Aimee Ibrahim, *The Al-Qaeda Threat: An Analytical Guide to Al-Qaeda's Tactics and Targets* (Alexandria, VA: Tempest, 2003), 53.

108. Ibid.

109. Osama bin Laden, interview by Hamid Mir, November 8, 2001, in Venzke and Ibrahim, *The Al-Qaeda Threat,* 54.

110. Matthew Bunn, senior research associate, Managing the Atom Project, transcript of statement before the House Committee on Government Reform's Subcommittee on National Security, Veterans' Affairs, and International Relations, *Federal Document Clearing House Congressional Testimony,* September 24, 2002.

111. Sulaiman Abu Ghaith, "In the Shadow of the Lances," June 2002, listed and summarized in Venzke and Ibrahim, *The Al-Qaeda Threat,* 110–11.

112. Ibid.

113. Ibid.

114. "Al-Jazirah Carries Bin Laden's Audio Messages to Iraqis, Americans," Doha al-Jazirah Satellite Channel Television, October 18, 2003, translated from Arabic by Foreign Broadcast Information Service.

115. Gordon Oehler, director, Nonproliferation Center, Central Intelligence Agency, transcript of testimony before the Senate Government Affairs Permanent Subcommittee on Investigations, "Proliferation of Weapons of Mass Destruction," *Federal Document Clearing House Congressional Testimony,* November 1, 1995.

116. Ibid.

117. Paul J. Smith, "The Terrorists and Crime Bosses Behind the Fake Passport Trade," *Jane's Intelligence Review,* August 2001.

118. Transcript of testimony of Ahmed Ressam in *United States v. Mokhtar Haouari,* July 3, 2001, 624.

119. Ibid., 626.

120. Sebestyen Gorka and Richard Sullivan, "Jordanian Counterterrorist Unit Thwarts Chemical Bomb Attack," *Jane's Intelligence Review,* 16, no. 10 (October 2004): 23.

121. Donna Watson, "MI5 Foil Fanatics Poison Gas Plot," *Daily Record,* April 7, 2004.

122. "Al-Aqsa Brigades Chemical Threat," Risk Pointers-CIR, June 29, 2006, *Strategic Intelligence Forum,* www.courcyint.com/crl/cr110486.asp (accessed November 18, 2004).

123. Ibid.

124. Bryant Furlow, "Biological, Chemical and Radiological Terrorism," *Radiologic Technology,* 75, no. 2 (November 1, 2003): 91.

125. Sopko and Edelman, testimony before the Senate Government Affairs Permanent Subcommittee on Investigations.

126. Ibid.

127. Ibid.

128. Ibid.

129. Ibid.

130. Furlow, "Biological, Chemical and Radiological Terrorism," 91.

131. Sands testimony before the U.S. Senate Foreign Relations Committee.

132. Ibid.

133. David Leppard and Nicholas Rufford, "U.K. Charges Four Suspects in Ricin Bust," *Ottawa Citizen,* January 12, 2003, A6.

134. Joby Warrick, "An Al-Qaeda 'Chemist' and the Quest for Ricin," *Washington Post,* May 5, 2004, A1.

135. Dana Shea and Frank Gottron, "Ricin: Technical Background and Potential Role in Terrorism," *Congressional Research Service: Report for Congress* (order code RS21383), February 4, 2004, 3–4.

136. Ibid., 2.

137. Ibid.

138. Ibid.

139. U.S. General Accounting Office, *Biological Weapons: Effort to Reduce Former Soviet Threat Offers Benefits, Poses New Risks,* Report GAO/NSIAD-00–138 (Washington, DC: April 2000), 7.

140. U.S. General Accounting Office, *Capitol Hill Anthrax Incident: EPA's Cleanup Was Successful; Opportunities Exist to Enhance Contract Oversight,* Report GAO-03–686 (Washington, DC: June 2003), 1.

141. Gregory Koblentz, "Pathogens as Weapons: The International Security Implications of Biological Warfare," *International Security,* 28, no. 3 (Winter 2003–4): 84.

142. W. Seth Carus, visiting fellow, National Defense University, transcript of prepared statement before the Senate Committee on Intelligence and the Senate Judiciary Committee's Subcommittee on Technology, Terrorism and Government Information, *Federal News Service,* March 30, 1998.

143. U.S. General Accounting Office, *Biological Weapons,* 7.

144. Ibid.

145. Ibid., 5.

146. Sands testimony before the U.S. Senate Foreign Relations Committee.

147. Ibid.

148. Ben Fenton, "Russians Knew of West's Germ Warfare Secrets," *Telegraph.co.uk,* December 2, 2005, www.telegraph.co.uk/news/main.jhtml?xml=/news/2005/02/12/nspies12.xml&sSheet=/news/2005/02/12/ixhome.html (accessed February 21, 2005).

149. Sands testimony before the U.S. Senate Foreign Relations Committee.

150. Ibid.

151. Ibid.

152. Ibid.

153. Koblentz, "Pathogens as Weapons," 86.

154. Ibid., 95.

155. Ibid., 97.

156. President George W. Bush, transcript of remarks at the 2002 graduation exercise of the United States Military Academy, June 1, 2002.

157. Ibid.

158. Ibid.

159. Ibid.

160. Vice Admiral Thomas R. Wilson, director, Defense Intelligence Agency, transcript of prepared testimony before the Senate Armed Services Committee, "Global Threats and Challenges," *Federal News Service,* March 19, 2002.

161. Malik, "The Stability of Nuclear Deterrence in South Asia," 345.

162. Ruth Wedgwood, "Al-Qaeda, Military Commissions, and American Self-Defense," *Political Science Quarterly,* 117, no. 3 (September 22, 2002): 357.

163. Sands testimony before the U.S. Senate Foreign Relations Committee.

164. Richard Daniel Ewing, "What the Neo-Cons Can't Tell Americans," *Asia Times,* September 14, 2004, www.atimes.com/atimes/Middle_East/FI14Ak01.html (accessed February 1, 2007).

165. Ibid.

166. Ashton Carter, John Deutch, and Philip Zelikow, "Catastrophic Terrorism: Tackling the New Danger," *Foreign Affairs,* 77, no. 6 (November–December 1998): 80.

167. Ibid., 81.

168. Ibid.

169. Ibid.

170. Commander James K. Campbell, United States Navy, transcript of prepared testimony before the Senate Judiciary Subcommittee on Technology, Terrorism and Government Information and the Senate Select Committee on Intelligence, "Chemical and Biological Weapons Threats to America: Are We Prepared?" *Federal News Service,* April 22, 1998.

Chapter 7

1. "List of Major Car Bombings in Lebanon," Associated Press, December 30, 1991.

2. Rohan Gunaratna, "Suicide Terrorism: A Global Threat," *Jane's Intelligence Review,* 12, no. 4 (April 2000): 52.

3. David C. Rapoport, "The Four Waves of Modern Terrorism," in *Attacking Terrorism: Elements of a Grand Strategy,* ed. Audrey Kurth Cronin and James M. Ludes (Washington, DC: Georgetown University Press, 2004), 62.

4. Mia Bloom, *Dying to Kill: The Allure of Suicide Terror* (New York: Columbia University Press, 2005), 17.

5. Raphael Israeli, "A Manual of Islamic Fundamentalist Terrorism," *Terrorism and Political Violence,* 14, no. 4 (Winter 2002): 25.

6. Leonard Weinberg, Ami Pedahzur, and Daphna Canetti-Nisim, "The Social and Religious Characteristics of Suicide Bombers and Their Victims," *Terrorism and Political Violence,* 15, no. 3 (Autumn 2003): 140.

7. Israeli, "A Manual of Islamic Fundamentalist Terrorism," 25.

8. Ibid., 27.

9. Adam Dolnik and Anjali Bhattacharjee, "Hamas: Suicide Bombings, Rockets, or WMD?" *Terrorism and Political Violence,* 14, no. 3 (Autumn 2002): 109.

10. Bloom, *Dying to Kill,* 123.

11. Dolnik and Bhattacharjee, "Hamas: Suicide Bombings, Rockets, or WMD?" 110.

12. Debra D. Zedalis, *Female Suicide Bombers* (June 2004), Strategic Studies Institute monograph, www.carlisle.army.mil/ssi/Pubs/pubResult.cfm/hurl/PubID=408/FEMALE_SUICIDE_BOMBERS.cfm (accessed March 26, 2007).

13. Scott Atran, "Mishandling Suicide Terrorism," *Washington Quarterly,* 27, no. 3 (Summer 2004): 68–69.

14. Intelligence and Terrorism Information Center at the Center for Special Studies, "Suicide Bombing Terrorism During the Current Israeli-Palestinian Confrontation," January 1, 2006, 2, www.intelligence.org.il/eng/eng_n/pdf/suicide_terrorism_ae.pdf (accessed November 3, 2006).

15. Yoram Schweitzer, "Suicide Terrorism: Development and Main Characteristics," in *Countering Suicide Terrorism: An International Conference, February 20–23, 2000, Herzliya, Israel* (Jerusalem: Gefen Books, 2001), 81.

16. Bloom, *Dying to Kill,* 6.

17. Serge Stepniak-Kravchinski, "Underground Russia," in *Voices of Terror: Manifestos, Writings and Manuals of Al-Qaeda, Hamas, and Other Terrorists From Around the World and Throughout the Ages,* ed. Walter Laqueur (New York: Reed Press, 2004), 89.

18. Walter Laqueur, "What Makes Them Tick?" *Washington Post,* July 24, 2005, T07.

19. Stephen Frederic Dale, "Religious Suicide in Islamic Asia: Anticolonial Terrorism in India, Indonesia, and the Philippines," *Journal of Conflict Resolution,* 32, no. 1 (March 1988): 39.

20. Ibid., 49.

21. Ibid., 52.

22. Ibid.

23. Schweitzer, "Suicide Terrorism," 78.

24. Atran, "Mishandling Suicide Terrorism," 68.

25. Bruce Hoffman and Gordon H. McCormick, "Terrorism, Signaling, and Suicide Attack," *Studies in Conflict & Terrorism,* 27, no. 4 (July–August 2004): 262.

26. "Russia's Toll of Terror: A List of Incidents Blamed on Terrorists in Russia Since October 2002," *Wall Street Journal,* September 7, 2004.

27. Ibid.

28. Sudha Ramachandran, "Killers Turn to Suicide," *Asia Times,* October 15, 2004, www.atimes/com/atimes/South_Asia/FJ15Df02.html (accessed February 1, 2007).

29. Ibid.

30. Ibid.

31. David Eshel, "Israel Reviews Profile of Suicide Bombers," *Jane's Intelligence Review,* 13, no. 11 (November 2001): 20–21.

32. Intelligence and Terrorism Information Center at the Center for Special Studies, "Suicide Bombing Terrorism During the Current Israeli-Palestinian Confrontation," 25–26.

33. Zeina Karam, "For One Groom, Wedding Will Be Remembered as Day of Carnage," Associated Press, November 14, 2005.

34. Jamal Halaby and Zeina Karam, "Details of Deadly Jordan Bombings Emerge," Associated Press Online, November 15, 2005 (Lexis-Nexis database).

35. "Jordanian Mass to Condemn Deadly Attacks," Agence France Presse, November 18, 2005.

36. Martin Chulov, "Chilling Confession of Failed Suicide Bomber," *Australian,* November 15, 2005.

37. Ashraf Khalil, "Iraqi Woman Calmly Confesses How She Tried to Blow Up Hotel," *Los Angeles Times,* November 14, 2005, A1.

38. Zedalis, *Female Suicide Bombers,* 2.

39. Arjuna Gunawardena, "Female Black Tigers: A Different Breed of Cat?" in *Female Suicide Bombers: Dying for Equality?* ed. Yoram Schweitzer (Tel Aviv: Jaffee Center for Strategic Studies, August 2006), 84.

40. Ibid.

41. Anne Speckhard and Khapta Akhmedova, "Black Widows: The Chechen Female Suicide Terrorists," in Schweitzer, *Female Suicide Bombers,* 63.

42. Ibid., 66.

43. Ibid.

44. Ibid., 67.

45. "PA Continues to Laud Female Suicide Bombers as Role Model," *Israel Faxx,* July 8, 2005.

46. Mira Tzoreff, "The Palestinian Shahida: National Patriotism, Islamic Feminism, or Social Crisis," in Schweitzer, *Female Suicide Bombers,* 19.

47. James Bennet, "Arab Press Glorifies Bomber as Heroine," *New York Times,* February 11, 2002, 8.

48. Ibid.

49. Robert A. Pape, "Blowing Up an Assumption," *New York Times,* May 18, 2005, A1, 23.

50. Ibid.

51. Ibid.

52. *White Paper: The Jemaah Islamiyah Arrests and the Threat of Terrorism* (Singapore: Ministry of Home Affairs, 2003), 15–17.

53. Atran, "Mishandling Suicide Terrorism," 74.

54. Hoffman and McCormick, "Terrorism, Signaling, and Suicide Attack," 255.

55. Intelligence and Terrorism Information Center at the Center for Special Studies, "Suicide Bombing Terrorism During the Current Israeli-Palestinian Confrontation," 116.

56. Ibid.

57. Ibid., 201.

58. Hoffman and McCormick, "Terrorism, Signaling, and Suicide Attack," 244.

59. "Background Briefing by a Senior U.S. Military Intelligence Officer; Combined Press Information Center, Baghdad, Iraq," *Federal News Service,* June 2, 2005.

60. Assaf Moghadam, "Palestinian Suicide Terrorism in the Second Intifada: Motivations and Organizational Aspects," *Studies in Conflict & Terrorism,* 26, no. 2 (March–April 2003): 65.

61. Mohammed M. Hafez, *Manufacturing Human Bombs: The Making of Palestinian Suicide Bombers* (Washington, DC: U.S. Institute of Peace Press, 2006), 26.

62. Schweitzer, "Suicide Terrorism," 75.

63. Kirk Semple and John F. Burns, "All-Day Suicide Blitz Claims 22 Lives in Baghdad," *New York Times,* July 16, 2005, A8.

64. Dolnik and Bhattacharjee, "Hamas: Suicide Bombings, Rockets, or WMD?" 114.

65. "Pakistan: Usama Bin Laden Urges Muslims to Launch 'Suicide Attacks' Against US," *Islamabad Ausaf* (April 9, 2003): 1, 7, translated from Urdu by Foreign Broadcast Information Service.

66. Dan Darling, "Special Analysis: The 12/04 bin Laden Tapes," December 30, 2004, www.windsofchange.net/archives/006101.php (accessed on January 21, 2007).

67. Robert A. Pape, "The Strategic Logic of Suicide Terrorism," *American Political Science Review,* 97, no. 3 (August 2003): 7.

68. Bloom, *Dying to Kill,* 1.

69. Hoffman and McCormick, "Terrorism, Signaling, and Suicide Attack," 249.

70. Ibid.

71. Israeli, "A Manual of Islamic Fundamentalist Terrorism," 28.

72. Hoffman and McCormick, "Terrorism, Signaling, and Suicide Attack," 271.

73. Ibid., 250.

74. Weinberg, Pedahzur and Canetti-Nisim, "The Social and Religious Characteristics of Suicide Bombers and Their Victims," 146.

75. Ibid.

76. Rana Sabbagh-Gargour, "'I Went to One Corner, He Went to Another. It Was a Wedding Party,'" *Times* (London), November 14, 2005, 3.

77. Weinberg, Pedahzur and Canetti-Nisim, "The Social and Religious Characteristics of Suicide Bombers and Their Victims," 148.

78. Neil Altman, "On the Psychology of Suicide Bombing," *Tikkun,* 20, no. 2 (March–April 2005): 16.

79. Hafez, *Manufacturing Human Bombs,* 34.

80. Intelligence and Terrorism Information Center at the Center for Special Studies, "Suicide Bombing Terrorism During the Current Israeli-Palestinian Confrontation," 8.

81. Moghadam, "Palestinian Suicide Terrorism in the Second Intifada," 73.

82. Hoffman and McCormick, "Terrorism, Signaling, and Suicide Attack," 253.

83. Intelligence and Terrorism Information Center at the Center for Special Studies,

"Suicide Bombing Terrorism During the Current Israeli-Palestinian Confrontation," 7.

84. Hoffman and McCormick, "Terrorism, Signaling, and Suicide Attack," 254 (quoting a cleric featured in the article "Letter from Gaza: An Arsenal of Believers," *New Yorker,* November 19, 2002, 39).

85. Ramachandran, "Killers Turn to Suicide."

86. Hoffman and McCormick, "Terrorism, Signaling, and Suicide Attack," 254.

87. Ibid., 261.

88. Pape, "The Strategic Logic of Suicide Terrorism," 1.

89. Michael Roberts, "Tamil Tiger 'Martyrs': Regenerating Divine Potency?" *Studies in Conflict & Terrorism,* 28, no. 6 (November–December 2005): 505 (quoting an interview conducted by Margaret Trawick).

90. Audrey Kurth Cronin, "Terrorists and Suicide Attacks," *Congressional Research Service: Report for Congress* (order code RL32058), August 28, 2003, 7.

91. Leonard Downie, Jr., "Prisoners End Fasting in Belfast," *Washington Post,* October 4, 1981, A1.

92. "IRA Claims It Is Stronger Because of Hunger Striker," Associated Press, December 4, 1981.

93. Intelligence and Terrorism Information Center at the Center for Special Studies, "Suicide Bombing Terrorism During the Current Israeli-Palestinian Confrontation," 112.

94. Cronin, "Terrorists and Suicide Attacks," 6.

95. "Jordan 'Bomber' Had Three Brothers Killed in Iraq," Agence France Presse, November 15, 2005.

96. Frank Gardner, "Combating Extremism and the Challenge of Security in the Middle East," *Asian Affairs,* 37, no. 3 (November 2006): 307.

97. Ibid.

98. Hoffman and McCormick, "Terrorism, Signaling, and Suicide Attack," 259.

99. Speckhard and Akhmedova, "Black Widows," 67.

100. Intelligence and Terrorism Information Center at the Center for Special Studies, "Suicide Bombing Terrorism During the Current Israeli-Palestinian Confrontation," 136.

101. Ibid.

102. Ibid.

103. Tzoreff, "The Palestinian Shahida," 20.

104. Ibid.

105. Ibid.

106. Moghadam, "Palestinian Suicide Terrorism in the Second Intifada," 72.

107. Hoffman and McCormick, "Terrorism, Signaling, and Suicide Attack," 250.

108. Richard D. Hecht, "Deadly History, Deadly Actions, and Deadly Bodies: A Response to Ivan Strenski's 'Sacrifice, Gift and the Social Logic of Muslim Human Bombers,'" *Terrorism and Political Violence,* 15, no. 3 (Autumn 2003): 38.

109. Summary of remarks by Ariel Merari, in "Israeli Experts View Terror, Homeland Security, Debunk Myths of Suicide Bombers," Tel Aviv University Workshop, February 22, 2005, translated from Hebrew by Foreign Broadcast Information Service.

110. Hafez, *Manufacturing Human Bombs,* 24.

111. Intelligence and Terrorism Information Center at the Center for Special Studies, "Suicide Bombing Terrorism During the Current Israeli-Palestinian Confrontation," 7.

112. Daphne Burdman, "Education, Indoctrination, and Incitement: Palestinian Children on Their Way to Martyrdom," *Terrorism and Political Violence,* 15, no. 1 (Spring 2003): 96.

113. Ibid., 107.

114. *Report of the Official Account of the Bombings in London on 7th July 2005* (London: Stationery Office, 2006), 2, http://news.bbc.co.uk/1/shared/bsp/hi/pdfs/11_05_06_narrative.pdf (accessed November 6, 2006).

115. Ibid.

116. *Intelligence and Security Committee: Report into the London Terrorist Attacks on 7 July 2005* (London: Intelligence and Security Committee), 11,http://news.bbc.co.uk/1/shared/bsp/hi/pdfs/11_05_06_isc_london_attacks_report.pdf (accessed November 6, 2006).

117. Ibid.

118. *Report of the Official Account of the Bombings in London on 7th July 2005,* 13.

119. Ibid.

120. Ibid., 14.

121. Ibid.

122. Ibid.

123. Ibid., 17–18.

124. Ibid., 18.

125. Ibid., 15.

126. Ibid., 14.

127. Ibid., 15.

128. Ibid., 20.

129. Ibid.

130. Ibid.

131. Thomas Catan, "Home-grown Killers in a Multicultural Mix," *Financial Times,* August 8, 2005, 4.

132. *Intelligence and Security Committee: Report into the London Terrorist Attacks on 7 July 2005,* 29.

133. Raf Casert, "Belgians Seek to Come to Grips with Fact That Suicide Bomber in Iraq Was One of Them," Associated Press, December 1, 2005.

134. "Six Charged with Terror Offences in Belgium," Agence France-Presse, December 1, 2005.

Chapter 8

1. Eric Lichtblau and James Risen, "Bank Data Sifted in Secret by U.S. to Block Terror," *New York Times,* June 23, 2006, A1.

2. Ibid.

3. Representative Geoff Davis (R-KY), testimony before a hearing of the House Committee on Financial Services' Subcommittee on Oversight and Investigations, *Federal News Service,* July 11, 2006.

4. Representative Patrick McHenry (R-NC), testimony before a hearing of the House Committee on Financial Services' Subcommittee on Oversight and Investigations, *Federal News Service,* July 11, 2006.

5. Rick Klein, "House Votes to Condemn Media over Terror Story," *Boston Globe,* June 30, 2006, A1.

6. Sheryl Gay Stolberg and Eric Lichtblau, "Cheney Assails Press on Report on Bank Data," *New York Times,* June 24, 2006.

7. Frank Rich, "All the News That's Fit to Bully," *New York Times,* July 9, 2006, 12.

8. "Following the Money, and the Rules," *New York Times,* June 24, 2006, 14.

9. Barton Gellman, Paul Blustein, and Dafna Linzer, "Bank Records Secretly Tapped; Administration Began Using Global Database Shortly After 2001 Attacks," *Washington Post,* June 23, 2006, A01.

10. James Risen, "Traces of Terror: The Money Trail," *New York Times,* July 17, 2002, 16.

11. *The 9/11 Commission Report: Final Report of the National Commission on Terrorist Attacks upon the United States* (New York: Norton, 2004), 172.

12. Chairman Michael G. Oxley, transcript of opening statement before the House Committee on Financial Services, "Dismantling the Financial Infrastructure of Global Terrorism," *Federal Document Clearing House Congressional Testimony,* October 3, 2001.

13. Juan Zarate, deputy assistant secretary, U.S. Treasury Department, transcript of testimony before the House Committee on Financial Services' Subcommittee on Oversight and Investigations, *Congressional Quarterly,* February 16, 2005.

14. Gellman, Blustein, and Linzer, "Bank Records Secretly Tapped," A01.

15. This term was used by former Secretary of State Colin L. Powell in November 2001. See Secretary Colin L. Powell, "Remarks on Financial Aspects of Terrorism at Office of Financial Crimes Enforcement Network," speech delivered in Vienna, Virginia, November 7, 2001, www.state.gov/secretary/former/powell/remarks/2001/5979.htm (accessed May 10, 2007).

16. Anne L. Clunan, "The Fight Against Terrorist Financing," *Political Science Quarterly,* 121, no. 4 (Winter 2006–7): 570.

17. Robert H. Kupperman, Debra van Opstral, and David Williamson, "Terror, the Strategic Tool: Response and Control," *Annals of the American Academy of Political and Social Science,* 463 (September 1982): 33.

18. Ibid.

19. Bernard Gwertzman, "President Sharply Assails Kremlin," *New York Times,* January 30, 1981, A1.

20. Galia Golan, "The Soviet Union and the Israeli Action in Lebanon," *International Affairs,* 59, no. 1 (Winter 1982–83): 10.

21. Ibid., 11.

22. Ibid.

23. "China Condemns Raid and All Acts of Terror," *New York Times,* April 16, 1986, A16.

24. Nigel Disney, "China and the Middle East," *MERIP Reports,* no. 63 (December 1977): 7.

25. Robert Alden, "U.N. to Debate Terrorism Despite China and Arabs," *New York Times,* September 23, 1972, 65.

26. Robert Alden, "China, at the UN, Backs 'Just' Wars," *New York Times,* October 4, 1972.

27. Lillian Craig Harris, "China's Relations with the PLO," *Journal of Palestine Studies,* 7, no. 1 (Autumn 1977): 124.

28. Ibid.

29. Ibid, 130.

30. Ibid.

31. "Bulgarian Ties to Red Brigades?" *Christian Science Monitor*, March 17, 1982, 3.

32. Lally Weymouth, "East Germany's Dirty Secret," *Washington Post*, October 14, 1990, C1.

33. Ibid.

34. Dan Cook, "A Terrorist's Many 'Connections,'" *Washington Post*, September 7, 1975, 33.

35. Ibid.

36. "Police Say Former Stasi Member Charged with Terrorism Arrested," Associated Press, September 8, 1992.

37. Bernard Weinraub, "Libyans Arm and Train World Terrorists," *New York Times*, July 16, 1976, 46.

38. Ibid.

39. Clunan, "The Fight Against Terrorist Financing," 574–75.

40. Somini Sengupta, "Canadian Cash Fueling Revolt in Sri Lanka?" *The Gazette* (Montreal, Quebec), July 16, 2000.

41. Somini Sengupta, "Canada's Tamils Work for a Homeland from Afar," *New York Times*, July 16, 2000, 3.

42. Jennifer Campbell, "Tamil Tigers Blacklisting Lauded," *Ottawa Citizen*, April 12, 2006, C5.

43. Michael Jonsson and Klas Karrstrand, "Money Problems—Tackling Terrorist Financiers in Sweden," *Jane's Intelligence Review*, February 2, 2007.

44. Honorable Walter B. Slocombe, under secretary of Defense for Policy, transcript of prepared statement before the House International Relations Committee, *Federal News Service*, July 23, 1998.

45. Linda Charlton, "Fund-Raising by a Group in U.S. Called Vital to I.R.A. Operations," *New York Times*, September 24, 1979, A1.

46. Bernard Weinraub, "Wilson Denounces U.S. Help for IRA," *New York Times*, December 18, 1975, 16.

47. *The 9/11 Commission Report*, 170–71.

48. Ibid.

49. *The 9/11 Commission Report*, 170.

50. Ibid.

51. Kurt Eichenwald, "Terror Money Hard to Block, Officials Find," *New York Times*, December 10, 2001, A1.

52. Ibid.

53. Ibid.

54. Jeff Gerth and Judith Miller, "Funds for Terrorists Traced to Persian Gulf Businessmen," *New York Times*, August 14, 1996, A1.

55. Eichenwald, "Terror Money Hard to Block," A1.

56. Ibid.

57. "Kuwait Officials Irked by U.S. Request to Check Charities," *Deutsche Presse-Agentur*, March 11, 1996.

58. Stefan Leader, "Cash for Carnage: Funding the Modern Terrorist," *Jane's Intelligence Review*, May 1, 1998, 36.

59. Ibid.

60. *The 9/11 Commission Report*, 170.

61. Brian Joyce, "Terrorist Financing in Southeast Asia," *Jane's Intelligence Review*, November 1, 2002.

62. "Terror Timeline: Ressam's Sorry Montreal Record," *The Gazette* (Montreal), May 15, 2005, D3.

63. Ian Mulgrew, "Ressam Gets 22 Years in Prison," *The Gazette* (Montreal), July 28, 2005, A1.

64. Ibid.

65. Chris Jasparro, "Low-level Criminality Linked to Transnational Terrorism," *Jane's Intelligence Review,* May 1, 2005.

66. Joanna Wright, "Interview: Antonio Maria Costa—Executive Director, UN Office on Drugs and Crime," *Jane's Intelligence Review,* March 1, 2006.

67. "Madrid Bombings Cost 105,000 Euros—Spanish Judge," *BBC Monitoring International Reports,* April 12, 2006.

68. Christopher Aaron, "Interview with Max-Peter Ratzel, Europol Director," *Jane's Intelligence Review,* November 1, 2005.

69. Tamara Makarenko, "A Model of Terrorist-Criminal Relations," *Jane's Intelligence Review,* August 1, 2003.

70. "Famous Cases: Willie Sutton," *FBI History—Famous Cases,* www.fbi.gov/libref/historic/famcases/sutton/sutton.htm (accessed May 8, 2007).

71. Clifton Daniel, "Terrorists Kill 4 in Tel Aviv in $180,000 Bank Hold-Up," *New York Times,* September 27, 1947, 1.

72. "British Say IRA Leaders Have Stolen Funds," *New York Times,* April 9, 1973, 12.

73. James Brooke, "13 Held in $7 Million Connecticut Theft," *New York Times,* August 31, 1985, 26.

74. Ibid.

75. Michael A. Sheehan, coordinator for counterterrorism, U.S. Department of State, transcript of prepared testimony before the House Committee on the Judiciary's Subcommittee on Crime, *Federal News Service,* December 13, 2000.

76. Mark Fritz, "Four More Reputed Red Army Terrorists Captured," Associated Press, June 15, 1990.

77. Henry Tanner, "Red Brigades Intimidates Italians but Fails in Effort to Start Civil War," *New York Times,* May 17, 1978, 25.

78. "Financing Is No Problem for the Red Brigades," *New York Times,* May 17, 1978, A14.

79. "Terrorists Land, Relinquish Money," *New York Times,* September 19, 1974.

80. Ibid.

81. "The Rise and Fall of the Symbionese Liberation Army," *American Experience* Web site, www.pbs.org/wgbh/amex/guerrilla/peopleevents/e_kidnapping.html (accessed May 8, 2007).

82. Sam Allis, "A Tough Trip Back to the Era of Patty Hearst," *Boston Globe,* May 23, 2005, B5.

83. Ibid.; Stephen Holden, "Even in the Days of Patty Hearst, It Was the Innocent Who Died," *New York Times,* November 26, 2004, 26.

84. Holden, "Even in the Days of Patty Hearst, It Was the Innocent Who Died," 26; "Patricia Hearst Writes of Role in Death at Bank," *New York Times,* December 5, 1981, 1.

85. Holden, "Even in the Days of Patty Hearst, It Was the Innocent Who Died," 26; "Patricia Hearst Writes of Role in Death at Bank," 1.

86. "Shultz Raps Ford Decision to Pay Argentine Ransom," *Wall Street Journal,* May 30, 1973, 3.

87. Ibid.

88. Sheehan, transcript of prepared testimony before the House Committee on the Judiciary.

89. Paul J. Smith, "East Asia's Transnational Challenges: The Dark Side of Globalization," in *Tiger's Roar: Asia's Recovery and Its Impact,* ed. Julian Weiss (Armonk, NY: M.E. Sharpe, 2001), 17–18.

90. Joanna Wright, "Afghanistan's Opiate Economy and Terrorist Financing," *Jane's Intelligence Review,* March 1, 2006.

91. *United States of America v. Pedro Antonio Marin, et al.* (superseding indictment), U.S. District Court for the District of Columbia, March 1, 2006, Criminal No. 04–446 (TFH), 9, http://files.findlaw.com/news.findlaw.com/cnn/docs/narco/usmarin306sind.pdf (accessed May 8, 2007).

92. Ibid., 6.

93. Ibid., 9.

94. Ibid., 21.

95. Ibid., 15–16.

96. Ibid., 16.

97. Simona Sapienza, "Keeping Money Out of Terrorist Hands," *RUSI / Jane's Homeland Security and Resilience Monitor,* May 1, 2006.

98. Martin A. Weiss, "Terrorist Financing: U.S. Agency Efforts and Inter-Agency Coordination," *Congressional Research Service: Report for Congress,* August 3, 2005, 46.

99. Ilias Bantekas, "The International Law of Terrorist Financing," *American Journal of International Law,* 97, no. 2 (April 2003): 315.

100. Clunan, "The Fight Against Terrorist Financing," 578.

101. Bantekas, "The International Law of Terrorist Financing," 315.

102. Clunan, "The Fight Against Terrorist Financing," 579.

103. "9 Special Recommendations (SR) on Terrorist Financing (TF)," Financial Action Task Force (FATF) Web site, www.fatf-gafi.org/document/9/0,2340,en_32250379_32236920_34032073_1_1_1_1,00.html (accessed May 8, 2007).

104. E. Anthony Wayne, assistant secretary, Economic and Business Affairs, U.S. Department of State, transcript of statement before the Committee on Senate Banking, Housing and Urban Affairs, *CQ Congressional Testimony,* July 13, 2005.

105. 50 U.S.C. § 1701–6.

106. *The 2001 National Money Laundering Strategy* (Washington, DC: U.S. Department of Treasury, Office of Enforcement, September 2001), 9.

107. Clunan, "The Fight Against Terrorist Financing," 585.

108. Chief Barry Sabin, Counterterrorism Section of the Criminal Division of the U.S. Department of Justice, transcript of testimony before a hearing of the Senate Committee on the Judiciary's Subcommittee on Terrorism, Technology and Homeland Security, *Federal News Service,* September 13, 2004.

109. Juliette N. Kayyem, former commissioner, National Commission on Terrorism, transcript of testimony before the House Armed Services Oversight Panel on Terrorism, *Federal Document Clearing House Congressional Testimony,* July 13, 2000.

110. Sabin, transcript of prepared testimony before the Senate Committee on the Judiciary.

111. Stephen C. Warneck, "A Preemptive Strike: Using RICO and the AEDPA to Attack the Financial Strength of International Terrorist Organizations," *Boston University Law Review,* February 1998, 213–14.

112. U.S. Department of the Treasury, Office of Public Affairs, "Treasury Department

Designates Burma and Two Burmese Banks to Be of 'Primary Money Laundering Concern' and Announces Proposed Countermeasures Under Section 311 of the USA PATRIOT Act," press release, November 19, 2003, www.treas.gov/press/releases/reports/js1014attachment.pdf (accessed May 8, 2007).

113. Nicole M. Healy and Judith A. Lee, "Ad Hoc Task Force on Professional Responsibilities Regarding Money Laundering: PATRIOT Act and Gatekeeper Update," *The International Lawyer,* 37 (Summer 2003): 631.

114. "Financial Crimes Enforcement Network; Anti-Money Laundering Programs; Special Due Diligence Programs for Certain Foreign Accounts," *Federal Register,* 71, no. 2 (January 4, 2006): 496.

115. See "Part 353: Suspicious Activity Reports," www.fdic.gov/regulations/laws/rules/2000–7500.html (accessed May 8, 2007).

116. Healy and Lee, "Ad Hoc Task Force on Professional Responsibilities Regarding Money Laundering," 631.

117. *The SAR Activity Review: By the Numbers* (Washington, DC: U.S. Department of the Treasury, February 2006), 2.

118. Ibid., 2–3.

119. "Treasury Department Designates Burma and Two Burmese Banks to Be of 'Primary Money Laundering Concern.'"

120. Marcus Noland, senior fellow, Institute for International Economics, transcript of statement before the Senate Committee on Homeland Security and Government Affairs' Subcommittee on Federal Financial Management, Government Information, Federal Services, and International Security, *CQ Congressional Testimony,* April 25, 2006.

121. Director Peter A. Prahar, Office of Africa, Asia and Europe Programs, Department of State, transcript of statement before the Senate Committee on Homeland Security and Government Affairs' Subcommittee on Federal Financial Management, Government Information, Federal Services, and International Security, *CQ Congressional Testimony,* April 25, 2006.

122. Ibid.

123. Daniel L. Glaser, acting assistant secretary, U.S. Treasury Department Office of Terrorist Financing and Financial Crimes, transcript of prepared remarks before the Latvian Commercial Bankers Association Conference, "The Fight Against Money Laundering and Financial Crimes," *Federal News Service,* September 14, 2005.

124. Bruce Zagaris, "Treasury Imposes Sanctions Against 2 Foreign Financial Institutions," *International Enforcement Law Reporter,* 20, no. 11 (November 2004).

125. Ibid.

126. Representative Dana Rohrabacher (R-CA), transcript of report before a joint hearing of the House Committee on International Relations' Subcommittee on Oversight and Investigations and Subcommittee on the Middle East and Central Asia, "Syria's Role in the UN Oil-for-Food Program," *Federal News Service,* July 27, 2005.

127. "Financial Crimes Enforcement Network: Amendment to the Bank Secrecy Act Regulations—Imposition of Special Measures Against Commercial Bank of Syria," *Federal Register,* 71, no. 50 (March 15, 2006): 13260–61, www.fincen.gov/noticeoffinalrule03152006.pdf (accessed May 8, 2007).

128. Ibid.

129. Ibid., 13263.

130. Ibid.

131. Ibid.

132. Guy Dinmore, "US Sets Sights on Iran's Financial Underbelly," *Financial Times,* February 28, 2007, 9.

133. Stuart Levey, under secretary, U.S. Treasury Department Office of Terrorism and Financial Intelligence, transcript of statement before the Senate Committee on Banking, Housing and Urban Affairs, *CQ Congressional Testimony,* April 4, 2006.

134. Clunan, "The Fight Against Terrorist Financing," 596.

135. Levey, transcript of statement before the Senate Committee on Banking, Housing and Urban Affairs.

136. Zachary Abuza, "Funding Terrorism in Southeast Asia: The Financial Network of Al Qaeda and Jemaah Islamiyah," *NBR Analysis,* 14, no. 5 (December 2003): 20–21.

137. "Indonesia: Article Details JI Funding, Noordin's Problem Getting Al Qaeda Funds," *Surabaya Post,* March 6, 2006, obtained from and translated from Indonesian by Open Source Center.

138. Statement of Stuart Levey, Under Secretary for Terrorism and Financial Intelligence, Department of the Treasury, before the Senate Banking, Housing and Urban Affairs Committee, reported in *Federal Document Clearing House Congressional Testimony,* April 4, 2006.

139. Michael Knights and Zack Snyder, "The Role Played by Funding in the Iraq Insurgency," *Jane's Intelligence Review,* August 1, 2005.

140. Daniel L. Glaser, acting assistant secretary, U.S. Treasury Department Office of Terrorist Financing and Financial Crimes, transcript of statement before the House Armed Services Subcommittee on Terrorism, Unconventional Threats and Capabilities, *CQ Congressional Testimony,* July 28, 2005.

141. Douglas Farah, "Al Qaeda's Road Paved with Gold," *Washington Post,* February 17, 2002, A01.

142. *The 9/11 Commission Report,* 171.

143. Ibid.

144. Walter Perkel, "Money Laundering and Terrorism: Informal Value Transfer Systems," *American Criminal Law Review,* 41 (Winter 2004): 183.

145. Ibid.

146. Chief Michael F.A. Morehart, Terrorist Financing Operations Section, Federal Bureau of Investigation, transcript of statement before the Senate Committee on Banking, Housing, and Urban Affairs, *CQ Congressional Testimony,* April 4, 2006.

147. The White House, "Fact Sheet on Terrorist Financing Executive Order," press release, September 24, 2001, www.whitehouse.gov/news/releases/2001/09/20010924-2.html (accessed May 8, 2007).

148. Ibid.

149. Hannah K. Strange, "July 7 Bombings 'Cost Just $1,000,'" *UPI,* January 3, 2006.

150. Ibid.

151. Ibid.

152. Kim Sengupta, "The 'Pounds 7,000 Terror Plot,'" *Independent on Sunday* (London), September 17, 2006, 16.

153. Kumar Ramakrishna, "Countering Radical Islam in Southeast Asia: The Need to Confront the Functional and Ideological 'Enabling Environment,'" in *Terrorism and Violence in Southeast Asia: Transnational Threats to States and Regional Stability,* ed. Paul J. Smith (Armonk, NY: M.E. Sharpe, 2005), 161.

154. For a more detailed analysis of al-Qaeda's ideology, see Christopher M. Blanchard, "Al Qaeda: Statements and Evolving Ideology," *Congressional Research Service: Report for Congress,* updated January 24, 2007, www.fas.org/sgp/crs/terror/RL32759.pdf (accessed May 8, 2007).

Chapter 9

1. DOD Commission on Beirut International Airport, *Report of the DOD Commission on Beirut International Airport Terrorist Act,* December 20, 1983, 33.
2. Ibid.
3. Ibid., 32.
4. General Paul X. Kelley, U.S. Marine Corps, Commandant, transcript of hearings before the U.S. Senate Committee on Armed Services, 98th Cong., October 25, 31, 1983 (Washington, DC: U.S. Government Printing Office, 1984), 53.
5. Ibid.
6. Ibid.
7. Ibid., 54.
8. Ibid.
9. Ibid., 86.
10. *Report of the DOD Commission on Beirut International Airport Terrorist Act,* 40.
11. Senator Sam Nunn, transcript of statement at hearings before the U.S. Senate Committee on Armed Services, 98th Cong., October 25, 31, 1983 (Washington, DC: U.S. Government Printing Office, 1984), 87.
12. Ibid., 88.
13. Kelley, statement before the Senate Committee on Armed Services, 88.
14. *Report of the DOD Commission on Beirut International Airport Terrorist Act,* 63.
15. Ibid., 123.
16. Dale L. Watson, section chief, International Terrorism Operations Section, Federal Bureau of Investigation, transcript of prepared statement before the Senate Judiciary Committee's Subcommittee on Terrorism, Technology, and Government Information, *Federal News Service,* February 24, 1998.
17. Ibid.
18. Substitution for the testimony of Khalid Sheikh Mohammed, Defendant's Exhibit 941, *United States v. Moussaoui* (Cr. No. 01–455-A), 4, www.rcfp.org/moussaoui/pdf/DX-0941.pdf (accessed March 26, 2007).
19. Ibid.
20. Ibid.
21. *The 9/11 Commission Report: Final Report of the National Commission on Terrorist Attacks upon the United States* (New York: Norton, 2004), 344.
22. Kelley, statement before the Senate Committee on Armed Services, 60.
23. Philip C. Wilcox, Jr., transcript of prepared testimony before the House Committee on the Judiciary's Subcommittee on Immigration and Claims, *Federal News Service,* January 26, 2000.
24. Paul K. Davis and Brian Michael Jenkins, *Deterrence and Influence in Counterterrorism: A Component in the War on Al-Qaeda* (Santa Monica, CA: RAND, 2002), 7.
25. Ibid., 4.

26. *The National Security Strategy of the United States of America* (Washington DC: The White House, 2006), 9–10.

27. Ibid., 9.

28. Ibid.

29. Ibid.

30. Ibid.

31. Ibid.

32. Interview with senior intelligence counterterrorism official, government of the Philippines, February 23, 2004.

33. Ronald Koven, "Italian Extremism Feeds on High Unemployment, Loss of Traditional Ties," *Washington Post,* April 27, 1978, A22.

34. Paul Pillar, "The Dimensions of Terrorism and Counterterrorism," in *Terrorism and Counterterrorism: Understanding the New Security Environment,* ed. Russell D. Howard and Reid L. Sawyer (Guilford, CT: McGraw Hill/Dushkin, 2004), 37.

35. Jonathan Fox, "The Effects of Religion on Domestic Conflicts," *Terrorism and Political Violence,* 10, no. 4 (Winter 1998): 60.

36. Samuel M. Makinda, "Global Governance and Terrorism," *Global Change,* 15, no. 1 (February 2003): 56.

37. Pillar, "The Dimensions of Terrorism and Counterterrorism," 37.

38. Richard K. Betts, "The Soft Underbelly of American Primacy: Tactical Advantages of Terror," *Political Science Quarterly,* 117, no. 1 (March 22, 2002): 19.

39. *White Paper: The Jemaah Islamiyah Arrests and the Threat of Terrorism* (Singapore, Ministry of Home Affairs, January 7, 2003), 15.

40. Davis and Jenkins, *Deterrence and Influence in Counterterrorism,* 17.

41. *The 9/11 Commission Report,* 53–54.

42. Based on author interviews with counterterrorism officials conducted in Southeast Asia from November 30, 2004, to December 9, 2004.

43. *The National Security Strategy of the United States,* 10.

44. Vice President Dick Cheney, transcript of remarks to the Conservative Political Action Conference, Crystal Gateway Marriott, Arlington, VA, *Federal News Service,* January 30, 2003.

45. Vice President Cheney, transcript of remarks at a Bush-Cheney 2004 Reception, Wakonda Club, Des Moines, IA, *PR Newswire,* October 4, 2003.

46. Barry Desker and Arabinda Acharya, "Targeting Islamist Terrorism in Asia Pacific: An Unending War," *Asia-Pacific Review,* 11, no. 2 (2004): 73.

47. Michael Slackman, "Saudis Round up 172, Citing a Plot Against Oil Rigs," *New York Times,* April 28, 2007, A1.

48. Desker and Acharya, "Targeting Islamist Terrorism in Asia Pacific."

49. Director of Intelligence Porter J. Goss, transcript of testimony before the Senate Select Committee on Intelligence, February 16, 2005, www.cia.gov/cia/public_affairs?speeches/2004/Goss_testimony_02162005.html.

50. James A. Baker III and Lee H. Hamilton, co-chairs, *The Iraq Study Group Report* (New York: Vintage Books, 2006), 2.

51. Frank Smyth, "Left, Right, the U.S. Out of Step in Iraq," *Asia Times,* September 24, 2004.

52. Andrew Kydd, "In America We (Used to) Trust: U.S. Hegemony and Global Cooperation," *Political Science Quarterly,* 120, no. 4 (Winter 2005–6): 620.

53. "Mistrust of America in Europe Ever Higher, Muslim Anger Persists," Pew Global Attitudes Project, March 16, 2004, 4.

54. Ibid., 3.
55. Ibid., 21.
56. Ibid., 14.
57. Ibid., 8.
58. *The National Security Strategy of the United States,* 10.
59. Stephen Van Evera, "Israel-Palestine," in *Flashpoints in the War on Terrorism,* ed. Derek S. Reveron and Jeffrey Stevenson Murer (New York: Routledge, 2006), 3.
60. Christopher M. Blanchard, "Al-Qaeda: Statements and Evolving Ideology," *Congressional Research Service: Report for Congress* (order code RL32759), January 26, 2006, 4–6.
61. C.L. Sulzberger, "Source of the Terror," *New York Times,* March 20, 1977, 171.
62. Petter Nesser, "Jihad in Europe; Recruitment for Terrorist Cells in Europe," in *FFI Rapport—Paths to Global Jihad: Radicalization and Recruitment to Terror Networks,* Proceedings of the FFI Seminar, Oslo, March 15, 2006, 14.
63. Ibid.
64. *The National Security Strategy of the United States,* 10.
65. Davis and Jenkins, *Deterrence and Influence in Counterterrorism,* 28.
66. Alan B. Krueger and David D. Laitin, "'Misunderestimating' Terrorism," *Foreign Affairs,* 83, no. 5 (September/October 2004), accessed May 16, 2007, from www.foreignaffairs.org/20040901facomment83502/alan-b-krueger-david-d-laitin/misunderestimating-terrorism.html.
67. Ibid.
68. *The National Security Strategy of the United States,* 10.
69. The U.S. government's National Security Strategy defines "transformational diplomacy" as "working with our many international partners to build and sustain democratic, well-governed states that will respond to the needs of their citizens and conduct themselves responsibility in the international system." See *The National Security Strategy of the United States,* 33.
70. *The National Security Strategy of the United States,* 11.
71. Pillar, "The Dimensions of Terrorism and Counterterrorism," 36.
72. Alberto Abadie, *Poverty, Political Freedom, and the Roots of Terrorism,* Harvard University, John F. Kennedy School of Government, Faculty Research Working Papers Series, RWP04–043, October 2004, 1.
73. Ibid., 3.
74. Ibid.
75. Ken Menkhaus, "Quasi-States, Nation-Building, and Terrorist Safe Havens," *Journal of Conflict Studies,* 23, no. 2 (Fall 2003): 14–16.
76. *The National Security Strategy of the United States,* 11.
77. Gerard Alexander, "The Authoritarian Illusion," *National Interest,* no. 77 (Fall 2004): 82.
78. Ibid., 80.
79. Walter Laqueur, "Reflections on Terrorism," in *The Terrorism Reader: The Essential Source Book on Political Violence Both Past and Present,* ed. Walter Laqueur and Yonah Alexander (New York: NAL/Penguin, 1987), 384.
80. Ibid.
81. Kumar Ramakrishna, "Countering Radical Islam in Southeast Asia: The Need to Confront the Functional and Ideological 'Enabling Environment,'" in *Terrorism*

and Violence in Southeast Asia: Transnational Challenges to States and Regional Stability, ed. Paul J. Smith (Armonk, NY: M.E. Sharpe, 2005), 162.

82. Egbal Ahmad, "Terrorism: Theirs and Ours," in Russell and Sawyer, *Terrorism and Counterterrorism,* 52.

83. Stephen Zunes, "Redefining Security in the Face of Terrorism," *Peace Review,* 14, no. 2 (2002): 238.

84. Thomas L. Friedman, "The 2 Domes of Belgium," *New York Times,* January 27, 2002, 13.

85. Testimony of Ambassador Dennis Ross, "Panel III of a Hearing of the National Commission on Terrorist Attacks upon the United States," *Federal News Service,* July 9, 2003.

86. Ibid.

87. *The National Security Strategy of the United States,* 10.

88. "The Conspiracy Theories," *Sunday Times,* August 13, 2006.

89. Erich Kolig, "Radical Islam, Islamic Fervour and Political Sentiments in Central Java, Indonesia," *European Journal of East Asian Studies,* 4, no. 1 (March 2005): 62.

90. Sidney Jones, "Who Are the Terrorists in Indonesia?" (commentary appearing in the *Observer),* www.crisisgroup.org/home/index.cfm?id=2150&1=1 (accessed March 26, 2007).

91. Stefan Theil, "9/11? It Never Happened," *Newsweek,* 142, no. 12 (September 23, 2003): 30.

92. *The National Security Strategy of the United States,* 10.

93. Ibid.

94. *National Military Strategic Plan for the War on Terrorism* (Washington, DC: Chairman of the Joint Chiefs of Staff, 2006), 18.

95. Davis and Jenkins, *Deterrence and Influence in Counterterrorism,* 18.

96. *National Military Strategic Plan for the War on Terrorism,* 18.

97. Davis and Jenkins, *Deterrence and Influence in Counterterrorism,* 5.

98. Walter Reich, "Understanding Terrorist Behavior: The Limits and Opportunities of Psychological Inquiry," in *Origins of Terrorism: Psychologies, Ideologies, Theologies and States of Mind,* ed. Reich (Cambridge: Cambridge University Press, 1990), 271.

99. Jerrold M. Post, "Terrorist Psycho-logic: Terrorist Behavior as a Product of Psychological Forces," in Reich, *Origins of Terrorism,* 38.

100. Rex A. Hudson et al., *Who Becomes a Terrorist and Why—The 1999 Government Report on Profiling Terrorists* (Guilford, CT: Lyons Press, 2001), 140–41.

101. Ibid.

102. David C. Rapoport, "The Four Waves of Modern Terrorism," in *Attacking Terrorism: Elements of a Grand Strategy,* ed. Audrey Kurth Cronin and James M. Ludes (Washington, DC: Georgetown University Press, 2004), 53.

103. Ibid., 56.

104. Walter Laqueur, *Terrorism* (Boston: Little, Brown, 1977), 58.

105. Paul Wilkinson, *Terrorism Versus Democracy: The Liberal State Response* (London: Frank Cass, 2001), 26.

106. *White Paper: The Jemaah Islamiyah Arrests,* 6.

107. Lee Harris, "Al-Qaeda's Fantasy Ideology," *Policy Review,* no. 114, August 2002, www.hoover.org/publications/policyreview/3459646.html (accessed May 16, 2007).

108. Laqueur, *Terrorism,* 128.

109. Rapoport, "The Four Waves of Modern Terrorism," 54.

110. Wilkinson, *Terrorism Versus Democracy,* 29.

111. Chris Quillen, "A Historical Analysis of Mass Casualty Bombers," *Studies in Conflict & Terrorism,* 25, no. 5 (September–October 2002): 288.

112. Quillen, "A Historical Analysis of Mass Casualty Bombers," 290.

113. Bruce Hoffman, *Inside Terrorism* (New York: Columbia University Press, 1998), 65.

114. Wilkinson, *Terrorism Versus Democracy,* 26.

115. Audrey Kurth Cronin, "Behind the Curve: Globalization and International Terrorism," *International Security,* 27, no. 3 (Winter 2002–3), 53.

116. Jessica Stern, "The Protean Enemy," in *Strategy and Force Planning,* 4th ed. (Newport, RI: U.S. Naval War College, 2004), 470.

117. *World Development Report (WDR) 2007—Development and the Next Generation: Regional Highlights—Middle East and North Africa,* http://siteresources. worldbank.org/INTWDR2007/Resources/1489782–1158076403546/WDR2007 RegionalHighlights_MENA_Aug29_draft6.pdf (accessed November 29, 2006).

118. Ibid.

119. Ibid.

120. "Pervasive Insecurity," in *Report of the National Intelligence Council's 2020 Project,* www.dni.gov/nic/NIC_globaltrend2020_s4.html#page96 (accessed November 30, 2006).

121. Robert L. Wilby and George L.W. Perry, "Climate Change, Biodiversity, and the Urban Environment: A Critical Review Based on London, UK," *Progress in Physical Geography,* 30, no. 1 (January 2006): 73–74.

122. Frank G. Hoffman, "Small Wars Revisited: The United States and Nontraditional Wars," *Journal of Strategic Studies,* 28, no. 6 (December 2005): 923–24.

123. Ibid.

124. Thomas Homer-Dixon, "The Rise of Complex Terrorism," *Foreign Policy,* no. 128 (January–February 2002): 57.

125. "The Contradictions of Globalization," in *Report of the National Intelligence Council 2020 Project,* http://dni.gov/nic/NIC_globaltrend2020.s1.html (accessed March 26, 2007).

126. Susan E. Rice, "The Threat of Global Poverty," *National Interest,* no. 83 (Spring 2006), 77.

127. Ibid., 78.

128. Graeme Hugo, "Population Geography," *Progress in Human Geography,* 30, no. 4 (2006): 517.

129. *Facts and Figures: Global Estimates and Trends* (Geneva: International Organization for Migration, 2007), available at www.iom.int/jahia/page254.html (accessed May 20, 2007).

130. Mark Galeotti, "People-trafficking Erodes Security in Former Soviet States," *Jane's Intelligence Review,* April 1, 2005.

131. Oscar Becerra, "Mexican People-smuggling Trade Worth Billions," *Jane's Intelligence Review,* December 1, 2004.

132. "The Contradictions of Globalization."

133. Jamal R. Nassar, *Globalization and Terrorism: The Migration of Dreams and Nightmares* (Lanham, MD: Rowman and Littlefield, 2005), 3.

134. Jessica Stern et al., "The Future of the Jihadi Movement: A 5-Year Forecast," *Chronicle of Higher Education,* 53, no. 9 (October 20, 2006): 64.

135. Jeremy McDermott, "Mexican Drug Trafficking Cartels Set Up Camp in Peru," *Jane's Intelligence Review,* 18, no. 10 (October 2006): 47.

136. Alexander Kupatadze, "Georgian Organized Crime Groups Spread in Europe," *Jane's Intelligence Review,* 18, no. 4 (April 2006): 42.

137. Ibid., 43.

138. Ibid.

139. Phil Williams, "Transnational Criminal Enterprises, Conflict, and Instability," in *Turbulent Peace: The Challenges of Managing International Conflict,* ed. Charles A. Crocker, Fen Osler Hampson, and Pamela Aall (Washington, DC: U.S. Institute of Peace Press, 2001), 109.

140. Ibid.

141. Ibid.

142. Tamara Makarenko, "The Changing Faces of Terrorism Within the Russian Federation," *Jane's Intelligence Review,* July 1, 2001.

143. Baker and Hamilton, *The Iraq Study Group Report,* 5–6.

144. McDermott, "Mexican Drug Trafficking," 45.

145. Tamara Makarenko, "Terrorism and Transnational Crime: Tracing the Crime-Terror Nexus in Southeast Asia," in Smith, *Terrorism and Violence in Southeast Asia,* 176.

146. Jorg Raab and H. Brinton Milward, "Dark Networks as Problems," *Journal of Public Administration Research and Theory,* 13, no. 4 (October 1, 2003): 413.

147. "Pervasive Insecurity," in *Report of the National Intelligence Council's 2020 Project,* www.dni.gov/nic/NIC_globaltrend2020_s4.html#page96 (accessed November 30, 2006).

148. Ana R. Sverdlick, "Terrorists and Organized Crime Entrepreneurs in the 'Triple Frontier' Among Argentina, Brazil, and Paraguay," *Trends in Organized Crime,* 9, no. 2 (Winter 2005): 84.

149. *National Security and the Threat of Climate Change* (Alexandria, VA: CNA Corporation, 2007), 1, accessed May 11, 2007, at www.SecurityAndClimate.cna.org.

150. Ibid., 44.

151. Michael E. Brown, "Ethnic and Internal Conflicts: Causes and Implications," in Crocker, Hampson, and Aall, *Turbulent Peace,* 210.

152. Ibid., 211.

153. "New Challenges to Governance," in *Report of the National Intelligence Council 2020 Project,* http://dni.gov/nic/NIC_globaltrend2020.s1.html (accessed March 26, 2007).

154. Ibid.

155. Martin van Creveld, *The Transformation of War* (New York: Free Press, 1991), 214–15.

156. Ibid., 197.

157. Ibid.

158. Niall Ferguson, "The Next War of the World," *Foreign Affairs,* 85, no. 5 (September–October, 2006), accessed on May 16, 2007, at http://web.ebscohost.com/ehost/detail?vid=10&hid=101&sid=9853bd96-dbd2-4548-af85-75178c19dc0d%40sessionmgr107.

159. Baker and Hamilton, *The Iraq Study Group Report,* 4.

160. Substitution for the testimony of Khalid Sheikh Mohammed, *United States vs. Moussaoui,* 51.

244 NOTES TO CHAPTER 9

161. Ibid., 12.
162. Ibid., 13.
163. Aldo Borgu, "Combating Terrorism in East Asia—A Framework for Regional Cooperation," *Asia-Pacific Review,* 11, no. 2 (2004): 50.
164. Joseph S. Nye, Jr., "Soft Power and American Foreign Policy," *Political Science Quarterly,* 119, no. 2 (2004): 256.

Index

Future terrorism
  climate change and, 187–188
  demographics and, 183–184
  desire to achieve "spectacular" results
    and, 189–190
  ethnic and religious identity and,
    188–189
  globalization and, 184–186
  quasi-states and, 187
  shaping, 183
  transnational crime and, 186–187

Gaddis, John Lewis, 47, 56–57
Gadhafi, Moammar, 50, 152
Gandhi, Rajiv, 17
Gap countries, 81
Garedat, Hanadi, 143–144
General Intelligence Department (GID),
  3, 122
Georgia (country), 114, 186
Germany, 10, 142
Ghazan, 97
Global politics. See International system
Global Salafi jihad, 98–100
Global war on terrorism (GWOT), 7
Globalization
  Americanization and, 67, 185
  chemical, biological, radiological, and
    nuclear technology and, 127
  "contagion" concept and, 79–80
  cultural, 65–66
  definition of, 64–66
  economic, 65, 80–81
  future terrorism and, 184–186
  gap countries and, 81
  importance of, increasing, 36
  information revolution and, 69–72
  interdependence versus, 64–65
  Internet and, 72–75
  marginalization and, 79–82
  migration and, 76–79
  movement against, 66–69
  "muscular," 56
  New Diaspora Order and, 76–79
  9/11 terrorist attacks and, 62–63, 82
  nonstate actors and, 52
  overview, 82
  political, 65
  Salafist campaigns and, 66–69

Globalization (continued)
  sovereignty and, 68
  television and, 69–72
  terrorism and, 7, 62–63
  "trade not aid" policy and, 81–82
  weapons of mass destruction and, 104
Goldman, Emma, 21–22
Goldstein, Bruce, 89–90
Goss, Peter, 173
Gottemoeller, Rose, 113
Government Accountability Office report,
  114–115
Government Accounting Office, 15, 125
Grievances as root cause of terrorism,
  177–178
Guevara, Che, 18
Gujarat episode (2002), 88

Haass, Richard, 55
Habash, George, 18, 33, 150, 152
Habeck, Mary, 100
Haddad, Wadi, 29
Haganah, 27
Haifa restaurant suicide bomber attack,
  143–144
Haig, Alexander, 150
Hamas, 67, 130, 136–137, 163
"Hard" power, 71
Harmon, Christopher, 11, 13
Harris, Lee, 39, 181
Harris, Lillian Craig, 151
Hart Senate Office Building anthrax
  letters, 124
Harvard University study, 176
Hassan Sabbah the Persian, 20
Hatred and suicide terrorism, 142–143
Hawala, 164
Haymarket Affair (1886), 24
Hearst, Patricia, 157–158
Hegasy, Sonja, 68
Hegel, G.W.F., 23
Hendrickson, David, 55
Herrhausen, Alfred, 30
Hezbollah, 36, 39, 129–130, 137, 163
Highly enriched uranium (HEU),
  109–110, 113, 115
Hijackings, 70, 182
Hill, Paul, 93
Hindu militants, 88

Vietnam War, 29, 180
Violence, 87–90, 155–159. *See also*
    specific acts of
Vishwa Hindu Parishad (World Council of
    Hindus), 89
Voigt, Helmut, 152

Wafa Idris, 135
"War on terrorism," 7, 59, 171, 174
Wardlaw, Grant, 75
Watson, Dale, 168–169
Wave model of terrorism
  definition of, 18, 51
  first, 21–25, 180–181
  fourth, 35–39, 118, 180–181
  international system and, 51
  learning from past and, 180–183
  overview, 18
  review of, 180–181
  second, 25–28, 180–182
  third, 29–35, 180–182
Weapons-grade plutonium (WGPU),
    110
Weapons of mass destruction (WMD).
    See also Biological weapons;
    Chemical weapons
  anxiety about, emerging, 107–112
  black market for, 104
  chemical, biological, radiological,
    and nuclear technology and, 7,
    104–107, 126–128
  counterproliferation efforts, American,
    114–115
  deterrence of, 126–127
  globalization and, 104
  Iraq and, 55–56
  "kill parity" and, 119
  mass casualties from, potential, 38–39
  overview, 128

Weapons of mass destruction *(continued)*
  post-cold war paradigm shift and
    demand changes, 117–120
    supply changes, 112–117
  proliferation of, 38
  radiological, 103
Weathermen, 34
Wells Fargo robbery (1983), 156–157
West Germany, 29–30, 142
Westernization, 67, 185
Wilcox, Philip, 170
Wilkinson, Paul, 34–35, 39
Williams, Phil, 186
Wilson, Harold, 153
Wilson, Thomas R., 65, 126
WMD. *See* Weapons of mass destruction
Woods, Randall, 53
World Development Report, 184
World Trade Center terrorist attack
    (1993), 17, 93, 154
World Trade Center terrorist attack
    (2001). *See* 9/11 terrorist attacks
    (2001)
World War I, 26, 48, 131, 178
World War II, 10, 26–27, 139, 150

Yeltsin, Boris, 125
Yemen, 75
Yousef, Ahmed Ramzi, 75, 154
Yugoslavia, 123, 125

Zada, Eden Natan, 90
Zarate, Juan, 149–150
Zealots, 19–20
Zelikow, Philip, 128
Zimmermann, Ernst, 30
Zionists, 27
Zunes, Stephen, 178
Zygo Corporation, 118

Paul J. Smith is an associate professor at the U.S. Naval War College in Newport, Rhode Island, where he specializes in transnational security issues related to East and Southeast Asia. He has contributed articles and essays on these and related subjects to such journals as *Fletcher Forum of World Affairs*, *Jane's Intelligence Review*, *Parameters*, and *Survival*. He is editor of *Human Smuggling: Chinese Migrant Trafficking and the Challenge to America's Immigration Tradition* (Washington, DC: Center for Strategic and International Studies, 1997), in addition to *Terrorism and Violence in Southeast Asia: Transnational Challenges to States and Regional Stability* (Armonk, NY: M.E. Sharpe, 2005). He has addressed academic and government audiences around the world on terrorism-related security issues.

Smith studied in the People's Republic of China, Taiwan, and the United Kingdom and is conversant in Mandarin Chinese. He earned his B.A. at Washington and Lee University, his M.A. at the University of London, and his J.D. and Ph.D. at the University of Hawaii, Manoa.